Under a Bad Sun

Under a Bad Sun

Police, Politics, and Corruption in Australia

Paul Bleakley

MICHIGAN STATE UNIVERSITY PRESS | *East Lansing*

Copyright © 2021 by Paul Bleakley

♾ The paper used in this publication meets the minimum requirements
of ANSI/NISO Z39.48-1992 (R 1997) (Permanence of Paper).

Michigan State University Press
East Lansing, Michigan 48823-5245

LIBRARY OF CONGRESS CATALOGING-IN-PUBLICATION DATA
Names: Bleakley, Paul, author.
Title: Under a bad sun : police, politics, and corruption in Australia / Paul Bleakley.
Description: East Lansing : Michigan State University Press, [2021]
| Includes bibliographical references and index.
Identifiers: LCCN 2020054485 | ISBN 9781611864007 (paperback ; alk. paper)
| ISBN 9781609176747 (pdf) | ISBN 9781628954425 (ePub)
| ISBN 9781628964363 (Kindle)
Subjects: LCSH: Police corruption—Australia—Queensland—Case studies.
| Political corruption—Australia—Queensland—Case studies.
| Police—Australia—Queensland—History—20th century.
| Queensland—Politics and government—20th century.
Classification: LCC HV8280.A5 Q4328 2021 | DDC 364.1/32309942—dc23
LC record available at https://lccn.loc.gov/2020054485

Book design and typesetting by Charlie Sharp, Sharp Des!gns, East Lansing, Michigan
Cover design by David Drummond, Salamander Design, www.salamanderhill.com
Cover art: detail from Police and protestors during a women's demonstration at the
Treasury Building, Brisbane,1977. © QUEENSLAND STATE ARCHIVES, IMAGE ID 2988

Michigan State University Press is a member of the Green Press Initiative and is committed to developing
and encouraging ecologically responsible publishing practices. For more information about the Green
Press Initiative and the use of recycled paper in book publishing, please visit www.greenpressinitiative.org.

Visit Michigan State University Press at *www.msupress.org*

Contents

1 INTRODUCTION

15 CHAPTER 1. Somewhere on the River Bend
33 CHAPTER 2. The End of the Green Mafia
47 CHAPTER 3. Rats in the Ranks
63 CHAPTER 4. Checking in at the National Hotel
77 CHAPTER 5. Jokers' Wild
91 CHAPTER 6. Vice City
107 CHAPTER 7. The Bodgie Squad Hits the Street
123 CHAPTER 8. Taking the Fight to the Streets
141 CHAPTER 9. If You Want a Friend in Politics
159 CHAPTER 10. Marching to a Different Beat
177 CHAPTER 11. The Curious Case of Constable Dave
193 CHAPTER 12. Dirt Files
211 CHAPTER 13. Joke's Over
223 CONCLUSION

233 ACKNOWLEDGMENTS
235 NOTES
275 INDEX

Introduction

Since she was eleven, Anne-Marie Tilley had taken a rather romantic view of the prostitution game. In the 1963 film *Irma la Douce*, the famous actress Shirley MacLaine plays a sex worker in Paris who falls in love with a white-knight police detective. Young Tilley loved everything about the life she saw on screen—a life of fancy clothes and even fancier people.[1] It wasn't her first exposure to the shadow world of vice. Her foster father had been a driver for one of Sydney's most notorious brothel madams, Tilly Devine. Had she asked him what the life of a sex worker was *really* like, Tilley might have been disavowed of any of the starry-eyed notions she had picked up from the cinema.

In the end, for better or worse, Tilley got her wish. It played out almost like she *was* in a movie. One night, she met a dashing man in a three-piece suit at a seedy nightclub in Sydney's Kings Cross. Hector Hapeta was sweet, a charmer. Before too long she moved in with Hapeta and began her career selling sex. By the time she had reached sixteen years old, Tilley was working the unlit laneways of the Cross. Prostitution was a career that defined Tilley's and Hapeta's lives for almost twenty years. Tired of struggling to make ends meet, they moved to sunny Queensland in the late 1970s to try their luck there. The industrious duo purchased the lease for a health studio, the Top Hat, in the heart of Fortitude Valley. Before too long, the

Top Hat became the first brothel in the Tilley-Hapeta vice empire.[2] In Brisbane, Tilley and Hapeta found a city where anything was possible if you knew the right person—and, more often than not, that person was a police officer.

On 11 May 1987, the Tilley-Hapeta empire could confidently claim to be the single biggest provider of prostitution in Queensland. Much of this was thanks to their long-standing relationship with the Licensing Branch, the division of the Queensland Police Force (QPF) responsible for controlling vice in the state. For the Licensing Branch, there was a major incentive to keep Tilley and Hapeta in business—corrupt officers in the branch received at least a million dollars a year from the Tilley-Hapeta organization. Tilley and Hapeta did not necessarily know where the money that they paid ultimately ended up. So, on 11 May 1987 when they sat down in their Spring Hill flat to watch ABC's current affairs program *Four Corners* they were, in some ways, as shocked as everybody else watching across Australia. While they had been warned that ABC journalist Chris Masters had been investigating Queensland's vice trade, Tilley and Hapeta had been told by their police handlers that everything would be fine. But no one quite expected the extent to which Masters revealed the connection between vice traders and corrupt police in Queensland. When Queensland police commissioner Terence Murray Lewis appeared on screen, Tilley was stunned. "Shit, you're my boss? This is going to get bad," she thought to herself.[3]

Masters's report, "The Moonlight State," did not hold back in demonstrating exactly what Queensland was like when the sun went down. His report opened with a topless woman gyrating on stage under a dim red light, pouring alcohol over her breasts and performing for a baying crowd of sweaty men. For decades Queensland had been led by ultraconservative premier Johannes "Joh" Bjelke-Petersen, a self-proclaimed moral crusader dedicated to preventing the moral decay of Australia's southern states from infecting Queensland society. From the very outset, "The Moonlight State" blew this perception out of the water. As Masters observed in the report's opening lines, "Despite some wholesome attempts to pretend otherwise, the Queensland government has not managed to stop the devil at the border."[4]

The QPF was the first to reckon with messy fallout from "The Moonlight State." Masters's story focused on illicit protection payments paid by the Tilley-Hapeta organization, as well as other players in the Queensland vice trade like Geraldo Bellino and Vic Conte. Masters interviewed former police officers, sex workers, and brothel managers. All told the same story: that the "Queensland system" of controlling the vice trade worked because everyone involved—police and criminal alike—had the "right attitude."[5] This "attitude" was that violence was bad for business, that vice could never truly be eradicated, and that the best alternative was to control it in a way that limited the fallout and allowed everybody to make money. Masters's investigation found that police corruption was pervasive, especially in the Licensing Branch who were responsible for ensuring that the "right attitude" was maintained by all participants in the vice industry.

Fortuitously, Premier Bjelke-Petersen was out of the country when "The Moonlight State" aired, and so it fell on his deputy premier Bill Gunn to deal with the fallout from the report. Gunn announced a judicial inquiry into the allegations of police misconduct. Led by local barrister Tony Fitzgerald, this commission examined in great detail the structural corruption that existed in the QPF. As it turned out, "The Moonlight State" was only the tip of the iceberg. Fitzgerald offered immunity from prosecution to any officer willing to go on the record to the inquiry and admit to corruption. Many took him up on his offer, revealing the inner workings of a system referred to colloquially as "the Joke." Officers were either in on the Joke or not, but those who were received a significant financial benefit for turning a blind eye to the activities of protected criminals. The money that people like Tilley and Hapeta paid to corrupt police was spread around the force, in a system that extended far beyond the Licensing Branch. Tilley wasn't wrong when she referred to Police Commissioner Lewis as her "boss." After more than a decade presiding over the QPF, Lewis was found guilty of official corruption in the aftermath of the Fitzgerald Inquiry and sentenced to fourteen years in prison.[6]

By the time he was done, Fitzgerald claimed the careers of many police. Lewis was sent to prison, as were three government ministers discovered to have misappropriated public funds. Even Bjelke-Petersen was forced to step down as state premier, just shy of his twenty-year anniversary in the role, and was put on trial for official corruption. A standing anti-corruption body, the Criminal Justice Commission (CJC), was created as a permanent successor to the Fitzgerald Inquiry, in response to the failure of oversight that was roundly blamed for allowing the systemic corruption to take root.

Quite rightly, the Fitzgerald Inquiry has been routinely cited in policing literature as an exemplar of how judicial commissions can create lasting, systemic change. Feeling the net around them closing, corrupt police officers fell like dominoes. First, the "bagman" Harry Burgess told Fitzgerald what he knew about the Joke—then his boss, Assistant Commissioner Graeme Parker, became the next star witness to tell all, and so it went on. In this manner, the Joke was revealed.

But this kind of "mercenary corruption," as scholars call it, was far from the only form plaguing the QPF. What about the other webs of corruption that existed in Queensland, most notably, the process corruption that was used by officers to control the Queensland public on a daily basis, that Fitzgerald described as "more widespread" than bribery and stand over?[7]

Like all systems, the rules of policing are open to interpretation and thus manipulation by the motivated officer. Corruption thrives where ordinary citizens are bestowed with power and authority over their peers. In no other job is this more pronounced than in policing, where the officer on the street enjoys a great degree of control over the criminal-legal process. Officers should rely on their professional judgment when exercising this discretion, however process corruption takes root where personal motivations compromise this. Whereas popular culture suggests that these "personal motivations" usually refer to criminals offering bribes for legal amnesty, the story of corruption in Queensland shows that process corruption is exercised for a variety of reasons, from protecting powerful members of society to the genuine desire to contribute to a "greater good," even when doing so means bending (or breaking) the rules. Unlike cliché vice-related bribery, there is no panacea for process corruption. The factors that underpin it are diverse, often hard to understand, and even harder to deal with.

Unfortunately, process corruption does not impact all members of the community equally. As Justice James Wood found in his late 1990s investigation into police corruption in neighboring state New South Wales, it "is often directed at those members of the community who are least likely or able to complain . . . in order to exercise control over sections of the community."[8] It strips the protection of the criminal justice system away from those who need it most, the communities that are already disenfranchised or otherwise marginalized. Process corruption is not simply about an officer's or a criminal's personal benefit, but the exercise of power by those who have it over those who do not. It is about reinforcing (or extending) the power dynamics within a society, to the detriment of those who are powerless to oppose it. In doing so, as the Queensland example shows, process corruption can be perpetuated over a prolonged period, comfortably coexisting with more stereotypical corruption involving bribery and protection of the vice trade.

Officers involved in mercenary corruption are typically motivated by extrinsic factors—the promise of receiving money for *not* acting on "victimless" crimes is often persuasive to an officer looking to supplement a meager income. This practice was particularly appealing to officers with, as "The Moonlight State" put it, the "right attitude" on policing vice. For them, controlling the vice trade required a rather pragmatic perspective. History and experience showed that it was near-impossible to eliminate "moral crimes" like prostitution and gambling. While society at large may have frowned on these behaviors, police often found that there was little support for enforcement in the areas where vice occurred most often. If prevention was too difficult to achieve, a new approach was needed. Instead of cracking down hard on vice, police would attempt to *control* it. Sex and gambling would be contained to proscribed areas or venues where it would be tolerated, and where police could keep a watchful eye on the industry. They found vice traders were willing to pay for the right to do business. Those who paid and followed the rules of engagement were permitted to carry out their business unmolested by law enforcement. Those who refused were pushed out, under threat of arrest or violence. Mercenary corruption in Queensland worked if all parties had the "right attitude." Criminals and police could both profit, while the public felt secure that vice was under control because it didn't encroach on the lives of the average, suburban Queenslander.

The public perception is that every other QPF officer was participating in mercenary corruption prior to the Fitzgerald Inquiry. This is not the case. Only a minority of officers were implicated in taking bribes, though far more were accused of willfully ignoring their corrupt actions. Tolerance of corruption has proven to be a challenging behavior to account for in policing throughout history. From an organizational standpoint, the reluctance to speak out on misconduct is a byproduct of a "blue brotherhood," an almost familial bond between officers, a sense of collective belonging, and an implicit trust in the colleagues who might someday hold your life in their hands. On the flipside, the costs of going against the brotherhood are severe: ostracization, harassment, and victimization. The history of policing worldwide is littered with examples of whistleblowers cast out from the blue brotherhood, serving as a cautionary tale for currently serving police. Whether the misconduct witnessed is taking a bribe from a drug trafficker or kneeling on the neck of a man in custody, the internal pressure to do the right thing and speak out is considerably curtailed by the fear of being exiled from this subcultural group—one that is not only powerful but spiteful when scorned.

Noble cause, or "white knight," corruption is distinct from mercenary corruption in that it is usually the result of intrinsic, philosophical motivations rather than personal gain. It is a form of process corruption in which police misuse their powers or break the rules in the pursuit of what they perceive as justice. There is no discernible benefit to the officer who practices noble cause corruption other than to act as a "good cop." The construction of the "good cop" is, of course, subjective. Often in these cases, the police conception of being a good officer differs considerably from public expectations. This form of corruption, cultivated with long-established traditions of rule-breaking in the police force and the experience of an imperfect justice system, is the kind Fitzgerald identified as pervasive in Queensland. Noble cause corruption occurs when an officer comes to the view that the goals of policing cannot be achieved using legitimate means, operating within the rules and regulations set out by the laws governing professional conduct. To properly serve what they perceive as the "greater good," the officer must make a choice: to play by the rules or to pursue criminals by any means necessary.

On a basic level, police doing whatever it takes to take offenders off the street is something that a community can support, at least in theory. Carl Klockars calls this the "Dirty Harry dilemma"—a situation in which a police officer breaks the rules, but their conduct is tolerated because the outcome meets the community's expectations of what the police should be doing.[9] Whereas police engaged in noble cause corruption see it as essential to accomplish their goals regardless of what professional ethics dictates, it is a consensus within democratic societies that even the pursuit of justice must be regulated. Abandoning the rules governing police would give too much power to law enforcement, giving them carte blanche to act however they see fit in the course of their duties. In Queensland, we are faced with a police force where noble cause corruption was tolerated at the highest levels, where internal police discipline barely existed, and where the bonds of the "blue brotherhood" were strong. The Queensland case shows the result of tolerating all forms of process corruption but is particularly concerned with the "noble" type that targets specific "undesirable" groups in the name of community cohesion.

The "Dirty Harry" method usually reflects a police culture that prides strict social control over softer, community policing. A culture like this does not develop in a vacuum. Despite police being tasked to enforce the laws impartially, there are intrinsic connections between policing and politics that permeate this boundary. When a political regime is more permissive of police taking firm action, regardless of the ethics, officers have freer rein to do so without fear of reprisal. This was certainly the case under Premier Bjelke-Petersen, who overtly gave Queensland police a green light to use extreme force against any enemies of his socio-moral agenda, from gay men to student protesters. Queensland was a state in which corruption of all kinds was tolerated, whether for mercenary reasons or to serve the "greater good." For most of the latter half of the twentieth century, the Queensland police were arbiters of the moral order at the behest of a conservative government who sought to repress deviance and dissent at all costs. Often, such governments are condemned as fascist states, and so too was Queensland under Bjelke-Petersen, referred to pejoratively by some as the "Hillbilly Dictator." The ultraconservative government Bjelke-Petersen led was elected by the people of Queensland time and time again, begging the question of whether the state-directed actions of the police in quashing dissent were, in fact, a legitimate exercise of democratic powers. Police were regularly called upon to control divergent subpopulations who were perceived as threats to "Queensland"—a shorthand for the Bjelke-Petersen government. Rock and roll fans, punks, protesters, communists, and gay men were all targeted by the government and, consequently, the Queensland police. Often, this involved process corruption being used by police to assert dominance in situations where following the ordinary rules of policing would not suffice. The use of excessive force on political demonstrators was not just routine but explicitly sanctioned by government.[10] It was a period where gay men lived in fear of being extorted by police who fabricated evidence to convict them of soliciting immoral acts. A time when confessions were beaten out of suspects in the interrogation room, and even if they were not, police presented a false, unsigned confession to the court anyway. With the government on its side, oversight of police was minimal, and there was little hope for justice for those who were on the receiving end of a baton or were sentenced to jailtime based on fabricated evidence.

Using a police force to quash opposition is an overt repudiation of democratic principles, casting the police as foot soldiers of a political movement rather than independent enforcers of the law as it stands. Here, though, is where process corruption becomes even more complicated: a government setting out to amend the law to legitimize the actions of police operating outside the standards we would typically expect, thereby vindicating the unwarranted use of extreme force and other discretionary powers afforded to police. When process corruption becomes enshrined in law, it is not (by definition) corruption. However, to understand the mutualistic relationship between a corrupt police force and a government that enables them, it is necessary to detach ourselves from the strict definition of corruption as being simply acting outside the rules. When a government and a police force are part of the same corrupt system, working towards the same agenda, the act of amending laws and police rules to permit behaviors that are considered by most to be inappropriate cannot be dismissed.

Here, police culture is on trial. Officers prioritizing loyalty to the badge over their duty to uphold the law is routinely cited as a causal factor in the evolution of corruption in Queensland. The term "blue brotherhood" is not used flippantly; research shows that the bonds that form between police officers are comparable to those commonly seen in traditional families.[11] This is understandable. Police officers are forced to trust their colleagues in an atypical way, compared to other professional settings. Officers follow each other into dangerous situations on a regular basis, and have to trust that their fellow police will do their job and protect them from harm. While this is reasonable, the expectation that fellow officers will "have your back" extends beyond the street. The blue brotherhood is a social structure where "peer pressure, social approval and sanction" bind an officer to the broader collective of policing.[12] Like any other social formation, these factors work in conjunction to shape an individual's self-conception. Ultimately, an officer exposed to the blue brotherhood begins to see "police officer" as their master role, an identity that supersedes all others they may also have.[13] Parent, child, citizen, football fan—to an officer whose self-perception is as a police officer first and foremost, none of these roles matters as much as preserving the blue brotherhood.

Such conditions breed corruption. An officer who is committed to the blue brotherhood can justify bending, or outright breaking, the law in order to do what he or she considers to be their "duty." They may see due process as an impediment that prevents them from doing their jobs or consider cutting corners as a viable method to expedite justice. Though motivated by noble concerns, in truth this behavior is no less corrupt than that of those in on the Joke who received bribes to protect vice operators. Mercenary and noble cause corruption are both predicated on a belief held within the blue brotherhood that police officers are above the law. If an officer breaks the rules, the brotherhood must support them, right or wrong. The blue brotherhood is propped up by police who decide not to participate in corruption investigations targeting other officers, a code of silence that consistently frustrated campaigns for policing reform in twentieth-century Queensland. This tradition was strong in Queensland. Without it, officers with a reputation for corruption like Lewis would never have reached the Commissioner's Office. From such lofty positions, senior police could better manage corruption on the endemic scale exposed by *Four Corners* in 1987 and later the Fitzgerald Inquiry.

For a historical criminologist, the story of corruption in Queensland is more than just the remnant of a long-gone era. Whereas crime historians are concerned with chronicling the past, the role of historical criminologist is to use the lessons of the past to better understand contemporary issues in criminal justice. While fields as diverse as geography, chemistry, and mathematics have all been readily accepted as useful additions to the pantheon of criminological studies, the readiness of the discipline to accept historical criminology has been relatively muted. This is predominantly the result of interdisciplinary division—a refrain common to this debate is that "historians study crime and criminal justice to contribute to historical knowledge, and social scientists study the past to build social knowledge."[14] Ultimately, these theoretical divisions are arbitrary. In truth, historical criminology exists on a spectrum extending from a purist historical research at one extreme to traditional, sociological criminology at the other. Every example of historical criminology research will fall somewhere along this continuum, and will borrow from both disciplines to different extents. This research draws on a range of archival sources to build the case that process corruption was pervasive in the QPF, sanctioned by a government who provided the police with whatever tools needed to enforce social control. Where the research enters into the realm of historical criminology, rather than just a historical recount, is in the instructive value it holds for contemporary practitioners.

Queensland is just one state in one country, but there are key lessons to be obtained from exploring how corruption became entrenched there and the impact it had on society. For one, it was not just here that diverse populations were targeted by process corruption in this era. Queensland provides a clear example of police being used to enforce the extant social order, but the same principles of corruption in pursuit of control can be observed around the world. The benefit of using Queensland as a case study lies in the overt, unapologetic nature of the process corruption that took place. It provides an extreme example of professional misconduct in action and can serve as a framework for understanding the way that noble cause corruption manifested in other, similar policing contexts. Queensland also showcases the way that the institutional safeguards that were put in place to prevent professional misconduct failed, allowing corruption to flourish.

Much attention has been afforded to the QPF's protection of the vice trade, but in reality, this was just the tip of the iceberg. What the failure to deal with vice effectively really showed was an inability, or unwillingness, of the QPF and the state government to take corruption seriously throughout the twentieth century. The state's resistance to addressing police corruption, at least for Premier Bjelke-Petersen, was not motivated by a desire to protect a relatively small group of Licensing Branch officers. What did motivate it was the desire to give police greater freedom to enforce an ideological agenda that suited Bjelke-Petersen. He routinely scuttled attempts to investigate police for excessive force against protesters, seeing the violence as an essential aspect of his own ability to maintain control by force. Similarly, police harassment of gay men was ignored because of their social construction in conservative Queensland as perverts or moral deviants. Disenfranchised young people, some of the most powerless in the state, felt the brunt of police persecution where, conversely, the powerbrokers propping up the conservative regime were routinely protected by police. There was an inherent lack of equity in policing Queensland that was accepted as the norm by a government that was, at the end of the day, more concerned with misapportioning blame for societal problems on others than it was on taking responsibility for the wrongs committed on its own watch.

Corruption in the QPF is a case that is extraordinary, but it is not entirely exceptional. Instead, it should be seen as a window into a culture where the ends justify the means, and any form of process corruption could be justified with the "right attitude." Queensland stands as a cautionary tale. It shows the influence that political interference in policing can have on fostering a tolerance of process corruption, which set the stage for the mercenary corruption revealed by the Fitzgerald Inquiry. The weaponizing of the QPF by the state government is often forgotten, lost among the shocking revelations of complex networks of mercenary corruption. It is treated as somehow separate, the product of an autocratic political regime that coexisted with the corruption revealed by Fitzgerald. In Queensland, political policing did not just coexist with the corruption revealed by Fitzgerald; it was an essential element of making the system work.

Reframing the story of process corruption in Queensland is essential, as for too long this narrative was controlled by the police themselves, using process corruption itself to shield corrupt officers and allies from public scrutiny. Controlling the narrative has been a challenge for researchers of process corruption, who are often required to set aside the official record or otherwise read between the lines to discern the truth. We see this in the 1964 National Hotel Inquiry, in which the police used every trick at their disposal to discredit witnesses and prevent the truth being revealed. The need to disentangle the true impact of process corruption in Queensland from the traditional narrative also impacts any reading of the archives, where the documents that shape our understanding are written in the hand of the very people accused of corruption. Often, the prevailing narratives around corruption in Queensland were carefully cultivated to minimize the influence that corrupt police had on the system as a whole. Lewis, for example, has often been portrayed as a lapdog and yes-man for Bjelke-Petersen, no more than a lackey of the dictatorial premier. Nothing could be further from the truth. Instead, Bjelke-Petersen relied on a cooperative police commissioner to enforce his agenda and willfully ignored consistent rumors that Lewis was corrupt to maintain their productive working relationship. If anything, it was Lewis who held the power, not the premier. Police are not simply the tools of the government they serve; no matter who the government of the day is, they have a commitment to enforce the law above political interests. Had Lewis chosen this path, Bjelke-Petersen's grasp on power would have been significantly curtailed, the Hillbilly Dictator unable to use the police force to play strongman politics.

The story of corruption in Queensland is a resounding indictment of the mutualistic relationship that can develop between governments and the police, especially in scenarios where a quid pro quo relationship emerged that served the interests of both groups. In Queensland, it was a recipe for disaster that must be avoided for the purposes of effective law enforcement. In the story of Queensland, echoes of police corruption from around the world can be heard. The selection of the corrupt Frank "The Big Fella" Bischof as police commissioner by the conservative Nicklin government on the basis of his political and religious affiliation in the late 1950s was reminiscent of the political machine Tammany Hall in nineteenth-century New York City, where jobs in the public service were given based on nepotism and cronyism rather than merit. The comparison goes further: just as the corrupt establishment presided over by William M. "Boss" Tweed was ultimately defeated by the Lexow Committee, it was the Fitzgerald Inquiry that would provide the deathblow to thirty years of conservative rule in Queensland.[15]

It was this nexus of police and politics that drove the persecution of the LGBTQI+ community, primarily gay men, in Queensland. The Bjelke-Petersen government incrementally gave police greater powers to target gay-friendly venues, forcing them out of business and forcing the city's gay residents underground.[16] The climate of fear was such that there was no Stonewall riot in Queensland like there was in New York City—instead, a frustrated resignation to being criminalized by the state and pursued by the police. The QPF's Licensing Branch exerted full control over Brisbane's vice trade from the 1950s until Fitzgerald ended their run. At the same time, half a world away, the Obscene Publications Squad of London's Metropolitan Police, the so-called Dirty Squad, extorted the pornographers and sex traders of Soho for protection money. Like their colleagues in the QPF, the

Dirty Squad allowed vice criminals to prosper, turning their attention instead to the left-wing activists of the alternative press.[17]

The use of police powers to repress dissent rather than control vice crime is a consistent theme of twentieth-century policing across the world, where police routinely clashed with protesters. The police crackdown on protesters at the 1968 Democratic Convention in Chicago culminated in what investigators described as a "police riot," a melee of violence designed to crush left-wing activism.[18] Much more recently, the same kind of "police riot" has been played out in cities across the United States as police clashed with demonstrators in the 2020 protests following the death in custody of African American man George Floyd. Those who believed we had moved on as a society since the chaos of the 1960s discovered this was not the case, as armed police stormed peaceful protesters with batons and tear gas in front of the White House, or drove squad cars into groups of demonstrators in New York City. Such scenes should not have come as a shock and instead are reflective of engrained patterns of violent police repression. The scene of a squad car driving into protesters bears uncanny resemblance to the actions of police in Queensland, who used the same tactics to disperse strikers in the state's capital almost a century earlier in 1912. The QPF likewise used excessive force to disperse the anti-apartheid Springboks protests in 1971, chasing down fleeing demonstrators and beating them to the point that they were hospitalized.[19] The QPF provides an extreme case of police corruption in the name of social control, but in no way was this a singular experience. It is, in many ways, universal.

The cause of corruption in Queensland cannot be narrowed down to any one reason, nor can it be ascribed to the influence of a single "rotten apple" officer. This is a debate that continues to inform our discussions of police reform in the twenty-first century. While progressive activists call for systemic change, or even to defund the police entirely, the often-conservative supporters of the blue brotherhood argue that the problems of policing are the work of bad actors who must be rooted out so the force itself can survive. In showcasing the example set by Queensland, the notion that rotten apples alone can cause such widespread damage to a police force is dispelled and, it is argued that it is systems (or lack thereof) that are truly responsible for endemic, tolerated misconduct.

Through archival research, it is possible to get to the bottom of what the real consequences of corruption were in Queensland. The Fitzgerald Inquiry performed a commendable job in exposing the Joke and forcing a purge of corrupt officers from the QPF, paving the way for meaningful reform. But, one way or another, the hearings could not go on forever. While Fitzgerald was (quite rightly) preoccupied with unravelling the threads of the Joke, the complex issues around noble cause corruption were left largely unattended. Perhaps this was a good thing. After all, it was far easier to construct the corrupt officers of the Joke as the villains of the story to the public, rather than the "good police" who occasionally cut a few corners to secure a conviction. The strength of the Fitzgerald Inquiry lies in its clear narrative: that a rogue element of the QPF received bribes to protect organized crime. But even Fitzgerald knew that this was just the tip of the iceberg.

The first step in understanding how a culture of corruption manifested in Queensland is to look back to its earliest days, when the very idea of "Australia" was still far away. Queensland had not existed for much more than a century by the time Bischof was appointed police commissioner. The QPF that he inherited was still nascent, still developing an identity. Into this state of transition stepped Bischof, twisting the ethos of the QPF into one that sanctioned corruption. He could not have accomplished this on his own, however. For this reason, the best place to begin this story is at the beginning—a time when Queensland was on the frontier of an emerging nation, and the shadow of Fitzgerald was no more than a distant threat that loomed on the horizon.

CHAPTER 1

Somewhere on the River Bend

Thomas Pamphlett had been lost for a long time when he set eyes on the HMS *Mermaid* on 29 November 1823. The ex-convict had set sail from Sydney with three others in March of that year, hired by settler William Cox to retrieve some cedar from the nearby Illawarra district, around fifty miles south.[1] It was a relatively straightforward mission and would have been completed quickly if not for a sudden change in the weather. Pamphlett and his crewmates came close to the Illawarra coast when a storm rolled in—the kind of classic Australian storm that comes out of nowhere with unforgiving and unrelenting ferocity. It was twenty-two days before the men saw land again. By the time the boat reached dry land one of their number, John Thompson, had succumbed to thirst. The others had survived on a steady diet of pork and rum, brought to trade for timber as was the norm in the boozy economy of colonial New South Wales.[2] Pamphlett's crew had no idea how far the wind had taken them and guessed that they had been blown farther south of Sydney. Setting off north, it was not long before they encountered one of the local Indigenous tribes of Moreton Island. The Indigenous people had never seen a European before and concluded that Pamphlett and his crew were the ghosts of their ancestors, returned to them from the clutches of death. The tribes took them in, fed them, and showed them how to live in this strange new world.

Pamphlett and his crew lived among the local tribes for around seven and a half months. Their Indigenous hosts taught them how to live off the land and gave the men the tools to explore the area so that eventually they could try to find a way home. After some time, Pamphlett's crew constructed a canoe and made it to the mainland. Hugging the coastline, they found themselves at the mouth of a vast river, so wide it was impossible to cross in their makeshift vessel. Instead, they turned up the river, searching for a better place to cross. Pamphlett's crew did not know it, but as their canoe floated down lazy river bends shadowed by looming volcanic cliffs they were making history—the first European men to chart what some Indigenous groups called Maiwar, later known simply as the Brisbane River.[3] The crew made it across the river farther upstream but returned to the river mouth and, from there, travelled north to Bribie Island. Here, the men separated. While the others went farther north in search of Sydney, Pamphlett stayed on Bribie Island. He lived among the native people, the Gubbi Gubbi, and was accepted as part of the tribe. He even allowed the Gubbi Gubbi to paint his body in red and white twice a day, but he stopped short of the ritual scarification that was common in the group. Pamphlett was fully painted on that day in November 1823 when the HMS *Mermaid* came into sight off the coast of Bribie Island.

The man leading the expedition of the HMS *Mermaid* was John Oxley, an accomplished explorer and surveyor-general of New South Wales. He had led successful surveys of the Lachlan River and Macquarie River over the past decade, but the expedition in 1823 was his most ambitious yet. He was selected by Governor Thomas Brisbane to go north and select a site to establish a new penal colony to house the most difficult convicts in New South Wales. Even though the colony was established as a place for British convicts to be transported to, the early nineteenth century saw a boom in the number of free settlers calling Sydney home. Tensions were rising between these settlers and the convicts and were only exacerbated by the reports of royal commissioner John Bigge, who found that mismanagement of convicts contributed to regular escapes and a high crime rate.[4] Brisbane sought a practical solution to his criticism: the creation of a new penal establishment for recidivist convicts, located far on the New South Wales frontier where convicts who escaped would have nowhere to run except into the harsh Australian terrain. Oxley was sent north to find a viable location for such a settlement. At first, he bypassed Moreton Bay, where Pamphlett and his crew had first landed. But after examining a different location, near modern Gladstone, Oxley found the conditions too poor to support habitation. Discouraged, he sailed south and, on 29 November, came ashore on Bribie Island to find Pamphlett, painted like an Indigenous tribesman, standing to welcome the HMS *Mermaid* on the white sand.

The plan for the Moreton Bay colony was born on the beach of Bribie Island, when Oxley met Pamphlett. It was a fortuitous meeting between a convicted criminal and a government envoy tasked with finding a location where the British colonial governments could punish its badly behaved convicts, under a regime so aggressive that even the worst recidivists would learn to fear. Even then, in its earliest days as a European settlement, the comfortable association between crime and government was a central part of Queensland's identity. The full realization of this partnership was still a long way off, however. For Pamphlett, Oxley offered the promise of a long-awaited return home to Sydney. He learned from Oxley that his crew's exploration of Maiwar never would have worked out—not only was Sydney more than five hundred miles away, but his crew had drifted north in the storm rather than south, taking them farther from their destination. Oxley could take Pamphlett home, but Pamphlett could offer Oxley something far more important. Pamphlett had lived among the Indigenous people for more than seven months, not just the Gubbi Gubbi but also others on Moreton Island, Stradbroke Island, and the mainland.[5] He knew the terrain and how to survive in this humid, subtropical landscape. He had explored Maiwar in his quest to cross the big river, unknowingly the first European to stumble across the future location of Brisbane. John Finnegan, one of his former crewmates, also returned to Bribie Island to assist Oxley's team. While Pamphlett instructed the Europeans on Indigenous culture, Finnegan retraced the crew's river expedition with Oxley. By the time the HMS *Mermaid* was ready to depart, Oxley was convinced the region around Moreton Bay would be a fine location for Brisbane's new penal colony and even one day a proper colonial settlement. As he sailed back to Sydney, Pamphlett would have thought he would never see Moreton Bay again. He was wrong. Ironically, the man so integral to the foundation of the Moreton Bay colony would return—as a convict once more. A little over a year after his rescue, he was convicted of theft and sentenced to seven years' imprisonment at the newly established Moreton Bay colony.[6]

Oxley returned to Moreton Bay to establish a settlement in 1824 after securing approval from Governor Brisbane. His first choice was Red Cliff Point (modern Redcliffe) on the coastline north of Maiwar, but this settlement was abandoned after a year in favor of a location with a more reliable water supply farther up the river at North Quay, the current location of the Brisbane central business district. By the end of 1825, the population of the new settlement officially registered forty-five men and two women, not including the local Turrbal people who also called the area, referred to as Mianjin, home.[7] The Turrbal, part of the Jagera people, occupied a vast area stretching from the mainland shores of Moreton Bay to the Great Dividing Range in the west. The Turrbal were a formidable people. Even Oxley, who encountered many Indigenous groups during his explorations, noted that the Turrbal were "about the strongest and best-made muscular men I have seen in any country."[8] The positive relations forged by Pamphlett's crew and the respect displayed by Oxley would not last, however. The trajectory of colonial settlement in Queensland followed roughly the same path that it did in Sydney and, farther abroad, in the Americas and Africa.[9]

As the Moreton Bay colony's population grew, so too did its size. By the end of 1830, a prisoner's barracks had been constructed to house up to a thousand convicts. Other buildings were constructed to house the troops responsible for these convicts, who made up most of the remaining population in this period. Because the colony was established as an outpost for recidivist convicts, there were limitations preventing free settlers from building in the area. There was little incentive to do so in any case. The legend of Moreton Bay was that it was a grim place, somewhere that even the most hardened convicts feared to be sent. Such a place was not somewhere that the average New South Wales settler wished to venture.

Fears of the harsh conditions of the Moreton Bay colony were exacerbated under the command of Captain Patrick Logan. The Scotsman was an experienced military man. He had served in the Peninsular War between Spain and Portugal and was a part of the Duke of Wellington's occupation force in Paris after Napoleon's defeat at Waterloo. Logan settled in Ireland after the Paris Occupation, but was soon called on for overseas service again. Two years after Pamphlett washed ashore in Moreton Bay, Logan was sent to New South Wales as part of the 57th Foot Regiment. He arrived in New South Wales on 22 April 1825, but it did not take long before his superior ability was recognized. Governor Brisbane selected Logan to head his personal project, the Moreton Bay colony. He arrived in the dreaded northern penal settlement in March 1826.[10] His time in Moreton Bay coincided with a rapid rise in the convict population. Though there were only seventy-seven prisoners in Moreton Bay when Logan arrived, by the end of his time as commandant in 1830, the convict population had risen to more than a thousand. His four years in charge of Moreton Bay was a period where the myth of the colony as a place of harsh punishment was largely justified. Logan believed in the severe treatment of convicts, forcing them to work from sunrise to sunset to build a new city on the river. The city of Brisbane emerged from the blood and sweat of convict labor under Logan, who ruled with an iron fist and did not tolerate bad behavior from his charges. Indeed, he was responsible for what might have been the first use of process corruption (namely, excessive force) in Queensland. A report from the New South Wales attorney general in 1827 noted that he ordered convicts to be whipped as many as 150 times as punishment, forcing Governor Brisbane's successor Ralph Darling to issue an order that no convict should be whipped more than one hundred times in a single day or more than three times for the same offense.[11]

Logan presided over the most notable period in Brisbane's history as a penal colony, before free settlers were permitted in the region. He was a notoriously harsh commander, but it was on his watch that the settlement on the river truly took shape. Like Oxley before him, Logan was an avid explorer and charted much of the area around Brisbane. It was on one such expedition that the brutal commandant would meet his end and be buried in a shallow grave northwest of Brisbane near Mount Beppo. He had set out with a small group of servants and convicts to explore to upper reaches of Maiwar. The expedition was repeatedly confronted by Indigenous groups armed with weapons, who warned Logan's party to turn back and return to Brisbane. He pressed on nevertheless, often riding ahead of the rest of the group to scout the area. On 17 October 1830, he was on one of these scouting rides when he disappeared. Searchers first found his horse, dead in a ditch and covered with tree branches. Logan's body was nearby, buried in a shallow grave. Despite speculation that he was murdered by the convicts in his party, furious after years of mistreatment at his hands, an autopsy later found that he had likely been killed with Indigenous weapons.[12] It seems that the Indigenous people who had threatened Logan throughout his expedition had, in the end, made good on their promise.

Logan's death highlights the precarious state of security in the early years of the Moreton Bay colony. The détente between European settlers and Indigenous locals that had been cultivated by Pamphlett and Oxley had well and truly ended under Logan's leadership. The opening of Brisbane to free settlers in the early 1840s only continued to fuel the tension. Exploration of the region in the 1830s had shown great potential for the development of an agricultural industry that was attractive to free settlers seeking to turn a profit. With convict numbers dwindling, down 75 percent from 1830 to 1838, the decision was made to close the Moreton Bay penal colony and open the area for settlement in 1842.[13] The arrival of free settlers was, in many ways, the final straw for local Indigenous tribes. Before 1842, the tribes saw the Moreton Bay colony shrinking in size, but the sudden influx of Europeans after the region was declared open for settlement put significant pressure on the area's resources. The expansion resulted in substantial clearing of land and the effective destruction of the traditional hunting lands of the Turrbal people. In response, the Turrbal found other means to gather food. Sometimes, it was necessary to hunt on the pastoral lands of the new settlers and use their herds as food sources to replace those that had been lost to development. It was not long before the struggles of sharing the land resulted in conflict with European settlers, who did not recognize the Turrbal's sovereignty.

The colony's response to the threat posed by the Turrbal was a policy of strict enforcement. The message was made clear to the locals even before the area was opened for settlement. Two Indigenous men were publicly executed by hanging at Brisbane's Old Windmill in July 1841 for the murder of surveyor Granville Stapylton and another European man the previous year. According to local legend, more than one hundred Turrbal were present at the execution, forced to bear witness to the brutal justice of the new colony.[14] Conflict in the settlement era was often fatal for the Turrbal. As was the case with the parallel displacement of Native Americans occurring in this period, the European settlers of Brisbane responded to the perceived threat posed by the local Indigenous population with deadly force, to the point that by the end of 1869 most of the Turrbal had died either from disease or gunshot. The hanging of the Turrbal men in 1841 was a public spectacle, intended to show the lengths the colonial government would go to when challenged. The intended effect was to strike fear into other Indigenous people and deter them from acting against the new European settlement. While not exactly equivalent the state lynchings of 1841, the use of police and the wider justice system to assert control would be a recurring theme throughout Queensland's history from this point on.

The former Moreton Bay penal colony might have been closed for good, but Brisbane remained a hard town in the mid-nineteenth century, where a person had to be tough and often ruthless if they wanted to prosper. There is little dispute that Australia, like so many other colonized nations around the world, was established on a foundation of settler colonialism, which Patrick Wolfe describes as "a structure rather than an event . . . [predicated on] the summary liquidation of Indigenous people."[15] In a settler colonial society, as Queensland was, the mechanisms of the state were tailored towards the replacement of Indigenous peoples, and the colony's policing model was no different. Even before the Queensland Police Force (QPF) was officially formed in the 1860s, the Native Mounted Police (NMP) was created in 1849 as a means primarily to protect the interests of white settlers spread across the vast, sparsely populated northern parts of the colony. Organized as more a paramilitary force than a civilian police service, the NMP was largely made up of Indigenous troopers led by white officers—many of whom, such as Alexander Douglas Douglas and Frederic Urquhart, would later become key figures in the early years of the QPF.[16] It was not just the NMP's role to serve as a vanguard watching over vulnerable northern pastoralists, however. The force was also actively involved in so-called punitive expeditions targeting Indigenous populations with extreme violence in retribution for crimes committed, whether actual or perceived. In one such punitive expedition in 1884, led by Urquhart, more than two hundred Kalkatungu people were massacred at Battle Mountain near Mount Isa, almost wiping out the entire tribal population in the name of colonial vengeance.[17] That men like Urquhart, capable of outright massacre, would be considered the best fit to help lead the QPF through its crucial early years speaks to the settler mindset that frontier Queensland was built on. It was place where European colonizers were emboldened to claim their "right" to what was classified as terra nullius, or no-man's-land. Resistance to accept the rights of this nouveau-landed gentry was not permitted by the colonial government, and as such, the style of policing that emerged in Queensland also reflected the settler colonial perspective that Europeans had the right (even *responsibility*) to supplant the traditional Indigenous owners of the land.

New migrants came to Brisbane with dreams of reinventing their lives. The rise of one Irish migrant, Patrick Mayne, embodied the at-times gothic nature of life in the colonial city. He came to New South Wales from Ireland in 1841, first to Sydney and then, after Moreton Bay was opened to free settlers, to Brisbane in 1846.[18] Like most Irish migrants, Mayne was a laborer. He worked as a butcher in a boiling down works at Kangaroo Point, across the river from the original settlement at North Quay. Boiling down was a less than glamourous process in which excess sheep carcasses were rendered down and converted into a fat called tallow that is used for candles.[19] The boiling down works was not a place for a man to make his fortune, and so it raised eyebrows in the city when Mayne purchased the lease of a butchery in downtown Queen Street in September 1849, only three years after arriving in Brisbane. Over the next ten years, he became one of Brisbane's leading businessmen with a diverse portfolio of houses, shops, hotels, and pubs. He even contributed funds to the building of St Stephen's Cathedral and was one of the city's most prominent Catholic residents. It was unsurprising, then, when he was elected alderman in 1859 as a part of Brisbane's inaugural city council.[20]

The question of Mayne's past lingered, however. How had he—a young, immigrant butcher at the boiling down works—managed to purchase the prime property on Queen Street where he made his fortune? There were rumors that he had made a confession to his priest on his deathbed in 1865 that the sudden wealth that he had used in 1849 to lease his butchery came from a rather grisly source—murder.[21] On 26 March 1848, an ex-convict named Robert Cox was murdered at the Bush Inn at Kangaroo Point. His body was mutilated and butchered into pieces by his killer, who spread his body parts around the crime scene in a bizarre, macabre tableau. Hours earlier, a drunken Cox had been at the Bush Inn accusing another ex-convict friend William Fyfe of having stolen £350 from him.[22] Fyfe's room was searched after Cox's body was discovered, and blood found there led to his arrest and, ultimately, his execution. But there was always speculation that Fyfe was not responsible for the murder. After all, no one had found the missing money in his room. But there was someone else who had been there that night, someone with a reputation for violence and who was desperate for the cash injection needed to get out of the boiling down works and into a shop of his own. Mayne, previously penniless and known for spending his weekly wages at places like the Bush Inn, purchased the lease on his butchery only a year later. That one of the city's most respectable residents might have built his fortune on a platform of death and theft was not a strange proposition in colonial Brisbane. For all the changes it had undergone since free settlement had commenced, Brisbane was still (in many ways) the same savage frontier town that it had always been.

Since arriving in Brisbane, Mayne transformed from a penniless immigrant laborer into a successful entrepreneur and politician. At the same time, the city he called home was also undergoing a period of seismic social change. Only a few years before, Brisbane was merely a British settlement under the greater colonial authority of New South Wales, governed from far-away Sydney. It was a cause of much discontent, particularly in the far north where even being governed from Brisbane was an unreasonable prospect. Though only a few decades old, Queenslanders already saw themselves as unique, with a distinct set of needs that were routinely ignored by an elitist southern plutocracy. The colonial government in Sydney was perceived to naturally favor the south, especially when it came to decisions that benefited the primary industries around Sydney at the expense of those in the north. Ironically given what was later to come, northerners saw the

Sydney elite as being politically corrupt and found it impossible to trust them to act in the north's best interests.

All of this changed on 10 December 1859 when the proclamation was read formally creating of the new colony of Queensland. The new colony began in the south at Point Danger and stretched west to the Great Diving Range, east to the Pacific Ocean, and north to the edge of the land.[23] With a new colony came the need for a new police force, and so the QPF came into existence on 1 January 1864. Queensland governor George Bowen's former aide-de-camp, David Seymour, was selected to head the new police force. Seymour continued in this role for thirty-one years and, more than any other individual, was responsible for shaping the cultural ethos of the QPF.[24] The warning signs of entrenched corruption in the QPF were already beginning at this early stage in the organization's history: Seymour, who refused to admit that his NMP were committing massacres of Indigenous people on the Queensland frontier, was described as "the force's greatest apologist ... [who] scorched any chance of effective reform during the 1870s."[25]

The Bread or Blood riots of 1866 presented Seymour's QPF with its first major test. A series of bad investments by the colonial government forced Queensland to suspend its extensive public works program. With many Queenslanders suddenly out of work and with no foreseeable end in sight, a series of increasingly volatile public demonstrations took place in the capital from July to September 1866. The conflict between the unemployed and the government came to a head on 11 September, when riot ringleader William Eaves told a crowd assembled outside the Treasury Building that "if we don't get bread, we will have blood."[26] The crowd, incited by Eaves's proclamation, decided to conduct a siege of the city's food stores, at which point Seymour and his colleague Police Magistrate William Massie determined it was time to read the Riot Act. In this era, this was tantamount of declaring a state of emergency. It gave police expanded powers to use whatever means necessary to disperse an unruly mob.[27] As Massie read the Riot Act to the assembled crowd, he was hit in the head with a rock, the first salvo in a prolonged street battle between rioters and the police. The Bread or Blood riots ended with the civilian ringleaders all being sent to prison for their actions directing the insurrection. By reading the Riot Act, the QPF had suspended the ordinary rules of conduct to bring the chaos to an end. In doing so, it set a precedent for social control that would reverberate in Queensland for more than a century.

The police response to civil unrest in Brisbane was not always to charge into action. When it suited their interests, the QPF found that inaction could be as powerful of a tool as excessive force. Inaction was certainly the policy of choice in the 1888 anti-Chinese riots, when the xenophobic political climate of the era bubbled over into a night of wanton destruction in downtown Brisbane. The race riots occurred on 5 May, the night of the Queensland parliamentary elections when anti-Chinese nationalist politician Thomas McIlwraith swept to victory over statesman and rival Samuel Griffith. McIlwraith, who had previously served as Queensland Premier from 1879 to 1883, returned to politics to contest Griffith's North Brisbane seat on a protectionist platform that called for repressive measures targeting Chinese migrants to be introduced.[28] Though Chinese migration in the nineteenth century occurred all over the continent, there was a particular influx to Queensland because its low European population was simply not enough to support the colony's thriving pastoral industry. Many of these jobs were filled with South Sea Islanders, but the Chinese also were part of this migratory pattern. More than twenty thousand Chinese had migrated to Queensland by 1877, and while many left after the state's goldrush ended, more than eight thousand stayed on, playing crucial roles in the banana industry and later moving across Queensland to major centers like Brisbane where they built their lives, opening businesses and starting families.[29]

Legislative moves to repress the Chinese population was not uncommon in the Australian colonies, where placing restrictions on Asian immigration was a popular response to the tensions with white miners in the goldfields of Victoria and New South Wales.[30] The same pressures had even led the U.S. government to issue to Chinese Exclusion Act in 1882, prohibiting the immigration of all Chinese laborers in an effort to slow the migration rate that began during the boom years of the California Gold Rush.[31] Far more than an alternative political view, anti-Chinese rhetoric was in many ways a norm in settler societies of the late-nineteenth century. McIlwraith's views went beyond the idea that these migrants were stealing the jobs of white Australians, however. He argued that the Chinese were an "inferior race people of low morals ... gamblers, drug addicts and sexual deviants, and accused of lusting after white women."[32]

On election night, as the results began to show that McIlwraith was going to be returned to power, two thousand of the new premier's supporters took to the streets in a booze-fueled celebration. Throughout the day, his team had supplied alcohol to those supporters who were out canvassing for McIlwraith, and by nightfall, there had already been several clashes between McIlwraith and Griffith voters—including one incident where Griffith himself was assaulted when he went to vote.[33] The McIlwraith contingent's drunken enthusiasm carried them to Frog's Hollow, the city's Chinatown, where it was not long before the first window was smashed, and the destruction began.

Rioting raged for hours, and all the while police stood by and refused to intervene. This was not uncommon for the period, both at home and abroad. In 1871, a crowd of more than five hundred Los Angeles residents similarly gathered at the edge of the city's Chinatown in response to the murder of local rancher Robert Thompson, shot dead coming to the aid of an injured police officer.[34] As the mob gathered, Los Angeles police (even including the chief, Francis Baker) came to the scene. As the mob encircled Chinatown, stopping any Asians from leaving the area, the police did nothing to win back control of the streets. Ultimately, the mob entered Chinatown. The result was far more disastrous than it was in Brisbane seventeen years later. Every Chinese-owned business was robbed, Asian residents were viciously assaulted, and up to twenty men were hanged in the street—some have described the 1871 riot as one of the largest mass lynching events in American history.[35] The stories of the Los Angeles massacre no doubt resonated in the minds of the Brisbane Chinese community as the Frog's Hollow riot grew increasingly out of hand.

As in Los Angeles, police in Frog's Hollow were reluctant to intervene and stop the mob, afterwards offering only the flimsiest of reasons for their inaction. Senior officers said constables on the scene chose not to disperse the crowd with a baton charge because "the majority of people in the street were respectable citizens and would probably have been injured had this been done." For the QPF, the safety of drunken, stone-throwing rioters was the priority, not the violent attack on Brisbane's Chinese. What could have informed this decision? Could it have been that McIlwraith's victory on an anti-Chinese platform signaled a turning of the tide that the QPF were reluctant to push back against? Whatever the reason, only a single person (later acquitted) was charged with malicious damage over the Election Night riot.[36] Remarkably, while many Chinese residents of Frog's Hollow were injured, most destruction was contained to property damage, and no fatalities were recorded. Even so, the riot and lack of political (and, in turn, police) willingness to protect the Chinese community spoke volumes about the selective nature of justice in the still young colony. In McIlwraith's Queensland, it seemed to be the case that you could get away with anything in the name of reinforcing the white European status quo.

The last decade of the nineteenth century was dawning. The federation of the

Australian colonies into one nation was fast-approaching. So much had changed since Queensland emerged as its own self-governed colony in 1859, but one thing remained the same: after all this time, Seymour was still the police commissioner. He had presided over a great expansion in the organization, one that was necessary to keep up with Queensland's growth. One of his lasting legacies was the establishment of a detective's branch which by the late 1890s was led by Urquhart, formerly of the controversial NMP. He was already notorious for leading the massacre of the Kalkatungu tribe of western Queensland in 1884, before joining the QPF and swiftly rising through the ranks to lead the detective's branch.[37] His time as an NMP commander gives insight into his views on aggressive justice and his later actions as a leader of the QPF. Mostly, it shows his propensity for disproportionate violence designed to deter further deviance. The royal commission into the management of the Criminal Investigation Branch (CIB) was called after Urquhart's team came under heavy criticism for its inability to solve a series of brutal murders that had captured the public's attention and stoked fear across the colony. First came the murder of a young boy in Oxley on 10 December 1898. Not long after came the triple murder of a brother and his two sisters returning home from a village dance in rural Gatton on 27 December.[38] Not used to dealing with mass casualty incidents like this in the normally sedate Queensland countryside, Urquhart initially treated the Gatton murders as a hoax and refused to act on a telegram about the incident for two days, showing, in the words of the commission, "a culpable indifference . . . to his duty to the public."[39]

The inquiry's criticism of Urquhart's handling of the Gatton murders was just the beginning of its highly negative portrayal of his professional capabilities. In its final report, the commission described Urquhart as displaying an "impulsive and exacting temperament [as well as] a vindictive and tyrannical nature."[40] The commission recommended his removal as head of the CIB, arguing that a man of Urquhart's personality was not fit to lead the colony's detectives. Urquhart was lucky. It was not the nature of the QPF or the colonial government to take directions from a mere judge, even if they had asked him to provide recommendations to improve the CIB in the first place. He remained in his position for a further six years, before being promoted to chief inspector of the QPF in 1905.[41] If presiding over massacres and bungled investigations was not enough to stunt his promising police career, neither was his "vindictive and tyrannical nature"—nor would it be enough to stunt the careers of many others who followed in Urquhart's footsteps.

The Australian colonies' federation into a united nation in 1901 was treated with healthy skepticism and profound lack of enthusiasm by many Queenslanders. When asked to vote on federation in an 1899 referendum, only 65 percent of qualified voters turned up to vote. Only 55 percent of those who did turn up at the ballot box voted in favor of federation, the lowest yes vote across the country.[42] The argument that the Australian colonies all shared a common culture and history that united them was a questionable proposition for Queenslanders. The colony had fought for its independence from New South Wales in the 1850s and had forged its own path as a society that was distinct from its neighbors. Yet here it was, only a few decades later, and Queensland was once more coupled to the domineering (and economically powerful) southern colonies. The same old problems immediately began to emerge. While Queensland argued against an exclusionary White Australia policy, in need of "colored" labor to sustain its agricultural industry, it found itself railroaded by inaugural prime minister Edmond Barton, who pushed through laws that severely curtailed Queensland's economic fortunes by precluding the use of migrant labor.[43] Indeed, Queensland threatened to withdraw from the federation altogether. The move was seriously considered by Queensland premier Robert Philip as a response to Barton's betrayal, but was shelved when the tide of public opinion shifted. The press began to lambast Philip's plan, going so far as to caricature the would-be secessionist as an American Civil War general carrying a blunt sword, mocking his lack of political power in the newly federated system. Though the Queensland independence movement never truly gained traction, it shows the reluctance of the state to become part of the newly born country of Australia.

The new state was once more playing the role of inferior northern cousin to the more diversified economies and established political elite of the south, just as it did before 1859, when Queensland first separated from New South Wales. Worse, these states represented everything that idyllic, rural Queensland was not. As the twentieth century dawned, both New South Wales and Victoria were feeling the effects of rapid, unsustainable growth that saw the development of working-class slums and, as a result, a criminal underclass. In this era, the concept of urban decay was rife, adding to the resentment of many Queenslanders who saw in their southern neighbors an immoral, corrupt society where dangerous ideas and behaviors were cultivated. That the leaders of societies like this would dare to tell Queenslanders what to do was bad enough, but the threat of those very southerners flocking north was a frightening proposition that fed into the moral panic around a "southern invasion" at least until the end of Joh Bjelke-Petersen's tenure as premier in the late 1980s.

Rebellion was always a part of Queensland's DNA, as was the critical role of the working classes, so it is unsurprising that the state became a hotbed for the labor movement in the early-twentieth century. The reputation it developed in later years as an arch-conservative bastion often obscures the truth of its past as the birthplace of the Australian Labor Party. One of Australia's first major industrial disputes, the 1891 Shearer's Strike united the labor movement behind a singular cause and showed the power of collective action.[44] It was barely tolerable for the government when it was happening in rural Queensland, but the power of collective labor became unacceptable when it reached Brisbane during the 1912 general strike. The strike began when 480 tram drivers in Brisbane were suspended from duty in January 1912 for showing support to the union movement. They took to the streets in protest. As thousands of retrenched workers took to the streets, the strikers publicly claimed that "there [were] not sufficient police in all of Brisbane to restrain them."[45] The challenge was issued, and conservative premier Digby Denham accepted it.

With tram company owner Joseph Stillman Badger calling on Police Commissioner William Geoffrey Cahill to have "police turn their firearms upon the strikers," Denham made the decision to swear in three thousand "Special" officers to supplement the police ranks.[46] Denham's decision to call in the Specials was not unusual, or even radical, for the time. Their use as "strikebreakers" became increasingly prevalent in the early twentieth century, as governments struggled with the threat posed by organized labor. Several years after Brisbane's 1912 general strike, the Canadian city of Winnipeg would go even further and dismiss its entire police force for refusing to sign an anti-union pledge, replacing them with a much larger force of untrained Special Constables. Unlike the situation in Winnipeg, Denham had the police firmly onside in Queensland. Instead of replacing incalcitrant officers, the recruitment of the Specials in 1912 was intended to bolster the strength of the QPF and present a show of force designed to deter the strikers and bring an end to the industrial action once and for all. The man placed in charge of the response to the strikers was well-acquainted with using extreme force to deter opposition: none other than the "vindictive and tyrannical" Urquhart.

The stage was set for a brutal battle. Armed with a force made up largely of untrained Specials, chances that Urquhart would use extreme violence to end the strike were high. On 1 February 1912, Urquhart showed his willingness to use such means. When protesters swarmed a beer truck on Roma Street, Urquhart ordered the officers under his command to mount a baton charge to disperse them. When this failed, he ordered his "car to be driven into the mass of strikers."[47] The fact that no one was killed by the police who drove at protesters was fortuitous, but this nevertheless shows the authorities' plain disregard for the safety of protesters. The beer truck incident was the final straw for Urquhart. The next day, he gave the order to shoot any protesters who refused to disperse during a demonstration in central Brisbane's Market Square. The incident on 2 February became known as the Baton Friday riot. It brought an end to the general strike at the end of a baton, as senior police like Cahill and Urquhart led a charge on strikers that resulted in a pitched street battle. Premier Denham rushed through new legislation to curtail the union movement in the aftermath of Baton Friday, trading on the community fears of a repeat of the violence.[48] This riot was a turning point for Queensland. Apart from the Bread and Blood riots, this was one of the first times the QPF was used by the government to forcibly crush left-wing opposition. It was a model of social control that would be used again in the future under the conservative rule of Frank Nicklin and, most notoriously, Bjelke-Petersen.

Civil unrest in Brisbane did not end with the Baton Friday riot, and when it returned Urquhart was, once again, at the center of the conflict. Five years after the general strike of 1912, he reached the pinnacle of his career, assuming the position of police commissioner on 1 January.[49] His time in charge of the QPF was in most ways unremarkable apart from his involvement in the 1919 Red Flag riots, where more than eight thousand Queenslanders took to the streets and laid siege to the Russian Hall in South Brisbane. The riots came in the aftermath of World War I, when there were fears in Australian politics about the influence of Bolshevik politics among the Russian émigré community. One of Urquhart's first acts as police commissioner was to attend a conference on 17 February 1917 on how to deal with the "threat" of "alien enemy suspects and agents." A policy developed at the federal level called on police around Australia to provide support to antisocialist vigilante groups in the fight against Bolshevism. Ever ready for conflict, Urquhart accepted the role as "permanent formal head" of the antisocialist movement and began "making the rounds of the extant patriotic organizations in Brisbane, dropping 'various hints' about the possibility of a more formidable coordination of loyalist forces."[50] Urquhart's new plan was more insidious: rather than riding directly into danger, in his new plan he would incite others to do the work for him.

Urquhart's plan came to fruition on 23 March 1919 when antisocialist vigilantes disrupted a left-wing protest against political censorship. The next night the antisocialists gathered again, this time marching on the Russian Hall. Police assembled outside as an estimated eight thousand descended on the venue, with Urquhart assuming command. He controlled the scene, to the benefit of the vigilante horde. Though standard procedure would have seen the police mount a bayonet charge to disperse the crowd, he ordered his officers to hold the line. The standoff lasted for two hours. In this time, scuffles erupted between police and rioters that ended with around twenty officers (including Urquhart) injured.[51] When détente was reached, it was because the police gave in to the will of the assembled mob. Police even gave the riot's ringleaders a guided tour of the Russian Hall to satisfy them that—in the words of historian Raymond Evans—"no Bolsheviks were hiding under any beds."[52] Afterwards, the mob was satisfied and willingly dispersed. In the 1888 Election Night riots, the QPF stood by as a conservative mob aggressively mounted a campaign of xenophobic violence. In 1919, the police stood against them only when they seemed set to tear the city apart searching for Russians to satisfy their bloodlust.

Brisbane settled into a phase of incremental, somewhat meandering expansion after the Red Flag riots. Several decades before in 1885 the colonial government had introduced the Undue Subdivision of Land Prevention Act, an early attempt at purpose-driven urban design intended to prevent Brisbane's center becoming overcrowded.[53] It provided a minimum size limit for residential properties that prevented the construction of the kind of terrace houses typical of inner-city Sydney or Melbourne. These terrace, or row, houses were reflective of a Victorian era design trend adopted as a means to enhance the residential capacity of the urban space by cutting the size of a property. The result was medium-to-high density neighborhoods populated predominantly by the working classes. The need for space mandated by the Undue Subdivision of Land Prevention Act in Queensland largely avoided the construction of terrace houses and inevitably pushed new residents to the city's outskirts, fostering a sprawling, semi-rural suburban environment.[54] Combined with the vast expanses of land available for development on the outskirts of the city and the increasing ubiquity of the motor vehicle in the late nineteenth and early twentieth centuries allowing for a suburban commuter lifestyle, the restrictive building laws prevented the evolution of the slums seen in the southern capitals. As a result Brisbane mostly avoided the poor social conditions seen elsewhere in Australia during this era. There were no razor gang wars or conflicts over control of vice. Instead, Brisbane fell into a slumber that could only be disturbed by the eruption of war in the Pacific.

Australia had been committed to World War II since the beginning, when Prime

Minister Robert Menzies announced on the wireless radio on 3 September 1939 that it was his "melancholy duty" to inform the Australian people that Great Britain had declared war on Germany, and "as a result, Australia is also at war."[55] When Japan entered the war in December 1941, dragging the United States into the conflict with the attack on Pearl Harbor, Australia found itself in a position it had never been in before: right in the middle of a theatre of war. In July 1942 the American commander of the Southwest Pacific Area, Douglas MacArthur, chose Brisbane as the site of the headquarters from which he would direct his campaign. The city was the northernmost location in Australia with the infrastructure needed to serve as MacArthur's headquarters, and it brought the Allied contingent far closer to the actual conflict zone.[56] It was also central to a controversial plan mulled over by the federal government that would see Australia concede the area north of Brisbane to a Japanese invasion, retreating to Brisbane to reinforce a line of defense that would protect the crucial industrial and agricultural regions in the south.[57] Prime Minister John Curtin denied his government had developed such a plan and, instead, stoked fears that abandoning northern Australia to the Japanese was actively considered by the Menzies-Fadden Opposition. Despite his rejection of the strategy, there is evidence to suggest Curtin's government was actively prepared to withdraw its defenses in the region to protect vital industry south of the Tropic of Capricorn.[58] The plan was referred to by MacArthur himself as "the Brisbane Line"—a rhetorical comparison to the Maginot Line established by France in the 1930s with similar objectives in mind.[59] Once again, a century after free settlement began, Brisbane was cast as the frontier of the Australian continent, the chosen venue of the country's last stand against Japanese invasion.

It was never Brisbane's choice to play host to the millions of Allied troops who passed through the city from 1942 to 1945, but its time as MacArthur's base of operations did more to change the culture of the city than any other event to that point. Brisbane had begun to forget its wild, colonial history in the early twentieth century. It was no longer the rough and tumble gothic town built by people like Logan and ruled by the likes of Mayne. It had calmed, and its citizens had settled into the doldrums of quiet, suburban life in the years before war broke out. But now it was alive again. The war brought with it unspeakable carnage, but for Brisbanites the influx of foreigners revitalized the city beyond measure. With the troops came changes to sexual norms and a demand for vice. Into this strange new world, born from the ashes of the old city, a new social order rose that openly rejected the old ways of doing business in Queensland and sought to overturn the "natural order" at every turn. This newfound permissiveness found a strident opposition in the moral crusaders of conservative Queensland, who saw the war not as a turning point but as an aberration in the otherwise parochial, traditional story of Queensland. The opposing forces of social progress and social conservativism ran against each other uncomfortably in the post-war landscape as Queensland struggled to find a new normal. From this chaos emerged a police officer with aspirations of greatness. His name was Francis Erich Bischof. By the time the 1950s came to an end, he would be Queensland's police commissioner.

CHAPTER 2

The End of the Green Mafia

In the 1950s, it was Jim Donovan's turn to sit in the commissioner's chair. He knew it, and, more importantly, the premier knew it too. The Allied occupation of Brisbane of 1942–1945 had shaken the foundations of the city, but it was now a time to return to the normal state of politics, where nepotism and sectarianism dictated the course of events. Donovan was a good police officer. He was honest, for one. Even better, he was a respected leader of men. Being an Irish Catholic didn't hurt either. Catholics tended to prosper in the government of Vince Gair, who was a part of the largely Catholic right-wing faction of Queensland's Labor Party.[1] Labor was split along sectarian lines between the Catholic workers and communists throughout the 1950s, with the feuding groups even splitting into separate entities in other states. But the Catholics were ascendant in Queensland. Gair's group consolidated power after he took office in 1952, and Irish Catholics—nicknamed the "Green Mafia"—had incrementally taken control of the public service after years of political appointments.[2] Donovan was well-placed to be the Gair government's choice to succeed Thomas William Harold when the time came for him to retire as police commissioner. He served as Harold's deputy, and in doing so, he felt like he was the natural successor. All that remained was to wait for nature to take its course and for the next Catholic officer of the Queensland Police Force (QPF) to claim his rightful place at the top of the force.

The collapse of the Gair government in 1957 gave Donovan reason to pause. The rise of the majority Protestant government of Frank Nicklin in its place posed a real threat to Donovan's career prospects. Even so, he had been groomed for the commissioner's job. For years he had been given opportunities to hone his skills and experience to the point that, even without the backing of a Catholic government, he was still the best person for the job, maybe even the *only* person for the job. When Nicklin announced that Harold was retiring due to ill health, Donovan was prepared and positioned to take over in a seamless transition.[3] The new premier's decision not to give Donovan the job that he had been waiting for was a reproach, not just to the deputy commissioner but to the entirety of the Green Mafia. It was a statement that, under Nicklin, there would be no more special treatment for Catholics, no God-given right to control the QPF. This was to be a new era of governance in Queensland, and there was no place for public servants with loyalties to "the other side." To the victors went the spoils. Donovan, to his regret, was not a victor. The man who benefited from Donovan's shifting fortunes did not have anywhere close to the experience of his rival. There were even suggestions that he might be corrupt, a hot-shot detective who sometimes bent the rules to make arrests and, even worse, could have taken bribes from illegal bookmakers. Despite all of this rumor and innuendo, Francis Erich Bischof (best known as just "Frank") had one thing going for him that Donovan didn't—he wasn't a Catholic.

There is a long tradition of religious sectarianism in the Australian public service. In many ways, it was an imported conflict borne from division that began in the mother country before Australia was settled. In Ireland, the eighteenth century had been an ascendant time for the Protestant minority while the Catholic majority suffered through poverty and famine. Social tensions came to a head in the 1798 Irish Rebellion when, inspired by the success of the recent American and French revolutions, a group of dispossessed Presbyterians and Catholics launched an assault on the Anglo-Irish establishment. Even with the support of troops sent by France to aid their cause, the rebellion was put down in brutal fashion.[4] It was at the very same time that the Irish Catholics were clamoring for political emancipation that settlement in Australia began, and there is no doubt that events back home influenced relations between English and Irish settlers in the new colonies. The continuation of the conflict in Australia resulted in a "suspicion and hostility" that contributed to a "mutually antagonistic relationship" between the two religious groups.[5] Although priding itself as an egalitarian nation, Australia did not hold the same opportunity for all new migrants. Traditional states of privilege were replicated. Wealthy settlers, typically English Protestants, invested their capital in order to become established as successful merchants or pastoralists. For many Irish Catholic migrants, there was no hope of this. Instead, they flocked to working-class professions where they could make a living and put food on the table.

It is unsurprising, then, that Irish Catholics would come to be closely associated with the union movement and later the Australian Labor Party. The country's existing political parties were dominated by members of the English establishment and (whether implicitly or explicitly) precluded Irish Catholic involvement. The Labor Party's formation after the 1891 Shearer's Strike gave a voice to working-class labor who, prior to this, had been largely disenfranchised in Australian politics. Much of this labor was Irish Catholic, but not all. From the beginning, the Labor Party provided a broad church for the working classes no matter their religious or ethnic background. For many police, it was a natural political choice. There is a strong tradition of unionism in policing, not to mention the sizeable Irish Catholic cohort in the police ranks around Australia.[6] In states like Queensland, where the Labor Party was in power, Irish Catholic support for the party in the police force translated to preferential treatment. In the background to his final report on police corruption, Fitzgerald notes that "patronage, rather than money, was the primary currency" of the Gair era.[7] In this climate, men like Donovan could expect to see their careers fast-tracked, sometimes at the expense of officers who were not in the Green Mafia. Corrupt in its own way, the system of nepotism was simply a fact of political life at the time the Gair government abruptly fell from power.

A truism of Australian politics (proven in recent years) is that internal division is far more prone to topple a sitting government than any external threat.[8] The same was true for Gair in 1957 when the right-wing Catholic contingent that ruled Queensland's Labor entered a fight to the death with the socialist forces of the union movement. For years the Gair faction prevailed over the more hard-liner elements of the labor movement in Queensland through sheer strength of numbers—the right-wingers controlled the government and, thus, power. But realities of governing are often hard, and Gair increasingly found himself unable to accede to the demands of the unions for better compensation and conditions. His decision to abandon the Labor Party's promise to offer three weeks of paid leave to workers because the state couldn't afford it was the final straw. Union activists Joe Bukowski and Jack Egerton mounted a successful campaign to incite delegates at a Labor Party conference in

February 1956 to vote in favor of reinstating the leave increase in the parliamentary party's platform.[9] After four years as state premier, Gair and his allies found themselves at an impasse with Queensland's labor movement, with both refusing to shift from their position. As a new year dawned, it was Gair's view that at the end of the day, he held all the cards. He was the premier of Queensland, a position of great authority from which he had staved off challenges from the militant elements of his own party before. Ultimately, the Labor Party would realize this and fall into line.

Gair was wrong. He was expelled from the Labor Party on 24 April 1957, more than a year after his start of his conflict with the unions. He didn't go quietly. On his expulsion, Gair took with him almost the entire Labor Party cabinet, all of whom were in firm agreement with their leader's stance on leave entitlements.[10] Desperate, the premier turned to an old enemy for support. Gair approached Nicklin, who led the state's opposition Country Party, and suggested an alliance that would allow Gair to remain in charge and give Nicklin's group power in a new coalition government. Nicklin was close to agreeing when his federal counterpart Arthur Fadden suggested that Nicklin might be better served by doing nothing at all. After months of floundering, a combination of the state's opposition parties voted to block supply to the Gair government, cutting off the money it had to govern. With no other choice, Gair was forced to call an election for 3 August 1957. On polling day, Nicklin's coalition swept to power with a considerable majority. His victory was the first time in twenty-five years that the state had elected a non–Labor Party government. Gair's fall reverberated in Queensland for years to come, but nowhere felt the impact more than the police force.

Nicklin came into power on a wave of change. In the space of a year, the Labor Party had destroyed itself. The once unassailable political machine was in tatters, and there was little chance that it would recover to provide a viable opposition any time soon. But the parliamentary Labor Party wasn't the only threat to Nicklin's power. Years of patronage had taken a toll on Queensland's permanent bureaucracy, and even with the Labor Party gone, there was still a profound Catholic presence in the public service. If the bureaucrats given jobs under the Gair government owed a debt to the Labor Party for their position, a shared Catholic heritage only exacerbated the risk for Nicklin. Although itching for the opportunity to rule, the Country Party were inexperienced at governing, and it had to be able to rely on the state's public servants for guidance. Nicklin had to be able to trust the information that he was receiving, and he could not do that while the remnants of the Labor Party remained in place. The police force was always on his priority list for restructuring and restaffing. It was vital that the premier be able to rely on the police to enforce his policies and keep order on the streets. But the QPF was dominated by the Green Mafia, which meant there were no guarantees that it would fall in line behind Nicklin's agenda.

Luck would have it that Nicklin got his chance to reshape the police force soon after his election. The sitting police commissioner, Harold, had only been in the role for a year and, by rights, should have been settling in for a long stretch in the job. But for some reason, the former government had chosen a man close to retirement age. Harold could have stayed in the role for several more years, but his age provided Nicklin with the chance he needed to force reform. Harold's days were numbered. It did not help that Harold and Nicklin had clashed almost immediately after the new government took the reins of power. Former premier Gair spoke in state parliament after Harold retired to cast doubt on the official reason for his ousting. Even though "ill health" was cited as the reason for Harold stepping down, Gair speculated that Nicklin had realized that Harold was "somewhat difficult . . . not a yes-man" and decided to replace him with a police chief that was more open to doing the government's bidding.[11] Whatever the real reason, the moment that Donovan had been waiting for had arrived: applications for the position of Queensland's eleventh police commissioner were open. There was considerable interest in the role, and the government received more than two hundred applications.[12] There were only two that were ever real contenders, though. One was the man groomed for the job: the dependable and honest deputy commissioner, Donovan. The other was a maverick, but a detective who "had runs on the board": the hotshot CIB chief, Bischof.[13]

Bischof, referred to in the QPF as "The Big Fella," was a force of nature. The country boy from rural Toowoomba weighed in at 220 pounds and was six foot two, a looming figure who was able to intimidate even the most hardened criminals. Born on 12 October 1904, he was raised on a dairy farm as one of nine children born to August and Sophia. The young Bischof was a dairyman, through and through. He grew up milking cows, and once he finished school, he took a job in a local cheese factory.[14] The life of a humble farmer was never in the cards for him, though. He was twenty-one years old, still working in the cheese factory, when a more glamourous job captured his imagination. Gone were the days of milking and churning—the Big Fella was going to become a police officer.

Bischof joined the QPF in 1925 and rose through the ranks quickly. Within three years he was promoted to detective, and then in 1933, he was appointed to the most prestigious posting: the Brisbane Criminal Investigation Branch (CIB).[15] It was here that Bischof flourished. The capital's CIB was the best of the best, staffed by the kind of hardnosed and heavy-drinking detectives that Bischof aspired to be. The most notorious cases in the state came through the Brisbane CIB, and its officers were often called on to travel around the state and lend their expertise whenever a major crime occurred in far-flung towns. His career was well on its way before the war reached Brisbane. In September 1941, he was sent to the mining town of Mount Isa to investigate the death of Greek migrant Naum Poplo and arrested Albanian miner George Elias for the crime in what was, at the time, one of the state's most prominent murder cases.[16] The Big Fella was making a name for himself in Queensland, but then the war came, and the normal course of events were (for a time) suspended. His march to the top would have to wait, for now.

Bischof had developed a reputation as "good police," a detective who got results on tough cases and, more crucially, was loyal to his fellow officers. Unlike some career-minded officers in the QPF, he was not a teetotaler or a moralistic wowser. He was certainly not a dour, serious Catholic like his boss in the CIB, Donovan. Bischof was a person that other men liked to be around. He was a drinker and was known to fancy a punt on the horse races every now and again.

Bischof's love for the track was seen as problematic by some. There were rumors that he did more than gamble. Some in the QPF had raised questions about why certain off-track bookmakers in Toowoomba had prospered when he was stationed there, and suggested that he might have had a hand in it.[17] The rumors persisted but did not have much of an impact. After all, he was not the only officer protecting illegal gambling in Queensland. In April 1951, Liberal politician Thomas Hiley accused the QPF of protecting a bookmaking operation in Ipswich where the principal offender, J. Marsden, was paying bribes to members of the Labor Party government.[18] There is little doubt that Catholic officers in the QPF were just as involved in protecting vice as Protestants like Bischof, so to tar him with the brush of corruption would have opened floodgates that the Labor Party government could not have stopped. So, Bischof was allowed to continue operating his protection racket unimpeded by his superiors. Even when he transferred to the Brisbane CIB, he allegedly continued controlling the gambling trade in his native Toowoomba. Moving to Brisbane did not slow him down—if anything, it just extended his opportunities to bring more vice operators into his protection scheme.

The free rein that Bischof was given to operate his protection racket came as a product of his successes as a detective. Since joining the CIB in 1933, he had cultivated a strong record of obtaining convictions. In fact, by the time he left to take up the police commissioner position, he could boast a clearance rate of solving thirty-two out of the thirty-three murder cases that he worked on.[19] There were rumors about his success here, too. It was an open secret in the QPF that one of the biggest weapons in Bischof's arsenal was his skill at "the verbal." Detectives in this era were aware that the most effective way to secure a conviction was to provide the court with a confession. Not only did it convince a jury beyond doubt that the offender was guilty, it also boosted the detective's career by giving the impression that the case was solved solely because of their professional skill. Unfortunately for police, suspects were usually reluctant to admit their wrongdoings in the interrogation room, and so the verbal was born. With the mandatory recording of all police interviews still several decades off, it was a simple task for the detective to draft a false confession and submit it to the court as an unsigned record of interview.[20] An accused would deny saying they did the crime, but it was their word against the police. There was usually more than one person in on the verbal. One-by-one, each officer attached to the case would stand before the court and testify that the tendered document was a genuine confession. The verbal was not a practice devised by Bischof. Its use in the QPF (and other police forces around Australia) was prolific, and Bischof mastered it at the feet of those who came before him, including the detectives that he idolized in the CIB.

Increasingly in the time since, critical research has undermined the usefulness of a confession, calling into question the coercive nature of police interrogations and the influence that such coercion has on a suspect's willingness to falsely admit guilt. Dylan J. French argues that most false confessions are the result of accusatory interrogation techniques deriving from the Reid Method, in which investigators are more focused on extracting a confession than probing a suspect for the truth.[21] In Bischof's case, however, there was no need to go to such lengths to pressure a suspect into admitting to something that they did not do. Absent modern recording equipment, it was more than enough for an officer to simply construct a confession out of thin air and, when the accused denied it, pose the question of who is more deserving of a jury's trust: an accused criminal or the police officer who caught him? False confessions continue to play a major role in miscarriages of justice around the world, but the ease with which a verbal could be committed made it particularly dangerous.

Bischof was alleged to have used the verbal in most of the cases he solved. It seems that the more prominent a case was, the more likely it was he would use the verbal to get a result. The conviction of Reginald Wingfield Brown in 1947 for the murder of his secretary, Bronia Armstrong, was one such case. Nineteen-year-old Armstrong was found strangled to death in Brown's office in the Brisbane Arcade on Queen Street in January 1947.[22] Bischof was not the lead detective on the case but (as he often did in big cases) found a way to become involved in the investigation. He was part of the team that interviewed Brown and, by the end of that conversation, police claimed to have obtained a statement from their suspect that indicated Brown, driven mad from sexual desire, had killed Armstrong. He was convicted but denied making admissions to Bischof and the other police that were later used against him in court. Brown was found dead in his cell at Boggo Road Jail nine days after being sentenced to life in prison, leaving a note claiming that he had been beaten and verballed by the police investigating Armstrong's murder.[23]

The same allegation was made in another of Bischof's most famous cases, the Southport Taxi Driver murder. On 22 May 1952, taxi driver Athol McCowan was battered to death in his car on the Southport Esplanade, south of Brisbane. The man charged with the crime, Arthur "Slim" Halliday was a recidivist offender who was released from Boggo Road in June 1949. Bischof told the court that Halliday was caught in a Parramatta hospital after shooting himself in the leg during a botched robbery. While in hospital, Bischof testified that Halliday admitted to having killed McCowan when he fought back while being robbed.[24] When Bischof said this in court, Halliday jumped to his feet and claimed the detective was lying. Even after being convicted and sentenced to twenty-three years in prison, Halliday continued to insist that he didn't murder Athol McCowan. In fact, he said he was 250 miles away when McCowan was killed.[25] Once again, the stench of the verbal lingered around one of the Big Fella's prize convictions. While the media reported on allegations of verballing, especially when made in the dramatic fashion Halliday did at trial, there was simply not enough public opposition to the practice to warrant a full investigation of how prevalent in was in this period. Overall, Queensland was still a conservative state. Even its Labor Party government was dominated by Catholics and Old Left trade unionists who, on the spectrum of leftist politics, erred towards the traditional. In such a society, support for the police was paramount, and thus, there was little incentive for government to investigate the practice of verballing and risk upsetting the status quo. So long as police were taking criminals off the street, the rumors of fabricated confessions were swept under the rug, ignored.

The Bulimba election fraud case was Bischof's first opportunity to show that he was not the servant of the Green Mafia or beholden to the Labor Party government.

The state election in 1950, as expected, saw Labor Party comfortably returned to power. But a close result in the south Brisbane division of Bulimba gave cause for greater scrutiny. While a Labor Party–held seat, the sitting member of Parliament for Bulimba had recently retired. A local painter named Bob Gardner was chosen to replace him as the Labor Party candidate, and after a tightly fought campaign, he won the seat. His victory was short-lived. After closer inspection of the ballot papers, electoral officers discovered that fake ballot papers had been lodged that helped him get across the line.[26] The CIB were called, and Bischof was sent to Bulimba to find out who was responsible for the fraud. Whoever rigged the election had obviously wanted Gardner to win, so it made sense to assign the case to Bischof. He was a successful detective, a Protestant Mason, and not part of the Green Mafia with its connections to the Labor Party government.

In the end, the result of the election was vacated, and in a rerun, Gardner won legitimately. Bischof's investigation found its culprit. He charged another member of the public service's Green Mafia, Chief Electoral Officer Bernard Maguire, with eight counts of forging ballot papers.[27] The Bulimba election fraud was not Bischof's usual murder investigation, yet did more for his career than any case that came before it. He proved he was not like other police, beholden to the Green Mafia and its masters in the state parliament. He was someone who went after the Labor Party establishment, revealing the unspoken truth that the public service was no more than an extension of the party, willing to commit corruption to ensure victory. The Bulimba case no doubt put Bischof on Nicklin's radar so that, when he became premier, the possibility of installing Bischof as police commissioner would have held great appeal.

The death of Mount Isa man Michael Jorgensen was a flashpoint that Nicklin hoped to resolve with the selection of a new QPF commissioner. Jorgensen was arrested on 7 February 1956, after police claimed he intervened and tried to incite another person to resist arrest. After spending the night in the Mount Isa holding cells, he complained to officers Paul McArthur and Eric Keith Murray that he was experiencing stomach pains. He was ignored at first, but he later died in hospital.[28] As usually happens whenever someone dies in police custody, a QPF team was dispatched to investigate the death. The team, led by Deputy Commissioner Donovan, recommended that McArthur and Murray be charged with unlawful killing. The investigation found that Jorgensen sustained his injuries during or after arrest, and that McArthur and Murray were the most likely culprits. Donovan's team discovered that they admitted to beating Jorgensen around the head when he refused to take his shoes off in the cells, and Jorgensen said in a statement before he died that the pair had also punched him repeatedly in the stomach during the altercation.[29] To make matters worse McArthur and Murray failed to obtain medical assistance for Jorgensen when he first complained of feeling unwell, further contributing to his death.

Despite Donovan's recommendations, the state prosecutor felt there was not enough evidence to secure a conviction and declined to pursue the case against McArthur and Murray. Commissioner Harold had, at first, been waiting for the outcome of the court case to take further action, but when prosecutors made the decision to not continue, Harold was free to make his own move. Citing the lies that were told to Donovan during the Jorgensen investigation, McArthur and Murray were fired from the police force on 15 November 1957.[30] The Jorgensen case was an embarrassment for the Nicklin government and showcased the headstrong nature of Commissioner Harold. For Nicklin, the prosecutor's decision to drop the charges against McArthur and Murray was a free pass. There would be no trial, no scandal, no claim for restitution. Even so, stubborn Harold insisted on keeping the scandal alive. If he was unsure about Harold's allegiance before, Nicklin was certain now. Harold could not be trusted to bend to the new government's will. He had to go and soon.

The dismissal of McArthur and Murray was one of Harold's last acts as police commissioner. It was not long before his "ill health" had become too much to bear, and the hunt was on for a replacement to take the commissioner's office. The Jorgensen affair had tainted Donovan almost as much as it had Harold. It was Donovan who started the entire thing, in Nicklin's eyes. If the deputy commissioner had held firm to the blue brotherhood of policing, McArthur and Murray would never have been charged in the first place. It was clear that, like Harold, Donovan was too honest for his own good. Then there was Bischof: successful, not tainted with a connection to the Green Mafia, and (as the Bulimba case showed) no friend to the Labor Party. The rumors of his corruption were certainly known to the selection panel. A few years earlier, in 1953, Bischof was awarded a promotion to take charge of the Toowoomba police district, his home turf. Not long before he was supposed to make the move, the transfer was cancelled. Then-commissioner John Smith claimed there were personal, domestic reasons for the cancellation. It is possible that concerns over Bischof's protection of bookmakers in the region may have influenced Smith's reconsideration of the decision.[31] In any case, the abortive promotion did little to slow Bischof's career advancement. When Donovan left to take on the deputy commissioner's role in 1955, it was Bischof who was selected for his plum position as officer-in-charge of the CIB.[32]

Bischof's wildcard reputation added to his appeal, from Nicklin's perspective. Harold and Donovan had shown in the Jorgensen case that there were clear risks when dealing with police officers who stuck too closely to the rules. Harold was willing to fire them for dishonesty, even though it was in his and government's interests to do nothing and let the entire case go away. Bischof did not have the same ethical hang-ups. Sure, it was possible (even likely) that he turned a blind eye to vice for his own profit, but those were victimless crimes. He was a master of the verbal, but he used it for good, to get justice for victims and get killers off the street. He was a maverick who bent the rules, but that could be beneficial to the Nicklin government—so long as he was *their* maverick, working in the best interests of the government. When it came time to interview the lead contenders, Bischof's performance in front of the selection panel pushed the decision over the edge in his favor. More than anything, Nicklin was obsessed about changing the way that Queensland operated. In his interview, Donovan said he believed things ran well in the QPF, and he was committed to maintaining "business as usual." Bischof, on the other hand, presented as a clear contrast. He came to the interview with new ideas for professional development and structural reform. Thomas Hiley, now Nicklin's treasurer, was on the panel and recalls Bischof saying "that his duty to the state outweighed his duty to any single officer."[33] Nicklin was sold. The coronation of Donovan would not go ahead. The Green Mafia was out, and the Big Fella was in.

The story that did the rounds in the CIB was that, when Bischof was told he was being appointed commissioner, he raced to the police building at Petrie Terrace as fast as he could "before anyone could take the position away from him."[34] Donovan was, of course, furious at the decision. He was the more qualified and the more experienced candidate for the office. It was cold comfort that Bischof would keep him on as deputy commissioner. He spent the rest of his career waiting for his chance to take down his rival from within.

Donovan was not the only QPF officer to register their concerns about Bischof's surprise promotion. Charlie Corner had a long history with Bischof. He had worked with the new commissioner on the Poplo case in Mount Isa in 1941. When Corner testified in that case, he contradicted Bischof's evidence in small ways, a possible resistance to the detective's characteristic creative recording of police statements.[35] Corner had other run-ins with Bischof after transferring to Brisbane to join the Licensing Branch several years later. After he arrested a sex worker for vagrancy at one of the city's brothels, Corner was called into the office of then-CIB inspector Bischof, who questioned him over the arrest. When the woman later attended court, she was given bail based on the recommendation of Inspector Bischof and subsequently left the city. Corner was told by several madams that Bischof was "collecting weekly" from the brothels in Brisbane in return for protecting their interests.[36] Corner lodged a formal complaint when Bischof became commissioner, to no avail.

Nicklin's move to take control of the QPF away from the Green Mafia came under fire in state parliament. Senior Labor Party politician Ted Walsh compared the decision to pass Donovan over to Adolf Hitler taking control of the police in Nazi Germany, a powerful allusion given that it was only thirteen years since the war ended. He noted that "it was he [Hitler] who, having corrupted the top of the Police Force, found it so easy to corrupt he whole of the force ... when he succeeded in corrupting the administration, it was easy for him to take over."[37] Bischof's critics were incensed that Donovan was not chosen, arguing that he was the more senior candidate and, as such, should have been chosen to take over from Harold. The support shown for Donovan among Labor Party politicians did not sway Nicklin. In fact, the fact that the Labor Party was going to bat so strongly for Donovan was proof that he had made the right choice, that Donovan was a Labor Party man who would not have served in the best interests of the Nicklin government. The premise that Donovan was senior and should have been given the job was dismissed by Nicklin, who argued that promotion should be based on merit and that Bischof was chosen with this principle in mind. He framed the decision to pick Bischof as a strike against the corruption of the Labor Party era, where patronage was traded in exchange for allegiance to the ruling party. Bischof's appointment was cast as the start of a new era of transparency in the QPF, but before that new era could begin, there would first be a reckoning with the past.

The decision to fire McArthur and Murray was still a sore point for Nicklin and Ken Morris, the Cabinet member responsible for police. As expected, McArthur and Murray had made the decision to fight their dismissal at the Police Appeals Board, and as a result, the scandal continued to threaten to erupt at any given moment. With Harold gone and Donovan under control, it might now be possible to end the Jorgensen affair once and for all. Who better to accomplish this than the new commissioner, a man who was reputed to have a loose relationship with the truth and would understand why McArthur and Murray had not told the whole truth to Donovan. They were scheduled to face the Police Appeals Board in February 1958, a month after Bischof's appointment. He had to act fast if he was to intervene in the process before it was too late. In one of his first moves as commissioner, Bischof broke protocol and intervened in the appeals procedure on behalf of the former Mount Isa officers. In a letter to Ken Morris on 3 March 1958, Bischof said that, after considering the case and reading Donovan's report, he came to the decision that dismissal would set a bad precedent for future cases. Because of this, he overturned Harold's decision to fire McArthur and Murray and reinstated both to their former positions in the QPF on 27 February 1958.[38]

It was just short of two years since Jorgensen's death, and finally, the scandal was almost at an end. Bischof, the man who had won over the selection panel by saying that the needs of the force superseded commitment to the blue brotherhood, had backflipped on his promise. Bischof's intervention with the Police Appeals Board was not a matter of him coming to the conclusion that McArthur and Murray had not lied to Donovan. In his letter to Morris, he admitted that the officers had not told the truth but took into consideration the stress they were under while being investigated for murdering Jorgensen.[39] Nicklin had gambled correctly when he predicted that Bischof would be open to bending the rules to get the result that he wanted. The end of the Jorgensen affair showed that Bischof would reject tradition when it suited him or even, if necessary, the Nicklin government. It also revealed that he had a keen ability to justify police misconduct, even in the most serious of cases. No one was ever charged with Jorgensen's death, and the whole sordid affair quickly faded from Queensland's collective memory. McArthur and Murray had their jobs back, and in Bischof, the premier had found a gifted new friend. No one saw the Big Fella coming.

From his position, Nicklin's choice to make Bischof the new police commissioner was a strike *against* corruption. Ironic as it may seem, for Nicklin this was a chance to take a stand against the tradition of nepotism that was the norm under his Labor Party predecessors. Presented with two options, Green Mafia favorite Donovan and outsider Bischof, Nicklin made a conscious decision to disempower the Catholics in the QPF and make it clear that, under his government, there would be no more "business as usual" in the promotions process. Admirable as his firm line against sectarian control of policing may have been, he could not know that putting Bischof in charge was akin to letting the fox into the chicken coop. Bischof's rise highlights the complex and often competing nature of corruption in a dynamic organization like the QPF. With the focus of anti-corruption in the late 1950s squarely set on sectarian nepotism, less political attention was afforded to police like Bischof, who allegedly took money to ignore "victimless crimes" like gambling and prostitution. In his haste to cleanse the police force of Labor Party loyalists like he did other state government departments, Nicklin ignored that simple fact that there is not just one monolithic "type" of corruption that exists in an organization like the QPF. Bischof may have been a rival to the Green Mafia, and he certainly did not benefit from the patronage of the Gair government, but this also did not mean that he was "clean." Faced with a binary choice, Nicklin chose to target political opponents rather than bribery and street-level corruption. In accepting this, the premier set the scene for three decades of rot in the police force, trickling down from the commissioner's office.

CHAPTER 3

Rats in the Ranks

On 22 January 1958 the law caught up with Raymond John Bailey as he tried to get into a car parked on a busy street in Mount Isa, an arid mining town in northwestern Queensland. He was returning to his car, a black 1938 DeSoto with South Australian plates, when two officers from the local Criminal Investigation Branch (CIB) emerged out of nowhere to take him into custody. Bailey had only been in town two weeks after making the long drive from South Australia, via the dusty roads of Australia's red center.[1] He brought his family with him, a wife and young son he told the detectives were at that moment staying in a caravan just out of town. Unwittingly, he had confirmed the suspicions of the Queensland police. Two days prior, local police received a call from their South Australian counterparts to be on the lookout for a black DeSoto connected to a man, woman, and fair-haired boy that had been spotted towing a caravan on the road to Mount Isa over a month earlier. It was, the South Australians believed, one of the only vehicles spotted in the area close to the Sundown station on 5 December 1958. The implications of that sighting were not good for Bailey: it made him one of the only suspects in the brutal slaying of Thyra Bowman, her fourteen-year-old daughter Wendy, and family friend Thomas Whelan.[2]

When the Mount Isa detectives got Bailey back to the station, local CIB chief

Glendon Patrick Hallahan took charge of interrogating his suspect. As the victims in the Sundown murders were shot dead, Hallahan asked him if he had a gun in his possession. According to the official record of the interview, Bailey denied this, but when Hallahan searched the DeSoto, he found a .32 caliber rifle.[3] This was not incriminating: the weapon used at Sundown was a .22 caliber gun. Even so, the discovery gave Hallahan cause to arrest Bailey for possessing an unlicensed pistol and continue his questioning. He searched Bailey's caravan, allegedly finding two packets of .22 caliber bullets. Bailey, again, denied owning such a gun and claimed the bullets were left in the caravan when he purchased it. Hallahan persisted, and eventually, the police record indicates that Bailey admitted to previously owning a .22 rifle that he had had with him when he left South Australia on the trip north towards Mount Isa. Later, in court, it transpired that he had stolen the .22 rifle from a man in South Australia, possibly explaining his reluctance to admit to possessing it.[4] Here, the record of the interview takes a strange turn. After repeatedly denying that he knew anything about the Sundown murders, Bailey suddenly had a story to tell. In a spontaneous confession, he blurted out, "I will tell you, I shot the young chap but I want to tell you how it happened."[5]

Hallahan, at twenty-five years old, had caught one of Australia's most wanted men. Not only that, he had done the unthinkable and forced a confession out of him that would ultimately see Bailey sentenced to death by hanging. Despite the prestige Hallahan had won, questions lingered. At his trial, Bailey asserted his innocence and that Hallahan had verballed him, producing an unsigned statement to secure a conviction.[6] The "confession" that Bailey had allegedly provided did not match how the Sundown murder victims were killed, and the .22 rifle was never located or tested to see if it matched the one used to kill the Bowmans and Whelan.[7] Despite all of the doubts, the court sent Bailey to the gallows. Within the Queensland Police Force (QPF), the case meant that Hallahan was now an officer on the rise. It did not escape the attention of new police commissioner Frank Bischof, who saw a certain talent in Hallahan. When the Big Fella visited Mount Isa, he met with Hallahan and, soon after, approved his transfer to the Brisbane CIB. From there, Hallahan would continue to build his career under Bischof's tutelage. The lessons the commissioner had to offer were not just about policework, however—the ambitious, talented Hallahan was about to get a crash course in corruption.

Bischof's mentoring of Hallahan was focused on bringing the ambitious young detective into a long-standing policing tradition, the protection one of the nation's most beloved recreational pastimes. Australians are some of the most prolific gamblers in the world.[8] In recent years, estimates have suggested that collective gambling losses in the country are around a billion dollars each year.[9] There is a long tradition of gambling in Australia, stretching back to the colonial era. Settlers played an ancient game called Two-Up, where pennies were tossed in the air and punters gambled on how the coins would fall. It wasn't long before horse racing tracks were built, and the first races at Sydney's Hyde Park took place in 1810.[10] There was a demand to place bets, and so the profession of the bookmaker emerged, a person who could calculate the odds and take bets on the outcome of races. Technically, before 1923, betting on races was completely illegal in Queensland. The first law to ban bookmaking was the Gaming Act 1850 and later, as the colony moved towards statehood, the law was once again recodified in the Suppression of Gambling Act 1895. Even when gambling laws were liberalized, a person was only allowed to take bets on races if they were physically present at the racetrack.[11] The law was designed to control the gambling industry as well as to protect punters from unscrupulous operators. In a time before wireless radios were commonly available, gamblers who weren't at the track had to rely on the honesty of their local bookie. Waiting for results to be published in the evening newspaper gave a bookie who was supposed to pay out a bet ample time to hit the road and disappear, he and the winnings never to be seen again. On-track betting could be regulated. It could be monitored by racing officials, and racetrack stewards or police could keep a close eye on problem bookies.

Technology was a game-changer for the betting industry. With races now being broadcast over the radio, a person no longer needed to attend a racetrack to place a bet. Off-track betting (OTB) saw a rapid increase in the early-twentieth century. Gamblers could either meet their local bookie at the corner pub or community hall, or even put in a phone call to place bets when unable to do so in person.[12] The bookie would offer starting price (SP) odds, numbers that fluctuated in the lead-up to a race based on variables ranging from past performances to weather conditions on the day.[13] The legalization of on-track betting did nothing to prevent the growth in the far more convenient OTB market. In the year before the law changed to permit on-track betting in 1923, there were three hundred people in Queensland prosecuted for gambling offenses. Just over ten years later, with on-track betting now well-established, the prosecution rate for gambling offenses had risen by 307 percent.[14] For Queenslanders, it was just not practical to go to the racetrack every time they wanted to place a bet, and even less so when there was a bookie in the area who could take a bet for them. The OTB market continued to boom, forcing the Hanlon government to call an inquiry in 1951 to determine if it was more beneficial to legalize OTB and regain some control of an industry that had proven difficult to stop.

The 1951 commission was sent around Queensland to gather information on OTB around the state. It found an illicit gambling market that was thriving in almost every city and town from the urban southeast to the tropical north. It was estimated that there were at least 980 criminal bookies in Queensland—on any given race day, police said there were 530 bookmakers operating in the Brisbane metropolitan area alone.[15] The QPF were losing in a war of attrition waged by SP bookmakers. The plan had been that, in allowing on-track betting, OTB would come to a natural end as gamblers would not need to seek out criminal operators to place their bets. Looking to the United States would have shown this hope to be problematic. When Belmont Park racetrack was opened in New York, it was hoped that regulated, on-track betting would send illegal bookies out of business. The plan did not work there and would not in Australia, either.[16]

For many Queenslanders it was an Australian tradition to put a bet on the races, not something to be criminalized. There was a smack of elitism about it, too. Even though on-track betting had been legal since 1923, structural factors meant access to the track was limited for working-class punters. For punters who could not take time off from work to go to the races or did not have the means to travel long distances to attend, it was not possible to legally place a bet under the "on-track only" rules. The proscriptive laws were even more restrictive for rural Queenslanders, for whom travelling to urban racetracks to gamble was not an option.

There were other stakeholders in the debate over legalizing OTB. The racing clubs were fervently opposed to legalization, in fear that legal OTB would have such a damaging impact on their ticket sales that it would no longer be profitable to run the races at all.[17] The commission suggested a compromise. It recommended that OTB be legalized in rural areas, far enough from a racetrack to make attending too burdensome for the average gambler.[18] The Labor Party government implemented this policy under Vince Gair in 1954, but the impact was minimal. The state's punters just could not quit their neighborhood bookmaker, no matter how criminal he was.

There was little incentive to "go legit" even for those SP bookmakers who operated in the now-legal rural areas of Queensland. Even though their operations were outlawed, a combination of social tolerance around gambling and the cooperation of local police meant the threat of arrest and prosecution was minimal. The willingness of police to look the other way on "moral crimes" like gambling and prostitution is not unique to Queensland. Vice is an ever-present problem for police, never more so than when it comes to areas referred to as "victimless crimes." Victimless crimes are those where the perception is that a person involved only harms themselves by taking part. When there is no risk that others will be hurt by a person's actions, there is less enthusiasm on the part of police and the community for seeing the law enforced in a punitive fashion.[19] What results is a policy of selective enforcement, where vice operators are able to practice their trade without the threat of police action as long as they stick to the rules set by police. In some communities, these rules are focused on social control. Sex workers are permitted to solicit in certain, contained areas, or drug dealers can sell their product as long as it does not find its way into the possession of children. Selective enforcement is, in these cases, focused on maintaining a certain standard of behavior in the community while nevertheless acknowledging that it is impractical to attempt to prevent all forms of social deviance from taking place.

The selective enforcement of vice in Queensland was not always undertaken with the best interests of the community at heart. The general acceptance of SP gambling as a victimless crime presented police with a win-win opportunity. It was possible to accede to the wishes of the community by tolerating illegal OTB and, at the same time, receive a financial boost by taking a cut from the enterprise for "protecting" a bookie's business interests. For officers serving in rural Queensland, this was a lucrative business model. Whereas in urban Brisbane there was a saturation of bookies operating, most country towns had only one or two SP bookies at any given time. Country folk might have been far-removed from the racetracks of Brisbane, but the demand for OTB in rural Queensland was strong. Behind closed doors, the SP trade was tolerated at the highest levels. When serving in the mining town of Mount Isa in the 1940s, Detective Charles Corner said that SP betting was "rampant" and that he was told by local politician Norman Smith that "it was Government policy for the hotels to trade behind doors."[20] Smith, the member of Parliament for Carpentaria, also happened to be the licensee of the Mount Isa Hotel and would have profited directly from the gambling trade that went on at the premises. Before becoming state treasurer in the Nicklin government, Thomas Hiley spoke out about the tolerated SP gambling that was an open secret in Queensland's regional centers. He claimed that one of the most prominent bookies in Ipswich, J. Marsden, was protected by police. Noting that Marsden was the brother of a Labor Party member, Hiley alluded to the existence of a "Premier's fund" where some of the proceeds of illegal gambling were sent to finance the campaigns of favored Labor

Party candidates.²¹ His claim was a swipe at the Gair government as well as at the corrupt police who protected SP bookmakers in the first place. Bischof's hometown Toowoomba is only fifty miles from Ipswich, where Hiley claimed bookies like Marsden were being protected. The rumor was that Bischof was the man in charge of the protection racket in Toowoomba, but there were whispers that his reach extended even further, encompassing much of western Queensland's rural towns.

The thing about Bischof was that he rarely worked alone. This became even more important after he was appointed Police Commissioner in 1958. The higher the Big Fella rose, the more power he accrued. That status was a blessing and a curse for a corrupt police officer. It meant he had the ability to protect criminal operators at a level that the average officer on the street could not, but it also meant that he was more visible and more vulnerable to being caught. The Big Fella had been making plans for this for a long time, at least since taking over the CIB in 1955. If he was not able to do the rounds and collect his illicit bribes any longer, others would have to take an active role in managing these rackets for him. For this, Bischof relied on the officers under his command in the CIB. Some had been groomed by him from an early stage in their careers, whereas others were transferred to the CIB purely because he saw their existing potential (even talent) for corruption. He had a legion of acolytes in the CIB, but three officers in particular emerged as his most trusted "bagmen." The trio became known in the police ranks as the "Rat Pack," a reference not only to the popular group of entertainers including Frank Sinatra and Dean Martin, but also this trio's devious commitment to doing what was necessary to keep Bischof's corrupt network afloat.²²

First among equals in the Rat Pack was the enigmatic detective Anthony "Tony" Murphy. At first, Murphy does not seem to have the background one might expect from Bischof's chief lieutenant. He was an Irish Catholic but not the Green Mafia kind. When he joined the QPF in 1944, the Irish Catholics were still firmly established, to the point that the CIB was jokingly referred to by some as "the Vatican." Even though Murphy did not put much stock in the Green Mafia, he appeared to be the quintessential Irish copper. It did not hurt to be seen as part of the Green Mafia in this era, and it possibly contributed to him being identified by the top brass as a star on the rise. He was sent to work in the Brisbane CIB in the early 1950s, at the time led by Irish Catholic factional leader Jim Donovan. If the powers that be thought Murphy could prove useful to Donovan, they were wrong. The young detective was not the type to offer blind loyalty to a person solely based on a shared heritage. He was calculating and valued relationships where the other person had something to offer him. It was no wonder then that he gravitated to Bischof, also a force in the CIB when Murphy arrived.[23] Bischof was a man on the rise, and with his vast experience in policing, the CIB chief had much wisdom to impart to his young protégé. Some of that wisdom made Murphy a better detective, possibly the best of his generation. Some, though, put Murphy on the path to the Rat Pack.

Murphy was not the only young detective in the CIB who saw the benefits of a close relationship with Bischof. The Ipswich-raised Terence "Terry" Murray Lewis was drawn to men who had power. His mother, a member of the Hanlon racing family, abandoned him when he was ten years old. He came home from school to find the house empty, with no explanation. It is possible that this childhood trauma, this feeling of powerlessness, stuck with Lewis. From then on, he determined never to be left behind again. He moved to Brisbane after school, moving in with his mother and her new husband. It was not a reconciliation. Staying with her was expedient, and Lewis was willing to suspend his personal feelings if it got him where he needed to go. He started out working at the Liquid Fuel Control Board, where he fell under the sway of one of his new mentors, a former QPF detective named Wally Wright. Wright took a shine to Lewis and, sensing potential in the young man, marched him to the police headquarters at Petrie Terrace to sign him up for training as a recruit.[24] When Lewis entered the CIB, he would have appealed to Bischof for a few reasons. For one, he was eager to please his superiors and was willing to do anything to get their approval. For another, Bischof was an avid punter, and for better or worse, Lewis was connected to racing royalty through his mother's family. Lewis quickly fell under Bischof's sway and became the second member of the Rat Pack.

The final member of the Rat Pack was more of a wildcard. He did not need someone like Bischof to mentor him to greatness. The fortunes of Hallahan were already on the rise before the two ever met. Hallahan had a lot in common with Bischof. He, too, was raised in Toowoomba, though he was the son of a milkman not a dairy farmer like Bischof.[25] He was slower to join the police force than the other members of the Rat Pack and was finally sworn on 18 February 1952 after trying several other careers, including time spent as an air force mechanic in Ipswich and sugarcane cutter in north Queensland. Before too long, he began to make a reputation for himself as a talented detective in the Mount Isa CIB. He was there at a pivotal time, when the town's police were effectively put on trial in the Jorgensen case.[26] Hallahan had bigger fish to fry, though. On 22 January 1958, as Bischof prepared to take on the job of police commissioner, Hallahan arrested Bailey on the streets of Mount Isa. He charged him with the triple murder of Thyra Bowman, Wendy Bowman, and Thomas Whelan on Sundown station in December 1957. The Sundown case put Hallahan on the new commissioner's radar. The rumors that he had verballed Bailey no doubt spoke volumes to his new boss—another "ace detective" with a notable tendency for the very same questionable practices. Bischof visited Mount Isa shortly after becoming commissioner. Not long after that, Hallahan was reassigned to the Brisbane CIB, where Bischof could put his talents to better use.

Gambling was far from the only vice where there was money to be made in Queensland. There was a long history of prostitution in the Sunshine State, stretching back into the colonial era. The first European residents of the colony were mostly convicts and soldiers, with only a small cohort of women in Queensland consisting of officers' wives and daughters. In general, the Moreton Bay penal colony was no place to bring a well-bred, cultured woman. When the region opened to free settlement there was minimal change in the gender demographics for some time. The new colony was a place of opportunity, but primarily for those who wanted to purchase pastoral land and make their fortune through backbreaking labor on farms.[27] It was not long, though, before the gender balance started to shift.

There is a persistent myth that frontier societies are exclusively masculine social arenas, but the facts do not bear this out. Take the case of America's westward expansion. Though the gender ratios of in places like California started off highly disproportionate (twenty-three men for every woman in 1860), the statistics show that the balance corrected itself quickly (two men for every woman in California by 1870).[28] The same is true for Queensland. Despite starting off as an almost exclusively male domain, the gender demographics in Queensland had shifted so that, by 1890, there was only 1.32 men for every woman in the state.[29] The close gender ratio does not reflect the culture of colonial Queensland, however. While women lived in Queensland, they were restricted by a strict set of Victorian era morals that demanded "respectable women" conduct themselves demurely and, for the most part, live a private life. Because of this, the most visible women in colonial Queensland were the ones labelled as "harlots"—mostly working-class women who did not conform to the modicums of respectability proscribed by colonial society and, thus, were often treated as prostitutes (whether that tag was accurate or not).

There was considerable demand for sexual services in colonial Brisbane, driven partly by the masculine culture and partly by the class barriers that precluded interaction between working-class men and women of a higher social standing. Brisbane was also a place that had a strong boarding-house culture into the early twentieth century.[30] Because of the restrictions placed on urban development by the Undue Subdivision of Land Prevention Act 1885, there was no scope for the kind of high-density building seen in the terraces of Sydney or Melbourne. For workers who needed to stay close to the inner city, there was a necessity to find shared lodging, often with several other young men. Boarding houses were a practical need in Brisbane but were limiting when it came to the sexual proclivities of their residents. For this reason, sex often occurred outside the home. At times, this involved clandestine public encounters with street walkers in laneways, but more often, it meant visiting one of the city's brothels. "Hubs of deviance" emerged. At one such hub, in an area of the inner city referred to as the East Ward, police noted no less than eleven separate brothels (or "bawdy houses") operated in a one hundred–yard radius.[31] Controlling prostitution was a challenge for police. The problem was not an absence of legal authority. The Act for the Prevention of Contagious Diseases gave them the power to arrest women for prostitution as a threat to the public health.[32] Vagrancy laws were also regularly used, with the provisions for immoral or obscene behavior giving police a broad scope to act where warranted. The introduction of the Criminal Code 1899 even made it an indictable offense to operate a brothel, giving police the power to act without the pretense of being an arbiter of moral authority. The issue of enforcement, instead, was a practical one. Because of its characteristic urban sprawl, there were any number of residences that could serve as "bawdy houses" around Brisbane. When police shut down a brothel, the operation did not stay closed for long. The women who worked there would be processed as summary offenders, released, and return to work at a new location, somewhere else in the area.[33] Policing prostitution was a constant struggle, and it was not one that the QPF were winning.

When war arrived in Brisbane in 1942, the existing demand for sexual services became even greater. With more than two million soldiers passing through Brisbane at some point in the three years that MacArthur made the city his base of operations, it was a boom period for Brisbane sex workers. The sheer amount of business that was up for grabs even drove migration to the Sunshine State, as sex workers from other areas of Australia moved to Brisbane and set up shop to get a slice of the market. The war was bringing major sociocultural changes to Brisbane, and for police, the visible practice of prostitution on the city's streets was a major concern. Many of the women recently arrived in Brisbane did not have any connections in the brothels and so took to street walking to ply their trade. The Criminal Code 1899 and a 1931 amendment to the Vagrants Act gave police the power to shut down brothels, but the rise in streetwalking forced them to rely once more on the Suppression of Contagious Diseases Act to get sex workers off the streets.[34]

There was, nevertheless, a recognition of the necessary role that brothels could play in keeping order on the streets. The tensions between recently arrived American GIs and the Australian troops entering late 1942 were at fever pitch. Most, if not all, of the strain was to do with women. For U.S. soldiers, Brisbane was considered "the best liberty port in the world . . . [a place of] milk and honey and pretty girls" who, in return, were enraptured by the Hollywood charisma of American men.[35] For their part, the Australian contingent were riled by American soldiers taking what was (in their view) rightfully theirs. The cliché "overpaid, oversexed and over here" became a mantra for the Australian soldiers as their U.S. counterparts continued to wine, dine, and dance with what seemed like every pretty girl in Brisbane.[36] The simmering feud exploded on 26 November 1942, Thanksgiving, when Australian soldiers clashed with American military police on the corner of Creek and Adelaide Streets, not far from MacArthur's base. Before long, news of the scuffle spread. It was the last straw. By the end of the night, close to five thousand people were involved in skirmishes across the city. Disgruntled Australian soldiers, releasing months of fury at the Americans, surrounded the Post Exchange near to where the conflict had begun. The Australians tried to relieve the American soldiers of their weapons by force, and in the chaos, an Australian soldier was poked in the chest with the barrel of a gun by an American GI. When his colleague, Edward Webster, grabbed the barrel of the gun in outrage, a shot was fired. Webster was hit in the chest, and died.[37]

The Battle of Brisbane (as it became known) was a flashpoint that went beyond the clash that triggered it. The violence was a physical manifestation of the rage felt by Australian troops that needed to be soothed if the allies were to get back to the business of warfare. If part of the problem was that American GIs were "stealing" the local women, then a potential solution was to provide an acceptable alternative: prostitution. Police had never managed to get a strong foothold in the fight to shut down the brothels and, to an extent, had given up believing that they could ever truly stop the sex trade by the 1940s. But rather than stopping it, the QPF could *control* it. The decision was made that certain brothels would be tolerated. Police would not harass the properties so long as the brothel operators and sex workers played by the rules and there was no trouble. To that end, some brothels in south

Brisbane were set up exclusively for the use of African American troops, with the QPF wishing to avoid an outbreak of racial tension that could cause problems for the new tolerated brothels plan.[38] The system worked. For the military and the government, the brothels provided sexual services that would hopefully prevent another incident like the Battle of Brisbane. For the brothel operators and sex workers, it was easier to turn a profit without the looming fear of police busting in at any moment. And for the police, it gave them the chance to stop chasing their tails and trying in vain to stamp out prostitution. The system of tolerance worked well—so well, in fact, that it continued after the war ended and the American GIs left Brisbane in 1945.

The existence of certain "tolerated" brothels was a fact of Brisbane policing from the end of the war into the late 1950s. Police in the CIB's Consorting Squad worked actively with brothel madams to ensure that the rules were followed. If a new girl wanted to start working at one of the four tolerated brothels, the madam would first check with their contact in the CIB to make sure the girl was an "acceptable" candidate for the role and did not come with baggage like a criminal record. Any person operating outside the system, whether independent or in an unsanctioned brothel, was dealt with harshly by the police. Some were charged for soliciting, others were taken by police to the New South Wales border and encouraged not to return. For some corrupt police, the policy of containment was an opportunity to make some cash. Even though their operations were tolerated, the sex trade was still officially illegal, and the brothel keepers and sex workers who worked at these establishments were at the mercy of the police. The officers who financially benefitted from the tolerated brothels mostly came from the Consorting Squad, who excused their presence in the brothels as a way of gathering intelligence on the criminal characters who frequented them. The sex trade was not, however, the jurisdiction of the Consorters. This was the Licensing Branch's turf, and every few months, it conducted raids on the premises where sex workers were taken in and booked.[39] There was no harm in letting the Licensing Branch do this. Not only did it give the impression to the public that police were actively enforcing prostitution laws, but the girls were taken in and charged under false names and failed to appear when the time came to face court.

The containment of prostitution to the tolerated brothels was a system of selective enforcement that was seemingly beneficial to everyone involved. Nevertheless, there was room for corrupt police to overreach, and in 1959, that is exactly what brought the entire scheme to its knees. At the time, Bischof had been commissioner for just on two years, and the Big Fella decided the time was right to take a vacation an hour to the south of Brisbane, on the beachside playground of the Gold Coast. He left Donovan, the deputy that he passed over for the Commissioner's role, in charge in his absence. The force was in safe hands, but Bischof underestimated the extent to which Donovan was willing to tear the entire police force down just to get at the new commissioner. Donovan had been waiting for the chance.

Fortune would have it that Leigh Hamilton walked in his door at a perfect time. Hamilton had started out working in one of the tolerated brothels but was seen as a "troublemaker" and left to start her own independent operation out of her apartment.[40] She had her operation sanctioned by the Consorters and kept up to date on her protection payments. In October 1959, with Bischof gone, Hamilton got a visit at her apartment from the Consorters. She said Lewis and Hallahan, two of the three Rat Packers, called in to tell her that her protection payments had doubled, and they would be back to collect the following week. She was furious. She had acquired a reputation as a troublemaker in the brothels for a reason, which is why it is perhaps not surprising that her next move was to go directly to Acting Commissioner Donovan to lodge a formal complaint.[41]

Donovan was ecstatic. How fortuitous that at the *exact* time that he was (temporarily) sitting in a position of power Hamilton came to him with accusations of corruption against two of Bischof's bagmen? The trap was set. Donovan told Hamilton to play it cool and agree to pay, and when Hallahan and Lewis came to collect the next week, the police would be there to catch them in the act of receiving a bribe. Accusations were one thing, but if Bischof's boys were caught red-handed, there would be nothing to do except kick them out of the force altogether. It would be a major blow to Bischof, cutting him off from some of his strongest allies in the QPF. The morning of the sting operation arrived, and the wheels were in motion for Donovan to pull off the coup of his career. There was one thing that he did not account for, though: the third man in the trio, Murphy.[42] On the morning of the raid, Murphy was working at CIB headquarters and heard that the sting was in progress. He tipped off his friends, and together the Rat Pack devised a plan. Before Donovan could spring his trap, Hallahan and Lewis walked into the office of acting CIB chief Bill Cronau and spun him a story. Hamilton had complained to them she was being stood over by someone else, and their plan was to go to her apartment, hide, and wait for him to arrive so that they could arrest him. Cronau was livid.

"You've been tipped off," he said. Get out of my office, you bastards."[43]

He might not have caught them red-handed, but Donovan still had enough on Hallahan and Lewis to demote them, sending the hot-shot detectives back to uniform for the first time in years.[44] When Bischof heard, he raced back to Brisbane to deal with the fallout. A major benefit of process corruption is its usefulness, not only in committing offenses but in covering them up as well. In concocting a story about their own sting operation at Hamilton's apartment, Hallahan and Lewis had given themselves plausible deniability that could explain their presence at the premises and their previous contact with her. This creative reinterpretation is often used to provide justification for actions that would otherwise be considered misconduct. In this case, they were able to wriggle out of a criminal charge by casting themselves as "good police"—a common tactic of police who engage in process corruption.[45] While the pair had managed to escape prosecution, however, Donovan's decision to demote them was a massive problem.

Bischof needed to change the narrative, get the heat off his Rat Pack, and give the impression that he was serious about policing prostitution. On his return from the Gold Coast, he made the decision to end the informal policy of more than a decade. He recommended to the state cabinet that it was time to close the tolerated brothels.[46] The state government was stunned. It wasn't pretty but tolerance worked. No friend of Bischof, Treasurer Hiley expressed concerns that the move would push sex workers out of the brothels (where they could be monitored and controlled) into the streets and bars of Brisbane. But, despite their reservations, the cabinet's hand was forced. The attorney general, Alan Munro, pointed out that if it became public that Bischof had recommended the closure of the brothels and the cabinet refused, it would be political suicide.[47] Munro's argument was persuasive. The cabinet voted in favor of Bischof's recommendation. The brothels were padlocked.

Initially, Bischof's plan to close the brothels was designed to change the narrative and get attention off the fact that two of his closest allies in the force were facing accusations of standing over sex workers for money. It worked, and before too long, Bischof reinstated Hallahan and Lewis to their previous positions. The closure of the brothels was politically expedient for Bischof. As commissioner, the process corruption that Bischof was able to engage in happened at a far higher level than the average officer on the street, and in this case, he was able to use his powers to manipulate the state cabinet into participating in his plan to divert attention from the actions of Hallahan and Lewis. The end of the tolerance period was beneficial to Bischof and his Rat Pack in other ways, too. Profiting from the protection of prostitution did not come to an end when the doors to the tolerated brothels were padlocked. Absent the controllability that the tolerated brothels provided, the sex trade simply changed venues. Just as Hiley predicted, sex workers became a standard in bars and hotels across Brisbane.[48] Sex workers no longer had the security of the brothels to fall back on, and so the protection of police officers became even more vital than before, opening up new markets for corrupt members of the force. Women like Shirley Brifman, who began working at the Killarney brothel after moving to Brisbane from north Queensland in 1958, now worked out of hotels and bars where they mingled with all sorts of people: laborers out for a drink after work, professional criminals, businessmen, lawyers, politicians, and, yes, even police.

Logically, the movement of prostitution out of brothels and into public bars and hotels should have resulted in the trade being practiced in a more clandestine manner, but this was not the case. Sex workers, now emancipated from the brothels, flocked to places like the Grand Central Hotel on Queen Street. Brifman was a regular at the Grand Central, along with friends like Lily Ryan and Val Weidinger, also former residents of the Killarney brothel.[49] No longer did the women have to wait for customers to step foot through the door at Killarney; now they set up shop in the lounges and parlors of the bar, watching the crowds of men and retiring to a rented room upstairs when a willing partner was located. For the corrupt police who made money from the prostitution trade, the protection scheme was slightly more complicated but the rewards much higher. Before, the police knew where the brothels were, and it was quite simple to make a stop to collect the bribes they were owed. In the new model, there were sex workers operating out of dozens of bars and hotels in the city, so the collection took far longer than it used to. But most of the sex workers they targeted now didn't have a brothel manager or pimp to take care of their interests. Some police made it a rule not to "work" with women who were being pimped out—independent operators only, please.[50] On one hand, the absence of gangsters and "bludgers" living off the earnings of prostitution prevented conflict between criminals over business. On the other hand, without a protector, the women were more vulnerable than ever to the pressure exerted predatory police seeking to extort them for protection money. For the Rat Pack, moving prostitution into Brisbane's hotels brought them even closer to the action. As sex workers like Brifman plied their trade in the bars (and later upstairs rooms) of places like the National Hotel, men like Bischof and his Rat Pack sat in the shadows, drinking and waiting to take their cuts.

A perplexing aspect of the Queensland police story is the question of how corruption was given the chance to flourish over such a lengthy period. The presence of a conspirator in the commissioner's office was a benefit, but Bischof alone was not responsible for the culture of misconduct that emerged in the QPF. However, his grooming of the Rat Pack—Lewis, Murphy, and Hallahan—provides great insight into how even the most talented and promising police could be convinced to join in unethical conduct. One of the great failings of the "rotten apple" concept is the argument that corruption is the product of rogue "bad" actors in a police force, officers with intrinsic personal failings that lead them down the wrong path. But when corruption becomes normalized on the level it did in Queensland, can we honestly attribute this to a cabal of "rotten apples"? Others take the analogy further, asserting instead that even one rotten apple can poison the entire barrel, dragging others into misconduct. While it is possible to suggest that Bischof was such a person, dragging the Rat Pack and their allies into corruption, this explanation too is questionable. The ace detective Hallahan, for example, had a reputation for verbals and other forms of corruption before ever meeting Bischof. Others, like Lewis, were taken under Bischof's wing from their early days in the QPF and more closely fit the "rotten barrel" theory. However, there is no common "cause" of corruption, and while useful from a conceptual standpoint, the rotten apple / rotten barrel fails to account for all corruption in a policing organization like the QPF where misconduct is so widespread. Bischof and the Rat Pack demonstrate that officers are enticed into corruption for a diverse range of reasons—some *are* simply rotten apples, whereas others are socialized to accept corrupt practices over time. Socialization is a powerful motivator for various reasons, not the least of which when it fosters in a context where even police who do *not* participate in corruption are driven to close ranks and go to extreme lengths to protect their "brothers" who are.

CHAPTER 4

Checking in at the National Hotel

If there was one thing that David Young could not stand, it was a drunk police officer. Unfortunately, in his line of work he came across a lot of them. Young was born into the hospitality business. The British expat worked in his parents' hotels growing up in sleepy Yorkshire, a rural region in England's north.[1] When the family moved to Queensland in 1949, they left the hotel business behind and opened a fruit farm at Woombye, a rural patch north of Brisbane known for its cultivation of exotic produce like pineapples and ginger. Young, once again, followed in his parents' footsteps and worked the farm but, after his father passed away, made the move the Brisbane where he returned to the other trade he knew best: the hotel industry. He started out working as a waiter at the Grand Central Hotel on Queen Street and, later, moved to the National Hotel at Petrie Bight when it opened a new restaurant in 1958.[2] He had been at the Grand Central before the closing of the brothels that occurred the following year, but was familiar with some of the girls who operated out of the hotel's lounge, including a young Shirley Brifman. When he said goodbye to the Grand Central, he had good reason to believe he would not see the likes of Brifman again, especially not at the National. His new bosses, the Roberts brothers, were close with Commissioner Frank Bischof, and the place was always crawling with police.

63

It was not long before Young realized how wrong he was. When Bischof closed the brothels in 1959, Young began seeing some familiar faces around the National. Even worse, the sex workers who were pushed out of the brothels did not at all seem worried about the police presence, even spending time drinking with the officers at their table. Over time, he came to recognize several police who were regular visitors to his workplace: Tony Murphy, Glen Hallahan, even Bischof.[3] All of them got special treatment. The police drank after hours and collected beers on Sunday when the law prohibited it, and they certainly seemed to ignore the sex trade going on at the hotel. It wasn't all bad. When Young had his own run-in with the Queensland Police Force (QPF) back in 1959, the intervention of senior police who were friendly with his bosses had meant that he was let off the hook.[4] For the most part, though, he was no fan of dealing with these special clients. Too often, the police were overly drunk, obnoxious, and licentious. They took whatever they wanted, and they did not pay. So, in late 1963, when the member of Parliament for South Brisbane Colin Bennett made claims in parliament that police were ignoring a prostitution ring operating out of the National, Young's ears pricked up.[5] Finally, someone was calling the police out for years' worth of bad behavior. When the premier, Frank Nicklin, called for any witnesses to come forward to support Bennett's allegations, Young put pen to paper. In doing so, he set off a chain of events that would almost bring the entire house down around the corrupt officers of the QPF.

Before the Roberts brothers took over the National in 1958, it was a losing prospect. The old pub enjoyed a prime position on the corner of Queen and Adelaide Streets, a stone's throw from the busy Brisbane River. The building was constructed in the 1880s and had the requisite wraparound porch typical of the Queenslander architectural style of the period.[6] Places like the National were common in Australia at the time, with licensing laws mandating that most pubs offer some accommodation to be able to serve alcohol.[7] The hotel had expanded upwards at some point before the Roberts brothers purchased the property. The lower levels were for drinking, while the upper levels hosted bedrooms. The presence of on-site bedrooms at most Brisbane hotels was a major reason that they became the central venues for the sex trade after the closure of the brothels. Not only could sex workers use the hotel's bars to locate customers, but when one was found, it was easy to take them upstairs to a rented room and complete a "date" without even leaving the premises. Despite its prime location, the National was in a state of disrepair by the late 1950s. Bad management had led to the building being rundown and the owners losing money. Experienced hoteliers the Roberts brothers, nevertheless, saw the site's potential. The hotel changed hands in 1958 and the plan to revitalize the National was set in motion.

The Roberts brothers saw the National as something more than a city pub. To them, the possibilities were endless. One of their first steps was to open a formal dining room and a steak house at the venue, in the hopes of attracting a new clientele. It was this restaurant that lured Young away from the Grand Central to work for the Roberts brothers at the exciting, all-new National. They also knew that simply putting their name to the National would attract new customers. The younger Roberts brother, Max, was technically the one responsible for running the National, but it was William "Rolly" Roberts who had the strongest connection to the police who would make the National their new home away from home. Rolly Roberts had, for the last year, been running the Treasury Hotel on George Street, directly across the street from Criminal Investigation Branch (CIB) headquarters. Rolly Roberts had made good connections at the Treasury—in a very short period, he had become a close friend of new commissioner Bischof.[8] It was Rolly Roberts's house on the Gold Coast that Bischof was staying in when the Leigh Hamilton incident occurred in 1959, very nearly ending the careers of Lewis and Hallahan.[9] The relationship between Bischof and Rolly Roberts meant that, from the outset, the National was a well-frequented venue for many police in the commissioner's circle. The plan to put the National back on the map was not in vain. By the early 1960s it was one of the most visited (and most profitable) venues in the city.

It was not Bennett's aim to open a can of worms to do with the National Hotel when he rose to deliver his speech in state parliament on 29 October 1963. The Labor Party politician was a consistent critic of the Nicklin government, and for the most part, his purpose on the day was to bring attention to a range of issues around disciplinary processes in the QPF that meant officers faced different treatment based on what faction they belonged to or if they were a friend of the commissioner. Bennett, a practicing lawyer, had represented several police officers in disciplinary or promotions appeals and, in doing so, became close to future police union boss Ron Edington. Years later, Edington admitted to feeding Bennett some of the information he used in his scathing parliamentary attacks on Bischof's administration.[10] However, amidst the accusations he laid out on 29 October 1963, there was one piece of information that Bennett had received from another, very different source: his client, Brifman. Bennett had represented her, and over the years, she came to trust him and gave him information about the sex trade operating under the noses of police at the National. As the time allotted to Bennett to speak ticked away, one passage of his diatribe stood out: "I do not wish to dally too long on this subject, but I should say that the Commissioner and his colleagues who frequent the National Hotel, encouraging and condoning the call-girl service that operates there, would be better occupied in preventing such activities rather than tolerating them."[11] The reference to the National was only one sentence of Bennett's speech, but it sent shockwaves through the parliament. He was not making general accusations. Here, he was pointing to a specific case where he alleged that Bischof and other police were "encouraging and condoning" prostitution. The police union called for a thorough investigation of the claims, and in turn, Premier Nicklin called on any person who had information on the conduct of police at the National to come forward.

Initially, no one did. This is quite possibly what Nicklin expected when he made the call for information in the first place. Notably, he did not call for *any* information about police corruption to do with prostitution—the premier had been smart. He only asked for evidence about misconduct at the National specifically. Doing so was a calculated move, limiting the potential fallout to one set of allegations at one venue alone. If that was the hope, his gamble did not pay off. First, an anonymous letter was sent to Labor Party leader Jack Duggan in which the writer claimed to have served alcohol to Bischof and other police outside the legal trading hours and alleging that police were not only aware of prostitution at the National but sometimes received "favors" from the sex workers that operated there.[12] The anonymous informant was Young, the waiter-turned-porter from Yorkshire. Young was a problem, but he was not the only National employee to come out in support of Bennett's claims. The hotel's former night porter, a Hungarian immigrant named John Komlosy, wrote to the *Sunday Truth* newspaper to claim that the staff of the National, including owner Max Roberts, were active conspirators in the prostitution ring operating there, and that police were also involved.[13] The public attention generated by the *Sunday Truth* article was the final straw. A week after first appealing for evidence, Nicklin announced on 11 November that a royal commission would be formed to investigate corruption in Bischof's QPF.

Bischof swung into action. There was nothing he could do to prevent an investigation now that Nicklin had announced it, but there were things that he could do to limit his exposure. His first priority was to make sure that the inquiry was limited in what it could investigate. He recognized that, between Bennett's specific reference to the National and Nicklin's subsequent call for witnesses from the venue, the narrative of the commission was already being shaped. In Australia, a royal commission is called at the request of the government to investigate a defined issue. Usually presided over by a judge, the commission typically has sweeping powers to subpoena witnesses, request documents and receive testimony under oath.[14] Once a commission has commenced, it is nearly impossible for a government to shut it down, which makes it a useful apparatus for investigating allegations of corruption that may involve politicians or public servants. Such a powerful entity can prove to be a major threat in a system where misconduct is widely tolerated, yet there is a weakness in the process that Bischof was able to manipulate to scuttle the National Hotel Inquiry before it truly started: the terms of reference. While a royal commission has considerable power, it is bound by the terms of reference set out before it begins, dictating procedural restrictions. The terms of reference set out what evidence a commission can and cannot examine, as well as the length of time that a commission has to report its findings.[15] From the outset, it was clear that Nicklin wanted the issue to be dealt with in short order: after announcing that the commission would be formed on 11 November, the first sitting day was set for 2 December, giving investigators only three weeks to prepare a brief of evidence.[16] The three-week period prior to the inquiry was chaotic. A little more than a week before the commission was due to begin, the assassination of John Kennedy in Dallas captured the world's attention. The media's focus was not on the small-scale allegations of after-hours drinking and sex at the National. Under this cover, with limited public scrutiny, the inquiry's team began to prepare its brief of evidence.

If the preparation time for the commission was restrictive, the limitations on what issues the commission were permitted to investigate were even worse. Taking his lead from Bennett's speech, Solicitor-General Bill Ryan issued terms of reference that were focused exclusively on the allegations made in parliament. The commission would investigate the specific allegations that members of the QPF allowed a call-girl service to operate out of the National and, further, that police had benefitted from a personal relationship with the hotel's owners by receiving "special treatment" like after-hours service of alcohol. The inquiry would be restricted to hearing evidence about a single venue (the National) over the preceding five-year period. The commission was not even given the power to examine the nature of the relationship between police and the Roberts brothers at the time that Rolly Roberts ran the Treasury, even though this was where the National's owners first became associated with Bischof and many other police implicated in corruption.[17] The terms were criticized as being "impossibly narrow" and purposefully designed to prevent a proper investigation from taking place.[18]

Initially, the attempt to limit the inquiry's fallout was blamed on the Nicklin government, who had shown that they were intent on dodging the political fallout that came with their maverick pick for police commissioner turning out to be corrupt. Certainly, this political consideration had a role to play in the process, but recent evidence suggests a more direct intervention by Bischof to shape the terms of reference to his benefit. In a 2017 book, journalist Matthew Condon relays a conversation he had with an anonymous informant who worked in Solicitor-General Ryan's office at the time of the National Hotel Inquiry. Condon's informant claimed that Bischof visited Ryan shortly before the terms of reference were due to be released and was "agitated and that he [Bischof] stated to Ryan that the terms of reference needed to be narrowed, they were far too broad in this [draft] document."[19] The informant said that, after Bischof's visit, the terms of reference changed. Though they had originally allowed for corruption in other venues to be part of the inquiry, the new terms kept the focus solely on the National. Without knowing the identity of Condon's informant, it is difficult to verify these claims, but if true, it would suggest that Bischof's first thought was not to allow the investigation to take its course. Instead, as ever, the commissioner's focus was on manipulating the legal processes to his own benefit, preventing the commission from entering into areas that he would not be able to control.

The man chosen to head the National Hotel Inquiry (now formally titled the Royal Commission Appointed to Inquire into and Report on Certain Matters Relating to Members of the Police Force and the National Hotel) was Harry Talbot Gibbs, a justice on Queensland's Supreme Court. An army veteran, Gibbs was appointed to the Supreme Court only two years earlier in 1961.[20] He would go on to be appointed to the High Court of Australia in 1967, and after that, he served as chief justice of the High Court for most of the 1980s.[21] Because he was a relatively inexperienced jurist, the decision to appoint Gibbs to preside over the commission was a surprise to some. His impartiality as a judge was questioned only three months earlier in parliament by Independent Tom Aikens, who speculated that Gibbs was only appointed to the Supreme Court for political reasons. He had campaigned for Nicklin's Coalition partners and the Liberal Party, and his brother Wylie was running as a federal Liberal candidate at the November 1963 election that took place only a matter of weeks after the National Hotel Inquiry was announced.[22] For whatever reason, Gibbs seemed to demonstrate preference for the QPF from the start and ruled in their favor on several procedural issues. For one, he did not object when Murphy was named lead of the commission's investigatory team, responsible for locating evidence (if any) of corruption. It was a strange choice. Murphy was one of the main officers accused of participating in misconduct at the National, yet he had been put in charge of leading the investigation. Gibbs, however, saw no conflict of interest.[23] That one of the key subjects of an inquiry was allowed to have such a prominent role on the team assigned to assist the inquiry is baffling, to say the least. From the inside, Murphy could influence what evidence was presented to the inquiry and, in doing so, shape the outcome of an investigation in which he had a very personal interest.

The police at the center of the National claims and their allies had done their best to cripple the inquiry before it began. The terms of reference were limited, there was little time to prepare a brief of evidence, a friendly commissioner had been selected in Gibbs, and Murphy was in control of the investigation. Even so, the floodgates opened, and others began speaking out about QPF corruption at the National. Former employees of the National gave evidence that women who they believed to be sex workers had regularly worked out of the hotel's bars and, when necessary, rented rooms. But none of them could provide evidence that money was exchanged for sex, and after all, casual sex was not a crime. One man, a New Zealand warehouseman named Basil Grove, told Gibbs he often saw men who had been pointed out to him as police officers drinking after hours, at times in the company of women who appeared to be sex workers.[24] Again, Grove's testimony was not solid. He could not prove the men he saw were police or that the women were sex workers. Even after William Ousley, a tax consultant and lawyer, came forward with a corroborating account, the testimony was treated as no more than hearsay and conjecture by Gibbs. Royal commissions are not ordinarily bound by the strict rules of hearsay evidence that traditional courts are, and this type of evidence is usually allowed as a way of forming circumstantial patterns of activity.[25] Under Gibbs, however, a stricter set of rules applied. He treated the National Hotel Inquiry as a courtroom, and as a result, much of the evidence provided by witnesses was shut down and treated as no more than unverified speculation.

Some witnesses received special treatment from Gibbs and the police assisting him. The Hungarian porter, Komlosy, had forced the government's hand to call the inquiry after giving his story to the *Sunday Truth* in November. Unlike most of the other witnesses, he had not just seen police drinking at the National. Komlosy said that he had been told about the prostitution ring at the National by owner Max Roberts himself, and more than that, he had "met Mr Bischof personally and served him" after hours.[26] When Komlosy stepped into the witness box on 9 December, the start of the inquiry's second week, he was confident in his assertions. When asked whether he recognized any of the police he served at the National, Komlosy said, "Yes, I just know Detective Murphy and Mr Hallahan . . . I was instructed that these gentlemen were friends [of Max Roberts] and they were always to be served at the hotel."[27] He was clear that, more often than not, Murphy and Hallahan came into the National after midnight, well past the time that the venue was legally permitted to sell alcohol. According to Komlosy, the pair from the Rat Pack treated the National like a clubhouse of sorts, coming in at all times of day, ordering around the staff, eating and drinking without paying. It was not just them, either. Komlosy said there were others, police that he did not know, that came in with Murphy and Hallahan at different times. All of them got drunk on the Roberts brothers' dime and, even worse, were far more aware of the prostitution happening at the property than they were willing to admit.

As the night porter, Komlosy saw things happening at the National that the average punter did not. When he started, he said that Max Roberts had explained the system to him and encouraged him to assist clients find "a date" wherever possible, all in the name of good customer service.[28] Komlosy would spend his nights in a small night porter's room and field calls from sex workers who operated out of the National. The women called in the middle of the night from the nightclubs and bars around town, asking if they could book a room for the night and if there was after-hours alcohol on offer.[29] Komlosy booked them in, and shortly after, the women arrived with male partners and checked in to the National. Some, like Brifman's friend Val Weidinger, actually had their own permanent rooms that were always booked. According to Komlosy, it was not just sex workers and their clients who showed up at the National in the middle of the night. In his article in the *Sunday Truth*, he spoke of a priest from St Stephen's Cathedral, the historic church partially funded by Patrick Mayne in the mid-nineteenth century, who regularly turned up between 10:30 p.m. and 2 a.m. and stayed until 5 a.m. He told of one particular night when he was forced to call the archbishop of Brisbane's residence because the drunken priest had gotten into a fight with two other men at the bar. Komlosy said two senior priests came to collect their colleague, dragging him out of the National at 4 a.m.[30] A drunk priest was the least of Komlosy's worries. For him, it was just another night on duty at the National.

Komlosy was dangerous. In his role as night porter, he had been privy to a lot of the vice that went on at the National. It was imperative for Murphy's investigatory team to find a way to bring him down. Xenophobia was a powerful option. It was the early 1960s, and Australia was not immune to the fear of communism that developed across the United States and western Europe. Consider the Red Flag riots in 1919, when eight thousand Brisbanites marched on the Russian Hall in a show of force.[31] The city had shown then that it rejected communism, and it would do so again when the time came. Now, more than forty years later, rhetoric casting Komlosy as a foreign threat was used to turn public opinion against the former night porter. When a lawyer appearing for the police union stepped up to question Komlosy, he did not ask about events at the National. Instead, he asked about a time the year earlier when Komlosy had been questioned for threatening Robert Menzies, the prime minister of Australia.[32] According to police, Komlosy was spoken to at Brisbane Airport after federal politician James Killen, who previously worked as a lawyer in Brisbane, alerted them that a strange man was lingering on the fringes of Menzies's group. The officer alerted on that day was, coincidentally, Murphy. He claimed that this was the first and only time he ever met Komlosy, issuing him a warning after the Hungarian said that in his country "they would put [Menzies] against the wall and shoot him."[33] Komlosy told a different story. In his rendition, he had gone to the airport with his ten-year-old son to greet Menzies when he arrived in Brisbane for a visit. He said he saw Murphy in the crowd and, knowing him from the National, approached him so that he could introduce his son to a "real copper."[34] Far from being the only time that the two had met, Komlosy's story was predicated on a long relationship with Murphy. For Murphy, it was essential to prove that he did not know Komlosy on a personal level because, if he did, questions might be asked as to why. To solve his problem, Murphy used a trick from his mentor Bischof's book. He relied on the natural suspicion of Eastern European migrants in conservative Cold War–era Queensland to verbal Komlosy, discrediting him by casting him as no more than a madman with an axe to grind.

Murphy's version of the airport incident was a critical blow to Komlosy's evidence. Komlosy was cast as a foreign devil. Lawyers for the police claimed that it showed his bad character and a history of lying that meant his testimony could not be believed. The attacks on Komlosy did not stop there. When another lawyer for police accused him of the "dirty business" of operating a prostitution ring without the consent of the National's owners, Komlosy spat back that the lawyer was "representing dirt." Komlosy was being taken down from the stand, but he was not going to go quietly. At one point, he asked Gibbs for the name of the counsel assisting the inquiry. Why? Because Komlosy recognized him and wanted to add his name to the list of people he had seen drinking illegally at the National after hours.³⁵ Eventually, after a week of testifying, Komlosy's time on the stand came to an end. He did not stick around long. On 21 February 1964, a few days before Gibbs was scheduled to hold his final sitting day, Komlosy and his family left Australia for Europe. He had received death threats warning against testifying about police corruption but had done so anyway.³⁶ Komlosy feared for his life, and he believed that nowhere in the country would be safe for him or his family. In the end, the effort to torpedo his evidence worked. In his final report, Gibbs said he found the witness to be "unreliable" and that his evidence contained "a curious compound of fact, hearsay, exaggeration, theory and invention, and perhaps even hallucination."³⁷ Komlosy was written off as mentally ill, his testimony no more than a vivid delusion.

Young received a different treatment. Instead, he was portrayed as a criminal. In many ways, he had helped get the ball rolling on the inquiry when he wrote his anonymous letter confirming Bennett's allegations. Because of this, he was the first to take the stand. He knew walking in that he was facing an uphill battle. Before the inquiry began, on 19 November, he received a late-night telephone call. The caller did not identify themselves, but referred to themselves "a friend." The caller had a story to tell. They told Young that police had gathered several sworn affidavits claiming that he was an abortionist. One of the affidavits was from a woman now living in Sydney who allegedly paid him £10 to perform an abortion on her at a city apartment block.³⁸ The affidavit was witnessed by a woman named "Val" who Young took to be Val Weidinger, the sex worker with a permanent room at the National. The allegations that he was an abortionist were patently false and showed the lengths to which the police were willing to go to discredit his testimony. Komlosy could be written off as a foreign basket case. He was easy to trigger on the stand, with the lawyers pressuring him to the point that he could not help lashing out at them, confirming his volatile nature in the eyes of the inquiry. Young was different. He was cool and calm, and would not be so easily rattled. He told the counsel assisting the inquiry, Lindsay Byth, about the call, and Byth, in turn, mentioned it in his opening statement on 2 December. Byth's decision to mention the abortion claim was, on the surface, an attempt to head off the campaign to derail the inquiry with the false allegation. By bringing it up just before he took the stand on 3 December, though, it put the idea in the public's mind early that he could not be trusted and that he was, in fact, a more vile criminal than the police he was blowing the whistle on.

Young started telling his story on the second sitting day. He told how Bischof was a regular guest of the Roberts brothers, how he served Murphy jugs of beer every week, and how he routinely booked rooms for women that were using the

National for the purposes of prostitution. He talked about the night he was arrested for serving alcohol after hours. Max Roberts had told him that a friend was picking up a delivery, and when a police officer turned up at the National, Young gave him beer as usual. When the Licensing Branch returned and charged him, Young was incensed and went to see CIB chief Norm Bauer to complain. Bauer, who was close to Bischof, made the charges go away and assured Young that the officer responsible had been given a stern talking to and told never to pull the same move at the National again.[39] When asked how he knew the rooms were being used for such purposes, Young was blunt: "I don't think I booked anyone into the National who had any luggage." He even pointed out two women sitting at the back of the room during his testimony, Lily Ryan and Val Weidinger, who he said were sex workers that operated out of the National. It was Lily Ryan, along with a sex worker named "Marg," who told Young about their police protection and how they were instructed to move their trade to the National by police after the Grand Central announced that it was closing down. Immediately after his testimony ended, both Lily Ryan and Val Weidinger testified that they had never been sex workers at all, let alone at the National. Investigators on Murphy's team failed to locate many of the sex workers that Young named, but the one called "Marg" would make a dramatic appearance at the inquiry in early 1964 under her real name: Shirley Brifman.

Brifman's name kept popping up at the inquiry. When Murphy was asked about her, he said he had not been able to locate her. When Val Weidinger was asked, she said she thought Brifman could be in Sydney now. Hallahan said he did not know Brifman very well, but from what he did know she was not a sex worker.[40] When Hallahan was in the box, the plan against Young started to reveal itself. As Hallahan spoke, Young realized he recognized the voice on the other end of the 19 November phone call. He was positive that it was Hallahan who warned him that the abortion claim would be made against him.[41] The detective was questioned about this on the stand and denied that he ever called Young. The problem with Brifman was not going away, though. The Rat Pack realized that she would have to appear at the inquiry after all. Years later, Brifman told internal affairs investigators that Murphy and Hallahan called her after every sitting day of the inquiry, coaching her on her testimony.[42]

Brifman flew into Brisbane on 28 January 1964 and went for a few drinks before arriving to tell her story. She was scheduled to give evidence after Bischof himself, who compared himself to Jesus Christ and complained that people in "high places" were attempting to "crucify him." Magnanimously, Bischof even quoted the Bible, imploring his fellow police to "forgive [Komlosy and Young] for they know not what they do."[43] Brifman was up next. She said she knew several police like Murphy and Hallahan but had never told Young that she was a protected sex worker under their control. Then came the death knell for Young. When the lawyer for the Roberts brothers asked if she knew Young, she said, "Yes ... David Young done an abortion on me."[44] Finally, the anonymous phone call came into focus. Brifman was the woman from Sydney who made the affidavit witnessed by Val Weidinger, at the behest of Murphy and Hallahan. While the claim was struck from the record as unproven slander against Young, the damage was done. Like Komlosy, he had been sunk by the Rat Pack.

The commission heard from a few more witnesses after Brifman's bombshell and wrapped up proceedings on 4 February 1964 after sitting for thirty-one days in total. There would be a two-month wait for Gibbs to file his final report, but the result was obvious to anybody who was paying attention. The police had done a good job in controlling the narrative. Most of the witnesses to corruption and vice at the National had no proof, and their evidence was dismissed by Gibbs as no more than hearsay. Others, sex workers like Brifman, were encouraged to perjure themselves at the inquiry to protect their friends in the police force and, in turn, the system of protection that allowed them to do business. Some witnesses, like Komlosy and Young, were more problematic and required more work to shut down. In the end, Young walked away with a reputation as an abortionist, and Komlosy was driven from the country in fear. The results for these whistleblowers was in stark contrast to that for the police who were at the center of the allegations. Bischof was so certain that his QPF was going to be exonerated by Gibbs that he ordered a party to be held on 4 February, the night of the final sitting day.[45] In what was either a bad taste joke or a case of pure hubris, the party to celebrate the inquiry's end was at a familiar venue: the National. Former state treasurer Thomas Hiley remembers being told about the party by someone who was there. He said that a drunk Bischof got on stage at one point and put his arm around three officers: Murphy, Hallahan, and Lewis. He thanked them for dealing with the threat of the National Hotel Inquiry and made a promise, saying, "I want you all to know that these are the boys who got me off this rap ... I'm going to look after them."[46] The fortunes of each rose and fell in the years that followed, but for the rest of his time as commissioner, Bischof kept his promise.

The National Hotel Inquiry was a whitewash. Unlike the Knapp Commission in New York City a few years later, the commission did not provide an inside look at the corruption taking place in the QPF. Whereas Knapp found endemic corruption, Gibbs saw nothing. If anything, the QPF came out of the National Hotel Inquiry stronger than ever, vindicated in the public arena. The failure of the commission to expose corruption at the core of the QPF was a clear argument for the dangers of process corruption in the way it was used as a defense for police accustomed to breaking the rules to get what they wanted. Benefit is not just measured in the amount of money in a person's pocket—what was more important was being able to survive and continue serving as a police officer. Ultimately, there was nothing about Bischof and the Rat Pack on a personal level allowing them to offer criminals protection. The power to engage in corruption came from their professions, and without it, their corrupt racket would collapse in an instant. Because of this, it was essential for police to defend their jobs if they were to continue to benefit, and as the National Hotel Inquiry showed, nobody who got in their way was safe.

The police were willing to go to any length to derail the National investigation—perjury, verbals, faking evidence—all to protect their jobs. Again, this shows the intimate connection between stereotypical police corruption and other, less focused-on forms. Here, process corruption was about corrupt police controlling the narrative and casting themselves as the victims of a vicious smear campaign, unfairly maligned by people who, as it turned out, were no more than "crazy foreigners" and "abortionists." The term "victimless crimes" often comes up when discussing mercenary corruption, with the premise being that police benefit from turning a blind eye to vice crimes where there are no real victims or, at least, not in the same sense as a sexual assault or murder. The smear campaign in the National Hotel Inquiry shows that such a perspective is inherently myopic—the "victims" of police corruption are many and varied, often the very people willing to take a moral stand by blowing the whistle on misconduct. The police had escaped the National for the moment, but the threat was not over. By the end of 1964, Bischof would have his showdown with Hiley over the protection of western bookies and be forced to bring the racket to an end.[47] It was the beginning of his downfall, and by the end of the decade, Bischof was gone.

CHAPTER 5

Jokers' Wild

Thomas Hiley could tell when the numbers didn't add up. The former national president of the Institute of Chartered Accountants had been in the profession for more than twenty years before being elected to parliament. He had continued to run his accountancy firm even after becoming the member of Parliament for Logan. He had been getting to put his skills to good use in the new Nicklin government. Hiley was named treasurer in 1957. It was a powerful position where he got to control the state's purse strings, which was important as the new government tried to course correct after twenty-five years of the Labor Party's capitulation to the unions. He was a senior member of the government and Frank Nicklin relied on his judgment, more than one might expect a Country Party leader to rely on a politician who belonged to a junior coalition partner. Hiley was different, though. Even in those years in the wilderness before Vince Gair's Labor Party imploded, people tended to respect Hiley. He was described by friend and foe alike as smart and hardworking and as a superior parliamentary performer.[1] He was a man of principles, too. Even though he had been replaced as leader by Ken Morris three years before the Nicklin government came to power, he never aspired to regain his position once the party was once more on the rise. There's no doubt that Hiley could have won over the party faithful and increased his power in the

Coalition government, but that wasn't him. He was a man who stuck to his word, kept his head down, and worked to make a better Queensland.

There was a lot to untangle in those early days in government, and the need to replace the recalcitrant police chief Tom Harold just added to what was already on Hiley's plate. He was no supporter of the Green Mafia, by any means, but there was something about Frank Bischof he didn't like. Earlier, in 1951, he and Bischof had clashed over the Bulimba election fraud when Hiley publicly accused Bischof of ignoring voter fraud in other divisions where it was more beneficial to the Country Party.[2] But as Hiley sat on the selection panel, he had to admit that Bischof had said all the right things about wanting to reform the police force, end patronage, and professionalize policing in Queensland. In the end, he put his reservations aside and got in line behind Nicklin to support his choice as police commissioner. There had always been something about Bischof that Hiley was suspicious about, though. Years passed and he survived one scandal after another. In a way, Hiley was happy that the police force was not his responsibility as treasurer—someone else could deal with the clean-up when the wheels fell off the entire thing. Then, in 1964, the scandal landed at his own doorstep. In a highly odd move, a group of illegal bookmakers from western Queensland, including Bischof's native Toowoomba region, reached out to Hiley with a story. The bookies were sick and tired of the extortionate protection payments that police were making them pay to operate. While they were happy to pay, could he do something about the amount?[3] He was flabbergasted. He asked what the bookies thought he, the state treasurer, could do about their problem. Talk to Bischof, they said. After all, half of the money ends up in the commissioner's office.

Earlier that same year, Bischof had been firmly in the crosshairs of the National Hotel Inquiry. While Gibbs had cleared the commissioner and his protégés of any wrongdoing, most believed that he was lucky, not innocent. The rumors of his corruption long predated the National Hotel, and his links to both bookmaking and the racing industry stretched back long before he became commissioner, even predating his career as a police officer altogether. So, when Hiley was visited by the western bookies in 1964, it was not difficult to accept the proposition that Bischof was at the head of a corrupt protection scheme operating in the regions. The bookies told Hiley that there were annual "fees" to continue operating: for large towns the price was $80,000 and $20,000 for smaller communities.[4] The system worked with around half going to local police and the other half going "to Brisbane," which to them was code for "Bischof."[5] The bookies told Hiley that it was not a problem to pay the annual fee, but other police had started to stand over them for more money, and it was starting to become an issue. The western bookies came to Hiley hoping to alleviate some financial pressure, but all their visit did was confirm the politician's long-held suspicions: the Big Fella was dirty.

The next step for Hiley was figuring out what to do next. It had been a miscalculation for the western bookies to go to him with their concerns. He was not part of the corrupt system, and there was no love lost between him and the police commissioner. When he brought up the possibility that they could get out from under Bischof's control by testifying against him, the bookies backed off. In general, the system of police protection worked. There was no way that they would ruin it by helping to bring down the man at the top. Without the testimony of the bookies, the solicitor-general told Hiley there was no firm evidence to bring charges against Bischof. Whatever Hiley chose to do, the legal route was closed. He brought his information to Bischof's superior, minister for police Alex Dewar, and the two men decided to confront Bischof head on. When he entered the meeting, Bischof was furious. He had beaten accusations of corruption at the National Hotel Inquiry earlier in 1964 and now here he was, facing more. Hiley and Dewar remained firm. The politicians outlined the case against Bischof and the details of the protection racket given to Hiley by the western bookies. The treasurer had collected more evidence, too: some of Bischof's old betting slips proving that the commissioner not only had a bad gambling habit but was in partnership with protected bookies as well.[6] While he had entered the meeting in indignant denial, Bischof left agreeing to stop the protection scheme at once. Not long after the showdown, he started taking an increasing amount of sick leave and, after a few years, stepped down as police commissioner.

Though a strike against endemic corruption, toppling Bischof was no panacea for all misconduct in the Queensland Police Force (QPF). Despite being police commissioner, Bischof did not have a monopoly on corruption, and so after his downfall, new actors in the Licensing Branch began to extend their grip on the protection rackets in Queensland. Jack Herbert was a former London police officer who joined the QPF on 7 July 1949, escaping the United Kingdom and, like so many Brits before him, destined for a new life in Australia.[7] It was ten years before he transferred into the Licensing Branch, a division of the QPF responsible for policing vice crime in the state from after-hours alcohol sales to prostitution and illicit gambling. Herbert told the Fitzgerald Inquiry in 1988 that it was not long after starting at the Licensing Branch that he was invited to join the corruption that was going on in the squad. Over drinks, Herbert's new workmates told him that it had been decided that he could be brought "in on the Joke." The setup of the Joke was simple. All Herbert had to do was steer clear of certain "protected" bookies. There was a list of the bookies who were "paid up" that was held at all times by an officer on duty who was in on the Joke—if they couldn't stop a raid from taking place, it was their job to call as many protected bookies as possible to sound the alarm. The punchline was even better. For doing this, he would receive £20 a month, a persuasive amount when considering the salary for an officer of his rank was only £90 a month.[8] Herbert was never one to miss an opportunity. He was up for a laugh and in on the Joke.

The Licensing Branch was a place where there was money to be made. When Herbert started in 1959, the Joke extended protection to starting price (SP) bookies, but as time went on, it expanded to offer the same corrupt deal to other forms of vice. Aside from gambling, Licensing Branch covered a diverse range of other crimes from after-hours alcohol sales to prostitution. The branch also laid claim to a new type of crime, one with the potential for great rewards: drugs. Vice providers had a choice: pay up or face the wrath of the Licensing Branch. The corrupt system only worked if those in on the Joke gave the appearance that they were doing their jobs effectively. If they didn't, there was a risk that someone would start asking questions or (even worse) corrupt officers could be transferred to a position with no chance to earn some extra cash. It was important that the branch continued to conduct raids and make arrests, but who to target? There was always a bookie or a brothel that thought they could get away with not paying their dues.[9] It wasn't long before their venues were raided and operations were shut down.

It was no good turning the police in. The brotherhood was strong, and a criminal who moved against one officer was considered to have moved against the entire force.[10] There was no escape from police control. The Jokers made sure of it. No warrant? No problem. Herbert was no stranger to forging warrants to get behind closed doors.[11] On occasion, there was no way to prevent a raid on a protected gambling site that had caught the attention of one too many honest police. The plan would be set in motion. Operators would be warned when the raid was set to take place so that, when police arrived, the situation would be controlled. Staff and punters with a criminal record would be sent home for the night, along with all the high-roller gamblers who were too important to lose. The only ones left were the "bunnies," minor gamblers who operators could afford to cut loose and didn't know much about how the operation worked.[12] It was a brutal system, but it worked.

After five years in the Licensing Branch, Herbert took over in 1964 as the chief organizer of the Joke. The organizer's job was an important one. It was not only up to him to collect and disperse the bribes amongst his fellow officers, but it was also up to him to make decisions about if a new officer in the Licensing Branch could be trusted to join the Joke. He had to be a discerning judge of character. One bad decision was all it would take to bring the whole house of cards crashing down. But as time went on, Herbert found this a much easier task than it first seemed. In his time organizing the Joke, not a single officer turned down his offer to get involved in the corruption taking place.[13] For some police, corruption was the entire purpose of wanting a transfer to the Licensing Branch. The normal trajectory of an officer's career meant them seeing some form of rural service before returning to Brisbane to join a unit like the Licensing Branch. Time in the country offered more than just a lesson in giving speeding tickets. Rural Queensland was a place where officers got a crash course in corruption. As Charles Corner found when he arrived in Mount Isa, protecting gambling was very much a team effort in country towns. The politicians sanctioned it, police protected it, hoteliers provided a venue for it, and the punters flocked to it.[14] The Licensing Branch was an attractive proposition for officers returning to Brisbane who were on the hunt for new opportunities to replace the ones they were leaving behind. The branch was responsible for policing all of those areas of vice crime that were most profitable for an officer on the take. It was Disneyworld for corruption.

Considering his affinity for racing and his interest in protecting bookies, it is somewhat surprising that Bischof never served a single day in the Licensing Branch. The protection racket in the Licensing Branch had been in action for a long time and was active in some form for the entire time that Bischof served in the Criminal Investigation Branch. For the most part, there was a tacit, unspoken gentlemen's agreement that corrupt police would not step on each other's toes. Herbert was aware that there were other police (like the Rat Pack) running their own corrupt networks in the force, but he left them to their own devices and focused on the protection scheme that he was responsible for. When Hiley confronted Bischof in 1964 about the western SP protection scheme, however, the terms of the gentlemen's agreement between the Joke and the Rat Pack started to change. Hiley was watching, and so Bischof was forced to cut one of his best revenue streams. Another new racket needed to be found to replace it, and moving in on the Licensing Branch seemed like a good proposition. Suddenly, the rats were on the doorstep, asking for their cut. After spending most of his career in the Consorting Squad, Tony Murphy transferred to the Licensing Branch in 1966. Herbert said he was aware of Murphy's reputation as Bischof's bagman and was told not to "let a day go by" without slipping the detective some cash to keep him onside. Herbert had no choice; Murphy was brought in on the Joke. The slow takeover had begun. Within a matter of weeks, Murphy suggested that Herbert include fellow Rat Packer Terry Lewis in his payment scheme, even though Lewis wasn't even a member of the Licensing Branch. He told Herbert that Lewis was close to the commissioner, so it would be useful to have him on board. It was impossible to say no to Murphy, so Herbert agreed.[15] For years, the Joke operated under the radar. Now, it had the Rat Pack's interest.

After the spotlight was shined on prostitution in Brisbane's bars and hotels in the National Hotel Inquiry, the sex trade was forced to evolve once again. First the street, then to the brothels, and then to the bars, and now, once again, the venue for selling sex changed. The rise of the massage parlor has been credited to Simone Vogel, real name Norma Pavich, who learned the sex trade under the notorious brothel proprietor Joe Borg in Sydney. When Borg was killed in a car bomb in May 1968, Vogel moved north. Brisbane was an untapped market compared to Sydney and, after what happened to Borg, seemed to be a much safer prospect. Vogel found a very different set of circumstances existed in her new home than what she was used to. There were few brothels, and the hotel-based trade was under a greater microscope than ever after the National Hotel fiasco. Necessity is the mother of all invention, though. Vogel has been credited with setting up the first "massage parlors" in Australia: venues masquerading as legitimate masseuse businesses but, in reality, sites where prostitution took place.[16] Like the "health studios" and "saunas" that were part of the sex trade in the United States, the massage parlor became a new paradigm for prostitution in Queensland, offering a modicum of plausible deniability to operators who could claim not to have known what was going on behind closed doors behind "massage therapists" and their clients.[17]

Setting up as a massage parlor did not protect brothel operators like Vogel from corrupt police looking to muscle in on the sex trade. Before too long, the parlor owners were under the control of the Licensing Branch. The smart ones, like Vogel, knew how the game worked. They paid into the Joke, just like the SP bookies before them. In return, the parlors were left alone or, if a raid was impossible to avoid, were at least warned and given time to prepare.[18] The parlors that refused to be a part of the Joke ran the risk of being targeted by the Licensing Branch and turned into an example of what happened when people did not cooperate. Former Licensing Branch officer Domenico Cacciola recalled that Herbert would often steal towels from parlors that were not in the Joke and give them to other officers in the squad. He told them to take them home, to have sex on the towels and bring them back. When the branch returned to the unsanctioned brothel where it had come from, Herbert returned the soiled towel and used it as proof that sex was taking place on the premises.[19] Corruption was a messy business, but someone had to do it. The parlor owners and the workers on the premises at the time were arrested and charged, and the parlor was shut down. Operators soon came to realize that it was useless to resist the Joke and either left town or started to pay into the system.

In 1970, a seismic shift in the QPF put corrupt police in more danger than ever before. The Big Fella had finally resigned in February 1969. At first, things continued as usual. He was replaced by Norwin Bauer, another Mason linked to the Rat Pack. But there was a move for change afoot driven by Max Hodges, a police minister who was set on reforming the QPF and moving past the era of corruption presided over by Bischof.[20] The government had barely escaped a scandal when Bischof dodged first the National Hotel Inquiry and then Hiley's investigation into the western bookies racket. Next time they might not be so lucky. It was important that his permanent replacement was someone clean, untouched by the Big Fella's malevolent influence. He landed on someone completely out of left field: Raymond Whitrod, then serving as the police commissioner of Papua New Guinea. Whitrod came with a reputation as a reformer, a man of impeccably honest conduct. When he first grabbed the reins of the QPF in September 1970, addressing corruption in the Licensing Branch was not initially treated as a priority—Whitrod was more concerned with going after Bischof loyalists in the Rat Pack. This focus shifted in November 1973 when former internal affairs boss Norm Gulbransen was named the new assistant commissioner. Gulbransen had been around the QPF for a long time. He had seen a lot in his time in the Crime Intelligence Unit (CIU) and knew a good deal about the rot in the Licensing Branch. He believed that the best way to deal with endemic corruption was to place someone in charge who could keep watch for it and, eventually, put a stop to it entirely. In July 1974, he chose Arthur Pitts to lead the branch.[21] The cleansing of the Licensing Branch had begun in earnest.

Pitts had his work cut out for him. The problems in the Licensing Branch were more than a case of rotten apples ruining the barrel. It was so ingrained in the culture that, in many ways, corruption *was* the barrel. A report released by the CIU in April 1974 noted that there were at least forty to fifty bookies operating in Brisbane, and more than that, "large scale businesses were being conducted with immunity because of collusion with the Licensing Branch."[22] Pitts came into the Licensing Branch with a mission. Within a few months of taking over, he had "created havoc" in the off-track betting (OTB) market, arresting seventeen major SP bookmakers who had (to that point) gone undetected.[23] Pitts left nothing to chance. He meticulously planned all raids and, to ensure no leaks, did not tell his fellow officers where they were going until the raid was already in progress and it was too late to warn the targets.[24] The campaign against SP waged by Pitts was, at its heart, a move against corruption in the Licensing Branch as well. Pitts sought to marginalize officers who were in on the Joke, transferring some out of the branch and keeping a close eye on others. For him, there was one big fish he really hoped to land: Herbert. Pitts did what he could to lure Herbert out, knowing that one day he would come to Pitts in an attempt to end the dismantling of the Joke. Pitts set up recording equipment on his home telephone so, when Herbert made the call, there was no denying it. He was offered $1500 each month to protect the operations of a select group of bookies.[25] In December 1974, both Herbert and his partner Neil Freier were arrested for attempting to corrupt the head of the Licensing Branch.

One of the risks of arresting the head of a corrupt police network is that, once caught, they have nothing to lose. If Pitts thought that his plan would end corruption in the Licensing Branch overnight, he was mistaken. Herbert had a lot of friends in the force, people who would do anything in their power to make sure that corruption continued. Too many careers were at risk to let Herbert go down, both in the police force and in the criminal world. The OTB industry was estimated to be worth around $50–60 million in 1974 and it would all disappear without the protection of friends on the inside.[26] Herbert was backed into a corner, and like a wounded animal, he fought back hard. Pitts was a crusader, but that didn't mean he was totally clean. Herbert waited, and before too long, a plan was hatched.

Less than a month before Herbert and Freier were arrested, Pitts had been involved in a raid on bookies Stanley Saunders and Brian Sieber on the Gold Coast, an hour south of Brisbane on the New South Wales border. With a team of three Licensing Branch officers, Pitts intercepted Saunders and Sieber's car on 20 November 1974 and charged the bookies with possessing materials used for illegal gambling. What seemed like an open-and-shut case was anything but that. Before they had been pulled over by Pitts's team, their car had crossed the border into New South Wales—a place where the Licensing Branch had no jurisdiction to operate.[27] If the court knew this, the case would be thrown out on a legal technicality despite Pitts having evidence that Saunders and Sieber were SP bookies. The only way to correct the mistake was to ensure that every officer on the raid was on the same page and was willing to tell the court that they had never crossed the border. It would be their word against Saunders and Sieber, and the word of four police officers was worth a lot more to the court. Pitts's plan would have worked if not for the fact that one of the team was Constable Frank Davey, and for whatever reason, Davey agreed to be Herbert's agent. As Pitts and the team met to get their stories straight, Davey wore a recording device that captured the entire conspiracy to commit perjury. Pitts's process corruption was clear on Davey's tape. When it was replayed, it was clear that he lied. He was caught in an exchange with another Licensing Branch officer, Cornelius William Horgan, saying:

> HORGAN: Okay. Well now listen; we didn't go across the border that day—or did we?
> PITTS: I did.
> HORGAN: But we've got to make up our minds whether we went across or stayed up there on the point.[28]

Herbert had outfoxed Pitts, using the Licensing Branch boss's own participation in corruption to wriggle free of the trap that had been set for him. With Pitts's integrity compromised, the case against Herbert and Freier fell apart. The charges were dismissed, and Herbert was free to continue his corruption, this time from outside the police force. He retired, but kept a close watch on the Licensing Branch, waiting for a chance to regain control. Pitts, once the QPF's most successful anticorruption crusader, was tarred with the brush of misconduct. He was disgraced and demoted, reassigned to the police Stores Depot to wait out the end of his career.[29]

Pitts drew a clear line between mercenary corruption and noble cause corruption. In his mind, to catch people like Herbert and the bookies that he protected, it was sometimes necessary to cut a few corners. He wasn't able to accept that mistakes were made on the Saunders and Sieber raid, and that it meant he would have to try again another day. For Pitts, the fact that he was a couple of feet out of his jurisdiction did not change the fact that Saunders and Sieber were guilty. Justice James Wood said in his final report into police corruption in New South Wales that noble cause corruption is an attractive prospect for even the most honorable officers, who see good policework go to waste because officers are constrained by a sense of due process that works to protect offenders, not victims.[30] Changing the location of the raid was a minor amendment to the case file to Pitts, not one that changed the brief of evidence in any real way. Yet, on tape, the crusading head of the Licensing Branch could be heard plotting to tell lies to get a conviction. Pitts had done fine work cleansing the Licensing Branch and going after people like Herbert, and then in one tape recording, he undermined everything he had achieved.

While Herbert and the Jokers dealt with the threat posed by Pitts, the Rat Pack had its own problems to contend with—a familiar face returned to Queensland to awaken the ghosts of the National Hotel Inquiry once again. Life had changed a lot for thirty-five-year-old Shirley Brifman since she was last in the Sunshine State. The girl from Atherton in the state's rural north had left in 1963, and aside from a brief return early the next year to front a royal commission, she had no intentions on returning. Things in Brisbane had gotten messy before she left. When it started, she was just doing what all sex workers had to do: she paid. Handing over a cut of your income to the police was simply the cost of doing business, a nuisance but no different to paying taxes at the end of the day. Brifman's problem was that she had gotten close with the tax collector, and it came back to bite her. She had learned the importance of keeping the police onside when working in the Killarney brothel in south Brisbane in the late 1950s, and when Killarney shut down, the good relationships she had made paid off.[31] She was close with the men pulling the strings. She forged a particularly close bond with two of Bischof's closest allies, who looked after her. One, Murphy, had a soft spot for her. Some feared Murphy, but the big detective never failed to make time for her. She was even closer to another member of the Rat Pack, Glen Hallahan—though he was, possibly, more of a dangerous prospect. Hallahan would meet her for sex and then, afterwards, smoke pot and talk for hours. He might have had the nickname of "Silent" in the QPF, but when he was with her, he loved to talk.[32]

It had been almost ten years since Brifman fled Queensland amid the uproar of the National Hotel Inquiry, putting Murphy and Hallahan in the rearview mirror in search of a new life in the Emerald City. The detectives from Queensland understood. It was a tough time in Brisbane, and having Brifman go south to keep a low profile for a while was a smart move. Hallahan had friends in Sydney that could take care of her. Before long, she was under the sway of Detective Fred Krahe of the New South Wales Police and set up as a brothel madam who, over the next few years, cultivated a client list that boasted some of the city's most prominent people.[33] Then, in a literal flash, her new life was turned upside down. Pictures were taken at the opening of one of her new brothels on 9 May 1969. They were later published in the newspaper and showed several police including the notorious Krahe.[34] Her friends started to disappear, including her one-time protector and lover from Queensland, Hallahan. It could have been a coincidence, but after a falling out between Brifman and Hallahan in mid-1970, the protected madam was charged with procuring a minor—her daughter—for the purposes of prostitution. Brifman's luck had run out. She was against the ropes. So when current affairs program *This Day Tonight* came calling she jumped at the chance to get her side of the story across. She went on TV on 15 June 1971 and spilled the beans. She told of paying protection money to the New South Wales Vice Squad for years and, even worse, admitted that she had lied to the National Hotel Inquiry on behalf of corrupt Queensland police.[35] The interview sent shockwaves through police on both sides of the border. Nowhere was safe for Brifman anymore. She knew Krahe and so she knew the risk she was in if she stayed. She packed up her family and went north, back to the city where it all started. Murphy and Hallahan also had a bone to pick with her, but she could handle them. She had another plan, too. One that could provide some extra security, just in case her former friends in the QPF got the idea she needed to be dealt with. On 2 July 1971, Brifman walked into a room with Assistant Commissioner Abe Duncan and offered to tell all about corruption in the police force.[36]

Although the way that prostitution was practiced had changed significantly since she was last in Queensland, most of the major players remained the same. The difference was that, since she left, there had been a change in the QPF's management. Bischof was out, and the reformer Raymond Whitrod was in, and he was no friend to the Rat Pack or the Joke. On Whitrod's first day as commissioner, he had barely touched down in Queensland before the officer sent to collect him from the airport warned him about the Rat Pack and the need for Whitrod to deal with Bischof's lieutenants if he really wanted to stamp out corruption.[37] Brifman's appearance on *This Day Tonight* in June 1971 was a problem, but her return to Brisbane shortly after had the potential to turn into a total disaster. Assistant Commissioner Duncan had tried to keep his meetings with Brifman under wraps as much as possible, on a need-to-know basis. She and her family were placed in a series of safe houses across Brisbane, and in return, she told Duncan and his team everything she knew about corruption in the QPF.[38] On *This Day Tonight* she said that when she was a sex worker in Brisbane, she paid corrupt police for protection. Duncan was particularly interested in this. Brifman told the National Hotel Inquiry in no uncertain terms that she *had not* paid any member of the QPF. If she was telling the truth now, then why had she lied to the inquiry in 1964?

The answer to that was simple, according to Brifman. She "lied because [she] was told to lie." She told Duncan that detectives Murphy and Hallahan had coached her before she gave evidence to the commission, calling her at night during the case to make sure she had her story straight. She also admitted that she lied to the commission to contradict the testimony of other witnesses, again at the Rat Pack's request. If the police were still uncertain that she was telling the truth, she had something to convince them. She gave Duncan letters that Murphy had written her over the past decade, proving that the pair had done more than just cross paths on the Brisbane vice scene.[39] Duncan's team had heard enough. On 4 February 1972, Murphy was charged with perjury based on Brifman's claims.[40] Before the accusations could be tested at trial and a month after Murphy was charged, she was found dead of a barbiturate overdose in her north Brisbane safehouse. Despite persistent claims that a third party was involved, her death was treated as nonsuspicious overdose.[41] The case against Murphy collapsed without the prosecution's star witness to tell her story. Once again, a member of the Rat Pack had escaped the trap set by anticorruption investigators. Murphy was back on duty, policing the streets of Brisbane. Not every corrupt officer had the same luck. By the end of 1972, a different member of the Rat Pack would be out for good.

The mission to force the Rat Pack out of the QPF was a multipronged campaign. At the same time Brifman was sitting in a safehouse giving Duncan the evidence he needed to charge Murphy, internal affairs boss Gulbransen was setting up a sting to catch Hallahan. The saying goes that madness is repeating the same action over and over again but expecting different results. If this is true, Hallahan was most certainly mad. He had almost lost his entire career in 1959 when Jim Donovan came so close to catching him in the act of receiving bribes from Leigh Hamilton. Now, on a balmy summer morning over a decade later, Hallahan was about to be caught doing the exact same thing again. It was around 9:30 a.m. on 30 December 1971 when the detective came strolling across the grass at New Farm Park, coming to a stop at riverside park bench next to a blonde in her early thirties named Dorothy Edith Knight.[42] The unlikely pair had known each other for some time. Hallahan met her years before, connecting her with other sex workers operating out of the inner city. They were already on Hallahan's payroll. Knight, too, started paying Hallahan at a rate of $20, to be paid each week at this exact bench in New Farm Park.[43] After some chat, she handed Hallahan the money, and as usual, he thanked her and went to return to his car. There was one very important difference about this day, however. Hallahan was not the only police officer in the park.

Unbeknownst to him, Knight had gone to the police several months before and blown the whistle on Hallahan's protection scam. So began the planning of an elaborate sting. Gulbransen was careful. His target had slipped the net before when someone tipped him off about a move against him. It was imperative that he did not see it coming this time. Gulbransen's need for a rock-solid case pushed the CIU to creative new methods. Before the meeting, Knight was fitted with the first-ever electronic listening device used in Queensland. It was not exactly a successful first outing. The bug was makeshift, and the batteries almost ran out right in the middle of the operation—no one thought to check them first.[44] But nevertheless, Gulbransen's team intercepted Hallahan as he left the meeting with Knight and, finding the bribe on him, charged him with two counts of official corruption.[45]

The heat was on for Hallahan. On 6 October 1972, the prosecution announced that it would no longer pursue the charges, and the case was dismissed. Because it was such a new technique, there were questions raised over the legality of the audio recording made during the sting. Even more curiously, the prosecution was having trouble making the argument that Hallahan had been protecting a sex worker stick. Under Hallahan's protection, Knight had never been charged as a sex worker since starting in the business in 1968. Ironically, without legal proof that she was a sex worker, it was hard to prove that he was being paid to protect her.[46] Even his own lawyers were shocked at how easy it had been to beat the charges. Hallahan, on the other hand, was so confident that he had not even shown up to face court. His lawyer, Des Sturgess, recalls that his client was concerned about the case until learning that magistrate Eddie Broad had been chosen to preside over it, at which point "relief flooded over Hallahan."[47] A criminal associate of Hallahan claimed that the detective pressured Broad, a judge who usually handled Licensing Branch cases, to dismiss the case against him, but this allegation was never proven.[48]

Hallahan may have dodged a criminal conviction, but his time in the police force was up. He could tell that, after coming so close to nabbing him, Gulbransen would never give up. Hallahan still faced departmental charges that, like in 1959, would likely see him demoted. The CIU would hound him until eventually he ended up behind bars. He wasn't going to let that happen. The CIU would stop pursuing him if he left the force. He resigned on the same day that he returned from suspension, the first member of the Rat Pack to walk away from the QPF.[49] Forcing one of the Rat Pack's most active members to walk away from policing shows the impact that even a small amount of pressure can create on systemic corruption, when supported by the commissioner's office. On the surface, it seems surprising that Hallahan was eventually caught in the same trap that Donovan had tried to set for him and Lewis in 1959 in the Hamilton case, pressuring a sex worker for bribes in amounts so high that she was willing to participate in an internal affairs sting. In the Hamilton case, Hallahan survived with the support of his mentor Bischof. But now Bischof was gone, and as a result the dangers of continuing to repeat the same stand over tactics were much higher. He beat the Knight case, but Hallahan might not have been so lucky on the next one.

Whitrod has been criticized in the past for not using his six years as police commissioner to effectively force out the Rat Pack, giving corruption the opportunity to rise once more after Lewis became commissioner in 1976. However, the Hallahan case shows that busting an endemic system of corruption does not require a series of successful anti-corruption operations. What is more important is to remove the safety net that emboldens officers to take part. The sting against Hallahan was not the most innovative and inspired operation in police history (and failed in court, no less), but it achieved its goals in that it showed Hallahan and the rest of the Rat Pack that there was nowhere to hide in Whitrod's QPF. If the Bischof-era rackets continued, those responsible would be found and prosecuted. Hallahan was a symbolic casualty of this new commitment to corruption-busting, and Murphy would have joined him if not for the untimely death of the state's star witness, Brifman. Five years before, Bischof's team was strong. Now, the Big Fella was gone. The Rat Pack were against the ropes, just waiting for Commissioner Whitrod's next move against them.

CHAPTER 6

Vice City

At the time he signed up with the Queensland Police Force (QPF) in August 1968, Bob Campbell never expected that it would get this bad. The teenager was dating a girl, and it just so happened that her father was a police officer. Campbell was, of course, looking to impress. His girlfriend's father said he could do some good on the force, and Campbell, tired of endless mundane days working in a bank, was craving the kind of adventure that came with chasing down the bad guys.[1] His parents did not approve. Joining the police force was not necessarily something to be proud of in the late 1960s, especially not for a strict Catholic family like the Campbells. Frank Bischof and his allies had avoided formal punishment at the National Hotel Inquiry, and yet in some corners, the mud had stuck. Nevertheless, Campbell went ahead with his plan.

He was sworn in on 10 December 1968 and, shortly after, was assigned to the Fortitude Valley police station in the heart of Brisbane's vice district. Nestled in the lowlands adjacent to Bowen Hills and Spring Hill, the Valley had been a thriving shopping district since the 1890s, but in the 1960s, the area had started to change for the worse. Urban sprawl and the closure of the tram line connecting the Valley to the rest of Brisbane caused a downturn in trade, and shops began to close.[2] In their place came the bars, the illegal casinos, and the brothels. Now, the Valley was

Brisbane's red-light district. There was no doubt that, at the Valley, Campbell would be right in the heart of the action.

Campbell saw action, but not in the way that he expected. Not long after starting at the Valley he started to realize that the true state of the QPF was exactly what his parents had feared. The police at the Valley barely worked, preferring to hang out in local pubs where they got drunk for hours for free. In return, the police ignored violations of the Liquor Act. Even when the pubs were shut, it did not stop them. A sergeant would stop by one of the nightclubs in the area, pick up some takeaway beers and bring them to a park where the officers could reconvene their drinking session.[3] Campbell was disgusted, to the point that he was thrilled to escape the Valley when he was called up for then-mandatory National Service in the military in April 1969. His reprieve was brief, though. When he returned to the QPF in 1971, it was not long before he found himself back in the Valley once again. There was a new commissioner now. South Australian Raymond Whitrod had taken over the year prior. The Valley police were still as lazy as ever but, aware that Whitrod's reformers were watching, at least gave the appearance now of doing some work.

Working in the Valley was tolerable for a time, but before too long, things returned to normal. When Whitrod was forced out in 1976, he was replaced with Terry Lewis. Campbell knew of Lewis. Since he joined in the 1960s, he had been hearing other police talk about him as one of Bischof's bagmen, a member of the Rat Pack along with Tony Murphy and Glen Hallahan.[4] Campbell felt the shift in the force. The Valley police returned to the old ways. Free drinks and the sex trade were in, actual policework was out. Even on the rare occasion that Valley cops *did* choose to act, the methods they used were unconventional, to say the least. Former Queensland police officer (later chief of the Australian Border Force) Roman Quaedvlieg recalls walking into a room at the Valley police station one day in the late 1980s to the odd sight of a detective dressed in a bird suit, beating a suspect with a rolled up newspaper.[5] When he questioned the practice, the other Valley police said the bird suit was a precautionary measure. The logic was that, whenever a suspect tried to complain about police brutality, the statement would be dismissed because no one would believe them when they said the culprit was a giant bird. The practice was allegedly so common in the Valley that, when too many suspects complained about the same bizarre set of circumstances, the giant bird costume was retired—only to be replaced with a chicken suit. Honest police like Campbell were, once more, ostracized. Day in and day out, Campbell became more frustrated with the state of the force. He waited for a chance to do something about it. Until he did, the party in the Valley raged on.

When Bischof walked away from the commissioner's job, he left a power vacuum in the police force. The officer who replaced him, Criminal Investigation Branch (CIB) boss Norm Bauer, was close to Bischof. He led the Mount Isa CIB in the late 1950s, where he worked with Hallahan on the Sundown murders before the pair transferred to Brisbane together in 1958.[6] For a remote mining town, Mount Isa was a flashpoint of corruption during the period. Apart from the whispers that Hallahan had perpetrated a verbal in the Sundown case, there was the 1956 death in custody of Michael Jorgensen and Charles Corner's accusations that police were protecting gambling at the town's pubs.[7] Bauer was aware of how policing worked in Queensland and was on board to continue Bischof's legacy. The problem was that Bauer was approaching retirement, with less than a year remaining before he reached the mandated age of sixty-five.

For Max Hodges, who was appointed police minister by Premier Joh Bjelke-Petersen in May 1969, it was a chance to act. Sending Bauer away on a months-long junket to study police forces around the world, Hodges brought in South Australian police chief John McKinna to audit the QPF and report back to Hodges on what was required to whip the force into shape. McKinna gave one recommendation that was more crucial than all others: Whitrod.[8] According to McKinna, the former commissioner of the Commonwealth Police was honest, fair, and effective. If Hodges wanted to reform the QPF, there was no other choice for the job.

Whitrod left the Commonwealth Police in 1969 to take up the role of police commissioner in Papua New Guinea, so when McKinna first reached out to him on Hodges's behalf, he was not interested in making another move so soon. Hodges was persistent. He went to Papua New Guinea personally to woo Whitrod and, eventually, secured his commitment to starting as QPF commissioner in September 1970. In his memoirs, Whitrod recalls having "little understanding of how entrenched corruption was" in Queensland before taking on the role.

If he was unsure, it was not long after his arrival that he was made aware. Sergeant Ken Hoggett was sent to collect Whitrod from the airport when he arrived in Brisbane from Papua New Guinea. Hoggett would not get a better chance than this. As the car approached the city, he turned to the new commissioner and said: "I don't know how much you know about the Queensland Police Force, but it's pretty corrupt." The Queensland premier in 1970 was Bjelke-Petersen, a former police minister, who advised Whitrod to not "lean too hard" on the QPF and not move too quickly to reform the force, or he could find himself losing the support of the rank and file.[9] It was obvious that, though Hodges was keen to see reform, Whitrod did not have the support of the man who ultimately called the shots.

Whitrod made it known from the outset that he was going to be a very different commissioner than what Queensland was used to. He set boundaries. He refused to give his private number to union official Merv Callaghan, setting the stage for a conflict between the union and commissioner's office that lasted for his entire tenure.[10] He set up a permanent squad, the Crime Intelligence Unit (CIU), to investigate corrupt police officers. The first task set for the CIU by Whitrod after its establishment was to combat the influence of the Rat Pack.[11] The CIU claimed Hallahan's scalp but could not make charges stick on Murphy or Lewis. Instead, Whitrod used his power to post the men to distant rural districts in Queensland's west. He was taking an axe to the corrupt structures of the QPF and, in the course of doing so, was making few friends amongst the old guard. One of his first targets was not the Consorting Squad or the Licensing Branch, however. The approach Whitrod took was more unorthodox. He went after the Juvenile Aid Bureau (JAB) and its longtime boss, Lewis.

The JAB was one of Bischof's pet projects, set up in 1963 after the Big Fella returned from a study trip to Europe. The unit's mandate was to devise new ways to deal with youth crime, and Bischof installed his protégé Lewis to lead the project.[12] The timing of Lewis's appointment was fortuitous. He left the Consorting Squad shortly before the National Hotel Inquiry and, as a result, managed to dodge being implicated in corruption alongside his former colleagues. The JAB was renowned for adopting a counsel-and-caution policy towards young offenders. Rather than charging them, the JAB officers acted as mentors and case managers to them.[13] It was, in many ways, a rare shining light amid the dark shadow of corruption in the QPF. Even so, the JAB's method was built on the same policy of discretionary enforcement favored by Bischof and his protégés in other areas of policing. Instead of cracking down strictly on young Queenslanders, as was the case in the 1950s, the JAB gave them a second chance at reform.

Though progressive for the time, counsel-and-caution was seen by some, even in the reformist camp, as turning a blind eye to the growing problem of youth crime. Partly the result of a general concern over discretionary policing, this reaction was also motivated by a desire to cleanse the QPF of any relic of the Bischof age under Whitrod. Just over two years after Whitrod's appointment, he and Hodges made their first strike against the JAB. Under Bischof, the squad was based on the same floor as the commissioner's office. Whitrod made the decision in November 1972 that the JAB should be moved to an off-site location, away from police headquarters, at Ampol House.[14] Now geographically marginalized, Whitrod and Hodges stripped Lewis's team of its power. The pair agreed that from 1 January 1973 the JAB would be seconded to the Department of Children's Services where the enforcement powers of its officers would be severely curtailed.[15] The JAB continued to exist, but for purposes, its role in the QPF was assumed by a new entity staffed by Whitrod loyalists: the Education Department Liaison Unit.

Whitrod and Hodges had dismantled Bischof's JAB in the matter of a few months. The move was more than just a petty one, though. With Lewis as the JAB boss, the squad had become a haven for police who were not on board with Whitrod's reformist agenda. Initally Whitrod was not interested in the JAB, which was, overall, a positive. If he did not see the importance of the JAB, he would not move to put one of his own people in charge of it and would leave Lewis to his own devices. By 1972, the list of officers attached to the JAB read like a roll call of those targeted by Whitrod under suspicion of corruption.[16] There is indication that Whitrod was aware of this and, further, supported moving suspected corrupt officers to Lewis's command. Whitrod's goal since becoming commissioner was to negate the influence of the Rat Pack. Yet on 31 August 1971, he signed the order to transfer Murphy from the Licensing Branch to the JAB. The move reunited Murphy with Lewis in the same squad for the first time in nearly a decade, not to mention the other police in the JAB who had been allies of the theirs during the Bischof era.[17] At first, this seems like a questionable move, putting two of the CIU's biggest targets together. But Whitrod was playing a long game. In transferring Murphy to the JAB, he removed a suspected corrupt officer from a position where he could continue his misconduct to a unit where there were few chances to solicit bribes. Not only that, Whitrod's plan to marginalize the JAB was underway. It was only just over a year after Murphy transferred to the JAB that Whitrod seconded the unit to Children's Services, cutting off whatever remained of its power. Whitrod used the transfers process to move his targets into position, seeming to give them what they wanted by reuniting them before delivering them a blow that left them languishing far on the outer fringes of the force's center of power.

Whitrod led the QPF in the mid-1970s, at the same time that Jack Herbert and Arthur Pitts were struggling for control of the Licensing Branch. In 1975, Herbert scored a pyrrhic victory when he got Frank Davey to record Pitts conspiring to commit process corruption. Even before his arrest, Herbert saw the writing on the wall that there was no room for him in Whitrod's police force. He retired from the QPF on medical grounds in October 1974, just before his attempt to bribe Pitts.[18] Whitrod appeared to be making ground in the fight against corruption in the QPF, but any progress evaporated in late 1976 when a series of events drove him to resign from his post.

Essentially, there were three events that directly contributed to Whitrod's decision to leave the QPF. The first occurred on 29 July 1976 when Traffic Branch inspector Mark Beattie was recorded on television news cameras during a protest over funding for tertiary students striking a female protester, Rosemary Severin, over the head with his baton, in contravention of the *Police Rules* on the use of force.[19] Though Whitrod pledged to investigate, he was shut down by Bjelke-Petersen and his cabinet, who ruled that no investigation would take place. By this time, the premier had come to regret the selection of Whitrod as police commissioner, at odds with Whitrod over the perception that he was "soft on crime" and, tellingly, Whitrod's resistance to aggressive action on Queensland's active left-wing protest movement. The premier was an outspoken supporter of police using force to suppress protest, and critics of the government argued that his decision to undermine Whitrod on the departmental investigation of Beattie was intended to give police "the green light ... to deal violently with demonstrators in future."[20]

The second event that pushed Whitrod to resign was, similarly, in regard to the premier's intervention in police disciplinary procedures. On 29 August 1976 police conducted a raid on Cedar Bay, a "hippy" commune in tropical north Queensland where around a hundred local officers (with the assistance of a naval patrol boat) were accused of using excessive force on residents and destroying property. The police believed the commune was the location of a large-scale marijuana crop, but after the raid, only two Cedar Bay residents were charged with the possession of an illegal substance. A meager crop of marijuana was found and ripped out of the ground by police—hardly enough to warrant such an aggressive raid, during which most of the Cedar Bay settlement was burned. When Whitrod set out to investigate the complaints of excessive force, Bjelke-Petersen intervened and instructed him not to pursue the matter further. Fed up, Whitrod ignored the premier and sent Assistant Commissioner Norm Gulbransen to Cedar Bay anyway.[21] The incident had echoes of the Jorgensen affair, when Commissioner Harold sent his own protégé, Deputy Commissioner Jim Donovan, to Mount Isa to investigate police involvement in Michael Jorgensen's death in custody.[22] In that case, the decision to ignore the premier's wishes was the first step towards Harold's dismissal. The same was true here. By going against Bjelke-Petersen's explicit instructions, Whitrod willfully put a target on his own back.

The third event and the last straw was the appointment of Lewis as assistant commissioner, against Whitrod's wishes. Whitrod found himself in an impossible position: to accept Lewis as assistant commissioner and let the fox into the henhouse or to resign in protest, unwilling to work with such a man.[23] Under significant pressure, Whitrod took the latter option and announced his resignation on 15 November 1976—the day Lewis's promotion was made public.

Whitrod was gone, and the premier was able to select Lewis as his successor, choosing a more acquiescent character for the commissioner's role. First, though, some action would have to be taken to satisfy the public that the QPF was no longer riddled with corruption. With the conduct of the police under a spotlight because of events like Cedar Bay and the seemingly never-ending trials of the Licensing Branch, the premier was forced to act. He called an inquiry into the enforcement of criminal law in Queensland to be overseen by Supreme Court judge Geoffrey Lucas on 18 November 1976, three days after Whitrod's resignation.[24] Like the National Hotel Inquiry before it, the Lucas Inquiry began swiftly. Lucas held his first sitting day on 26 November and reported on 29 April 1977, by which point Lewis had been named Whitrod's replacement as QPF Commissioner.[25] Lucas was not tasked with investigating mercenary corruption in the force. Instead, he was given the responsibility of looking at how its systems could be improved to better serve the Queensland public. In this sense, Lucas was more concerned with process corruption, where police cut corners to make a case stick or otherwise became socialized to accept that corruption was, sometimes, necessary. Lucas's findings were reminiscent of those of the Mollen Commission in New York City in the early 1990s. Like Mollen, Lucas found that the QPF had "tolerated a culture that fostered misconduct and concealed lawlessness by police officers."[26]

Drawing on the experience of police themselves, such as the recently exonerated Herbert, Lucas issued a raft of recommendations to eradicate process corruption. He suggested improvements like limiting terms of service in "at-risk" squads like the Licensing Branch. Lucas called for the mandatory recording of police interviews to prevent verbals as well as an end to arrest quotas, which he believed drove police to commit process corruption to make arrests.[27] Lucas was, in some ways, ahead of his time, and many of his recommendations were subsequently acknowledged by police around the world as being best practice. In the United Kingdom, for example, the Police and Criminal Evidence Act introduced in 1984 made (as Lucas recommended) audio recording of police interviews mandatory, and enshrined a suspect's right to legal representation. The implementation of recording protocols in the United States has followed a (typically) more fragmented trajectory but also began to be widely adopted in the 1980s. At the time of the Lucas Inquiry, however, his ideas were still new and, for many, controversial. Bjelke-Petersen was vehemently critical of recording police interviews and, as such, was backed into a corner, obliged to act on Lucas's recommendations yet, at the same time, firmly resistant to doing so. His response was, once more, to turn the process itself against the Lucas Inquiry. After the government received the Lucas's final report, the premier instructed Lewis to head a small team tasked with reviewing the inquiry's findings. Perhaps unsurprisingly, this committee did nothing, and as a result, most of the Lucas Inquiry's recommendations were not implemented on Lewis's watch.[28] Indeed, by the time of the Fitzgerald Inquiry ten years later, the recommendations still sat gathering dust somewhere in the commissioner's office.

In the meantime, Lewis got down to the business of governing. Choosing a new inspector for the Licensing Branch was at the top of his to-do list. Since Pitts's fall from grace, the Licensers had been rudderless. Herbert's loss was being felt, too. He was corrupt and the organizer of the Joke, but even so he had served in the Licensing Branch since 1959. His retirement left a major gap in the squad that had yet to be filled. To add insult to injury, the Licensers were also the focus of the ongoing Lucas Inquiry, now entering its third month. No one in the branch was left untarnished in the turmoil of the previous few years. Lewis's eventual choice, Alec Jeppesen, was no exception. He was a central figure in the Lucas Inquiry. As one of Pitts's top lieutenants, he was also featured on the recording that brought down his boss, counselling other Licensers on how to commit perjury effectively in the Southport betting trial.[29] Maybe Lewis thought Jeppesen was someone he could work with, someone on board with process corruption. If so, he was wrong. Jeppesen, for all his faults, was firmly opposed to the mercenary corruption in the force. He conspired to put bookies in prison, not to protect them. Anticorruption reformers like Whitrod, Gulbransen, and Pitts were all gone or otherwise neutralized. Jeppesen, in his new role, was one of the last in a position to fight corruption in the QPF from the inside.

Jeppesen's time at the Licensing Branch sparked a struggle over control of prostitution that originated before the closure of the tolerated brothels. As was the case then, the Consorting Squad and Licensing Branch went to war over who was responsible for policing the lucrative sex trade. Both groups had some jurisdictional claim. Selling sex was technically a licensing offense. However, the Vagrants,

Gaming and Other Offences Amendment Act 1971 empowered the Consorters to arrest women who solicited clients "for immoral purposes."[30] When the Licensing Branch was under the control of the Joke, the Rat Pack were happy to let them take the lead on policing sex, especially after Murphy joined in 1966. Now, Jeppesen was on a crusade to shut down the array of illegal brothels, massage parlors, and escort agencies that started to emerge once again on the Brisbane vice scene in the Whitrod era. That could not be permitted—the sex industry was too profitable for corrupt police. So commenced a "private tug-of-war" for control that began in earnest when Murphy was appointed by his old friend Lewis in 1977 to a rather ironic position: chief of the internal affairs unit, the CIU. From the beginning, Murphy began turning the CIU to his own ends. He dismantled the anticorruption squad from within and at the same time made his first grab for prostitution. He argued that the CIU needed access to the brothels and parlors to gather intelligence, but Jeppesen disagreed. The Licensing Branch boss brought the matter to Bjelke-Petersen in 1978, who agreed that the Licensers should be in sole control of prostitution. The premier told Murphy to keep his nose out.[31]

Despite the official verdict on who could police prostitution, the Rat Pack continued trying to wrestle control from Jeppesen for the two years that he oversaw the Licensing Branch. Another of Pitts's former Licensers, Domenico Cacciola, said that some of Murphy's Consorting Squad came to him when he was stationed at the Fortitude Valley CIB and "reminded [him] on more than one occasion that they ran the Valley and to stay out of their way."[32] He said the Consorters were out of control in this period, doing rounds of the brothels standing over the managers and workers for protection money and, on occasion, demanding free sex. Another supporter of Jeppesen in the Licensing Branch, Salvatore Di Carlo, backed up Cacciola's experience at the Fitzgerald Inquiry. He told Fitzgerald that the police were aware that Murphy wanted prostitution under his control, and if he could not get it away from the Licensing Branch, he wanted his friend Lewis to take a more drastic action and place the branch itself under his command at the state CIB.[33] Getting Lewis into the top job returned to the Rat Pack a level of control it had not held since the Bischof era ended several years earlier, including, importantly, the power to alter the very structure of the force. Lewis could change the playing field. If prostitution *had* to be under the Licensers, the commissioner could just give the Licensers to Murphy.

Another of Lewis's new powers was to order internal investigations. When Licensing Branch officer Brian Marlin came to see him on 24 November 1978, he had a story to tell about his boss. He told Lewis that Jeppesen was corrupt, that he was stealing from the QPF in a scam where he made payments to "criminal informants" that did not exist and pocketed the cash.[34] Lewis put two of his best men on the case, Brian Hayes and Syd "Sippy" Atkinson. Hayes and Atkinson were part of the old guard—remnants of the Bischof era with a reputation for committing verbals. The Jeppesen investigation was a hit. The rumor was that Lewis told Atkinson and Murphy that whoever of them destroyed Jeppesen would be handed the first available assistant commissioner job.[35] Atkinson was incentivized to find dirt, and he did. He found one of Jeppesen's informants who said he often signed off on payment slips that quoted a figure far greater than he received, suggesting the shortfall went into Jeppesen's wallet.[36] It was crucial evidence in the case against Jeppesen. Conveniently, the informant just so happened to be a person who also informed to Atkinson. Whether this personal relationship influenced his statement against Jeppesen is not known, but it did not matter. On 13 February 1979 Jeppesen was transferred out of the Licensing Branch.[37]

The insidious part of process corruption is that it is often masked under the guise of good practice. No one could argue that Lewis, once informed of allegations against Jeppesen, should not have investigated. By the same token, though, the outcome of the investigation was a foregone conclusion. The hunt was on to claim Jeppesen's career, and the commissioner set out a clear incentive for investigators to find some reason to force the transfer of the Licensing Branch chief. The plan had worked. Anxious not to repeat past mistakes, Lewis sought out expert advice before replacing Jeppesen: the corrupt ex-Licenser, Herbert.[38] There are few reasons for the commissioner to consult a disgraced former detective, none good. Considering Herbert's area of expertise, it is a good guess that Lewis hoped to select an officer who was going to be open to restarting the Joke. Ross Rigney, the officer Herbert suggested, was another bad choice. When Herbert approached him about "getting something going" with a new corruption scheme in the branch, Rigney turned him down.[39] Herbert's records, supplied to the Fitzgerald Inquiry, show that no corrupt payments were registered during Rigney's time at the Licensing Branch, possibly explaining why after only a year of service he was transferred and replaced with Noel Dwyer.[40] This time, Herbert was more careful. Before suggesting him to Lewis, Herbert tested Dwyer by offering him a bribe to drop charges against bookie Terence McMahon. Dwyer agreed and, unknowingly, put himself at the top of the list to by the next Licensing Branch boss.[41] Finally, the Joke was alive again. The new boss had none of the moral concerns about the Joke that his predecessors did. Dwyer was in the job to make money. After almost a decade of contending with first Pitts then Jeppesen and Rigney, the Joke was, once more, back in action.

The firm control of police was a hallmark of Queensland's vice trade in the 1980s. Unlike the criminal free for all seen in other states, the second Joke placed restrictions on the amount of people who were able to enter into the sex and gambling business. Essentially, vice was provided by one of two groups. The first was led by the Bellino brothers, Antonio and Geraldo. The Sicilian-born Bellinos were fringe players in Brisbane's nightlife before opening Pinnochio's nightclub on Ann Street in the Valley in 1971. While Antonio ran the club downstairs, Geraldo and Luciano Scognamiglio operated an illegal casino upstairs. Former employees told Fitzgerald that detectives like Murphy and Atkinson patronized the Bellino casino from the early 1970s, and Geraldo was paying Murphy so that the casino could keep operating. By 1974 the group (which now included Vic Conte) had gone into partnership on a larger illegal casino at 142 Wickham Street, above the infamous Bubbles Bathhouse brothel. When the Bellinos brought experienced flesh-trader Geoff Crocker into their operation, the "Syndicate" was born. Crocker was responsible for running brothels and massage parlors, Conte looked after gambling and Geraldo Bellino served as "managing director" overseeing the entire operation.[42] In their years in the Brisbane vice world, members of the Syndicate all had experience with police like Herbert. When Dwyer was installed as the Licensing chief Branch, Herbert came to him with a proposition: protect the Syndicate, permit experienced operators like Bellino and Crocker run the show, and rake in the profits.

If the Syndicate represented the vice establishment in Brisbane, then Hector Hapeta and Anne-Marie Tilley were most certainly the youthful interlopers on the scene. The couple from Sydney arrived in Brisbane in 1978, at the peak of Jeppesen's reign at the Licensing Branch. Tilley was the brains of the organization, Hapeta the muscle. She had been a sex worker in Sydney for years, but at the ripe age of twenty-three, she was looking to be her own boss. She came to Brisbane to rent a massage parlor from Syndicate member Crocker, and soon after, she and Hapeta got to work establishing their new empire in Brisbane.[43] Before too long, Hapeta and Tilley were purchasing properties all over the inner city and setting them up as brothels, or escort agencies. The operation benefited from the general lack of interest around prostitution under Dwyer, but they were not formally part of the Joke until 1981, when Tilley was caught up in a raid and sentenced to two months in prison. After the raid, the pair realized that something would have to be arranged if they were to continue operating in Brisbane. Hapeta approached Dwyer who, after conferring with Herbert and Conte (representing the Syndicate), agreed to protect their businesses in future.[44] Another Licenser, Harry Burgess, was tasked with being Tilley's primary contact in the Joke. At the peak of their arrangement, Hapeta and Tilley paid as much as $23,000 a month. It seems the historical relationship between the police and Syndicate members paid off. Despite having a more diversified portfolio that included gambling, the Syndicate only ever paid a maximum of $17,000 a month to corrupt police.[45]

Vice was being reorganized in Brisbane. The Valley was at its epicenter. By 1981, Campbell had been languishing at the Valley police station for most of his career. He tried on a few occasions to alert someone about the corruption he was witnessing. He wrote to Lewis when he took over as commissioner and, when the boss did nothing, escalated his complaints to Police Minister Tom Newberry. Five weeks later, Newberry responded, referring him back to Lewis. Campbell knew he was starting to be noticed, though. Not long after his letter-writing campaign began, he was transferred out of the Valley. Like Pitts before him, Campbell was being sent to the Stores Depot as punishment for making waves. He worked for six months in the Stores Depot before being moved, again, to Woolloongabba. At his new station, Campbell was the target of relentless abuse, constantly threatened with violence by drunken police for "not being a good Joh Bjelke-Petersen supporter" and buried in paperwork that kept him away from more active policework.[46] The harassment escalated to the point that his family received threats to blow up his children while they played in the street. His family lived in fear, all because he refused to keep his mouth shut about corruption in the force. The powers that be were not listening to him, but he was at the end of his tether. He could not get satisfaction from the QPF or the state government, so he had to go around the system. He picked up a pen and wrote to ardent anticorruption campaigner, Kevin Hooper.

Hooper was elected to parliament as the Labor Party member of Parliament for Archerfield in 1972 and made a name for himself as a strident critic of the government, particularly on issues of corruption. On 13 October 1981 he made a speech in parliament naming the Bellinos and other alleged Syndicate members as "godfathers of the mafia" in Queensland.[47] Campbell was impressed. The next day he started writing to Hooper, telling all about the corruption that he witnessed in the force. He told no one that he was feeding Hooper information, which the politician then used in parliament to attack the government and police force. Campbell did not even tell his wife, but somehow Lewis knew. A record in his diary dated only twelve days after Campbell first wrote to Hooper reads, "Saw Col Chant (union executive) re . . . S/Const Campbell, Woolloongabba, info to K. Hooper MLA."[48] How Lewis knew was a mystery. Was he conducting surveillance on Campbell? Was he monitoring Hooper's mail? In any case, Campbell had crossed a line, and the commissioner had him firmly in his sights.

In late 1981, Campbell gave evidence to Hooper revealing that the commissioner had tried to interfere with a drink driving charge for prominent National Party donor Ted Lyons. Lewis knew exactly who Hooper's source was.[49] Campbell was pushed out of the force, leaving for good on 28 February 1982. On his way out, he took one last swipe at the police. He recorded an interview with ABC's *Nationwide* program to put his observations about corruption on the public record. Three days after his last day as a police officer, the program aired. Campbell accused the QPF of masterminding organized crime in the state and, further, doing so with "the full protection of the National Party in this state."[50] The police and government rushed to slander Campbell's character, but the *Nationwide* interview did what it was intended to do. On 1 October 1982, after months of fighting the allegations made in the program, Murphy tendered his resignation citing "the slander emanating from that program" as a major reason. Murphy, then assistant commissioner, was at the peak of his power, but Campbell's interview had, in his view, torpedoed any chance of ever becoming commissioner when Lewis stepped down. Campbell was driven out of Queensland to make a new life in Tasmania. In the struggle for the soul of the QPF, the force had won this round. Not all was lost, though. The Rat Pack was now down to one member.

Life continued as normal in the QPF after Campbell left. The *Nationwide* program revealed some dark areas of the force, however the public's memory was short-lived, and the allegations were soon forgotten by most. Meanwhile, the Syndicate and the Hapeta-Tilley organization continued to flourish under the protection of the Queensland police. The influence of the vice traders was not limited to the Valley, or even Brisbane. The Bellino family had a strong presence in tropical north Queensland, and as such, the Syndicate treated the town of Cairns as an extension of its territory. Because it was far from the center of power in Brisbane, sometimes the Syndicate's activities in Cairns slipped through the cracks in the system. An illegal casino operated by Crocker and another Syndicate member, Allan Holloway, attracted the attention of the Licensing Branch in mid-1982.[51] Six Licensing Branch officers from Brisbane flew to Cairns to conduct a raid on 24 July 1982, along with the now-assistant commissioner Atkinson, who had been promoted since bringing down Jeppesen in 1979.[52] Atkinson gave the order to "bust some tables" at the casino, telling officers to break the equipment so that Crocker and Holloway could not easily reopen the venue after the raid was complete.

Atkinson's attempt to shut down the Syndicate's casino was crippled before it began. Burgess had been sent to Cairns in advance to conduct surveillance on the property and get things in order for the upcoming raid. Standard practice was for Licensing Branch officers to enter the casino undercover, observe gambling going on and then return to make arrests. Burgess told Atkinson that he had been recognized, though, so a stealth operation was off the table.[53] Shifting course to an overt raid, Atkinson instructed his men to confiscate any instruments of gambling they found, but again Burgess had bad news. He had obtained a warrant under the Vagrants Act, not the Racing and Betting Act. The Vagrants Act did not give police permission to seize gaming implements. While Crocker and Holloway were arrested in the raid, the Syndicate was able to retain all the equipment needed to reopen their casino straight away. There is no proof that Burgess was paid to intentionally scuttle the raid on the Cairns casino, but there is a strong possibility that this was the case. Burgess had worked at the Licensing Branch for some time and was aware of the nuances of the legislation used to conduct raids. The decision to obtain a warrant under the Vagrants Act could be seen as a concerted decision to prevent the police from shutting down the casino entirely—especially as the protection scheme set up between the Licensing Branch and the Syndicate was well established at this point. The foiled 1982 raid is yet another case where a simple procedural move was able to protect vice operators in a subtle, yet consequential, way.

At the time he took over as commissioner, Lewis was handed a force where corruption had been under constant attack from Whitrod's reformers for years. Herbert had been forced out, and the Joke in the Licensing Branch was dead. Hallahan, too, was forced out under pressure from Whitrod's CIU—the same unit came so close to nabbing Murphy for perjury as well. Lewis and his allies had been marginalized in the JAB, shifted away from the halls of power by Whitrod with a single pen stroke. Before the end, Lewis and Murphy were moved away from Brisbane, cast out to the rural west to keep them far away from the profitable urban vice trade. The hope remained that the Rat Pack would be in the ascendant once again, and that hope was realized with the help of a state premier who sought to undermine Whitrod at every turn. The battle for the QPF was not fought between the Rat Pack and Whitrod in the end. It was a struggle for supremacy between the commissioner and the premier, with Bjelke-Petersen actively playing spoiler to Whitrod's attempts at reform and scuttling them at every possible opportunity.

After the Beattie incident and Cedar Bay, the premier realized he needed a friend in the force who was willing to do the bidding of the government, no questions asked. He found that man in the form of Lewis, and perhaps sooner than he may have anticipated, Lewis became Bjelke-Petersen's man in the force. The relationship was mutually beneficial. Lewis could do what Bjelke-Petersen asked to enforce the government's policies, and in return, the premier could be trusted not to look too closely at corruption.

Vice was back on the map in Queensland with Lewis in charge. For as long as the Syndicate and the Hapeta-Tilley group kept paying, there would be no problems. Lewis also set out to expand his horizons when it came to making a buck or two. He met with Jack Rooklyn of the American Bally organization and arranged to offer protection to in-line gaming machines that were at that point illegal in Queensland.[54] Rooklyn was a businessman with ties to both the United States mafia and the organized crime milieu in the southern states. With the help of former police officer turned state cabinet minister Donald Lane, Lewis and Rooklyn set about introducing a whole new dimension to the gambling landscape in Queensland.[55] That the QPF commissioner felt comfortable meeting in person with an underworld figure like Rooklyn speaks volumes of the confidence with which corruption was carried out in the 1980s. There was, as Campbell said on the *Nationwide* program, a sense that corrupt police were being protected by members of Parliament with a vested interest in their continued success. Part of this vested interest was undoubtedly the involvement of politicians in mercenary corruption in return for financial gain.

There is another crucial element to this political protection that needs to be considered, however. Whitrod was not forced out by Bjelke-Petersen because he fought against mercenary corruption in the QPF. He was cast aside because he refused to enforce the premier's political agenda. It is essential to understand the extent to which political coverage for corruption was purchased through the QPF enthusiastically supporting the government. There are some who argue that the police serve the people, and as the parliament represents the people, it cannot be "corrupt" when police follow the orders of an elected government. For this reason, examining the use of process corruption in these circumstances is usually more open to interpretation than stereotypical bribery is. Where the logic that following government orders *is* serving the people falls apart is when the practices adopted by police cross an ethical line. Whitrod was willing to apply the law, yet drew a line on casting aside all police ethics to do so, as the premier demanded. Because of Whitrod's intransigence, his relationship with the government soured and sent the premier looking for a new commissioner who would be more willing to accede to his autocratic directions to repress all public enemies, real or imagined. He found it in Lewis, who was more than willing to perform the role demanded of him by Bjelke-Petersen if it resulted in the Rat Pack and their allies returning to power. The bargain these men struck was not new, however. In reality, the quid pro quo began long before Lewis became commissioner, at a time when he still walked the beat under the watchful eye of CIB chief Bischof.

Frank "The Big Fella" Bischof in 1951. By the end of the decade, Bischof would be police commissioner.
© JOHN OXLEY LIBRARY, STATE LIBRARY OF QUEENSLAND.

The Green Mafia's Jim Donovan (*left*) and Frank Bischof (*right*) were rivals for most of their career.
© JOHN OXLEY LIBRARY, STATE LIBRARY OF QUEENSLAND.

Glen Hallahan (*front right*) in 1964, shortly after the conclusion of the National Hotel Inquiry.
© QUEENSLAND POLICE MUSEUM (CC BY 2.5 AUSTRALIA LICENCE).

Terry Lewis, police commissioner and later prisoner.
© QUEENSLAND POLICE MUSEUM (CC BY 4.0).

Raymond Whitrod, reformist police commissioner.
© QUEENSLAND POLICE MUSEUM (CC BY 4.0).

Johannes "Joh" Bjelke-Petersen on his wedding day in 1952, not long after he entered parliament. © JOHN OXLEY LIBRARY, STATE LIBRARY OF QUEENSLAND.

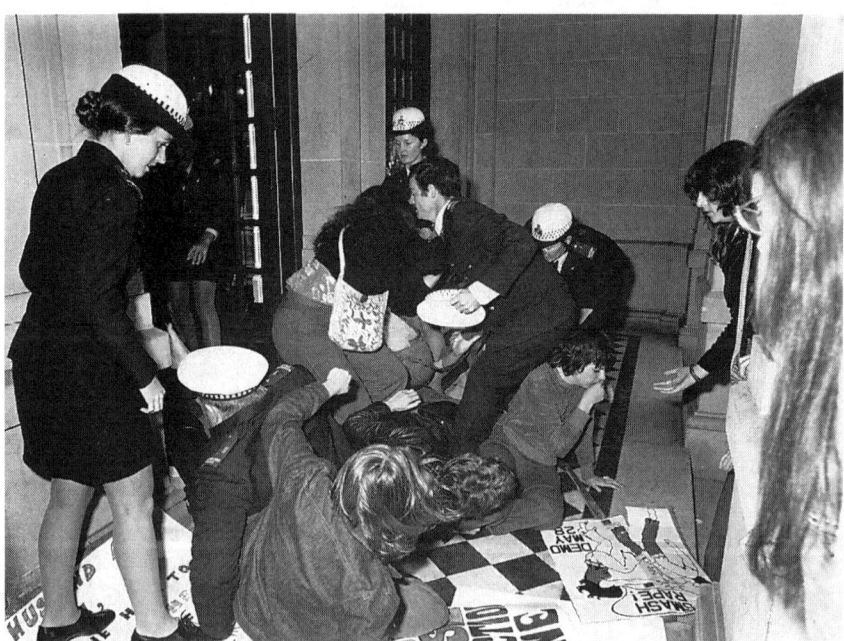

Police and protestors during a women's demonstration at the Treasury Building, Brisbane, 1977. © QUEENSLAND STATE ARCHIVES, IMAGE ID 2988.

Anti-apartheid protesters march during the July 1971 Springboks tour. © QUEENSLAND POLICE MUSEUM (CC BY 2.5 AUSTRALIA LICENCE).

The National Hotel, venue of choice for police and sex workers in the early 1960s.
© JOHN OXLEY LIBRARY, STATE LIBRARY OF QUEENSLAND.

Chris Masters reports outside QPF headquarters for *Four Corners* in 1987.
© FOUR CORNERS, ABC NEWS, 1987.

CHAPTER 7

The Bodgie Squad Hits the Street

If there was one thing that Danny Simmons thought that he was better at than boxing, it was dancing the jive—and he considered himself to be a *very* good boxer. He won the featherweight title in New South Wales in 1945, just after the war in Europe came to an end. Simmons was sixteen when World War II broke out and signed up as soon as he was able, two years later. During the time he was away serving his country, his dream of being a professional boxer was born.[1] With the war winding down, he came back to Australia and turned that dream into a reality. He beat reigning state champion Sid Knight on points to claim the belt, going twelve rounds at Leichardt Stadium in Sydney on 7 June 1945.[2] That was just the way he was. Whenever he wanted something, he grabbed at it with both hands. Sometimes that attitude did not make him friends. People said the notoriety went to Simmons's head after he won the featherweight title. He had a bad habit of going to dance halls, cutting in on a girl and her partner, and simply saying, "I am Danny Simmons."[3] He was confident in his reputation, and for the most part, he was right. His reputation certainly made him alluring to girls who fancied a bad boy. It was, of course, far less appealing to the men who he roughly pushed out of the way in his arrogance. Which is why, when he was shot dead on 1 May 1951, some believed that his murderer was one of the young bodgies whose girl Simmons had stolen.[4]

In many ways, Simmons was the quintessential 1950s bodgie: a slick-haired bad boy in jeans and leather jacket, just like James Dean. The term "bodgie" was an Australian term for the young men who were part of the rock and roll subculture that swept the globe in the post-war period, a product of the fascination with American popular culture that was brought by the U.S. troops deployed across the world during the previous decade. Some bodgies, so the newspapers said, even spoke with a phony American accent, such was the influence of the "bodgie cult."[5] Bad boys like Simmons were made to be bodgie leaders, with the perfect look and the rebellious attitude to match. At the time that he was murdered, Australia was on the precipice of a moral panic over the threat posed by bodgies. A disregard for authority was central to the bodgie culture, and to conservative Australian society, the bodgies were the first step towards a decline in respect and morals amongst the country's youth. Bodgies and their girlfriends (referred to as "widgies") were promiscuous, got drunk, and even smoked marijuana. These were all behaviors that contributed to young people turning into delinquents and, from there, falling into a life of crime. Events like Simmons's murder reinforced what the state already believed. If the bodgies were not dealt with swiftly, the result would be chaos on the streets. As the New South Wales police began to hunt for Simmons's killer, plans were being made in the boxer's hometown Brisbane to strike at the bodgie threat head-on. The seeds of the Bodgie Squad were being sown.

At the time of Simmons's murder, the bodgies were seen as more than just another passing teenage fad. The country experienced major sociocultural changes after World War II. The war years brought rapid industrialization to Australia. As was the case in other Allied nations, the absence of men sent abroad to fight resulted in women becoming an essential part of the workforce. Unlike other places, the economic boom that World War II created lasted for decades after the war's end in Australia. The early 1950s were a time of middle-class prosperity where the archetypal nuclear family lived the Australian dream in the suburbs, in a house with a white-picket fence and a vast backyard for children to play.[6] Under these prosperous postwar conditions, a collective social conservatism began to emerge, similar to that which occurred at the same time in 1950s America and Churchill's conservative Britain. In Australia, the conservative era was embodied by long-serving prime minister Robert Menzies. Though he was considered a social liberal (for his time, anyway), Menzies's greatest contribution to the national political discourse was his affirmation of the "respectable middle-class family as the bedrock of modern Australian society."[7] Initially serving as prime minister from 1939 to 1941, he spent the later years of World War II building his credentials as a champion for the middle class—a group that he coined the "Forgotten People."[8] Borrowing from the "fireside chats" pioneered by U.S. president Franklin D. Roosevelt, Menzies spoke directly to the Australian people via radio, pitching a message that "the home is the foundation of sanity and sobriety; it is the indispensable condition of continuity; its health determines the health of society as a whole."[9] His rhetoric spoke to the increasing population of Forgotten People who believed they had been left behind in a two-party political system where one side represented the interests of working-class labor and the other represented the interests of the wealthy elite. When the war ended, Menzies swept back to power and served as prime minister for almost two decades, from 1949 through until 1966.

However, the Menzies era was competing with a significant repositioning of Australian cultural norms. Previously a southern bastion of British culture, the influx of American troops in World War II saw the country looking increasingly towards the United States. Though Menzies represented the core values of traditional British society, Australia's youth were becoming fascinated with American culture—including a then-new music genre, rock and roll. Rock music was an amalgam largely influenced by African American musical styles such as rhythm and blues, jazz, and gospel. When it exploded onto the airwaves in the early 1950s, the music was criticized and accused of corrupting young (usually white) fans. Young people across the United States and, later, Australia were suddenly wearing leather jackets and tight jeans, smoking, and generally mimicking the behaviors of teen idols like James Dean and the "King of Rock" Elvis Presley. For a conservative society that saw "sanity and sobriety" as essential to societal function, the rock and roll–loving "bodgies" were no meaningless trend. The social deviance they represented posed a real threat to the society that was being built by (and for) the Forgotten People.

The bodgie cult of the 1950s was not the first time that the Queensland Police Force (QPF) had been forced to fight for the soul of state's youth. In the late 1800s, as Queensland marched towards statehood, the colony was grappling with the rise of the larrikin. The term "larrikin" has entered Australian slang, a word used to refer to someone with a streak of mischief in them—an Aussie joker with a heart of gold.[10] In modern Australia, the larrikin label is typically worn as a badge of honor, but in the nineteenth century the larrikin was as big a social problem as the bodgie of the 1950s. When the term first came into general use in the 1860s, a larrikin was "any apparently lowborn young person who spent time in the streets and engaged in uncouth behavior."[11] Larrikins gathered on street corners, generally making a nuisance of themselves, smoking pipes, and harassing people who happened to pass by them. When it came to social disruption, they were comparable to the "slogging gangs" found in Britain in the same period, who used the streets as gambling dens or warzones, depending on the day.[12] The rise in larrikinism has been attributed to an increased rate of industrialization. As improved manufacturing technology was introduced to Australia, textile workers found themselves out of work or in professions where casualization rates were high.[13] Hotspots of larrikinism in Brisbane were in areas that the manufacturing industry once called home: south of the river at Woolloongabba, and north of the river at Petrie Terrace and Spring Hill.[14] The connection between precarity in these professions and larrikinism was not lost on the state. In sentencing a "larrikin" offender in 1884, a Brisbane magistrate noted that many larrikins who came through his courtroom "claimed fraternity" with the clothing and footwear industry that was experiencing a decline at the time, implying a degree of correlation between socioeconomic status and social deviance.[15]

The QPF drew on the physical characteristics associated with larrikins to target young people, just as they did years later with the bodgies. A larrikin was "clean-shaven in an era when masculinity was expressed by facial hair" and wore unusual clothes such as bell-bottomed trousers, waistcoats, and pointed-heeled shoes.[16] If a young person was targeted by the police as a larrikin, officers could use several methods to assert control over them. The most common legislation used was the Vagrancy Act, which gave the police the power to arrest any person they found to be "idle and disorderly" or associated with "rogues and vagabonds."[17] The Vagrancy Act was open to interpretation. The definition of terms like "idle" or "rogues" was not set out in the law, and it was up to the officer on the street to determine whether someone warranted arrest. The more moral panic around larrikinism rose so too did the police's propensity to treat larrikins as people covered by the Vagrancy Act, making them increasingly vulnerable to police action. The police's response continued to harden into the 1890s, especially after the murder of William Dobson on Christmas Eve 1891 by a fifteen-year-old larrikin, Arthur "Spider" Fay.[18] Dobson's murder signaled to police that larrikinism posed a real threat to order in Queensland, and matters were only exacerbated further by the formation of larrikin "pushes" in the early 1900s, gangs of youths who fought each other in the streets and threw stones at police who tried to intervene in the violence.[19] Like the slogging gangs of industrial Britain, immortalized in BBC's *Peaky Blinders*, Brisbane's larrikin pushes experienced increasingly repressive crackdowns by police as their conduct became more unruly and violent.[20] As often happens with youth trends, the era of the larrikin fizzled out in the early 1900s, much to the relief of the QPF and urbane Queenslanders.

Larrikins were not, however, the only youth subculture to give the QPF cause for concern. As the state entered a quieter post-war era, the bodgie served much the same role as the larrikin before him as a scapegoat for Queensland society to blame for a decline in social values. "Bodgies" were young men like Simmons, who dressed and acted as if they had just stepped straight off the set of *Rebel Without A Cause*. The bodgie culture was as much about persona as it was aesthetic. For a young man to be a bodgie, he had to do more than wear leather and ride a motorcycle. He was expected to reject the conservative norms that were prevalent in the Menzies-era 1950s. The female bodgie, or the "widgie," was similarly someone who cast aside traditional values, instead taking a more modern, permissive view on the world. Music was central to the lifestyle, especially the new, energetic rock and roll.[21] Initially, both rock music and the bodgies and widgies who loved it were treated as a fascination more than a threat. An article published in the *South Coast Express* on 16 March 1951, shortly before Simmons's murder, referred to an upcoming "battle of the bands" contest to be held in Brisbane and noted that "the bodgies and widgies will turn out in force ... the stage won't be the only entertainment."[22] Later that year, at a dance hosted at Brisbane City Hall, more than 1,500 non-bodgies (dubbed "squares") showed up to watch 500 bodgies and widgies do the jive, a dance developed to complement rock and roll music.[23] The threat of the bodgie was not, at this early stage, treated seriously. The fact that a dance for the bodgies was held at City Hall suggests that there was no fear of the council being associated with hoodlums who were responsible for eroding the moral fabric of society. Instead, it indicates the existence of a permissive attitude in a city that had become used to the American cultural influence during its time as a wartime base for U.S. troops in the 1940s. If Brisbane was tolerant of the Americanized bodgie culture in mid-1951, it was short-lived. By the end of the year, the QPF campaign to smash them was on in earnest.

There is no doubt the murder of Simmons, a prominent Brisbane bodgie, contributed to the changing attitude towards bodgies and widgies in Queensland. Though he was raised in Sydney, he moved to Brisbane in 1949. The former boxing champ started working as a bookmaker's clerk, a job he possibly got through connections of his uncle John.[24] John Hayes, known to most as "Chow," was a powerful figure in Sydney's violent underworld. He had lived a life of crime since he left school at eight years old, becoming a fixture in the Sydney razor gang wars in the 1920s and 1930s. He was put on trial for the New Year's Day murder of gangster Eddie Weyman, but acquitted. He even shot the de facto partner of vice queen Kate Leigh, yet in the way that only hardened criminals can, Chow and Kate remained close into the early 1950s.[25]

Simmons was living on Wickham Terrace in Brisbane's Fortitude Valley in 1951, but came to Sydney to visit his uncle several weeks before his death. He wasted no time making enemies. Ten days before he was shot, he got into an altercation over a girl with a local bodgie. When he was found in Chow's Ultimo home on 1 May 1951, police put the word out that they thought the murder was the result of a lover's quarrel, though this was most likely a case of intentional misdirection. Police knew Chow and knew that if Chow thought Simmons's murder was a strike at him, a new gangland war could be sparked.[26]

For the QPF, the shooting confirmed their worst fears about bodgies. Queenslanders had been treating the southern states of New South Wales and Victoria as an existential threat since the colonial era. The state was seen as a fiefdom, with a culture of its own that was at constant risk of being negatively influenced by the more cosmopolitan, immoral southern states.[27] Rarely was the larrikin trend mentioned without reference to its origins as a Melbourne fad, and likewise, bodgies were routinely characterized as a southern threat in 1950s Queensland. Even in the news reports of Simmons's death, there was an effort to distance malignant bodgie culture from Queensland. Journalists noted that he was not a native Queenslander and "fitted perfectly into the bodgie world of Sydney."[28] If he had just stayed in Brisbane, he might have been safe from Sydney's violent bodgie thugs—such things simply did not happen in Queensland. The suggestion that Simmons put himself at risk by going to Sydney is true, but not for the reasons that anti-bodgie critics thought. Police found that, in fact, his murder had nothing to do with a feud between Sydney and Brisbane bodgies. It was a simple case of mistaken identity. When he fired two shots into the back of Simmons's head, Chow's gangland rival Bobby Lee thought he was actually shooting Chow.[29]

Simmons's murder did not trigger an all-out gangland war as the Sydney police predicted, but directly led to one of the most notorious murder trials in New South Wales history. Almost a month after the shooting, on 29 May 1951, Chow walked into the Ziegfield Club and in the middle of the crowded room shot Bobby Lee dead.[30] At the trial, Chow went head-to-head with ace detective Ray Kelly, nicknamed "Verbal" for his propensity to fabricate confessions to secure a conviction.[31] In the end, after three trials, Kelly's story won out. Chow was sentenced to death for the revenge killing, later commuted to a fifteen-year sentence when the death penalty was abolished in New South Wales.[32]

Simmons turned out to be an accidental victim in a southern gangland feud, completely unrelated to his bodgie lifestyle. Nevertheless, his murder reflected a growing panic over bodgie-related crime. Once again, a theme emerged of police blaming a corruptive southern influence for Queensland's bodgie problem. This was made clear in the police case against Lewis Owen Stanton and Alan Edward Green, who faced court in Brisbane shortly after Simmons's murder in December 1951. In their early twenties, Stanton and Green were charged with stealing a car in Fortitude Valley. They had intended to drive across the New South Wales border, along with two seventeen-year-old girls who were found with them when they were caught.[33] Noting that the men were "members of the bodgie cult," police prosecutor Cecil Risch made a point of telling the court that Stanton and Green were not from Brisbane and had stolen a car explicitly to travel to the bodgie mecca, Sydney.[34] The case against them was more than just a standard car theft. From the way that Risch constructed the incident, it was presented as a case of southern bodgies coming to Brisbane and not only committing crimes but corrupting young local girls, spiriting them across the southern border and luring them into the clutches of the so-called bodgie cult.

The closing months of 1951 marked an apparent rise in crimes committed by southern bodgies in Brisbane. Seventeen-year-old Donald McDonald from New South Wales faced court in Brisbane charged with motorcycle theft, a stereotypically "bodgie" act. The police prosecutor, again Risch, labelled McDonald a bodgie and told the court that the teenager had pledged to "dissociate himself from the 'bodgie' cult and remain out of trouble at all times" in return for a more lenient sentence.[35] Note the language used by Risch in both cases: the bodgie lifestyle was being treated as a "cult" by the Queensland judicial system, something that was coercive and deviant rather than a rational choice. To some extent, this meant that they were often seen as needing rehabilitation, not punishment. McDonald's promise to reform his bodgie lifestyle in return for a second chance from the court was common in the period and highlights that bodgie culture was considered the core issue facing the QPF, far more than any particular criminal action. Views on the culture shifted considerably in 1951. What started as a fascination that drew thousands of spectators to jive dance contests earlier in the year was now being treated as a serious threat to safety. The murder of Simmons showed the potentially fatal repercussions of a bodgie lifestyle. The series of court cases involving southern bodgies that came before Brisbane courts later in the year only reinforced the problems. Once a southern problem, bodgies were the barbarians at the gates of Queensland, heading north in droves to corrupt the state's youth.

The moral panic over bodgies was starting to filter into the psyche of the Queensland public. Two days after McDonald vowed to leave the lifestyle behind in court, a *Sunday Mail* report stated that at least six bodgies and widgies had been fired for their membership in the "cult" in Brisbane that week.[36] There was still a reluctance to blame young Queenslanders for bodgieism. The same article that reported the firings noted that the rising rate of delinquency was due to a "vicious Sydney bodgie class coming to Brisbane and influencing the 'locals.'"[37] Casting them as an external threat gave Queenslanders the chance to blame outsiders for social problems in the state, absolving them from taking an introspective look at the changes happening in their own society. Stoking a fear of "the other" is a common tactic of social control, framing issues in such a way that the public willingly give the police the moral authority to aggressively pursue the scapegoated population as a solution to the issues of concern.[38] One of the first steps to address the bodgie threat was the formation of "blitz squads" in mid-December 1951, perfectly timed to coincide with the Australian summer holidays. Twenty officers from the QPF's Traffic Branch were seconded to specialist squads that were sent to the oceanside resort areas of the Sunshine Coast and Gold Coast for the Christmas period.[39] The blitz squads were nominally formed to supplement the local police and help deal with an influx of holidaymakers, but had a more specific responsibility to prevent the bodgies and widgies expected to flock to these towns from causing problems.

By the mid-1950s the bodgie population in Brisbane had grown to the point that police like Risch described the city as being at risk of being "plagued with this teenage type of thug such as [*sic*] causing trouble in the south and overseas."[40] He made this statement during the sentencing of eighteen-year-old Lionel Farnham, convicted of possessing an offensive weapon in May 1954. He was caught carrying a brass-studded piece of lead pipe when police responded to an assault in the south Brisbane suburb Woolloongabba, a suburb that was once a haven for the larrikin. In this incident, a man was assaulted by a "gang of bodgies ... [who were] operating round hamburger stalls on the southside, intimidating people."[41] The case was the last straw for a police force that had been struggling to keep the bodgie wave at bay for years by this point. Now, as far as the police were concerned, vicious bodgies were flagrantly cruising around the southside and beating ordinary Brisbane residents with deadly weapons. If the state was to avoid going the way of its southern neighbors, the police had to act. Several days after the Woolloongabba assault, QPF commissioner John Smith gave the order to "smash 'bodgie' hoodlum gangs" in a concerted push to drive the deviant group out of Queensland once and for all.[42]

Smith described the bodgies as "a pest [that] should be eradicated before they become really troublesome and dangerous," and police were ordered to treat them as "potential criminals" whether they had committed an offense or not.[43] Bodgies were profiled based on their appearance. Young men wearing "draped suits, narrow trousers, and colorful jumpers ... [with] long haircuts" were on the police's radar, subject to a move-on order under the Vagrancy Act just as the larrikins before them had been.[44] The zero-tolerance policy bore fruit almost instantly. Smith gave the order to "smash" the bodgies in May, and by early July, the media was reporting that "bodgies and widgies have gone underground in Brisbane" and that "the cult is now dying" as a result of the QPF's actions.[45] Finally, after years of inaction, the QPF took decisive action. The connection between bodgie culture and crime had by this point become so ingrained that any person who even *looked* like a bodgie was treated as a criminal, with police given free rein to move them on wherever they saw fit. The QPF's renewed push was a clear case of social control designed to placate a fearful public. While gangs of young bodgies indeed were responsible for some anti-social behavior in Brisbane, the targeting of the entire community was a gross overcorrection that equated all bodgies with deviance. The strict enforcement was directed from the top, and as it would be in later years, social control was exercised with the full sanction and approval of the state.

Smith's campaign worked to begin with, but within two years the bodgies returned again, pushing the Queensland police to take even more repressive measures. For the two years between 1954 and 1956, the public fear over bodgies largely subsided in the state. Even so, there remained some discussion of youth crime and the links to bodgie culture in the public discourse. Labor Party police spokesman Arthur Jones vowed to "wipe out the bodgies" in 1955 in response to reports that members of the group were committing acts of petty nuisance such as vandalizing public property. For the most part, however, the threat was considered to have been dealt with until late 1956, when a clash between bodgies and police at a rock and roll concert reignited the campaign to wipe out the bodgies in Queensland. In October 1956, a rock and roll concert held at St Francis Hall in Elizabeth Street attracted 650 attendees and was described in the media as the first wave in a bodgie resurgence in Brisbane. The responsibility for this looming threat fell to the Criminal

Investigation Branch (CIB) chief, Frank Bischof, who was vocal about the need for "systemic action" to "clean up" the city's youth.[46]

Bischof got his chance in 21 November 1956 when police were dispatched to raid a rock and roll festival at Brisbane Stadium, ostensibly to stop the three thousand–strong audience from dancing in the aisles. There were no initial reports of crowd violence, however the mere temerity of young concertgoers to ignore orders to return to their seats was enough to trigger Bischof's officers. The police took their refusal to bend to the rules as incitement, and set about creating the very anarchic melee they were supposedly there to prevent. For the young patrons on the receiving end, the actions taken by police were perceived as heavy-handed, sparking an outbreak of violence where "many punches were thrown and young men were felled by being struck across the head with police handcuffs."[47] Police were indiscriminate in their use of violence at the Brisbane Stadium. Not all concertgoers fit the description of stereotypical bodgies, and most were simply music fans who came from all walks of life. In the end, it was not bodgies that were the target of violence at the stadium, but rather *any* young person who refused to cower in the face of an aggressive police force. The aggression of police in the rock and roll riot was partly inspired by the relentless yearslong campaign against bodgies, but what was more important was showing what could happen to those who challenged the conservative values of the state, in which showing a deferential respect for the police was paramount. For Bischof, the rock and roll riot presented a challenge to the QPF's authority from the youth of Brisbane. It was a challenge that the Big Fella could not back down from.

Bischof's experience at the rock and roll riot showed him that it was not enough to haphazardly target rock and roll concerts, where police were sure to be outnumbered by large groups of angry bodgies who could put up a good fight against his officers. Using his mandate to smash the bodgies, he formed the Bodgie Squad, an informal collection of officers under his CIB command who were given a roving brief to travel the city and, where possible, target bodgies. The new "squad" was important to Bischof, as indicated by the list of police who were assigned to it. Some of his favored officers were part of the Bodgie Squad at one point or another including all three members of the Rat Pack, future state politician Don Lane, and future acting commissioner Ron Redmond.[48] As before, the Bodgie Squad were given the power to act against bodgies under the provisions of the Vagrancy Act, familiar to the members of the team from their experience using it in the Consorting Squad.

Using the Vagrancy Act was difficult when it came to bodgies, though. The police needed to prove that bodgies were idle, disorderly, or associating with known criminals. The fact was that most of them were employed, and many did not have criminal records. The bodgies were, for the most part, young people who loved rock and roll and dressing in the fashion of the bodgie culture. The challenges of using the Vagrancy Act meant the Bodgie Squad were often forced to take a different, more aggressive strategy. This strategy was grounded in process corruption, in this case excessive and unnecessary use of force. The Bodgie Squad were known as being "ready to bash first and ask questions afterwards." Local musician Brian Gagen recalls the Bodgie Squad would "bust a lot of heads and run them into walls and all sorts of things," while others remember that the Bodgie Squad "roughly moved on [young people] when caught loitering; or [they were] made to stand for ages by police at the footpaths edge, with their heels painfully suspended over the gutter."[49] The force used was intended to intimidate bodgies into submission or, on some occasions, to provoke them into an act that warranted arrest. For example, John and Aileen McCourt used to run a dance hall in the southern suburb Mt Gravatt, which the Bodgie Squad, including Bischof himself, once raided during the middle of an event and began harassing bodgies and widgies, going so far as to touch teenage girls on their breasts in an attempt to trigger their bodgie partners to attack them, after which they could be arrested.[50]

One of the most notorious practices adopted by the Bodgie Squad was the enforcement of a strict dress code on Brisbane's youth. The deviant bodgie lifestyle had been, since the early 1950s, strongly connected to the rock and roll aesthetic. Part of the Bodgie Squad's mission to address the public's concern over bodgies was to prevent the outward expression of the lifestyle on Brisbane's streets. It was common for members of the Bodgie Squad to locate a bodgie, approach them and tell them to "get rid of that haircut, get rid of those clothes."[51] There is anecdotal evidence to suggest that, sometimes, this policy was forcibly enforced on bodgies who resisted the police's suggestions. Former nightclub bouncer John Wayne Ryan remembered clearly an incident in the early 1960s where Tony Murphy and Hallahan, two members of the Rat Pack, herded a group of bodgies into a laneway on Elizabeth Street after finding them outside a club. He says Murphy "forced them to remove their jackets ... [then] forced them to put on collared shirts and ties."[52] The purpose of forcing bodgies to change their outfits was twofold. It was a visible representation that police were removing the bodgie culture from Brisbane, but more importantly, it was a demonstration of the police's ability to exert control over the city's youth and force them into compliance. In some ways, the Bodgie Squad was a precursor to the corrupt networks that developed in the QPF in later years. When Bischof became commissioner in January 1958, he naturally gave preference to officers he trusted from his time in the CIB. The officers who served in the Bodgie Squad could be trusted to do whatever was necessary to enforce order on the streets and, like Bischof himself, were not opposed to bending the *Police Rules* in the name of "good policing." These officers were loyal soldiers who were willing to follow his orders, even when they went against the professional ethics of policing. It is not coincidental, either, that many of the officers attached to the Bodgie Squad would be named at the Gibbs Inquiry in 1963 as being involved in corruption alongside Bischof at the National Hotel.[53]

The Bodgie Squad's success reflected on Bischof and contributed to his professional record ahead of his tilt for the commissioner's job. Alex Dewar, who led a commission on juvenile delinquency in the late 1959, told parliament that Bischof was "ideal" for the commissioner's role because of his proven strength in "dealing with young people who tend to stray off the track." Going further, Dewar said that Bischof's experience in running the Bodgie Squad had proven "his belief that every policeman should have a big heart and be capable of a human understanding of all problems."[54] Even Bischof's predecessor as commissioner, Tom Harold, praised his CIB chief's efforts in saying that the Bodgie Squad's success was the "dividend of a firm but fatherly approach by police officers ... police went up to these young people, gave them a talking to, and in most cases received co-operation."[55] The public portrayal of the Bodgie Squad's actions was far removed from the experience of the young people who were targeted. What was presented to the government and the public as a conciliatory outreach strategy was, in reality, a strict crackdown designed to push bodgies out of the public view and assert the ultimate authority of the QPF to dictate order on the streets.

As Bischof moved into the commissioner's office and his old protégés in the CIB began to work on their own career advancement in the early 1960s, the old Bodgie Squad quietly disappeared from view. The panic over bodgies had begun to subside in any case. The widespread popularity of rock and roll music softened the perception of rock fans as deviant, thanks in part to iconic bands like The Beatles and The Rolling Stones.[56] Considering the role that The Beatles played in moving rock more into the mainstream, it is somewhat ironic that one of the last major conflicts between the QPF and rock fans in this era came during the band's tour in 1964. Their global success had changed the public's views on rock, but in

Queensland (and especially in the QPF) there was still a fear that rock and roll was inherently connected to deviant behavior. When The Beatles touched down at Eagle Farm Airport on 29 July 1964, there was almost as many anti-Beatles protesters as there were fans waiting to catch a glimpse of John, Paul, George, and Ringo. The protesters were rowdy even before the band touched down. Around a dozen of them were ejected before The Beatles arrived after a number of brawls broke out between them and the band's fans. Firecrackers and smoke bombs were thrown onto the tarmac, along with a variety of bottles and other projectiles.[57]

The mood at the airport was tense already but became even worse when the band eventually arrived. As the band stepped off the plane, a "black rain of projectiles crash[ed] down upon the unsuspecting Beatles ... eggs, tomatoes, pieces of wood and rotten fruit showered [down on them]."[58] The reception received by The Beatles in Brisbane was never again repeated in their career to the same extent. Despite the incident receiving international attention, the QPF recorded no arrests of anti-Beatles protesters, only going so far as issuing move-on orders and ejecting them from the airport. Instead, CIB chief Norm Bauer apportioned blame for the chaos to the journalists who were present to report on the band's arrival. He alleged that the journalists were responsible for agitating the crowd, inciting young fans to crush against the fence-line to take photos of them in a state of euphoria described around the world as "Beatlemania."[59] Bauer claimed it was this mania, stoked by the media, that had caused the riotous conduct that greeted The Beatles, not the antics of the anti-Beatles contingent who had been throwing projectiles in the period before the band arrived and, more than likely, were responsible for throwing more items at the band as they attempted to leave the airport.[60] The suggestion that journalists and fans were the root cause of the Eagle Farm incident is reflective of his reluctance to put the blame where it logically belonged, on the anti-Beatles protesters. Instead, it suggests some form of solidarity with the protesters who were perpetuating an anti-rock agenda that the Bodgie Squad themselves had steered in years gone by. Though the Bodgie Squad itself was no more, there was still an element of the QPF that believed in the work that the unit had accomplished and, in turn, gave tacit support to anti-rock vigilantism when it broke out in the more conservative sectors of the Queensland public.

Time passed and, by the 1970s, a new music-oriented panic had emerged to replace rock and roll. Punk music was openly anti-authoritarian, built on the concept that the state was a repressive body that infringed on personal freedoms. This made it a perfect outlet for Brisbane's youth who, by this point, felt like they were living under a police state overseen by state premier Joh Bjelke-Petersen. Brisbane became a hub for punk music, with bands like Razar and The Parameters coming out with songs targeting the police state with titles like "Pig City" and "Taskforce (Undercover Cops)."[61] For the QPF, the former success of the Bodgie Squad meant that a model already existed to deal with the social threat posed by Brisbane's punk scene. Terry Lewis, a former member of the original Bodgie Squad, ordered the creation of the Regional Task Force after becoming commissioner in 1976. The Task Force was a squad of twenty officers who were sent into "trouble spots" with a sweeping mandate to deal with any incident that posed a threat to the public order.[62] This roving brief put them on a collision course with Brisbane's punks, who prided themselves on "implicit counter-capitalist and counter-cultural emphases . . . which contained residual and emergent political opposition to the National Party regime."[63]

The QPF took a multipronged approach to combatting the punk threat, using some of the process corruption tactics that were successful against the bodgies to do so. Bands like The Saints were known for their "scorched-earth" policy at shows, resulting in violence and property damage that meant few venues in Brisbane were willing to host them.[64] Because of this, The Saints set up their own club, Club 76, in a rundown residential property at Petrie Terrace where punks could gather to watch bands play. The police responded to the opening of Club 76, and other similar venues, with a campaign of harassment involving repeated raids, breaches under the Liquor Act, and, ultimately, the intervention of the Health Department to shut the venue down.[65] The strategy worked, forcing The Saints to move to London where they became pioneers of the global punk scene alongside bands like the Sex Pistols.[66] Other police strategies were more insidious, like monitoring people associated with the punk scene by members of the intelligence-gathering Special Branch. Radio announcer Amanda Collinge worked for alternative station 4ZZZ when she was approached at a press conference by an unknown man she presumed to be part of Special Branch, who "started asking questions that indicated he knew a hell of a lot about me" and made it clear he knew what car she drove and where she lived.[67] This subtle form of intimidation was reinforced by the Task Force's violent response to punks on the streets. For many punks, the only way to avoid being harassed by police was to dress "normally." Just like it was with the larrikins and bodgies before, police used the punk aesthetic to target young people for attention, sometimes stopping to search them three times on a single stretch of road if they looked "out of place."[68]

Punk concerts were deemed potential "trouble spots" in Brisbane, and thus, the Task Force was expected to police them strictly. On one occasion, at an event sponsored by 4ZZZ on 24 June 1978, concertgoers were met with a reception committee of Task Force officers as they left the venue. The police had positioned themselves strategically between the hotel's exit and the parking lot, and began arresting people as they passed, holding them in the city watchhouse overnight before releasing them without charge.[69] The events promoted by 4ZZZ were given special treatment by the Task Force, until a clash at a concert held at Caxton Street Hall on 30 November 1979 caused the QPF to implement a policy of not granting licenses to 4ZZZ-sponsored events in future. The concert, which was in fact not sponsored by the station, ended with police arresting punks at random on the street outside the hall. Violence broke out between police and punks attempting to intervene in the arrests, resulting in twelve people being taken to watchhouse and one, Annette Wenck, being "beaten outside the hall, then being grabbed, slapped and pulled around... eventually released with a black eye, bloodied nose and bruises across her body."[70] Previously, the police targeted concertgoers outside venues or at least needed some excuse to raid licensed concerts. Now, under the new policy of not issuing licenses to 4ZZZ events, no excuse was needed at all. Simply holding a concert at all provided cause enough for police to disperse gatherings of punks, often with bloody results.

There was zero tolerance for different or alternative lifestyles in Brisbane, where the demand for police to deal with the moral panic around delinquency was so strong that it gave police carte blanche to act in whatever way necessary to assert the social order. Part of the problem with corruption exercised for the purposes of social control is that there is often an unspoken approval of it within some sectors of the community. It is, as Carl Klockars described, the Dirty Harry dilemma. There will always be some who believe the police should use whatever powers at their disposal to impose order on the streets. The problem rests in who determines what a threat to order looks like. While most would agree that an armed gunman causing chaos in a crowded street constitutes such a threat, others take this concept further in arguing that police must be proactive in combatting sociomoral threats to society. The moral panic around the bodgies saw them accused of a gamut of societal woes ranging from violence and drug use to inspiring promiscuity in teenage girls. Because of this fear, there was a real pressure from the public and the government for police to take action to combat the threat posed by these young delinquents. As such, the Bodgie Squad was widely seen as a humanitarian enterprise, preventing deviance by having police reach out to young people. In reality, the reaching out that was performed by the squad was usually either to give a swift slap around the head or to hand over a white-collared shirt and tie for bodgies to change into. Though unacceptable conduct by today's standards, this enforcement of conformity enjoyed the tacit approval of a largely conservative public conditioned by the media and government to believe that the bodgies presented a tangible threat to Queenslanders' way of life.

Even when the bodgie trend subsided, the impetus on police to enforce a moral standard among Brisbane's youth persisted. It is ironic that, while bodgies were seen as a southern import, the punk scene in Brisbane boasted a native anti-authoritarian sentiment that was one of the strongest in the country. The punks of Brisbane were motivated by growing up in "Pig City"—a police state where alternative lifestyles were not tolerated and forcibly repressed by the QPF on behalf of the conservative state government. While certainly not the intention, the QPF's harassment of Queensland's youth was partly responsible for the punk culture that fermented the pushback against the state in the late 1970s and into the early 1980s. Such is the risk of continuing to enforce a traditionalist perspective that is generally out of step with changing societal norms. Whereas the strict repression of bodgies was largely accepted in conservative post-war Queensland, by the rise of the punk scene in the late 1970s, the police were faced with a population that was increasingly accepting of progressive views that were antithetical to those espoused by the Bjelke-Petersen government and, in turn, enforced on the streets by the police. The clashes between punks and the police were far greater than those between the QPF and bodgies in decades past, driven by the explicitly political messages conveyed by punk music. In fact, politics underscored much of the civil conflict that Queensland experienced in the 1970s and 1980s. The firm repression of the protest movement by the QPF was a central point of agreement between the state government and the police force, and one where using process corruption in pursuit of social control was considered the norm.

CHAPTER 8

Taking the Fight to the Streets

Aged only eighteen, young Peter had never experienced anything like the pure chaos outside the Tower Mill Hotel that night. Like so many other students of the era, he was no stranger to taking to the streets to register opposition to the government of the day. Usually he and the other activists from the University of Queensland were out protesting the conservative rule of Joh Bjelke-Petersen, but this event was bigger than that. The South African Springboks rugby union team were visiting Brisbane, and the city's protest movement had come out in force to oppose the racist system of apartheid that existed in that country.[1] The state government was intent that the often-rambunctious student protesters did not embarrass Queensland on the international stage, so Bjelke-Petersen used his powers as premier to call a state of emergency before the Springboks team even arrived. He gave the police carte blanche to disperse protests in whichever way they saw fit, including the use of extreme force if necessary. Anticipating clashes, Queensland Police Force (QPF) officers from around the state started flocking to Brisbane, ready to act as loyal servants of the state and boost the ranks of the local Brisbane police.[2] If anything, the state's extreme response to the threat of protest only served to galvanize the movement further. By the time the Springboks arrived in Brisbane on 22 July 1971, more than four hundred demonstrators had gathered

| 123

outside the Tower Mill, right across from the Old Windmill that had stood vigil over the old city since the colonial era.

Tensions were already high at 6 p.m., when police gave the final order for the anti-apartheid protesters to disperse. Most of the demonstrators moved to comply. The Springboks were in town for a few more days, and the big action was planned for two days' time, the day of their match. As the protesters started to leave, however, something happened. Suddenly, the police outside Tower Mill rushed the protesters, forcing them to run. The hotel was set on a rise, and across the road, a fifteen-foot cliff face separated Wickham Terrace from Albert Street below. Police chased down the scattering protesters. Some were caught and beaten. Others were thrown down the cliff face on Wickham Terrace, tossed into the dark depths of the city. Peter escaped the first wave of violence, running for the safety of the union stronghold on Edward Street, Trades Hall. One day, twenty-five years later, Peter Beattie would be elected premier of Queensland. Tonight, though, he was just another protester in the sights of a QPF caught in the red mists of war. He made it inside Trades Hall with a few others seeking sanctuary, but their safety was short-lived. Before long, the door burst open and three police officers stormed in. In an instant, he was set upon. A woman tried to come to Peter's aid as the police beat him. It was no good. She received a beating for her troubles, too.[3] The attack on Peter continued. The future premier had learned a hard truth in the Trades Hall that night: politics in Queensland was a vicious business.

The siege on Trades Hall was not the first time that a left-wing political movement was subject to the repressive control of a conservative mob in Brisbane. The scene was reminiscent, on a far smaller scale, of the Red Flag riot in 1919 when eight thousand right-wing vigilantes trapped members of the city's Russian community in the Russian Hall in South Brisbane in a campaign to stop the rise of Bolshevism.[4] Since then, however, the protest movement in Queensland had experienced a period of calm. Apart from the Battle of Brisbane in 1942, there were no real cases of major civil unrest in the city from the Red Flag riots in 1919 until the post-war period of the 1940s.

The years following World War II were tough in Queensland. As was the case in countries around the world, the return of soldiers and end of wartime industries meant a deficit in jobs. The struggle of unions to fight the government for new investment in jobs, as well as better pay and conditions, resulted in a surge in industrial action in Brisbane not seen to such an extent since the 1912 general strike. Despite his reputation as a "worker friendly" Labor Party premier, Ned

Hanlon passed a new raft of laws designed to curtail protest action in 1948. The new Industrial Law Amendment Act sparked furious condemnation from the trade union movement, particularly as it gave police the power to arrest strikers without a warrant and to order an end to strikes.[5]

The expanded police powers were intended to bring an end to a month-long period of industrial action by Queensland rail workers, who sought wages on par with those paid in other states. Passed by state parliament on 9 March 1948, the laws prompted a protest march just over a week later, on St Patrick's Day. Demonstrators gathered at Trades Hall on Edward Street—the same place that a young Beattie would later seek refuge during the Tower Mill fracas. Around 150 marchers began to move towards Central Station, but before long the QPF closed in on them and began to beat the assembled group with their batons.[6] In the melee that resulted, five protesters were arrested and two were hospitalized with injuries that came from violent clashes with the QPF. One of the men hospitalized, Fred Paterson, was a state member of Parliament (MP). Paterson, the MP for Bowen and the only Communist Party politician ever elected in Australia, received treatment for concussion, scalp lacerations, and potential brain damage after the incident, later called the "St Patrick's Day Bashing."[7] While trying to prevent police beating protesters with their batons, Paterson was hit across the back of the head by Detective Sergeant Jack Mahoney, a plainclothes member of the Criminal Investigation Branch (CIB) who had been drinking at the nearby Gresham Hotel before being called to respond to the union march.[8]

Ordinarily, the police beating of a state politician would be cause for reflection, but Hanlon stood by his QPF. The premier came out publicly to describe the police actions towards the protesters as "characterized by the greatest patience and tolerance."[9] No further action was taken to investigate the bashing of Paterson. By ignoring the violent conduct of the Queensland police, Hanlon reinforced a traditional view in Queensland: that, in cases of civil unrest, police should have the full power and authority to use extreme measures to maintain order on the streets. Despite operating on different ends of the political spectrum, this is something that Hanlon and his later successor as premier Bjelke-Petersen had in common. Hanlon's refusal to investigate the allegations of police brutality against Paterson echoes in Bjelke-Petersen's scuttling of Whitrod's attempts to investigate police violence in the mid-1970s. At their core, both premiers were motivated by the same overarching belief that the supremacy of the state *must* be asserted, sometimes with extreme force, to allow for stable and orderly governance. This fundamentally conservative perspective was, as the Paterson case shows, not limited to the right-wing of Queensland politics, but also permeated the traditionalist left who controlled the state Labor Party.

The Old Left that controlled Queensland Labor Party in the 1950s was, to some extent, in the decline in the mid-century leftist political scene. Around the world, a New Left was emerging that rejected the traditions of Marxist class-based struggle in favor of a broader progressive opposition to the conservative politics of the 1950s. In theory, the New Left was designed to be a democratic movement without the autocratic structures of Old Left labor movements. There was good reason for left-wing Australians to see the Old Left as no longer being an effective vehicle for dissent. In 1951, Prime Minister Robert Menzies had passed a law dissolving the Communist Party and branded its members a "traitorous minority."[10] The Communist Party took the Menzies government to the High Court of Australia to challenge the dissolution, forcing a national referendum on whether the party should be banned. The 1951 referendum was defeated but only by the bare margin of just over half a percent.[11] The close result revealed an Old Left establishment that found itself against the ropes and struggling to survive in the conservative Cold War era of the 1950s. This was especially true in Queensland, where the Catholic-dominated Gair government already skewed to the social right of the Labor Party. For many young Queenslanders concerned with regressive social policy more than the economics of class, the state Labor Party simply could not represent the political interests of a rising New Left.

When Frank Nicklin toppled Vince Gair in 1957 and formed the first non–Labor Party government Queensland had seen in twenty-five years, the relationship between protesters and the government was already strained. The conflict between the state government and the unions in the mid-1950s did not help, and though organized labor welcomed Gair being forced from office, the rise of a conservative premier like Nicklin was not expected to soothe the tension in any meaningful way. However, the new premier differed from his predecessor in one crucial way: whereas Gair lost his position because he was committed to an austerity budget that would not let him improve the pay and leave system for workers, Nicklin was committed to a program of infrastructure development and capital works that kept workers employed for most of the 1960s.[12] Absent their perennial conflict with organized labor, the QPF turned their focus to the young bodgies who posed a cultural threat to Queensland that all sides of politics could agree on. It was not until 1967 that the first wave of the New Left reached Brisbane and brought with it problems for Nicklin. Whereas the Old Left was focused on winning better conditions for labor, the New Left was centered on the more existential issues connected to identity politics: racism, sexism, and colonialism.[13]

Political organization was changing, not just in Queensland but around the world. In 1960, American student activist group the Student League for Industrial Democracy changed its name to Students for a Democratic Society (SDS), a recognition of the shifting priorities of the New Left. Over the next decade, SDS emerged as an influential force in the radical protest movement. Indeed, the SDS served as inspiration and a model for Queensland's own premier New Left student organization, Students for Democratic Action (SDA). The group was formed by political activists attending the University of Queensland and consisted of several activists who went on to be significant leaders in the Australian protest scene, such as Brian Laver and Mitch Thompson. While an independent organization, the SDA had links to its American SDS counterparts from the outset. Several American students and scholars who were members of the SDS (now at the University of Queensland) were instrumental in forming the SDA, as well as creating its organizational charter.[14] It is unsurprising—given this history—that the SDA quickly established itself as a radical organization that advocated for the type of New Left causes common in the era, such as opposition to the Vietnam War, denuclearization, and civil rights. However, none of these causes provided the spark for the 1967 conflict that was fought between SDA-led protesters and the Nicklin government. The clashes of that year were about something even more essential to the future of the Queensland protest movement: the right to march itself.

A city bylaw introduced in 1897 dictated that it was a requirement for any group that wanted to hold a public procession or street march to seek the permission of Brisbane council authorities before a demonstration could go ahead, along with giving the police commissioner at least twenty-four hours' notice before the event went ahead. The rules were tightened by the Traffic Act 1905, giving the final decision on protest permits to the QPF commissioner and setting a prohibitive fee to obtain a permit.[15] The rules set out in the Traffic Act 1905 were rolled over into the Traffic Act 1949 when the law was reformed, with the clauses related to public protest remaining mostly intact. Brisbane's New Left protest movement was developing at the same time as its equivalents in other countries, with its growth becoming ever more rapid in the run-up to the Vietnam War.[16] In July 1967 Sven Condon, a leader of the Civil Liberties Co-ordinating Committee (CLCC) wrote to Nicklin to express the protest community's issues with the Traffic Act provisions, such as the arbitrary power given to the Traffic Superintendent to refuse permission to march and the exorbitant $1 fee for each placard or sign carried in the march.[17] Condon's letter ended with a note that the CLCC intended to march in support of amending the Traffic Act on 11 July 1967, later delayed until September.[18]

Nicklin was not ignorant to Condon's criticism. He sought out the advice of Commissioner Frank Bischof to canvas his opinions on whether changes to the Traffic Act needed to be considered. Bischof was firm in his support of the current laws. In a letter to Nicklin dated 7 July 1967, the commissioner said, "The Police Force of this State has always exhibited maximum restraint in the exercise of their powers and ... is not given to provoking incidents" with protesters, no matter their political persuasion.[19] Bischof's version of the QPF's record on policing protest was a fantasy. There was a long tradition of the force aggressively policing protest in Queensland, dating back to the colonial period. The use of force in crushing public dissent on the streets of Brisbane dated back to the reading of the Riot Act in the 1866 Bread or Blood riots, and since then the city had seen various cases like the 1912 general strike that were characterized by brutal clashes between the public and Queensland police. While the Nicklin era had been relatively peaceful on that front so far, one did not have to look too far to find cases like the St Patrick's Day Bashing in 1948.

Bischof told Nicklin in his 7 July letter that there was no need to amend the Traffic Act to placate the student protest movement. He argued that there were legitimate enforcement reasons to limit the number of signs that protesters could bring to a demonstration, claiming that there was a real threat that the placards might be used as weapons against police in the event of a confrontation.[20] As the commissioner pressed for Nicklin to stay the course on the Traffic Act, the student protesters made good on their promise to push the government for reform. A relatively small group of 180 protesters march on Parliament House on 5 September, only to find themselves turned back by ninety officers under the command of CIB chief Norm Bauer.[21] Bauer was a staunch ally of Bischof's, brought to Brisbane to head the CIB in early 1958, shortly after Bischof took charge of the QPF. Before that, Bauer had served as head of the CIB in Mount Isa. He was transferred to Brisbane by Bischof at the same time as his Mount Isa workmate, the Rat Pack's own Glen Hallahan.[22]

The interaction on 5 September was generally peaceful, though there were reports that some of Bauer's men got into physical clashes with the marchers.[23] Two days later, the Nicklin government attempted to strike a compromise. The premier agreed to lower the waiting time to process a permit to seven days, down from fourteen, and to remove the $1 fee for carrying signs.[24] What it would not do, however, was strip the QPF traffic superintendent of the right to arbitrarily deny a permit, one of the CLCC's most important demands. The student protesters were unsatisfied, insisting on Nicklin's complete capitulation to their demands. Representatives from the University of Queensland student union met with Nicklin on 8 September and told him that a march would go ahead that afternoon in protest of his decision. Initially the march was denied a permit by the police, but when it became obvious that the demonstration was going to proceed regardless, the QPF rushed through an approval.[25] Sanctioning the protest was mostly a tactical move. It undercut the protest's impact as a defiant challenge of the permit system and thus lessened the impact of the act.

That afternoon, around 3,900 marchers took to the streets. At first, the protest moved through the city with few problems. When the protesters reached the busy intersection of Roma and Makerston Streets, there was a sudden shift in the QPF's approach to the event. Mid-march, the protesters were told their permit had been revoked because police felt that traffic was being obstructed. Rather than disperse as directed, however, a group of marchers staged an impromptu sit-in at the intersection. The QPF later reported there were 124 protesters arrested as a result of the 8 September march, mostly charged with failure to comply the lawful instruction of a police officer. Here, the perspectives on events differ. Traffic Superintendent L. E. Hughes, who gave the order to revoke the permit, later said that "at no time did [he] observe Police using unnecessary force in order to make an arrest."[26] What Hughes considered "unnecessary force" is up for debate. Other witnesses, like the Reverend Colin Arkell, wrote to Nicklin after the incident to protest the aggressive response of police, noting that "the impression gained was that the police enjoyed the roughness of their actions as if they were settling a score."[27] The trade unions called for Nicklin to ensure police were properly disciplined for using excessive force, perhaps remembering their own experiences at the business end of a police baton.[28] Thompson, a prominent Brisbane activist and CLCC leader, circulated a pamphlet to state politicians in June 1968 pointing out that the promises made by Nicklin had not been kept almost a year after the protests.[29] Aside from the removal of the $1 fee on signs, no changes had been made to the Traffic Act.

The failure of the Nicklin government to keep its promises to the protest movement further enflamed tensions between the two parties. By this time, Nicklin was no longer premier, having stepped down in January 1968 after more than a decade in power due to poor health.[30] He was replaced briefly by Jack Pizzey who, at the time of the 1967 protests, had served as minister for police. The student protest movement was unlikely to win concessions from Pizzey, but as it turned out, they would not have much of a chance to negotiate with the new premier. He died from a sudden heart attack on 31 July 1968, just short of seven months after taking over.[31] Traditionally, the party in a coalition that holds the most seats is the one that takes the primary role in forming a government. At the time of Pizzey's death his Country Party held twenty-six seats in the parliament, seven more than the Liberal Party. Even so, there were serious discussions about respected Liberal leader Gordon Chalk taking over as premier on a permanent basis.[32] Several senior members of the Country-Liberal coalition held concerns about the abilities and suitability of Pizzey's deputy, Bjelke-Petersen, to lead Queensland. For his own part, Bjelke-Petersen was furious that Chalk had been sworn in as premier immediately after Pizzey's death, which he thought was his right as the next most senior member of the Country Party.[33] The whispers of keeping Chalk in the position lasted less than a week, after Bjelke-Petersen threatened to use his prerogative as the new Country Party leader to withdraw from the coalition unless he was named premier. He got his wish on 8 August 1968, being officially sworn in as the thirty-first premier of Queensland.

Bjelke-Petersen was born in the Hawke's Bay region of New Zealand's North Island, a picturesque region renowned for its world-class wines and rolling green hills. He was barely walking when his father, a Lutheran pastor, moved the family across the Tasman Sea to make a new life in Australia in 1913.[34] The family settled in small-town Kingaroy, a rural hamlet in southeastern Queensland known as the "Peanut Capital of Australia."[35] Young Bjelke-Petersen did not have an easy time of it growing up, fighting a bout with polio that left him with a limp for the rest of his life.[36] He left school aged fourteen, working the land and making a career for himself as an agricultural entrepreneur. He was elected to the Kingaroy Shire Council in 1946 and, after gaining the endorsement of Nicklin, was endorsed to run as the Country Party candidate for Barambah at the 1950 election. While a young CIB detective named Bischof set about investigating Labor Party's involvement the Bulimba election fraud, the new MP for Barambah was settling into the life of a state politician. Bjelke-Petersen remained on the fringes of the Nicklin government for years and proved a thorn in the premier's side on a range of issues. Finally, in late 1963, Nicklin brought Bjelke-Petersen in from the cold. He would rather have the maverick outsider on the inside, in cabinet, rather than having him agitating from the backbenches.[37] He offered Bjelke-Petersen the job of minister for works and housing, a broad portfolio with responsibility for much of the state's public construction program. Nicklin did not just hand him the job. He told him that he could join cabinet, so long as he was willing to fire four hundred workers under the authority of the Department of Works and Housing straight away.[38] It was a no-brainer. For the one job he coveted, Bjelke-Petersen would gladly trade four hundred others. He used his new job wisely. A former disgruntled backbencher himself, he knew the power his position gave him. It was within his power to decide where state money would be spent, and he used that power to buy the gratitude of his former friends on the backbench. The favors he gave out were paid back when the time came in January 1968 for him to stand for deputy leader of the Country Party. He was elected unopposed, clearing the way for him to storm to power in the wake of Pizzey's death only a few months later.[39]

There could not have been a more ill-suited person to assume the position of Queensland premier in the late 1960s than Bjelke-Petersen. It was a time of new social movements, protest, and activism. Bjelke-Petersen, on the other hand, was an arch-conservative Lutheran with little tolerance for the long-haired, dope-smoking hippies that he saw as corrosive to the state's moral fiber. The protest movement that he inherited was galvanized in its opposition to a government it believed had betrayed them the year before.

The new Brisbane protest movement was highly active and operated out of places like the Foco Club. The Foco Club was a venue located on the third floor of Trades Hall on Edward Street. Its location was a tangible reflection of its role as the intersection between the music scene and radical politics in Brisbane for the two years that it operated.[40] For conservative politicians, the Foco Club was "Australia's most evil and repugnant nightspot," but for the patrons it was a place to gather and regroup in the early years of the anti–Vietnam War protests. Cofounder Laver, also a leader of the SDA, described it as a place for political activists to enjoy some "collective R 'n' R," comparable to soldiers having time off in between deployment to a theatre of conflict.[41] The founding of the Foco Club has been heralded as the true "arrival" of the 1960s in Brisbane, somewhat belatedly compared to other Australia states, but when it did arrive it took a shape that was in some ways more aggressive than its southern equivalents.[42]

Though student marches in September 1967 were partly organized by key Foco Club and SDA members like Thompson, the most significant clashes of the year occurred prior to the demonstration against the Traffic Act. The state visit of South Vietnamese president Marshall Ky was a rallying point for the local activist community, resulting in a demonstration outside his hotel in Brisbane that marked the first serious clash between police and protesters. The clash began when Queensland Peace Committee secretary Norma Chalmers held a one-woman sit-in at the lobby of Lennon's Hotel on 20 January 1967. From a practical perspective, a sit-in conducted by a single person like this did little to obstruct the operation of the hotel, but was instead symbolic. Every moment that Chalmers sat in the Lennon's lobby was an affront to the police tasked with ensuring a smooth visit for President Ky. There was great potential for embarrassment if her sit-in was to continue too long, both for the QPF and more importantly the politicians who wanted to showcase that, unlike its southern neighbors, Queensland was a place where the radical left would not be tolerated. After twenty minutes, police moved to physically remove her from the premises. In the process of this, Chalmers was "manhandled by police, kicked by one or more of them when she was on the ground, and suffered a broken heel bone and bruising."[43] Upon her removal, violence broke out as police then moved to disperse the demonstrators outside Lennon's. Fifteen were arrested, and many more went away with injuries as a result of the incident. Key players in the protest movement saw police action during the Ky visit as much more than just a reaction. SDA leader Laver was told prior to the event that police were planning to "vegetablise" him, hurting him so badly he was unable to cause further problems as part of the movement.[44] The aggressive actions of police on the day seem to vindicate this rumor, contributing to the warlike relationship between the QPF and the protest movement moving forward.

Despite the open antagonism between the protest movement and police in Queensland, there were relatively few major cases of violence during the Vietnam War protests of the early 1970s. Partly, this was due to the singular nature of the activist community in Brisbane. Whereas the Vietnam Moratorium marches in southern states were collaborative efforts between sections of the New Left and the old guard trade unions and Labor Party, the activist community in Brisbane mostly avoided working with "establishment" political groups.[45] The Old Left and especially the Labor Party were seen by many as ineffective campaigners and out of step with the ideological priorities of young New Left activists. The central role of the Labor Party in organizing the Moratoriums was immediately problematic for the more radical protesters in Brisbane, many of whom were members of the CLCC or patrons of the Foco Club. The schism was confirmed after the first Moratorium on 8 May 1970, when Laver was refused permission to address the assembled crowd of around ten thousand people.[46] He was incensed at what he saw as an attempt to wrestle control of the movement from the local groups that had been on the frontlines, and he threatened to withdraw his substantial contingent of supporters.

The subsequent Moratorium actions in Brisbane attracted far less of a crowd, potentially due to the reluctance of the radical local activists to participate. Instead, local activists adopted a more direct approach. When a group of pro-war students at the University of Queensland invited South Vietnamese ambassador Luic Tuong Quang to a meeting on 4 September 1970, the anti-war protesters struck, blockading the meeting and effectively holding Quang hostage on campus.[47] A combination of uniformed police and Special Branch officers responded to free him, resulting in a pitched hour-long battle in which several police came away with injuries requiring hospitalization, including an officer who ended up with a broken arm.[48] This incident was the final straw for Bjelke-Petersen, no friend to the protest movement before but now livid at the perception that they had won a victory over the police. The premier demanded that unruly university students were brought "under control," setting the stage for a showdown the next year when the Springboks came to town.[49]

The Quang incident showed the lengths that the Brisbane activists were willing to go to when an opportunity presented itself. Both with Quang and earlier with Ky the local protesters had struck when a visiting dignitary was in town, knowing full well that acting at that exact moment was important to maximize the impact of their actions. Because of this, Bjelke-Petersen was determined to not be caught off guard when it was announced that the South African Springboks rugby union team would play in Brisbane during their six-week tour of Australia in mid-1971. The system of apartheid, where black South Africans were segregated and disenfranchised by the white minority, was a cause célèbre for the global New Left movement, almost as much as the Vietnam War, and so the chances of activist disruption on the same level as the Ky and Quang altercations were high.[50] The game was scheduled for 24 July, and almost two weeks before, the premier called a state of emergency designed, in his words, to ensure the safety of the visiting Springboks team. The state of emergency issued on 13 July gave the police sweeping powers to arrest or detain any person considered to be a threat to the public order, similar to the powers bestowed by the reading of the Riot Act during the Bread or Blood riots more than a century prior.[51] Unlike the use of the Riot Act in the 1860s, though, Bjelke-Petersen's calling of a state of emergency was preemptive. The decision was made not in response to a threat, but to crush resistance before it even began.

The state of emergency placed police on a war footing, perhaps necessary given the guerrilla tactics and antagonistic rhetoric used by Brisbane activists during this era. Even so, it was a radical move from the conservative premier, virtually suspending the civil liberties of Brisbane citizens in the name of repressing dissent. The decision gave the QPF carte blanche to use whatever tactics necessary to disperse political demonstrations in the name of securing the safety of the Springboks.[52] The new rules of engagement gave police the power to arrest protesters without having to provide cause, but did not explicitly grant them the right to use excessive force in doing so. Permission for that was given informally by the premier, who told Ron Eddington from the police union that officers would "not be penalized for any action they take to suppress" the protests, virtually offering immunity to police who used excessive force to disperse protesters.[53] The message was passed down to the police who were gathering in Brisbane to prepare for the tour. The official police logbook on the day the state of emergency was declared noted that 569 officers were being mustered for duty from around the state, many travelling to Brisbane in convoys from rural or regional areas to supplement officers in the capital.[54] Many of these nonlocal officers were being housed at the Enoggera army barracks, living together and preparing to lock horns with the urban "hippies" that Bjelke-Petersen considered enemies of the state. The atmosphere at the Enoggera barracks further primed the police for action to the point that, by the time the Springboks arrived on 22 July, the QPF was ready for action.

Bjelke-Petersen was right. Local activists had plans for the Springboks tour. The first anti-apartheid demonstration took place a day before the team even touched down in Brisbane, on the afternoon of 21 July. Demonstrators were issued a permit by the QPF to march from the University of Queensland to the Roma Street Forum, where speeches would then be made to the assembled group.[55] A funny thing happened on the way to the forum, though. The march deviated, making its way through the city streets to Parliament House instead. There, marchers were met by the Public Order Squad, a group of QPF officers established by Commissioner Raymond Whitrod as a specialist team trained in crowd control.[56] Forty-two protesters were arrested during this first march, and a report on the Springboks tour suggested that police were not shy in using the powers vested in them by Bjelke-Petersen's state of emergency. Ordinarily, police were required to first give directions to protesters to disperse before taking more aggressive action. Under the conditions of the state of emergency, this was no longer necessary. One protester said "he was accosted by police who kicked, kneed and punched him, pulled his hair, and pushed him to the ground . . . no directions were given by the police involved."[57] The state government pointed to the incident as proof of the need for the state of emergency, with protesters unwilling to follow the rules even when granted a permit. There is little evidence that the Parliament House deviation was a planned act, however. Police radio logs from the day show that SDA leaders Laver and Thompson were at the Roma Street Forum as promised when the clash occurred, suggesting that the decision to head for Parliament House rather than the forum was an impromptu and unsanctioned move, not a premeditated act of civil disobedience.[58]

The clash on 21 July pales in comparison to the events of the following night, when police moved to aggressively disperse the crowd gathered outside the Springboks' hotel at Tower Mill. This was the incident where police were observed chasing down fleeing demonstrators and tossing them roughly down the fifteen-foot cliff that borders Wickham Terrace.[59] Young demonstrators like eighteen-year-old Peter were pursued by police, hungry for conflict. Even when he sought refuge in the Trades Hall, he was not safe. Three police, all from regional areas, entered the building without need for a warrant, thanks to the state of emergency in place. One officer, Lindsay Daniels, reportedly set upon Peter and beat him to the point that doctors initially suspected that he had sustained spinal damage.[60] Peter and the others in Trades Hall were seeking shelter when the police violently assaulted them and certainly did not pose a further threat to civil order. Yet Daniels was not punished for his attack on Peter. He claimed that he was being held hostage by the protesters in Trades Hall, a dubious claim that was nevertheless supported by the other police with him at the time.[61] He escaped charges, but Peter was not so lucky. While still recovering in hospital, the future premier was charged with disorderly conduct for his altercation with Daniels, most of which he spent being beaten on the floor of Trades Hall.[62]

There was a lull in the conflict on 23 July, with protesters and police recovering from the violence of the days before. On 24 July, hostilities resumed. Initially, police prepared for a protest at the RNA Showgrounds, where the Springboks were due to play that evening. The plan soon changed. Special Branch officers embedded undercover with the protesters fed intelligence back to the QPF command that, rather than disrupting the rugby match, the demonstrators intended to regroup at Tower Mill, now a symbolic location after the violence that occurred two days before.[63] Police gathered to blockade Tower Mill under the personal direction of Commissioner Whitrod. The mood was tense, with police "grinning in anticipation" at protesters and heard chanting "paint them red, flog them dead," a reference to the perceived communist leanings of many in the New Left.[64]

The details surrounding Whitrod's decision to order police to disperse the protesters are clouded. Whitrod said he gave the order after Sister Eunan of the nearby Holy Spirit Hospital complained that her patients were being disturbed by the noise from the protest. According to police radio logs, however, Sister Eunan did not contact Whitrod until 5:55 p.m., while the commissioner gave the order to disperse over an hour earlier at 4:41 p.m.[65] Additionally, the fact that protesters had begun to use projectiles to smash windows at the hotel was used as another justification for action. The problem with this is that glaziers who later fixed the windows said that, in their professional opinion, the windows looked as though they had been broken from the inside, not from projectiles thrown from a crowd that was chanting "no rocks" in the period just before their dispersal.[66] The circumstances around the dispersal order are unclear, though there are several potential explanations. One is that Whitrod, having issued the order earlier than necessary, sought to provide justification for the police actions after the fact to cover his own conduct on the day. The other is perhaps more persuasive, given his reputation for not tolerating excessive force in the QPF. It is possible that police acted autonomously, against his orders. If this was the case, Whitrod may have felt it necessary to revise the timings of events at Tower Mill to retrospectively give permission for the dispersal, to avoid giving the public impression that the police were not under his control. Whatever the reason, the logs suggest that Whitrod's explanation of what happened at Tower Mill on 24 July was inaccurate and obstructive, a form of process corruption designed to protect the blue brotherhood of police from reproach over what happened after the dispersal commenced. Just like the clash at the same location two days before, police were described as having gone "berserk" when they charged at protesters, a confrontation that resulted in serious violence.[67]

The conflict around the Springboks tour was a turning point for the policing of protest in Queensland. Before, police had resorted to violence but there had always been a reluctance to overtly advocate for the use of force against protesters. Now, the floodgates were open. Bjelke-Petersen gave them permission to use violence during the Springboks tour, and what he found was that the QPF were willing to serve as loyalist spear-carriers for the state government, cultural warriors who could be sent into battle against the leftist vanguard who opposed the conservative government and all it stood for.[68] More than any other reason, it was Bjelke-Petersen's determination to use the police force to crush dissent that forced Whitrod from his job. When the premier moved to intervene not once but twice in Whitrod's attempts to investigate excessive force complaints in 1976, his position was no longer sustainable.[69] All autonomy to manage his force had been stripped, and by the time the third strike of Terry Lewis being named assistant commissioner came, Whitrod had his bags packed and was ready to check out of Queensland altogether.

In Lewis, Bjelke-Petersen once again had a police commissioner that he could do business with. On his departure, Whitrod described Bjelke-Petersen's control of the QPF as being at a level that "resembles Goering's Gestapo in Nazi Germany."[70] Though hyperbolic, Whitrod's concerns about political involvement in policing were very real. Lewis was more than willing to accede to the premier's will. The new commissioner had learned at the feet of Bischof, and was aware of the importance of currying favor with powerful men. The premier's preference for using the QPF as his attack dogs was made evident on 4 September 1977, less than a year after Lewis became head of the QPF. He ordered Lewis not to issue any permits for political protests from then on, saying, "the day of the political street march is over ... don't bother applying for a march permit, you won't get one."[71] Bjelke-Petersen's edict was not supported by new laws but the application of old provisions in the Traffic Act giving police the final say on issuing permits, the same rules that the 1967 protesters fought to have removed. The premier relied on the compliance of Lewis to achieve its general ban on protest, leveraging the political power he had over the commissioner to ensure cooperation. The enforcement of the ban on protest was, in itself, a form of process corruption that was conducted in full public view, with the premier and police commissioner working in conjunction to implement total ban without it having to be passed in the state parliament.

Lewis used his administrative powers to deny any protest permit that came across his desk from 1977 to 1979 and, when protests went on regardless, used a strategy of extreme force to dissuade further displays of opposition to Bjelke-Petersen and his government. Lewis established a permanent unit to replace the Public Order Squad called the Regional Task Force. The primary responsibility of the squad was the violent repression of events that contravened the ban on street marches.[72] The result of the protest ban was the opposite of what the state government wanted but predictable given the history of dissent in the state. As was the usual pattern in Queensland, when the government cracked down on protest, the activist movement responded with an even greater show of force than before. The protest ban gave birth to the Right to March movement, during which thousands of Queenslanders came together to call for a return to the basic principles of free speech. The first major action of the Right to March movement came on 22 October 1977, a date intended to host a rally in opposition to uranium mining in Queensland's north before the government ban was imposed. A horde of more than three thousand protesters faced down 460 police officers in King George Square, outside Brisbane City Hall. The confrontation lasted over four hours, and ended with 418 taken into police custody.[73]

The ban on protest was, conversely, inspiring an increase in civil disobedience and causing even more problems for Lewis's police than ever before, but the new commissioner was determined to stay the course. It was important that he remained in Bjelke-Petersen's favor. Rumors of Lewis's involvement in corruption as Bischof's bagman continued to circulate, however it would not be a problem as long as he kept the premier satisfied by acceding to his demands on protest. For Lewis, enforcing the protest ban was more pragmatic than ideological, a way to use the Premier as cover for the corruption in the QPF.

Eventually, the ban on street protest became unsustainable. After two years, more than two thousand people had been arrested for defying the ban, and the Right to March movement was only growing stronger.[74] Someone had to blink, and in the end, that person was Commissioner Lewis. He gave permission for an anti-uranium mining protest to go forward on 9 August 1979, just under two years after Bjelke-Petersen had proclaimed the "day of the political street march" was over.[75] The state government and QPF stance towards public dissent remained firm, yet the blanket ban on protest was made a thing of the past. The premier might not have liked backing down to the protest movement, but it was necessary for him to accept it. At a Brisbane byelection in late 1978, support for his National Party candidate had dropped to just 10 percent, signaling a potential electoral rout at the approaching 1980 state election if Bjelke-Petersen did not act to satiate the increasing rejection of his political agenda. In the end, the premier's plan to regain political support worked, and the National Party recorded their highest ever vote at the 1980 poll.[76] By the time the Commonwealth Games came to Brisbane in 1982, a more rational approach to protest had emerged in Queensland. Despite the considerable potential for the Bjelke-Petersen government to be embarrassed on an international stage, permits were issued for street marches during the event, and even though the QPF arrested many protesters, there were few cases of violence, and none on the scale of the Springboks tour eleven years earlier.[77]

Criticism of police responses to political protest was not unique to Queensland in the 1970s, nor has it ceased to be a contentious area in the years since. The aggressive and repressive response of police forces around the United States to the 2020 Black Lives Matter protests shows that this is not a matter of rotten apples or rotten barrels in specific law enforcement agencies but a cultural problem in policing in itself. The same treatment that faced civil rights protesters in the late 1960s United States echoed in the violent dispersal techniques used by police in the 2020 protests, where batons and tear gas were liberally used to turn American streets into virtual warzones. The images of peaceful protesters fleeing from police violence in terror was reminiscent of the 1971 Springboks protests, or the beating of Rosemary Severin in 1976. When U.S. president Donald Trump performatively marched from the White House to a nearby church after clearing the area of protesters with tear gas, you could almost envisage Bjelke-Petersen doing the same, flanked on either side by the loyal police who made up "Joh's Army." In the 2020 protests, however, there were also signs of the same determination and hope that ultimately allowed the Right to March protesters to overcome state oppression in late 1970s Queensland. The refusal of the Black Lives Matters protesters to back down in the face of police aggression displays the very same determination to hold fast in the face of a government who consistently showed callous disregard for human rights, and freedom of speech. In the late 1970s, the tenacity of protest movement forced the government to blink first.

With the movement growing ever stronger, Lewis was no longer able to serve as Bjelke-Petersen's attack dog against protesters. However, it did not mean that the commissioner was not useful to the premier. It was not just protesters that were a threat to Bjelke-Petersen's rule. Sure, the Premier could protect Lewis and the QPF, but the commissioner could protect his friends in parliament, too.

CHAPTER 9

If You Want a Friend in Politics

The rest of the city was winding down for the year, but Sergeant Len Bracken and Constable Peter Carmichael were still hard at work in the early hours of 18 December 1981. The last few weeks of December were a time for celebration, making the roads dangerous. Christmas parties were in full swing across Brisbane, and more than usual, the police were forced to deal with people hitting the road after indulging in one too many drinks. So, when Bracken and Carmichael noticed a Rolls-Royce swerving erratically on the South East Freeway at 1:20 a.m., there was nothing unusual about it.[1] The only strange thing was that the officers rarely got to get so close to such a nice car on one of these stops. The gentleman behind the wheel was certainly intoxicated, though he refused to take a roadside breath test to confirm the fact. Again, this was nothing unusual for officers on a drink driving stop. No one wanted to get arrested, and drunk people tended to be more belligerent in any case. There was a protocol for this. Bracken and Carmichael took the driver into custody and transported him to the city watchhouse. He was handed over to the Breath Analysis Section and, after some persuasive discussion, agreed to be tested. Despite the lengthy period between the time he was pulled over and the time he eventually gave his breath sample, the driver still registered a blood alcohol reading of 0.12—at the time, slightly less than double the legal limit in Queensland.[2]

Carmichael set about writing up the charge sheet. Meanwhile, the officer in charge of the watchhouse, Dante Squassoni, took pity on the driver. He was an older gentleman in his late sixties, and by now, it was 2 a.m. All that he was asking for was to make a phone call, and Squassoni was happy to oblige. After all, the driver was not going to be able to drive himself home after this, so it might be useful for someone to come to the station to collect him. After a short conversation, the driver handed the telephone to Squassoni. There were no family members on the other end of the line. It was Squassoni's boss, the commissioner. In short order, Terry Lewis made the police at the watchhouse acutely aware of the mess that they had stumbled into. The elderly gentleman in the cell was Edward Houghton Lyons, referred to by some as "Top-Level Ted." As Lewis told Squassoni on that 2 a.m. phone call, Lyons was a close confidante and right-hand man of Joh Bjelke-Petersen.

The year before the premier named Lyons as the chairman of the Totalizator Administration Board (TAB), a state body responsible for legal off-track betting in Queensland. In fact, he was coming from the TAB Christmas party in Albion at the time of his arrest. Lewis should know; he was at the party too, coming along as Lyons's special guest.[3] The simple drink driving case had quickly turned into a political hot potato. Squassoni passed the phone to Bracken. In another room, unaware of the drama unfolding, Carmichael continued to draft Lyons's charge sheet. Shortly after, someone (later, Carmichael could not recall if it was Bracken or Squassoni) came to him, telling him about the commissioner's call and that, as a result, the Queensland Police Force (QPF) would not be pursuing charges against the TAB chairman. Bracken and Carmichael were furious, gave Lyons the keys to his Rolls-Royce, and told him to drive himself home. The charge sheet and breath analysis certificate were scrunched up, tossed in a wastepaper bin.[4] The papers did not stay in the garbage for long though, and when they reemerged, the extent of political influence on Queensland policing was put on display for all to see.

Australia was not immune to the almost insatiable hunger for capital accumulation that afflicted Western consumer culture in the 1980s. The term "yuppie" was popularized in a 1980 article in *Chicago Magazine*, coined to describe the "rising tide ... [of] young, urban professionals rebelling against the stodgy suburban lifestyles of their parents."[5] In this sense, the yuppie was a cultural repudiation of the wistful 1950s era banality championed by Robert Menzies—more important was making money that could in turn offer a heightened stimulation, often through lavish spending on consumer goods. Yuppie culture at first seems to be incompatible with the strict social conservatism of the Bjelke-Petersen era. However, the premier and his allies were nothing if not pragmatic. While true that Bjelke-Petersen desired a moral society, he also had an obsessive longing to see the kind of investment that would make Queensland the most prosperous state in Australia. His government incentivized property development, rolling out the red carpet for the construction of major tourism resorts and foreign-owned buildings in the state capital.

The concessions made to Queensland developers such as Keith Williams and Mike Gore by the state government gave rise to what became known as "the white shoe brigade," an informal group, based in southern Queensland resort town the Gold Coast, that benefited from the premier's largesse and, in response, supported his government.[6] Unlike the stylish and urbane American yuppie, the white shoe brigade attracted its name from the perception that members could not hide their working-class origins, obvious by their ostentatious choices of apparel such as patterned, Hawaiian-style shirts and white-leather shoes.[7] For the premier, development was essential to Queensland's success, and as such, the white shoe brigade became part of an unofficial advisory group that governed the state from behind the scenes, a sort of "kitchen cabinet" for Bjelke-Petersen. Though not a property developer, Lyons and friends of the premier like him were members of this social set. So too was another public servant, who regularly accepted the hospitality of the white shoe brigade during holidays to the Gold Coast: Police Commissioner Lewis.

One of the legacies of the Fitzgerald Inquiry was its exposure of the deep connections that existed between the QPF and the Bjelke-Petersen government. For some, this has resulted in the false impression that politicization of the police force was a historical aberration, forged by the perfect storm of an authoritarian premier and a compliant, corrupt Police Commissioner. History shows that this is not the case. Since its formation, the QPF was used by state governments of all political persuasions to crush dissent and support the status quo. It is not illegal, unethical, or corrupt to support the interests of a democratically elected government, especially in times of civil unrest. This is the problem with process corruption that occurs for political reasons. If a government is complicit in justifying suspensions of ordinary rules of conduct, the legalization of otherwise unethical practices becomes a form of misconduct that can be practiced in plain sight, without fear of reprisal. When the premier suspended the usual rules of conduct in the 1971 state of emergency, what resulted was a period of aggressive repression. Not all repression of political repression was so overt, however. The practice, coined "high policing" by criminologist Jean-Paul Brodeur, is a form of enforcement that recognizes the importance of serving the "higher interests" of the state over the individual interests of its citizens—putting collective safety and stability above individual rights and freedoms, in many cases.[8] Following these utilitarian principles, there was a division of the QPF that had worked behind the scenes since the late 1940s to collect intelligence on any person or group that posed a threat to state security. Its name was Special Branch.

In the post-war era, squads like Special Branch were formed in most major police forces around the world. This was the time of perhaps the world's greatest ideological conflict, the Cold War, and the carnage of World War II was still fresh in mind, as was the experience of fascism. The rise of fascism showed the risks governments courted by letting political or social movements evolve into unstoppable, dangerous behemoths. For Queensland, the creation of Special Branch was a response to the threat posed by the union movement during the 1948 railway workers strike.[9] Though a Labor Party premier, Ned Hanlon saw real danger in permitting the unions to bring the state to a grinding halt with industrial action. It set a bad precedent, showing that special interest groups could get what they wanted if they caused enough damage. Hanlon rushed through new laws to ban strike action, resulting in the St Patrick's Day Bash where Communist member of Parliament (MP) Fred Paterson was beaten by police.[10] Creating Special Branch was designed as a more lasting response to the ever-present threat of political activism. Arthur Jones, the minister for Home Affairs, announced that it was the new Special Branch's responsibility to "obtain details of any organization or individuals who may be regarded as a potential menace to law and order."[11] The "potential menaces" Special Branch targeted varied, from communists and neo-Nazis to protesters in the anti-war or feminist movements of the 1970s. Police files were opened for every person believed to be engaged in subversive behaviors and included personal information and records of surveillance designed to support a brief of evidence if police decided it was in the public interest to take them off the streets. Brodeur claimed that high policing was fundamentally about putting the interests of the state above the individual liberties of citizens. Though seemingly a noble commitment to the "greater good," one of the risks of high policing emerges when the interests of the state become conflated with the interests of those *running* the state—the politicians and bureaucrats at its head. In the wrong hands, a unit focused on high policing like Special Branch can be transformed into a powerful personal or political force, used to suppress "dangerous" (read: opposing) ideas. This was exactly what was in the Special Branch's future as Queensland marched—reluctantly, for some—towards the volatile, progressive future of the 1970s.

For Premier Bjelke-Petersen, the Special Branch's role was more than just taking photos of protesters from afar. He envisaged a Special Branch that was active in infiltrating subversive groups and destabilizing them from the inside. Former Special Branch officer Domenico Cacciola said it was common strategy for members of the unit to go "undercover" in radical groups like Civil Liberties Co-ordinating Committee (CLCC) or the Communist Party to gather information. On other occasions, officers cultivated informants from within the activist community, preying on internal group politics or using coercive strategies to encourage them to feed intelligence back to the branch. The groups in Brisbane that were targeted "never knew that half the people at their meetings were dogs, giving their secrets to the cops . . . a meeting wasn't over for five minutes before we knew what they had been talking about."[12] The strategy of internal destabilization was not unique to Queensland's Special Branch. It was the same general approach used by the U.S. Federal Bureau of Investigation's COINTELPRO, which sought to disrupt American political groups by infiltrating them, spreading disinformation and turning members against each other.[13] The operations of Special Branch were shrouded in secrecy. Part of the squad's power was that radical groups did not know where the leaks in their organization were coming from, so it was paramount that covert informants were protected and undercover Special Branch officers were not exposed. Because of this, the actions of Special Branch officers avoided scrutiny at a far greater rate than the regular rank and file of the QPF.

Referring to the Queensland Special Branch, historian Ross Fitzgerald observed that "secrecy is the bottom line of corruption."[14] In the Bjelke-Petersen era, that secrecy provided the coverage needed to gather intelligence on all political opponents of the government, criminal or not. The use of Special Branch to collect information on the Labor Party opposition began before Bjelke-Petersen, when Frank Bischof served as commissioner under Frank Nicklin. Addressing state parliament on 20 September 1960, Labor Party MP Pat Hanlon accused Special Branch of spreading hearsay and rumors about members of the Labor Party who were suspected to be communist sympathizers. Hanlon said that he "did not accept that they [Special Branch] are infallible" and accused the police of collaborating with government ministers to abuse the privilege of their position by circulating this information and using it for political benefit.[15] Spying on activist groups like CLCC was one thing, but providing the sitting government with information on their rivals, also elected politicians, was on a different level entirely. The argument made by the state government and the QPF was that a person's position as a politician did not provide them immunity in the event they were found to be a threat to the Queensland public. In reality, though, the Special Branch's function as a source of political dirt on the Labor Party helped reinforce the power and control of the conservative government. The flow of information was one-sided; there was no sharing of compromising information on conservative politicians shared with the Labor Party opposition, for example. This could be seen as the privilege of government, with the police under no obligation to share sensitive material with politicians outside of government. Even so, the result remains the same: the sharing of Special Branch intelligence on Labor Party politicians with the state government was part of a corrupt compact between the two groups, one with major consequences for the Australian political environment.

The Colston affair in 1975 was a prime example where QPF intelligence was used to reshape the face of politics, this time on a national scale. In 1975, Australia was facing one of the biggest political crises it ever faced. The federal Labor Party had been elected in 1972 on a sweeping platform of social reform, but by 1974, it was being prevented from implementing its vision for Australia by a Senate that refused to pass the government's legislative agenda. Gough Whitlam, the Labor prime minister, first called a double dissolution election to resolve the issues preventing him from getting laws passed. In Australian politics, a double dissolution is an exceptional circumstance where, unable to pass laws because of a political deadlock between the Senate and House of Representatives, a government dissolves *both* houses of parliament in their entirety and forces every Senator and MP to contest their seat at an election. While Whitlam retained power at this election, he was returned with a reduced majority that made his job even harder.[16] A series of scandals forced Whitlam to fire several senior Labor Party senators, and when Queensland senator Bertie Milliner died on 30 June 1975, the vacant seat was crucial to the Labor Party keeping the coalition opposition from taking control of the Senate entirely.[17]

Standard practice when a casual vacancy like this came about was for the deceased senator's party to nominate a replacement, who was then formally approved in a vote by the parliament of the state that they represented. The Labor Party nominated Mal Colston, a former teacher, to replace Milliner, but before the vote in parliament could take place, Liberal MP David Byrne anonymously received a police file on his desk in state parliament with information that Colston was investigated by the QPF in 1962 and was suspected of arson. The investigating officers on the case believed Colston was tired of his rural service as a teacher, and thought that setting fire to the school would result in a transfer back to Brisbane.[18] No charges were laid, but the revelations were enough to give Bjelke-Petersen an excuse to reject the Labor Party's suggestion to nominate Colston. Instead, he selected Albert Field as Milliner's replacement, a Labor Party member openly opposed to the Whitlam government. Field refused to support Whitlam's agenda, and as a result, the Opposition gained control of the Senate. The federal government was, again, in deadlock. While the prime minister of Australia leads the national government, they are not the head of state in the same way as a president of the United States of America might be. Instead, the British monarch retains this role, acting through a proxy—a governor-general appointed by the Crown to oversee Australia. The position of governor-general is that of a ceremonial figurehead in practice, however in the context of the political crisis of the 1970s, Governor-General John Kerr took unprecedented action. To break the political stalemate, Kerr exercised his power as the Queen's representative to dismiss the Whitlam government, in effect firing the elected government of Australia.

The police file that found its way onto Byrne's desk was central to Australia's biggest political crisis. However, despite its considerable historical importance, the origins of the document have never officially been determined. Few people had access to both confidential police files and Byrne's office. One of them was Donald Lane, a former Special Branch officer turned Liberal MP for Merthyr in 1971.[19] Lane, a staunch acolyte of the government and friend to the Rat Pack, has long been suspected of being the source of the document, continuing a career-long practice of feeding beneficial police intelligence to the government to assist in political point-scoring. When he took over as police commissioner in 1970, Raymond Whitrod conducted an assessment of the QPF and found that Special Branch officers had "frequent access" to Bjelke-Petersen that went beyond the normal police-government relationship. Whitrod, who was central in creating national domestic spy agency the Australian Security Intelligence Organization earlier in his career, was critical of the extent of Special Branch surveillance in Queensland. He claimed that "the range of people investigated seemed unjustifiably large and selection appeared to be based on the personal judgements of investigators rather than on a systemic analysis of threats." Despite his reservations about the Special Branch, Whitrod failed to reform the unit during his six-year tenure as commissioner. In his view, the Special Branch was too close with the premier, and any attempts to change the way that the unit operated would be a lost cause.[20]

The year after the Colston affair, pressure mounted on Whitrod to resign as police commissioner. Partly, this was a result of the premier's intervention in Whitrod's attempts to investigate accusations of excessive force in the Cedar Bay raid and the Severin incident. There was also a push coming from within the government to remove him, however. A campaign to undermine the commissioner led by the Rat Pack's chief supporter in Parliament House, Lane. Before entering politics, Lane joined the Queensland police in early 1952, a week before Glen Hallahan was sworn in as a police officer.[21] Lane was from Warwick, a rural town in the Darling Downs farming region, not far from Hallahan and Bischof's hometown Toowoomba. He was a country boy, so when the sixteen-year-old Lane moved to Brisbane to train as a police cadet, he was shocked by the sometimes uncouth nature of urban life. He was so appalled that he told his father about his fellow cadets' behavior, causing him to rush to Brisbane to remove his son from the corruptive environment of police training camp.[22] Lane was given permission to attend training during the day, returning to off-site lodgings organized by his father each evening—a luxury not extended to his apparently less privileged peers. Shortly after Lane was sworn in as a police officer, he was sent to the northwestern mining town Mount Isa to learn the ropes. Far from the prying eyes of corruption-busters in Brisbane, it was a frontier town where vice was broadly tolerated behind closed doors. In Mount Isa, Lane served alongside the likes of future commissioner Norm Bauer and ace detective Hallahan until the pair were transferred to the Brisbane Criminal Investigation Branch (CIB) in 1958 after their success on the Sundown murders case.[23] Lane replaced Hallahan in the Mount Isa CIB, but it was not long before he too followed the trail back to Brisbane, joining Hallahan at the Consorting Squad.[24]

The country boy from Warwick had learned a lot about how the world worked since last time he was in Brisbane as a cadet. His time in Mount Isa showed him that, though crimes like gambling and prostitution could never be truly eradicated, police could control them if they worked with vice operators rather than against them. He became known during his QPF career as "Mr 10 percent," a nickname referencing the protection fee he normally charged sex workers to operate.[25] When the National Hotel Inquiry began in 1963, Lane was one of the eighty-nine detectives who were legally represented before the commission, concerned they might be implicated in corruption.[26] He was also part of Tony Murphy's team of investigators, nominally assisting the inquiry but, in reality, digging up dirt on witnesses against police like John Komlosy and David Young.[27] Perhaps it was during this time that Lane got his first taste for political intelligence gathering, because in 1967 he transferred into Special Branch where he spent the remainder of his career spying on threats to the state. His secondment to Special Branch coincided with Bjelke-Petersen's rise to the premier's office, and if Whitrod was correct that Special Branch had unprecedented direct access to the premier during this period, it was likely Lane's first contact with Bjelke-Petersen. The premier must have liked what he saw in Lane. By 1971, the Special Branch spy was selected to run as the Liberal candidate for the Fortitude Valley-based seat of Merthyr.[28] The election was held on 24 July 1971, the day that the contentious Springboks rugby match was being held just down the road. As police and protesters clashed once more at Tower Mill, the results started coming in: Lane, former QPF officer, was the new MP for Merthyr.

Though he left the QPF in 1971, Lane remained close to Lewis and other serving police, many of whom were targets of Whitrod's aggressive campaign to clean the force of corruption. Lane was vocal in his opposition to Whitrod, speaking in favor of disciplinary action against Arthur Pitts after the Southport bookmakers' case in March 1976 and supporting the removal of Whitrod ally Max Hodges as police minister later that same year.[29] He called on Hodges's replacement, Tom Newberry, to sanction Whitrod for his rumored use of "kill sheets"—quotas forcing police to make a certain number of arrests that Lane argued was akin to "bounty hunting."[30] Lane described Whitrod in state parliament as "that clown" and noted that "no commissioner in the history of the Police Force has had so many votes of no confidence in him."[31] There is evidence that the pressure Lane put on Whitrod to resign was part of a concerted plan to remove him and install a new commissioner who was more friendly to the Rat Pack and the government. Gregory Early, who served as assistant to both Whitrod and Lewis, believed Lane to be part of a cabal of officers including Rat Packer Murphy, police union president Ron Eddington, and Special Branch boss Les Hogan to overthrow Whitrod and replace him with Lewis.[32] A letter sent by Early to Lewis on 15 November 1976, the day of his appointment as commissioner, supports this. In it, he says he spoke to "Shady" two weeks earlier, who alluded to the fact that change would be occurring in the commissioner's office.[33] "Shady" was Lane's nickname, and the letter suggests that plans were afoot to remove Whitrod long before he ultimately decided to resign his post.

Forcing Whitrod out removed any potential threat the reformist commissioner posed to Bjelke-Petersen's use of the police force as a political weapon. Under Lewis, police went from sharing damaging information on Labor Party MPs with the government to more actively serving as Bjelke-Petersen's attack dogs whenever the Labor Party got too close to landing a blow on the regime. Often, these blows were to do with the questionable dealings of the Bjelke-Petersen government. Even aside from the corruption in the QPF, the government was mired in controversy surrounding political donations and the National Party's business dealings. In July 1983, Labor Party leader Keith Wright alleged that senior bureaucrats close to the premier had corruptly granted a $331 million contract to a company called C. Itoh and Co. Ltd. to build a power station.[34] The claim was that the government permitted the company to offer a tender after the period had closed and other tenders had been revealed, allowing them to undercut the competition and claim the contract for themselves. After Wright's comments in state parliament, the premier rang the commissioner's office personally and instructed his staff to interrogate Wright about the source of the information. Notes from the conversation state that the Bjelke-Petersen said, "Wright must not get off the hook . . . Get him in a corner so he has no feathers left so I am in a position later on, when I get the report, to say he had absolutely nothing to tell the police."[35] The premier explicitly instructed the police on the best way to trap Wright, maneuvering him in such a way that his information could be discredited as without basis. The premier's intervention was purely political. Rather than letting the auditor-general do their job and investigate the deal properly, Bjelke-Petersen sought to use the QPF to scuttle the allegations. It worked. A month later the auditor-general determined that the government had not acted improperly in the power station deal.

The active intervention of police in protecting the interests of the government was not restricted to attacking their opponents. On some occasions, it was up to loyal members of the force like Commissioner Lewis to prevent police action being taken against friends of the government, as well. The drunk driving case of Lyons was a prominent example of this tendency. Lyons was Brisbane born and bred, schooled at the prestigious St Joseph's College in Nudgee. He was a renowned businessman who made a name for himself as chairman of the Katies fashion label, making a profitable trade selling women's clothes at the same time that Bjelke-Petersen was presiding over the violent Springboks tour. He became close to the premier around this period, changing his party allegiance from the Liberals to the Country Party after hearing Bjelke-Petersen speak at a business function.[36] Virtually from then on, Lyons held sway over the premier as one of his closest advisers. He was described by some as "the Rasputin of the Queensland economy" and "acted as an extra-parliamentary politician for 20 [sic] years."[37] Through his friendship with the premier, Lyons was named chairman of the TAB in June 1980, to the dismay of Bjelke-Petersen's coalition partners in the Liberal Party who fought his appointment as an act of political nepotism. There is some merit to this. Russell Hinze, a powerful figure in the government in his own right, revealed much later that he was only given the Racing portfolio in December 1980 on the condition he push through Lyons's appointment to the TAB in a corrupt quid pro quo.[38]

Because he was close to Bjelke-Petersen, Lyons also came to know the premier's other top lieutenant, Lewis. While the premier had a strong professional relationship with both men, Lyons and Lewis were closer on a social basis, which is why Lewis was invited to the TAB Christmas party on 17 December 1981.[39] After Lyons was taken into custody for driving under the influence in the early hours of the following morning, Lewis told arresting officer Bracken that "other than my mother he's about the only bloke in the world I'd like to do something for... take him home."[40] Bracken did not follow Lewis's order to take Lyons home, incensed by the commissioner's intervention. Nevertheless, he did tell his partner Carmichael to "forget about" the charges, and Carmichael threw out the charge sheets and breathalyzer results before the pair released Lyons, following him as he drove himself home in his Rolls-Royce to ensure the still drunk businessman did not do any damage to himself or others.[41] A funny thing happened while Bracken and Carmichael were gone, though. Another police officer at the watchhouse that night, Brian Cook, retrieved the documents relating to Lyons's arrest from the wastepaper bin. Cook was furious that Lyons was released because he had powerful friends. Enough was enough. Cook passed the evidence off to the only person in the police force he could think of that might know what to do with it: the constant thorn in Lewis's side, Bob Campbell.[42] By this point in late 1981, Campbell had been passing embarrassing information about the force for some time to Kevin Hooper, the Labor Party MP for Archerfield, who used it as ammunition against the government in parliament. This time, Hooper acted as a conduit. The document prepared by Carmichael, retrieved by Cook, passed to Campbell, and handed to Hooper found its way into the hands of *Sunday Mail* journalist Ric Allen and, on 20 December 1981, became a frontpage story.[43]

Even as the story was about the break in the *Sunday Mail*, Lyons and Lewis continued to conspire to hide the commissioner's role in protecting his friend. The pair "concocted a story which borders on the ridiculous" and claimed that Lyons had been released at 2:30 a.m. to attend an important business meeting, and that it was always the intention of police to charge him via summons at a later time.[44] This story requires its audience to believe several strange propositions, most importantly that Lyons was holding meetings in the early hours of the morning after a drunken Christmas party. In any case, with their attempted cover-up rumbled, there was no option but to charge Lyons with drink driving as Bracken and Carmichael originally intended. He faced court on 28 January 1982, was fined $175, and was banned from driving for four months.⁴⁵ The implications for Lewis were serious, too. If the article was correct, the commissioner had personally intervened to protect a powerful friend. There had always been allegations that Lewis was corrupt, but this time there seemed to be evidence: not only the documents retrieved from the wastepaper bin, but at least three police officers involved in the arrest and detention of Lyons who knew about the instructions to leave Lyons alone.

An inquiry was held to investigate the claims that Lewis had misused his position, led by Liberal Attorney-General Sam Doumany in 1982. Doumany found no evidence that Lewis colluded to make Lyons's arrest disappear. Contrary to what the *Sunday Mail* article said, Doumany found that Bracken and Carmichael had driven Lyons home and that the charge sheet that he eventually went to court on was signed before the newspaper article came out, confirming that the police always intended to issue it regardless of the public furor.⁴⁶ Though the results of the Doumany investigation vindicated Lewis at the time, the Fitzgerald Inquiry found otherwise when it revisited the events in the late 1980s. Carmichael told Fitzgerald he provided a false statement to Doumany confirming Lewis's story about the Lyons arrest. He said Lewis did not instruct him directly to lie, but that he "didn't want to expose an attempted cover-up" for fear of the repercussions for his career.⁴⁷ Carmichael had a point. At a meeting with internal affairs investigators about the leak on 22 December 1981, Campbell was told that he was going to be transferred to a rural police station effective 4 January 1982, a move to get him away from a position where he could continue to harm the Lewis administration.⁴⁸

Controversy around Lewis's relationship with Chief Crown Prosecutor Angelo Vasta was another area of contention throughout the 1980s. Not long before Lyons was arrested, police in Brisbane arrested Alfred Thompson and Steve Kossaris, both twenty-one years old, who were accused of a series of bank robberies around the city. The pair were known as the "Bikie Bandits" for their preference for using motorcycles to flee the scene of their crimes.⁴⁹ When police arrested Thompson and Kossaris, they were held in separate cells overnight before making full confessions. Later, both claimed that police supplied them with heroin before they made their admissions, saying that an officer told them that they "look[ed] pretty sick" before offering the men, both addicts, narcotics. Thompson even went so far as to say that one of the officers at the watchhouse held his arm for him while he injected the heroin after it was brought to his cell.⁵⁰ Six officers were charged as a result of the Bikie Bandits case, four for supplying drugs to prisoners and a further two for committing perjury at Thompson and Kessaris's trial.[51] As chief prosecutor in Queensland, Vasta was asked to prepare a report as to whether the case against the officers should proceed. While in the process of compiling this report, he called Lewis. According to Lewis's meticulous diary entries, the call was about "police charged over Bikie Bandits" among other matters. Though Vasta denied any "significant discussions" on the case took place during the phone call, he filed a report only days later where he found that "notwithstanding the argument that there was [a] *prima facie* case, it should not proceed."[52] A few weeks later, on 2 September 1983, a nolle prosequi was formally entered, and the charges against the six police officers involved in the Bikie Bandits case were dropped. That night, a party was thrown at the home of one of the police accused in the case. In attendance were all six newly cleared officers, along with Commissioner Lewis and his special guests, Lyons and Vasta.[53]

Vasta was named the next Justice of Queensland's Supreme Court a matter of months later, on 13 February 1984. Two years later, his association with Lewis was again in the spotlight. Vasta sued the satirical magazine *Matilda* for defamation over a series of articles beginning in September 1985 that he said gave the implication that he could not discharge his duties as a judge because he was beholden to the powerful triumvirate of Bjelke-Petersen, Lewis, and Lyons.[54] As part of the defamation case, Vasta said he was "acquaintances" with the trio "but they are not friends as suggested in the article."[55] The commissioner also went to bat for Vasta, vowing that he had "not had close contact with him." Vasta's attempt to distance himself from the Lewis and the others came back to bite him a few years later, when the watchful eye of the Fitzgerald Inquiry turned to the old defamation case.

On 19 October 1988, with Lewis on the stand, counsel assisting Fitzgerald tendered a copy of a letter Vasta sent to Lewis in November 1985 where he told the commissioner that he would "always treasure [his] friendship." Yet, less than a year later, both made sworn statements that there was no personal relationship between them.[56] The target was Lewis, proving he committed perjury in the defamation case, but Vasta was collateral damage. He, too, had been less than honest in the *Matilda* case. Less than a week later, Vasta was instructed to stand down as a justice of the Supreme Court by Chief Justice Bob Andrews.[57] An act of parliament passed on 8 June 1989 formally removed him from his position, the first time a judge had been removed by a parliament in Australian history. Lewis put himself on the line to protect Vasta, to lie for him and support his protestations that he was not unduly influenced by Lewis and the others. As in the Lyons case, though, Lewis's protection eventually ran out. When the heat turned to exposing the commissioner's corruption, the façade fell and took Vasta's career with it.

Lane was another political scalp claimed when the Fitzgerald Inquiry turned its attention to corruption in the political realm. Even though he was a member of the Liberal Party, the lesser partner in the coalition, Lane had the ear of the premier and, in 1983, changed his party affiliation to become a National Party member when the coalition dissolved and Bjelke-Petersen's party began to govern in its own right.[58] Lane's privileged position in the government gave him power to direct the judicial process in ways that even his old friend the police commissioner could not. Lewis could advise the premier, but at the end of the day, he was only able to operate under the conditions that the elected parliament set for him. Lane's election had changed the status quo. Now, corrupt police had a partner in Parliament House who sat at the table that made decisions like whether to fire Whitrod or what new laws should be passed. Lane could not just capitalize on the criminalization of vice—he created the conditions that corrupt police could profit from.

Since the mid-1970s, Lane had been a close associate of Sydney businessman (and U.S. Mafia associate) Jack Rooklyn.[59] Despite Rooklyn's questionable reputation, Lane enjoyed a social relationship with him, even visiting him in Sydney and spending time vacationing on his yacht. In 1970s Queensland, poker machines were banned. However, a similar type of in-line machine was legalized in 1974. In-line machines operated in a similar way to banned poker machines, but were intended for amusement purposes only. Even so, they were routinely used as substitute poker machines in Brisbane, with hosts illegally "paying out" wins in cash.[60] After Jack Herbert was forced to resign from the QPF in the wake of his attempts to bribe Pitts, he joined the Queensland branch of Rooklyn's operation, acting as a conduit between in-line gaming operators and corrupt officers in the police force.[61] Former Art Union executive Roy Clapper told Fitzgerald that Herbert charged $10,000 a year to secure police protection for the machines he operated.[62] It was around the time that Herbert joined Rooklyn's operation that he organized a meeting with Lane, his former colleague and now state politician sitting on the parliamentary Justice Committee, which, at that time, was reviewing the status of in-line machines.[63] For the system to work it was essential not only that in-line machines remain legal, but that the ban on poker machines also remained in place. Though legalizing poker machines would be a boon to gambling operators like Rooklyn, it would mean that corrupt police were no longer able to collect the protection money that they were currently receiving from operators of in-line machines. Lane was in a prime position to influence these decisions, and given his connection to both Rooklyn and Herbert, it is likely that he advocated a continuation of the existing laws to promote their interests in the Justice Committee.

Lane was affiliated with the U.S. Mafia and corrupt Queensland police, yet it was his misuse of ministerial expenses that eventually brought him down. At the time, Queensland politicians were entitled to claim reimbursement for meals, travel, and other miscellaneous expenses incurred while carrying out parliamentary business. Lane admitted to falsely claiming for costs that were not in the course of his political duties, resulting in more than two dozen charges of misappropriating public funds. He submitted his resignation on 30 January 1989, just five months before the Fitzgerald Inquiry handed down its final report.[64] In testimony to the commission on 15 November 1988, he said it was standard practice in the Bjelke-Petersen era to use state money to cover personal expenses. Even as his corruption began to emerge, the premier continued to go to bat for Lane, saying that if Lane was guilty of a crime then "every member of parliament in Australia should be jailed for 50 years . . . everybody takes their family out to dinner in politics."[65] The tolerance of process corruption shown by Bjelke-Petersen was telling. For the previous eighteen months he had been facing down allegations that he turned a blind eye to the mercenary corruption taking place in the police force, yet even now the premier was still showing public support for the same sort of behavior carried out by one of his own ministers. The final nail in Lane's professional coffin was hammered in by none other than Herbert, his former partner in corruption. Herbert admitted that both he and his son John had unlawfully registered to vote in Lane's electorate Merthyr before the 1986 election, claiming that it was done to commit electoral fraud and boost Lane's chances of being reelected.[66] Lane only won the 1986 election by a meager thirty-one votes, and the idea that others might have also illegally registered in Merthyr called the entire result into question. Lane was sentenced to twelve months in prison on 3 October 1990 on after being found guilty of twenty-seven counts of misusing public money in the order of $4538.17.[67] Unlike the much longer prison sentence given to Commissioner Lewis, Lane was released on a community control order after only seven weeks, never having been found guilty of any misconduct associated with his relationships with Rooklyn, Herbert, or Lewis.

Use of the QPF as a political force was not the invention of Commissioner Lewis, or even Bjelke-Petersen. There was a long tradition in Queensland of using the police to reinforce the status quo and, later, as a vehicle for a utilitarian form of high policing designed to protect the interests of the government in the name of security and stability. The mandate of Special Branch to gather intelligence on dangerous groups and individuals was a noble one, but the secrecy of the squad and its closeness to the politicians in power meant that too often it erred into a grey area where the best interests of politicians were conflated with the best interests of the state. The branch began to take orders from the premier, not the commissioner, during the Whitrod era, using the intelligence it gathered to undermine the enemies of both the police force and the conservative government. Sometimes, this simply meant providing Bjelke-Petersen with information to score points against rivals like Wright. Other times, it meant taking down would-be politicians like Colston and, with him, the entire Labor Party government of Australia.

The cozy relationship between police and government only consolidated under Commissioner Lewis. He was part of an elite group in Queensland that included people like the premier, Lyons, and Vasta. This group protected each other in personal and professional ways, sometimes corruptly. Lewis was empowered to personally intervene to make charges against Lyons disappear and commit perjury to support his friend, Judge Vasta. When Brodeur established the concept of "high policing" in 1983, he talked about how police could be used protect a government from external threats. What he described, though, was not a "secret police" that worked to support a government's political and personal interests, but instead a police force that was dedicated to defending a state's structures and interests. The issue in Queensland was that, over time, the interests of the state became conflated with the interests of the government. As far as the premier was concerned, he led a state at war with left-wing, communist attackers who would destroy the social and moral fabric of Queensland. In this fight, he considered himself as a moral messiah. From his perspective, he alone stood in the way of the state's ruin at the hands of an immoral political movement set on dismantling the conservative society he had built. On that basis, he waged a war using the QPF as his foot-soldiers.

With the premier seeing his government's survival as the last bulwark in conservative Queensland's defenses, his interests became inherently tied to those of the state. High policing, thus, was carried out just as much to protect Bjelke-Petersen and his allies as it was to defend the legitimate interests of Queensland democracy. The police actions to protect its allies were as much about averting threats to the establishment as they were protecting personal friends, and they were reflective of a corrupt nexus that existed in Queensland in the era. If that nexus were personified, it would take the shape of Lane, who bridged the gap between corrupt police and corrupt politicians and worked for years to promote the interests of his former police colleagues in government. Police in Queensland were inextricably linked to political actors, trapped in a death spiral that only ended when the Fitzgerald Inquiry brought down both Bjelke-Petersen and Lewis. Before that, though, the police worked diligently to enforce the government's agenda. No cause was more important to Bjelke-Petersen than asserting his vision of moral order in Queensland. Public enemy number one? The gay community.

CHAPTER 10

Marching to a Different Beat

It was a cold night in the middle of winter—at least to the people of Brisbane, so used to being nestled in the warm embrace of the Sunshine State. Like so many other couples across the city, Max and James spent this Sunday night in early July tucked away in bed at Max's flat in Kangaroo Point, a suburb on the southern banks of the Brisbane River with sweeping views over the growing metropolis on the other side of the water. Max was a dress designer, a career choice that reflected a creative flair that was somewhat unusual for men in 1950s Brisbane, where rugged masculine archetypes were the norm and men were expected to "act like men." His partner James, on the other hand, had a far more conventional job—he worked in a bank. There was an age-gap between the couple: James was thirty-nine years old, roughly twelve years Max's senior. James and Max's relationship was a mature and committed one, but even so the pair had not yet lost the passion of new love. They did not live together on a full-time basis, so they looked forward to their time together.[1]

Max and James did not notice that there was anyone else in the bedroom until the light was abruptly switched on and all hell started to break loose. Standing at the foot of the bed were James Clough and Charles Hackett Scanlan, senior detectives with the Queensland Police Force (QPF). Unbeknownst to Max and James, the two detectives had been watching them for some time before they broke into the apartment to interrupt their cozy night in. The police had been tipped off to Max and James's illicit affair by Max's landlady, who had gotten her hands on love letters sent by the pair and supplied them to her friends in the force. She then took things a step further, providing Clough and Scanlan with a ladder and drill that the detectives used to make a hole through the wall of Max's apartment. For how long Clough and Scanlan watched Max and James from this spot is unclear. What is clear is that Max and James were in the throes of passion when the police finally made the decision to enter the property and arrest them both.

Max was charged with having "carnal knowledge" of James, who was charged with the no less serious charge of having permitted it. When the case came before court, both men pleaded not guilty to committing an offense. Under Queensland law at the time, police had to have proof that penetration had occurred in order to obtain a conviction, and with neither Max or James willing to testify against each other, the only evidence that it had even taken place was the testimony of Clough and Scanlan. The police officers said that they had witnessed sex taking place from their hole in the wall. Lawyers for Max and James argued that, with the lights off in the apartment, it was impossible to tell what was happening in the bedroom. Alas, the jury were not persuaded by this argument. Max was sentenced to four-years imprisonment, though he managed to have this reduced to nine months on appeal. James was less fortunate, receiving a five-year sentence and eventually being released after serving two-and-a-half years in prison.[2]

On first look, the Kangaroo Point case reflects nothing more than the continuation of the police's role as arbiters of social control in Queensland. Since its foundation as a separate colony in June 1859, there were laws on the books in Queensland regulating male same-sex acts. Most of these early colonial laws were carried over from the British system, which provided the basic principles of jurisprudence for each of the colonies that eventually came together to form Australia in 1901. Statutes prohibiting male homosexuality had originally entered into British law with the collapse of the ecclesiastical courts in the sixteenth century, a time when many acts previously treated as "moral offenses" were assimilated into civil law system. The Buggery Act 1533 was one of the first to enshrine moral offenses in British common law. The act, which remained in place for nearly three hundred years, made anal intercourse punishable by execution. Execution continued to be a potential punishment for sodomy under British law until 1861, when the Offences Against the Person Act was passed. This new law set a tariff of up to ten years in prison for sodomy convictions. Queensland formally repealed the death penalty for male same-sex offenses in 1865. However, there is no evidence that any executions were ever carried out for such a crime in the new colony. In all cases where the death penalty was applied for a homosexual offense in colonial Queensland, judges commuted the sentence to a term of imprisonment instead. Even then, there was very little public support for applying the death penalty in such cases, and the rationalization of the law in 1865 to repeal the death penalty was generally accepted (even welcomed) by Queenslanders.[3]

When Queensland became a state of a newly federated Australia in 1901, a review of all the colony's existing laws took place. The debate over the inclusion of same-sex acts in the Criminal Code 1899 was surprisingly progressive by the standards of the period. Then-premier Samuel Griffith, later Australia's first chief justice, argued vehemently in parliament that it was impossible to police the sexual habits of citizens and that there was no public support for this type of moral policing in Queensland. He said:

> There are some things which to every decent-minded man are criminal and ought to be so treated, and there are others which, although they are thought wrong, stand upon a different basis from that which we consider a crime ... As practical men we should bear in mind that we are dealing with human nature as it exists in the world.[4]

If Griffith had succeeded in rationalizing the criminal code at this early stage, almost a century of criminalization experienced by the gay community in Queensland could have been avoided. Instead, his call for repeal was dismissed by the Queensland parliament, and several statutory offenses were included in the Criminal Code 1899. Under section 208 of the act, anal intercourse became punishable by up to fourteen years in prison, and even an *attempt* to commit anal intercourse (essentially, solicitation) could earn an offender a seven-year sentence. In some ways, the Criminal Code 1899 went further than previous legislation. Moving past a preoccupation with anal sex, the act also outlawed acts of "gross indecency"—a term that was intended to cover nonpenetrative acts like masturbation or oral sex. Any person found to have committed an act of gross indecency (or even having attempted to commit one) was liable to be sentenced to up to three years in prison. There was a gendered aspect to the laws around homosexuality in Queensland. It was not against to law to identify as being LGBTQI+, but rather the sexual acts themselves that were criminalized.

The language used in the Criminal Code 1899 was a remnant of the colonial era and explicitly prohibited acts such as anal intercourse and male-on-male "gross indecency."[5] While the Criminal Code 1899 caused gay men to be vulnerable to prosecution if they practiced their sexuality, it left a loophole in state law that meant that, while it was illegal to be a practicing gay man, it was technically legal to be a practicing gay woman in Queensland.

The specific criminalization of male homosexuality in Queensland gives the impression of a colonial society attempting to deter behavior that was socially constructed as deviant and, in turn, reinforce a conservative status quo. While there is some merit in this perspective, it is ultimately reductive. There were as many sociocultural factors at play in Queensland that supported the development of a vibrant LGBTQI+ subculture as there were that contributed to its repression. Queensland was burgeoning frontier society where many young men from around Australia and the world came to make their fortunes on the vast expanses of arable land that were on offer. The hypermasculine gender dynamics of colonial Queensland resulted in a colony and later a state that historian Raymond Evans describes as "rambunctious, brash, violent and larrikin" with little tolerance for bohemian, "femininized, or otherwise divergent forms of masculinity.[6] At the same time, a profound gender imbalance led to a notable increase in the rate of situational homosexuality in Queensland, in which otherwise "straight" men had clandestine sexual relationships with other men due to a lack of access to women and often considerable alcohol consumption. Intentionally distanced from the "feminized" masculinity traditionally associated with gay men, men engaged in this practice mostly "passed" for straight and conformed to the heteronormative paradigms of colonial Queensland society. Importantly, men who had sex with other men in this frontier culture often did not self-identify as being homosexual. This is common in settler societies where traditional masculinity has a privileged position. In Europe, situational homosexuality was widespread in the late-nineteenth century through all-male military battalions, exploratory expeditions, and penal colonies.[7] Even the most persistent model of masculinity, the American cowboy, participated in same-sex relationships. With limited access to women on the frontier of the Wild West (with some exceptions), the lines between male socialization and homosexuality became increasingly blurred to the point that "bachelor marriages" between cowboys were not unusual.[8] In each of these scenarios, men experienced a shared existential conflict: the drive for physical intimacy, yet the need to reject any identification with a deviant, feminized sexual lifestyle.

Rapid urban growth in the colonial period also contributed to the way that same-sex relationships between men were practiced in Queensland. Situated in the state's southeast corner, Brisbane served as a natural hub for most of those who came to Queensland searching for employment opportunities. It did not take long before the city's infrastructure reached capacity, fostering what has been referred to as "boarding house society" where migrant workers—mostly men—were forced to live in close quarters with each other, sharing the limited accommodation that existed or sleeping rough on the streets of the capital. Whether gay or straight, this scenario meant a distinct lack of privacy for Queenslanders looking to have a sexual relationship. Privacy was especially limited for gay men. While their straight counterparts could still have sex with women in the presence of those men they shared accommodation with or use the services of a brothel, these options did not exist for the gay men who sought to practice their sexuality in a covert manner. Under these conditions the first "beats" began to form, a subcultural development for Brisbane's gay community that had lasting implications on the way that homosexuality was policed in Queensland well into the future.

The "gay beat" is a feature of LGBTQI+ communities around the world, referred to in other places with terms like "cottaging" in the United Kingdom or "cruising" in the United States. It refers to the use of communal public spaces by the gay community as venues for sexual encounters. In an era where male same-sex acts were formally criminalized, there was a real absence of places that gay men could go to safely meet each other and strike up a relationship. The beats filled this gap. In Brisbane, beats existed in secluded areas along the Brisbane River, while others could be found in the abandoned quarries of inner-city Spring Hill or near train and bus stations in the city's central business district (CBD).[9] Using these kinds of places gave those who attended a degree of plausible deniability. Men could provide a reasonable explanation for being in these spaces if seen by someone they knew and discreetly maintain a façade of heteronormativity. This was an incredibly important rationale for using public spaces as beats considering that many men frequenting these areas were not openly gay. In his ethnographic observation of beats in New York City in the 1970s (referred to as the "tearoom trade"), Laud Humphreys found that 38 percent of those attending beat spaces identified as neither gay nor bisexual and an additional 24 percent were characterized as "covertly" gay men, often living outwardly heterosexual lives outside of the beat.[10] If the cultural pressures of traditional masculinity in Humphreys's New York City were strong enough to foster a clandestine beat culture, the social conditions driving this covert practice in colonial

Brisbane were even more aggressive. Beats were governed by a set of implicit rules and codes that assisted men in recognizing others who were there looking for sex. A man who wanted to solicit another man for sex might maintain eye contact, simultaneously brushing against them or otherwise making physical contact. The signs could be subtle, like a wink or nod of the head, or they could be overt and verbal, like asking if the other man had a cigarette lighter that they could use.[11] In any other context, these would be treated as ordinary nonsymbolic interactions. The beat space itself imbues them with a meaning that is only understood by those partaking in these covert subcultural rituals.

There is an abiding view that gay beats are inherently transitory venues for sexual activity—places for opportunistic trysts, used for sex before returning to their intended purpose. The historical tradition in Brisbane shows that this is most certainly not the case. Court records show that the same locations were used over long periods of time. The same quarry in Spring Hill featured as a venue for male same-sex offenses in criminal trials more than a decade apart in 1914 and 1925.[12] Even more profoundly, gay men were arrested for same-sex acts that occurred at the beat under the Victoria Bridge from as early as the 1890s until after decriminalization in 1990, meaning that it had nearly a century-long history as a gay space in Brisbane.[13] That the same spaces were routinely used is not coincidental. The unwritten rules had to have been learned from somewhere. Not knowing the signals marked the individual as an outsider to the beat, a potential risk, and prohibited them from participating in the sexual encounters. It must be assumed, therefore, that the specific methods of signaling intent and the "rules of the beat" were passed down on a subcultural level in an expression of community-building behavior. However, as noted, these signals would not have the same meaning if not for the context of the space in which they were used. It stands to reason, then, that not only were the rules transmitted within the gay community, but so too were the locations where men could solicit for same-sex encounters. Instead of a convenient and temporally fleeting location for public transgression, this suggests that the beat was a semipermanent space with considerable subcultural significance to the gay community.

The semipermanent nature of the beat is fascinating from a subcultural standpoint, yet from a practical perspective it also allowed members of the QPF to target men who used these spaces. As the case of Max and James highlighted, the post-war period was typified by the renewed efforts of police to reassert the moral order in Queensland. While it was a catalyst for social change across the country, there is arguably nowhere in Australia that felt the sociocultural impact of World War II more directly than Brisbane. The capital served as the headquarters for the Allied forces in the Pacific region from July 1942 until the formal cessation of conflict in September 1945. Serving as a major regional outpost triggered extensive changes in Brisbane, not the least of which being the influx of American servicemen who were stationed there during the war. In the three-year period from July 1942 to September 1945, around two million American troops were posted to Brisbane.[14] For the most part, civilian police in Queensland were not responsible for policing the troops. That responsibility fell to the military police, most of whom did not prioritize the policing of moral offenses committed by troops.

Views on sexual morality experienced a significant shift in 1940s wartime Brisbane. Prostitution became increasingly tolerated and organized, largely because of the increased demand for sexual services that accompanied the arrival of American troops. Seen as another "moral offense," homosexuality was also not actively policed in this era. Although the real rate is impossible to ascertain, estimates suggest that anywhere from eighty thousand to two hundred thousand visiting American servicemen were either gay or open to same-sex encounters in wartime.[15] A combination of factors led to the development of a relatively open gay scene in Brisbane in the mid-1940s, partly the result of lax enforcement of same-sex offenses and, in other ways, influenced by elements of gay culture introduced by soldiers from around the world. In any case, just as the American troops were leaving Brisbane in 1945, a visible gay community emerged that was a prime target for police harassment in the years that followed.

For a police force that was desperately seeking to reassert its authority in the wake of three years of military rule, the Pink Elephant affair was an early sign that moral offenses were in the firing line once more. During World War II, gay culture in Brisbane was centered on the city's coffeehouses, where a mix of gay men, lesbians, bohemians, and artists regularly gathered to socialize. Of these coffeehouses, the Pink Elephant Café on Adelaide Street was one of the best-known—and most notorious. It was dimly lit and atmospheric, the closest thing to a nineteenth-century French salon that Brisbane had. Constable Joseph Larkin told a Brisbane court that the reputation of the Pink Elephant among police was that it was "a den of vice, and a place where undesirables congregated." On further questioning, he admitted that the only "undesirables" that he ever found at the Pink Elephant were "effeminate-looking men," which indicates that there was a clear conflation in the police force of the post-war era between gay men and social "desirability," as well as, seemingly, their corrosive effect on traditional masculinity, to the point that a gay-oriented café could be described as a "den of vice."[16]

These perceptions reached boiling point on 2 October 1946, when two detectives from the Consorting Squad entered the café on the hunt for "a pervert who had been stealing rings and money." One of these officers, Scanlan, should be familiar—he was one of the two officers involved in the sting operation leading to the arrest of Max and James in 1950. After entering the Pink Elephant, Scanlan's partner Merton Hopgood accused city commission agent Douglas Morton Murray of using obscene language and took him into custody. Murray later claimed that Hopgood and Scanlan were drunk when they came to the Pink Elephant and that Hopgood had viciously beaten Murray after taking him into custody.[17] The charges against Murray were ultimately dismissed because an appeals court judge found Hopgood and Scanlan's evidence "untrustworthy," but negative publicity surrounding the case had irreparably damaged the Pink Elephant.[18] Focusing in on the salacious nature of the café as a gathering place for the gay community, the local tabloid press had constructed the venue as a place that "reeked of perversion."[19] Because of this, owner Frank Mitchell closed the café and left Brisbane shortly after Murray's trial concluded. Shutting the Pink Elephant was more significant than the closure of a single establishment. It showed that police harassment could force Brisbane's gay community underground—if not by direct force, then by portraying them as "perverts" and "deviants" in order to tarnish their reputation on the public stage.

Harassing the patrons of gay bars to force their closure was a strategy that was commonplace around the world in the years after the Pink Elephant incident. Only two years after Scanlan and Hopgood drunkenly stumbled into the Brisbane café, the San Francisco Police Department launched its own campaign to force the gay-friendly Black Cat Bar out of business. Just as the QPF referred to the Pink Elephant as a "den of vice," police in San Francisco brought charges against the Black Cat's owner Sol Stoumen for "keeping a disorderly house."[20] Stoumen successfully won a case against the State of California in the Supreme Court affirming his right to serve the gay community in 1951, but not unlike the case of the Pink Elephant more than a decade prior, continued targeting by local police forced the Black Cat's closure in 1963. Harassment continued to be a method used by police to assert control over gay bars in the years that followed, notable as a key factor in the 1969 Stonewall riot in New York City.

Criminalization of homosexuality (or, more accurately, gay sex acts) was an area of law that was changing in many jurisdictions around the world in the twentieth century. In 1955, the American Law Institute voted to decriminalize consensual sodomy—in essence, among other things, legalizing gay sex—and, as such, did not include these anti-gay laws in their drafting of a Model Penal Code for the United States.[21] The problem with a federalized system like the United States, however, is that it is the responsibility of individual states to adopt legal "guidelines" such as the Model Penal Code. With widespread moral opposition to homosexuality in some states, the decriminalization of consensual sodomy and other gay sex acts remained inconsistent across the country. Ultimately, criminalizing gay sex was determined to be an infringement on citizens' Fourteenth Amendment rights to exercise their personal liberty by the U.S. Supreme Court in *Lawrence v. Texas*, though not until 2003.[22] Meanwhile, in the United Kingdom, reform occurred much earlier. A commission led by Sir John Wolfenden convened in 1954 to consider changes to a raft of offenses, including homosexual crimes. When the Wolfenden Report was released in 1957 it rejected both criminalization *and* medicalization, finding that homosexuality should no longer be treated as a crime or illness.[23] Despite this firm recommendation, change was still slow. As in Australia, the United Kingdom was experiencing a period of resurgent conservatism that stifled attempts at instituting the Wolfenden reforms. After a decade, gay sex acts were eventually decriminalized in the Sexual Offences Act 1967.[24]

Similar to the United States, Australia is a federal system where most criminal law is crafted by the states rather than the national government. Because of this, the road to decriminalization was patchwork, and while several states started the reform process in the 1970s, gay sex continued to be criminalized in others until the 1990s. It was not a public inquiry like Wolfenden's that triggered change in Australia but a shocking death. The brutal killing of Adelaide academic George Duncan, a gay man, in 1972 triggered a shift in public opinion, and by 1975 the South Australian government became the first in the country to decriminalize homosexuality.[25] Duncan, a university lecturer, had been thrown into the River Torrens close to a popular gay beat. Witness reports caused police to believe that the offenders were a group of Vice Squad officers who were known for harassing gay men on the beat, though this was never proven. Other southern states gradually began to follow South Australia in decriminalizing homosexuality over the next decade, yet in the deep north of Queensland the Bjelke-Petersen government remained firm in their moral opposition to the "perverse" sexual practice. The premier was at the forefront of the campaign to eradicate the gay community from Queensland, placing the blame for the state's apparent moral decline on its southern neighbors. In August

1984, Joh Bjelke-Petersen publicly referred to gay men as "insulting evil animals who should go back to New South Wales and Victoria where they came from in the first place."[26] The instinct to blame more liberal, urbane southern states for Queensland's perceived moral decline was not a new one, nor was it original to Bjelke-Petersen. The same explanation was offered by police for the bodgie culture of the 1950s, the "hippie" activism in the 1960s, *and* the punk scene in the 1970s—all of which were also treated by Queenslanders as a southern import.

The threat of being exposed as a gay man was key to the agent provocateur sting used by Queensland police in the 1960s as a means of extorting members of Brisbane's gay community. In policing parlance, this was a tactic in which an undercover officer incited a target to commit an unlawful act. The agent provocateur strategy inevitably raises a few ethical concerns, not the least of which is where the blurred line between provocation and entrapment lies. In most jurisdictions, the distinction is an arbitrary one. It is usually considered to be a legitimate tactic if there is a reasonable belief that the offender had preexisting intention to commit the crime in question, while an unlawful entrapment has occurred if the offenses incited by the agent provocateur never would have happened absent the intervention of undercover police. When it came to policing the gay population of post-war Queensland, the agent provocateur approach was routinely employed as a way of securing convictions against gay men. As noted earlier, the laws governing gay sex necessitated that police satisfied a burden of proof that an offense had taken place. Because of the closed nature of the gay community at this time, and the rarity of consensual sexual partners testifying against each other, reaching this standard of proof was often a challenge for police. As a result, they were forced to adopt innovative covert strategies to achieve their goals. Officers in the Kangaroo Point case went to the extent of drilling a hole in the wall of an adjoining apartment solely so they could visually witness Max and James having penetrative sex, which in turn allowed them to lay charges on the couple. In the beat space, a different covert strategy was needed—one that required police officers to pose as gay men themselves.

Section 211 of the Criminal Code 1899 made it a crime for a man to perform an act of "gross indecency" with another man or even to make attempts to solicit such an act. There was no need for police to prove that any sexual contact had occurred, only that an attempt had been made. Of all the anti-gay provisions in the Criminal Code 1899, this was the one that required the lowest standard of proof to be achieved and opened the door for the use of agent provocateur techniques. The role of the covert operative in these cases was simply to elicit a sexual advance from another man, making the known beat spaces around the city fertile hunting grounds for officers looking to make arrests. The beat spaces thrived because their locations were well-known within the Brisbane's gay community, but the Queensland police were also privy to this information. It was a case of institutional knowledge, handed down by senior officers with years of experience policing the city's gay spaces. As the attention of police turned to reasserting the moral order in the post-war period, the safety of the beat space was intrinsically compromised. In a sense, these spaces became traps for gay men. The very nature of the beat was that men approached strangers and solicited sexual acts, a risky proposition at the best of times, but even more so when any of these strangers could be an agent provocateur.

William Nation Leslie, a forty-one-year-old schoolteacher, was arrested on 6 September 1967 after visiting the Eagle Street public toilet block in Brisbane's CBD. In his version of events, he had driven into town from suburban Coorparoo and enjoyed a few scotches before doing some shopping on nearby Queen Street.[27] At this point, the need to relieve himself became too much for him to bear, resulting in his fateful visit to the nearby public facilities. If this is true, it was an unfortunately timed bathroom break. The toilet block under the iconic Fig Tree on Eagle Street was a notorious and well-attended gay beat in the middle of the Brisbane CBD and a regular target of police sting operations. Leslie claimed to be unaware of the salacious reputation of the Fig Tree toilets, yet when Detective John Fulton approached him and offered to buy him a drink, Leslie responded in a way that indicates he was aware of the subcultural cues that dictated interactions on the beat. If Leslie was telling the truth and he was not aware of the Fig Tree beat, his agreement to join Fulton in his car for a cigarette was, once again, a very unfortunate coincidence. The trap was sprung the moment that Leslie stepped into the car. Fulton's partner Lawrence Welldon appeared out of the darkness and told Leslie that he would be charged under section 211 of the Criminal Code 1899 for attempting to solicit a sexual act from Fulton.[28]

The threat to charge Leslie for solicitation is a curious one, and it is unclear if his actions genuinely constituted a breach of the criminal code. Consider that, in 1950, police went to extreme lengths to observe Max and James having sex in order to provide the evidence required for conviction. Leslie had not overtly propositioned Fulton, nor had he even physically touched the undercover officer. From a sociological perspective, we can analyze his actions and speculate that he did know the subcultural procedures of the beat, and that his actions may have constituted a prelude to solicitation. Nevertheless, there is considerable doubt whether these subtle cues would have been treated as indisputable evidence of an offense in a court of law. What mattered in this case was that Leslie believed that he was vulnerable to prosecution for solicitation, because it was not long after Welldon appeared to arrest him that a proposition was made. Initially driving Leslie towards the police station for processing, Welldon and Fulton abruptly stopped not far from the Fig Tree toilets on Creek Street. The officers told Leslie that they would forget charging him with a crime in return for the $7 in his wallet and a further $100 to be paid on the following Monday.[29] Leslie was a teacher at a Church of England school and a married man. Desperately seeking to avoid the public humiliation and repercussions of facing court as a gay offender, he agreed to the offer and was released from "custody."[30]

Leslie was certainly not the first person extorted by Welldon and Fulton after being entrapped in the beat space. The pair were arrested for a similar incident earlier in 1967 where they were seen in a public bar receiving $200 from another man they accused of solicitation and making "a threat that he would be locked up if he did not comply."[31] After this case was brought to the attention of police investigators, Leslie's name was discovered in Welldon's and Fulton's police notebooks along with scores of others who it must be assumed were targeted as part of their racket. Unusually for police officers in the 1960s, Welldon and Fulton faced court for their crimes and were sentenced to five years in prison. While these two rogue operators were taken off the streets, the threat to Queensland's gay community was by no means eradicated. At the time of the Welldon and Fulton case, around 25 percent of gay men in Brisbane reported having experienced violence, blackmail, or otherwise negative experiences with the police.[32] It can only be assumed that this number was in reality much higher. As Leslie's case showed, blackmailers like Welldon and Fulton preyed on men who had much to lose from being publicly revealed as gay or at least as men who sought out same-sex affairs. These statistics are derived from the openly gay community, and so if the clandestinely gay population was also included, it is probable that the rate of harassment was significantly higher. Blackmail and extortion of the gay community continued long after Welldon and Fulton, becoming ever more organized and sophisticated as it did.

Aside from the fear of public exposure that plagued Queensland's gay community during this era, the tangible threat of violence was viscerally reinforced by the murder of Gary Venamore in November 1968. A significant number of the men targeted in beat spaces preferred to maintain their anonymity, understandably deciding not to be open with their sexuality at a time when conservative values were once more on the ascent in Queensland. Venamore was different. He was a social animal, referred to around Brisbane as "the gay, witty, exuberant life of the party" and known as someone who liked a drink (perhaps a little too much at times).[33] Ross Beer, lead detective on Venamore's case, called the victim a contradiction, someone who was a ladies' man and playboy when sober, but "when he got on the drink he was a raving homosexual." Indeed, Venamore was out with work colleagues in the city's bars on 5 November 1968—the last night of his life. At about 8:30 p.m. that night, he left his colleagues and told them he was going home. He didn't. Instead, he ended up at Petrie Bight, an area of the city known for the thriving vice trade that operated out of its bars and hotels. He wasn't seen for two hours from the time he left his colleagues in the CBD until 10:30 p.m., when he arrived at the door of the Playboy Club.[34] Investigating officers suggested that Venamore might have spent some or all of that time cruising the beat for sex. After all, he would have had to pass the Fig Tree toilet block on his walk from the city to Petrie Bight. It is only speculation that he went to a beat on that night, but it fits the police narrative that his murder was a gay-related crime, perhaps the product of an unwanted advance by the victim on his killer.

The last confirmed sighting of Venamore alive was when he left the Playboy Club at around 2:30 a.m. along with two unidentified men. Several hours later, his badly beaten body was pulled from the Brisbane River. His liver was ruptured, and it appeared that he had been bashed. Bruises on his wrists led medical examiner John Tonge to believe he was thrown into the river by at least two men. Tonge estimated Venamore had drowned at around 4 a.m.[35] Because of this, as well as the antemortem bruising on his wrists, it was clear that Venamore was still clinging to life when he was thrown into the water. He was not the first gay man in Queensland to be murdered in brutal fashion, but the ultraviolent nature of his death and his social prominence meant that the case received more attention than it might have otherwise. Two of the state's most decorated detectives, Beer and Glen Hallahan, were appointed to lead the investigation. Despite this, the trail of Venamore's killers very quickly went cold. The failure of the investigation was blamed in part on the reluctance of the gay community to cooperate with police. Because of Venamore's sexuality and the suggestion that he had a history of attending beat spaces, Beer and Hallahan attempted to interview as many members of the city's gay community as possible in the hopes that they might be able to provide information that led to the killer. At almost every turn, they were confronted with a brick wall of silence.

Those who did talk told Beer and Hallahan that there had been many vicious bashings of gay men in Brisbane in the period prior to Venamore's death, but that the community feared that reporting these incidents would lead to victims being exposed as gay and putting themselves at risk of further harassment, if not criminal prosecution.

Venamore's case was not the only murder investigation impacted by the gay community's reluctance to cooperate with police. Eight years later, the murder of Rex Kable Keen at the Lennon's Plaza Hotel was another investigation that came to a screeching halt because of the deep distrust of police. Keen, a forty-six-year-old from regional Bowen, was found stabbed to death in his hotel room in August 1976 while visiting the capital for a medical appointment. Shortly before his death, he had been seen drinking with another man at the Carlton Crest Hotel.[36] He was last seen in his hotel room by room service staff, who also saw a man in the room matching the description of Keen's drinking partner from the Carlton Crest. The presence of this unidentified man led police to believe that Keen might have been the victim of a gay tryst gone wrong. Items had been taken from his hotel room, and police believed that he could have been targeted for robbery by an offender preying on gay men.[37] For almost forty-three years, this line of inquiry could not be dismissed because, as with Venamore's case, Brisbane's gay community were paranoid about the repercussions of revealing themselves to the police. A suspect was ultimately arrested and charged with the murder of Keen in June 2019.[38]

Under the circumstances, gay men were right to be fearful of exposing their sexuality to police. After his work on the Venamore case, Hallahan had the idea for a lucrative new venture. Like Welldon and Fulton before him, Hallahan set his sights on Brisbane's beat spaces—in particular, the Fig Tree toilet block on Eagle Street. His plan was detailed in a statement from whistle-blower Shirley Brifman, a former sex worker turned brothel madam who enjoyed both a professional and personal relationship with Hallahan for much of the 1960s. Brifman told internal affairs investigators that Hallahan decided to add the extortion of gay men to his portfolio of corrupt dealings after his involvement in Venamore's case, when he realized that the patrons of beats would pay any price to avoid being identified as gay. One night, lips loosened by a combination of alcohol and marijuana, he told her: "The businessmen who are homosexuals you would not believe it . . . We pulled in the businessmen one by one and the businessmen would arrive at the Eagle Street toilets, meet different ones and leave with them."[39] Unlike Welldon and Fulton's agent provocateur strategy, the approach Hallahan took to extortion was more passive and hands-off. He told her that he set up recording cameras outside the Eagle Street beat. Considering his record of using police resources to support his corruption, it is very possible that he used Queensland police property to do this, claiming it was necessary to identify a suspect in Venamore's case, or a similar pretense. After reviewing the tapes, Hallahan would pick a target and bring them to the station for questioning. Most of the time, he focused on the "big fish." If what he told Brifman is correct, there were a number of prominent businessmen who used the Eagle Street beat. It was a fact well-known to Hallahan that the more a person had to lose, the more that they would pay to keep their sexual preference secret. After presenting his target with the video recordings of them, Hallahan made an offer: a hefty lump sum payment or charges would be laid. In some instances, he told Brifman that cash was substituted for a favor to be named at a later date. He evidently remembered the threat of the National Hotel Inquiry earlier in the 1960s and knew that holding blackmail evidence against powerful individuals was a good way of protecting himself if ever again exposed to the same type of risk. Whatever blackmail material that Hallahan had, it did not protect him totally, because by 1971 he had been forced from the QPF, the result of a separate internal affairs investigation into his long-suspected corrupt relationship with sex workers.[40]

On this matter, like so many others, the Queensland police acted as enforcers of government policy on the streets. From the perspective of the Bjelke-Petersen government, this was a completely justified use of police powers to monitor and deter a group seen as subversive and who posed a tangible threat to the collective values shared by all Queenslanders. The uptick in enforcing anti-gay laws had driven the community underground during the immediate post-war era, and once again the police were issued a directive to enforce the moral order. Being labelled as "outlaws" had a real impact on the gay community in the early 1980s, a time when the LGBTQI+ population internationally were being forced to reckon with the existential threat of HIV/AIDS. In fact, the police crackdown in Queensland was a contributing factor to worsening the impact of HIV/AIDS in the state. Local campaigner Phil Carswell claims "it was made clear to [him] that anyone openly identifying as a spokesperson for a gay organization would be subject to Special Branch and other police scrutiny and harassment... there was a genuine and well-founded fear of actual physical violence."[41] The fear of prosecution or worse once again dissuaded the gay community from gathering in public, or seeking advice from support groups about how to avoid contracting HIV or what to do if it did happen.

This passive social control of the gay community was not the only way that

Bjelke-Petersen sought to use the police to enforce his puritanical version of sexual morality. Aside from the HIV/AIDS scare, the early 1980s also saw a concerted campaign by the government to conflate gay men with pedophilia as a means of justifying increasingly repressive laws. Focus turned to the increase of "gay bars" in the city, a phenomenon that the government insisted represented a shift in the state's moral fabric even though gay-friendly venues had existed in Queensland since at least the coffeehouse era of the early twentieth century. Gay bars across the city were placed under regular police surveillance. Ultimately, state cabinet agreed in 1985 to amend the Liquor Act to make it an offense to serve "drug dealers, sexual perverts or deviants or child molesters on licensed premises."[42] While not explicitly referring to the gay community in the text of the law, Attorney-General Neville Harper was vocal that the amendment was designed to ensure that "these gay bars will not be allowed to continue and to prosper."[43] These laws were yet another example of the Bjelke-Petersen government seeking to extend the powers of police, effectively providing them carte blanche to harass the gay community in what was previously one of their few safe spaces to gather in public.[44] Just as moves towards decriminalization of homosexuality were gaining traction in other states around Australia, conservative Queensland tightened the noose around its LGBTQI+ population, further straining relations between police and the gay community.

Right until the end of his tenure as premier, Bjelke-Petersen fought a ceaseless battle against Queensland's gay community. Shortly before his removal from power in 1987, he once again used the police as stormtroopers in his moral crusade. On 31 August, coordinated police raids on the University of Queensland and Griffith University occurred. The target? Condom vending machines that had been placed in the universities' bathrooms. With condom vending machines prohibited under the Health Act, Queensland universities were forced to comply, but they turned a blind eye to condom machines that were installed in student union buildings in contravention of the law. Bjelke-Petersen asserted that these vending machines were the beginning of a "slippery road" and said that, rather than practicing safe sex, gay Queenslanders should "stop that horrible lifestyle they're living in."[45] Cabinet records from 1988 show that he was highly concerned with "preventing the spread [of HIV/AIDS] into the general heterosexual population," and so it is curious that he would remove condom machines also presumably used by heterosexual couples to practice safe sex.[46] However, under the premier's strict Lutheran worldview, it was not just gay sex that was sinful, but all premarital intercourse. Condom vending machines were not *just* a reflection of gay immorality, but symptomatic of a broader moral permissiveness that he had been fighting against since at least the 1960s. Police responded to Bjelke-Petersen's order to remove the condom vending machines with enthusiasm, smashing windows to gain access to them and using crowbars to pry them off the walls. The destructive potential of the QPF was once more harnessed in pursuit of the Bjelke-Petersen's moral agenda. He sanctioned all police action, no matter how excessive it was. Sixteen years before, he had told police to use whatever means necessary to disperse the protests against the Springboks. Here, again, the police were given carte blanche to break their way into university campuses and forcibly rip condom machines from the walls. Amid a sweeping HIV/AIDS epidemic, the Queensland police acted at the behest of their conservative paymasters to put the gay community and sexually active Queenslanders in general at increasing risk of harm.

Less than a year after the anti-condom campaign, with Fitzgerald continuing to reveal the extent of corruption in Queensland, Bjelke-Petersen and Police Commissioner Terry Lewis were removed from power. The election of the Goss Labor Party government in 1990 marked an end to more than three decades of conservative rule in the state. One of Wayne Goss's first policy initiatives was to reform the Criminal Code 1899, decriminalizing homosexuality in line both with the recommendations of the Fitzgerald Inquiry and the precedent set by most other states in Australia. Decriminalization put a legislative end to much of the discrimination and harassment faced by Queensland's gay community. Even so, after such a lengthy tradition of aggressive enforcement, it was inevitable that a cloud of suspicion and distrust shadowed the police and community relations for a long period of time after. For many, the process of decriminalization was not the result of a gradual shift in community attitudes as it was in other places. Whereas other states like South Australia slowly came to the decision to reform anti-gay laws, decriminalization in Queensland came with the change of government and an overhaul of the entire system of policing. It was only a matter of a few years between legislative reform and the most senior public figures in Queensland referring to the gay community as "evil," "deviant," and "perverts." Changing the law might have meant that gay men were no longer threatened with jail time for their sexual preferences, but the fear of police harassment in the community continued for some time after decriminalization. A new compact had to be negotiated between the community and police, one that had its foundations in a recognition of historical wrongs. For many who lived through the violence and fear of the criminalization period, this reconciliation will never be achieved—the wounds of the past remain too strong to overcome.

Twentieth-century Queensland has been routinely described as a police state, a place where any deviance no matter how minor could result in police harassment and persecution. Arguably, there is no community that felt the moralistic rage of the police state more than gay Queenslanders. Some, like Venamore, never received justice. Some, like Max and James, were thrown in jail. Some, like Leslie, were blackmailed and extorted. Some never received the help they needed during the HIV/AIDS crisis, in fear that doing so might put them at greater risk of harassment. They were called "evil perverts" by the political establishment and treated with disdain by police. The case of Queensland's gay community was a clear example of how virulent strains of puritanical moralism can infect a police force. The historical evidence does not suggest that all police were homophobic. Some no doubt were, but the archival record shows something even more sinister. Police used the criminalization of gay men not as a chance to prosecute their own moral agenda but instead to line their pockets. The state may have been responsible for putting a target on gay men, but it was corrupt police who often set their own price.

The criminalization period was not a time when gay men were rounded up en masse to be imprisoned for their sexual preference, as the Criminal Code allowed for. What was more important was the threat that the anti-gay laws posed, ever-present and threatening to destroy their lives. Understandably, gay men were willing to do anything to evade going to prison for who they happened to love. Police were acutely aware that this disposition made gay men easy targets for extortion. Though police executed the Criminal Code's provisions against sodomy relatively rarely as the years went on, criminalization allowed the informal victimization of gay men to continue into the 1990s, when decriminalization took place as part of a raft of post-Fitzgerald reforms. Here we see a different case of the government-police connection working together to facilitate corruption. Criminalization of gay men was mutually beneficial, a pillar in the conservative Bjelke-Petersen agenda on one hand and, on the other, creating easy prey for industrious and corrupt police. No matter the rationale behind criminalization, mercenary or political, the QPF's treatment of the gay community represents a stain on the history of the force that will not easily wash away—or be forgotten.

CHAPTER 11

The Curious Case of Constable Dave

Sergeant Peter Gallagher never knew exactly what he was walking into when he arrived at work. As one of the top cops in the Brisbane Criminal Investigation Branch (CIB), it was his job to take charge of a diverse range of crimes in the capital, major and minor. He was especially notorious for his aggressive approach to shoplifters. Store security guards from across the city called him directly when they collared an offender, confident that the straight-as-an-arrow officer would actually go through with prosecuting them.[1] Some days it was shoplifters and other petty criminals, but other days were more complicated. When Gallagher arrived to work just before 6 a.m. on 19 January 1984, he immediately knew it was going to be one of those more complicated days. Sitting in the foyer of the police building was a disheveled, panicked teenage boy. Gallagher approached the boy, asking what he was doing there. Ricky Garrison had a story to tell about a man named Paul Breslin. He said that, at some point in the early hours of the morning, Breslin picked him up somewhere near Victoria Bridge, a historical gay beat in the Brisbane central business district (CBD). Garrison was taken to one of Breslin's properties, an apartment at the high-end Coronation Towers in the inner-west suburb Auchenflower, where Breslin drugged and sexually assaulted him before putting him into a taxi and sending him away.[2] For some police, it would have been

178 | Chapter Eleven

a strange and unbelievable story, but not Gallagher. Before Garrison even finished telling his tale, Gallagher was planning his next move. He already knew Breslin. More than that, he raided another of his Brisbane properties only two years before.

Gallagher gathered a team, and taking Garrison with him to identify the Breslin apartment, the team headed straight for Coronation Towers. When he knocked on the door of Number 24, there was no answer. It was not going to be easy to bust the door down. The flat was equipped with three deadlocks in addition to its normal lock.[3] Gallagher knew Breslin was in there, though. He caught glimpses of the curtains moving and thought he saw someone peering through the window watching the police as they gathered outside. Eventually, one of the team called a locksmith friend who gave them access. This was legal under the police rules, the severe nature of the crimes alleged by Garrison justifying warrantless entry under the principles of "fresh pursuit."[4] The team found Breslin in bed, claiming he did not hear the police banging on his door yelling to be let in. The police went to work. The scientific team found traces of semen on Breslin's couch, where Garrison said some of the offenses had taken place. There were other questionable finds in the apartment, too. Gallagher's team discovered a baton and two sets of police-issue handcuffs. One officer, Barry Krosch, found something even more curious: a photo album. Amongst the pictures inside the album were images of a familiar face, not just to police but to a lot of children in Queensland. He called Gallagher over to show him what he found: pictures of the prominent Queensland Police Force (QPF) public relations officer, David Warren Moore, in compromising positions with other young men.[5] Gallagher was shocked but not surprised at the content of the pictures. He had seen pictures like this (maybe even the very same ones) before, two years ago, on the first time he raided one of Breslin's properties. For two years, there had been concerns about "Constable Dave" and the company he kept. Over the course of the next year, those concerns provided a spark that created a firestorm that would burn through the QPF, all the way to the commissioner's office.

The criminalization of gay acts in Queensland was not as simple as a binary, antagonistic relationship between gay men and police. Inevitably, many police serving in the QPF were part of the LGBTQI+ community albeit unable to openly practice their sexuality for fear of the repercussions. There was a real danger to gay officers in the late 1970s, a time when the QPF was described as being a "fearful workplace for homosexuals" where gay police lived in "absolute fear [of being exposed] like it was the Nazis."[6] Brian Marlin was a Licensing Branch officer close to Inspector Alec Jeppesen. He turned on his boss and alleged that Jeppesen was corruptly claiming "informant" payments, causing Terry Lewis to call an investigation that, in the end, led to Jeppesen's demotion.[7] By assisting in the removal of Jeppesen, who was an impediment to the reestablishment of the Joke in the Licensing Branch, Marlin ingratiated himself to the Lewis regime and proved his worth as a police officer who was firmly on board to support the new commissioner in whatever way he could. Without the official support of his superiors, Marlin launched a one man crusade against the LGBTQI+ community in the late 1970s, going undercover at beats and gay bars and writing confidential intelligence reports on aspects of LGBTQI+ culture in Brisbane from the signals used at gay beats to lists of "suspected persons" that he witnessed during his "operations." Some of those he listed as going to LGBTQI+ hotspots in the city were police, and he was not reluctant to turn in his fellow officers, setting him apart from other members of the blue brotherhood who prided themselves on loyalty to the uniform. When completed, Marlin's dossier went to CIB chief Tony Murphy, who ordered surveillance on several of the locations Marlin identified, like the Hacienda Hotel and Rose's Café in Fortitude Valley.[8] Just as Marlin said, serving police officers were among the many people who were witnessed participating in the LGBTQI+ community.

This was not Marlin and Murphy's only collaboration dealing with LGBTQI+ officers. Shortly after, a campaign to root out lesbian officers in the QPF began that was directed personally by Murphy. Despite female same-sex relationships not being illegal under the Queensland Criminal Code, Murphy and Marlin pressed on and in 1977 began calling female officers in for questioning about their sexual preferences. There was little justification behind which female officers were targeted. One of the officers investigated, Lorelle Saunders, noted that "about every policewoman that was doing any active work or stirring to get active work was interviewed in relation to the issue."[9] Most were labelled as former Raymond Whitrod supporters, and it is possible that the Lesbian Investigation was a cover used by Murphy and Marlin to harass female officers seen as being threats to the new commissioner. In cases where two female officers were found to actually be in a sexual relationship, the force used its powers to transfer them to separate locations around the state. Whitrod ally Jill Bolen and her partner were transferred to the regional towns of Mount Isa and Longreach respectively, which Bolen describes as a purposeful "witch hunt" designed to disrupt relationships and ramp up the pressure to force the "enemies" of the Rat Pack out of the police force entirely.[10] Despite this, lesbian officers were not the subject of the same degree of fervent harassment as gay male officers, which comes down to subcultural perspectives on masculinity—in the QPF and, crucially, conservative Queensland society in general. For the predominantly male QPF, a gay man on the force called into question the inherent masculinity of policing in a way that lesbian officers did not. The greater level of intolerance towards gay men was, thus, not simply an aversion to same-sex relationships in general, but rather the challenge that gay men represented to the hypermasculine cultural norms many Queensland police subscribed to.

At the same time that Lewis's QPF was actively working against LGBTQI+ officers in its ranks, a young constable named Moore was just starting to emerge as a rising star of the force. After joining up with the QPF in 1974, at the zenith of the Whitrod era, he did time in some of the least appealing areas of the force: the Mobile Patrols and Operations. Secondment to both sections was often seen as punishment, a way of getting difficult or nonconforming officers "out of the way" and into a place where there was no real policework happening. Moore was a born performer, active in the local Brisbane theatre scene. It was one such extracurricular activity that put him right in the sights of Commissioner Whitrod. He was performing in a play at Brisbane City Hall in 1976, when he sent an invitation to the boss, never expecting him to actually come. But Whitrod, committed to supporting his junior officers, took Moore up on his invitation and was impressed by the young officer's skills on the stage.[11] When Moore requested a year of sabbatical to travel to London and attempt to make a career as an actor, Whitrod approved the request. Unfortunately, Moore was not successful and returned home with his tail between his legs in six months, resigned to a career languishing in Operations again, manning the police switchboard. However, Whitrod had other ideas. Still a huge fan, he created a position for the thespian at the Police Academy directing crime reenactments, and from there, Moore became a public relations officer for the force—after the commissioner, the face of the police in Queensland. He was lucky that he came back when he did. Had he waited much longer, his patron Whitrod would have been gone, replaced by a new commissioner in late 1976 who may not have given him the shot he needed to keep his dreams of the limelight alive.

In the role of public relations officer, Moore was in his creative element. He was put in charge of the branch and spent his time delivering presentations to schoolchildren or designing crime prevention leaflets that were distributed to the community, telling citizens to keep their doors locked and how to stay safe on the mean streets of Brisbane.[12] His dreams of an actor's life were long gone, so much so that when he was instructed to make an appearance on popular children's morning show *Super Saturday* in 1980, he was reluctant. The show had called the QPF asking for an officer to appear and tell young viewers about important topics such as road safety or "stranger danger." Despite his reservations, he made the trip to the Mount Coot-tha television studio. Adding insult to injury, his costar for the morning was a puppet. Agro was a haphazard Muppet-like character created by studio floor manager Garry Rhodes, and was notorious for telling jokes wildly inappropriate for kids' television that nevertheless flew over the heads of the children while their parents turned red and cried with laughter.[13] As usual, when it was time for Moore's segment, he found himself being harassed by Agro, who called him "Constable Economy" in parody of his actual rank, Constable First Class.[14] Moore returned fire though, impressing the program's producers and proving a hit with the audience. When he returned to work the next week, he was told that he was being given a regular weekly spot on *Super Saturday* where he would banter back and forth with Agro while at the same time informing children on how to stay safe. The character of "Constable Dave," the smiling face of the Queensland police, was born.

In the early 1980s Moore was easily the most recognizable police officer in Queensland, and maybe even the country. Even aside from his appearances on *Super Saturday*, he had an active media profile. He was friends with the local ABC Radio announcer Bill Hurrey and was regularly on his popular show.[15] He appeared at a never-ending stream of community events, cutting ribbons and smiling for the camera. Moore was highly recognizable, which was part of the reason why Drug Squad officer G. M. Jones quickly recognized him when he spotted Moore at the Hacienda on the night of 14 April 1982.

For a long time, the Hacienda had been a meeting place for members of Brisbane's LGBTQI+ community. Several years earlier, it had been one of the venues included in Marlin's report on the gay community in the city, and since then, the bar was a constant subject of police monitoring. Jones was there that night, undercover, watching out for one of the drug deals that often took place in one of the bar's dark corners, but he found something else entirely. He reported that he encountered Moore unexpectedly at the Hacienda, which Jones described as "a known gathering place for large numbers of homosexuals . . . [who] gathered at the end of the bar at the rear exit." He said that, at around 9:45 p.m., a group of three men that included Moore entered the bar and joined the group of apparently gay men at the end of the bar. Jones said Moore seemed "well known to this group" and, on several occasions, placed his arm intimately around the shoulders of some of the men.[16] In an addendum to Jones's report, his superior noted that "it appears obvious that Constable MOORE has homosexual tendencies" and that it should be brought to the attention of his superiors, given his position working with children and the prohibited nature of gay sex in 1980s Queensland.[17]

Jones's report was not the only warning sign about Moore in 1982. He began associating with an eclectic crowd after rising to prominence on the back of *Super Saturday*. Apart from ABC presenter Hurrey, he also became close to an executive with the Ford motor company named Breslin, an unusual character originally from coastal central Queensland town Gladstone. Like Moore and Hurrey, Breslin spent a lot of time in places like the Hacienda, but he was also fascinated with police. He was a frequent visitor to and patron of the Police Club at the QPF headquarters, one of the few "civilians" to spend much time at the venue.[18] Breslin visited Moore one day in 1982 when the constable was working the desk of a careers fair at the Exhibition Showgrounds in Bowen Hills. At the next stall over were representatives from the South East Queensland Electricity Board (SEQEB) who began chatting with Moore and Breslin. When the fair ended for the day, the group decided to continue their conversation at Breslin's apartment on Alice Street in the CBD. The men started drinking, and many of them tried on Moore's police uniform, while he in turn wore one of their SEQEB uniforms. At some point, Breslin snapped a photo of the encounter, later placed in a photo album kept at the apartment.[19] There the photograph remained to be found during a raid on Breslin's flat on 23 December 1982. The raid was conducted because Breslin was believed to have been impersonating a police officer, even going so far as to wear a uniform that he had somehow acquired.[20] When police, including Gallagher, found photos of Moore swapping uniforms with other men in that very flat in the album, along with other more obscene pictures, their suspicions were piqued. Their discoveries were put in the report of the raid and the dangers of Moore's associations were, once again, firmly placed on QPF's radar.

The police report on the Alice Street raid was brought to the attention of Deputy Commissioner Syd Atkinson, who was already aware of the concerns around Moore's sexual behavior. Shortly before the raid, he was forced to speak to Moore directly about an "allegation that he [Moore] had been seen with another male person in the vicinity of public toilets at Stafford," known for being a gay beat. Having seen the photos of Moore found in Breslin's apartment, Atkinson said he felt there was "nothing untoward" in the pictures, and after warning Moore about his associations, he was satisfied that no further action needed to be taken.[21] Nevertheless, a pattern was starting to emerge that turned even more sinister when Juvenile Aid Bureau (JAB) officer Mike Garrahy took the statement of a teenage boy who claimed that Moore and Hurrey propositioned him on 4 September 1982. Garrahy was alerted to the issue by the boy's father, who had overheard Hurrey ask his son if he was "still interested" in making pornographic movies at an event for the Shaftesbury Centre, a facilitator of opportunities for young people who needed extra support.[22] On further questioning, the son told his father than he was offered $200 to take part in producing three pornographic films by Hurrey and Moore.[23] He rejected the offer but did not report it because he was aware of Moore's position in the QPF and "was afraid of repercussions."[24]

Garrahy then interviewed the teenager. He confirmed the story that his father had told Garrahy, noting that he first became associated with Hurrey and Moore when Moore gave him the phone number for a business called "Jobs for House Boys" at the opening of a Salvation Army Church in Nundah. From there, he turned up to work at a flat in Brunswick Street, the heart of Fortitude Valley, owned by Hurrey. After doing some cleaning, the boy said that both of them gave him alcohol and forced him to watch hardcore pornographic films, before taking him out for dinner at the high-profile Lennons restaurant in the CBD where the offer to make pornographic films was made over the meal.[25] Though Moore was not present when Hurrey made the offer, the boy became aware that Moore knew about it when he bumped into him at the event at the Shaftesbury Centre where, in between signing autographs for children, Moore casually asked him if he was going to take Hurrey up on his offer.[26]

Garrahy was incensed that Moore, a police officer, could have been involved in the sexual molestation of a minor. He wrote a report detailing the allegations and sent it to his boss at the JAB, Frank Rynne. Since taking over the JAB in late 1981, Rynne and his fellow officers felt any investigation had become increasingly aware that a ring of prominent local figures was alleged to be molesting young men in Brisbane, but this was the first direct accusation of Moore. Rynne was cautious. He found Garrahy to be an unreliable officer who sometimes overdramatized things, but these allegations were serious enough to investigate and pass up the chain of command nonetheless. When Rynne told Tony Murphy, now assistant commissioner, about the Moore allegations, he recalled that Murphy said something along the lines of "the dirty bastards, I can't stand them, see what's in it." Taking the lead from Murphy, the JAB boss took the issue to Commissioner Lewis, who took the same view. Lewis told him that "rumors are not evidence, go flat out," which Rynne took to mean that he should continue looking into the allegations.[27] Even so, the Moore investigation hit a brick wall. Other JAB officers claim that Rynne told them that Moore was a serving police officer and the case would be taken over by internal affairs, with JAB officer Kerry Kelly claiming to have been "dissatisfied with ... reluctance by the police hierarchy to act quickly" on the evidence against Moore.[28] Moore was under close scrutiny as 1982 came to a close. Senior police like Atkinson had even alerted him to the rumors that were circulating about his sexuality in police circles. But despite the accusations piling up against him, he continued serving in his role as the face of the QPF both on children's television and in the community.

More than a year passed between the Alice Street raid in 1982 and the second raid on Breslin's apartment in Coronation Towers in January 1984. Now, though, Gallagher was not simply dealing with Breslin's impersonation of a police officer and lewd photographs. He was dealing with a case of Breslin kidnapping, drugging, and sexually assaulting someone.[29] The photo of Moore in Breslin's album was the same one found in 1982, but this time Gallagher was not going to let the evidence of Moore's association with Breslin out of his hands. He kept the picture, being sure never to leave it somewhere where it could be easily stolen by one of Moore's allies in the police force. Moore was, in many respects, the commissioner's golden boy. Unlike other police who rose through the ranks in the Whitrod era, Lewis recognized Moore's potential as the smiling face of the force and, in turn, became a strident protector of the rising star. With Lewis onside, Gallagher knew that the blue brotherhood would rally around Moore, despite the rumors about his sexuality that would ordinarily put him at risk of being ostracized within the QPF. In the end, Gallagher began posting the photo to himself over and over again, resending it whenever it arrived in the mail so that it was never in his possession at any given time. If a senior officer asked to see them he could honestly say that he did not have it.[30] It was a seemingly paranoid move, but Gallagher had reason to believe that there were forces in the QPF that were intent on protecting Moore and his associates.

Shortly after Breslin's arrest, one of Gallagher's informants came to him saying he knew that Moore and others were involved in producing child exploitation material, recruiting "actors" and bringing them to the home of a local businessman where pictures were taken. The pictures were kept in a safe for a short period of time, before being put on aircraft and transported to other members of the network around the country. Gallagher believed the intelligence was legitimate and secured a warrant to search the safe. There was nothing there. He believed that his operation was compromised because he told several other officers about the plan before it went forward, increasing his fear of corrupt operators within the force working against him. Shortly after the Breslin raid, Gallagher—a well-respected twenty-year veteran of the force—was suddenly transferred from his senior post at the Brisbane CIB to the purgatory of Beenleigh police station, another place where "difficult" officers were placed to punish them for speaking out against members of the force.[31] With the Breslin trial soon to take place, Gallagher was called at Beenleigh and told that the informant who gave him information about Moore had been arrested and was being held at Woolloongabba station. When he arrived, he went to check the records to see what his informant had been arrested for. There was no record. He believed he was being targeted, intimidated by corrupt police into keeping his mouth shut about Moore and the other high-profile individuals who Gallagher believed were a part of the molestation ring.

Despite the apparent attempts to sideline Gallagher, the case against Moore and Hurrey continued to escalate throughout 1984. The rumors about Moore were brought directly to Lewis by the mother of one of the officer's alleged victims. She claimed to be in possession of ten photographs of her underage son engaged in sexual acts with a variety of older men including Moore.[32] Lewis remained firm, refusing to stand Moore down from his prominent position on television or from any other duties that required him to be close to children. By late 1984, however, Lewis had lost control of the situation. Unable to actively target Moore, police had nevertheless proceeded to investigate accusations against Moore's friend Hurrey, and by October, they were ready to strike. Hurrey's residence was searched on 20 October 1984 as the result of complaints from several students of a nearby school in Fortitude Valley that he was involved in either propositioning or sexually assaulting them. Most of these young men also accused Moore of participating in their abuse. When police searched Hurrey's Brunswick Street apartment, they found exactly what the victims told them was there: a considerable cache of pornographic films, indecent images of underage teen boys, and small quantities of amyl nitrate, a chemical drug used by many in the gay community in the 1980s to loosen muscles in preparation for anal sex.[33] Hurrey was arrested on 3 November and, eighteen months later, was found guilty of charges ranging from the usual anti-gay provision of permitting sodomy to indecently dealing with a boy under seventeen years old. He was sentenced to five years in prison, but he walked free after serving less than half of his sentence.[34]

The allegations gathered in preparation for the Hurrey raid were collated in a report given to Lewis by JAB officer Mark McCoy a week after Hurrey's arrest. The stories of the witnesses who gave statements to the police suggest a pattern of predatory behavior that existed since at least 1982, the exact time that the accusations raised by Garrahy to Lewis.[35] Like the boy who initially spoke to Garrahy in 1982, some of the boys in the 1984 case also met Moore through community events—one even alleged that the first time Moore assaulted him was in the public toilets at the same Salvation Army Church in Nundah where Moore first met the 1982 victim.[36] The same victim was also taken to Hurrey's apartment on Brunswick Street to watch pornographic films with Moore and Hurrey, before being sexually abused by Hurrey while Moore watched. Other victims also alleged the same general process took place with them, with Moore luring teenage boys to Hurrey's apartment where they were plied with alcohol, watched pornography, and then were sexually assaulted. Two of the young men corroborated each other's story that Moore sometimes adopted a feminine personality referred to as "Mildred" and also maintained a sexual relationship with Hurrey, along with the teen boys the pair targeted. One victim was left with physical marks from his abuse, described as "love bites" left by Moore, who also gave the teenager "gifts" such as a pair of police handcuffs and a gun, neither of which was recovered in the later police investigation into Moore's conduct.[37] Though police were fairly swift to arrest Hurrey after the raid, there continued to be a reluctance to pursue action against Moore, despite the fact that it appeared most of Hurrey's crimes were inextricably linked with Moore as coconspirator.

Police Minister Bill Glasson was not aware of the chaos he was about to face until Hurrey's arrest on 3 November when the premier's press secretary Allen Callaghan told him that he had "problems . . . [with] Dave Moore." It was clear that, while the police minister was not kept in the loop about Moore, the premier's office was very aware of the allegations against the face of the police force. Glasson called Lewis two days later, asking about Moore's exposure in the Hurrey case. He said Lewis "scoffed" at the idea that Moore was involved with Hurrey, ignoring the connection made between the pair by Garrahy in 1982.[38] Lewis told Glasson that there was a "lack of evidence" that Moore was involved in child sexual abuse, justifying his decision not to move him from his role in the public relations branch.[39] If Glasson ever believed Lewis's denials, that came to an end on 14 December 1984 when Moore was charged with five counts of indecently dealing with underage boys along with several other charges related to conspiring with Hurrey to molest underage boys between 1982 and 1984.[40]

In the days that followed, Garrahy called Glasson's office to fill the minister in on the aborted 1982 investigation into Moore. Glasson was intrigued, especially given that Lewis just told him that there was no reason to suspect Moore was involved with Hurrey or child sexual abuse at all. He called Garrahy in for a conversation on 19 December 1984, where Garrahy outlined the entire history of allegations against Moore over the past two years. He told Glasson that JAB officers believed the 1982 case was sabotaged, with the Crown Law office deciding not to proceed because of an insufficient brief of evidence. He suggested that evidence went missing from the brief before it reached the prosecutors' office, through the intervention of someone in either the JAB itself or the commissioner's office, where it was sent before being passed on to the prosecutor's office. Garrahy said that he and his fellow officers felt any investigation into Moore was "off bounds... a hopeless situation" and being "hushed up" because of Moore's close relationship with Commissioner Lewis. Garrahy said the brief sent to prosecutors in 1982 was not the only case of information related to Moore going missing. He alleged that Jones's report on Moore being at the Hacienda also "was lost" for the two years between 1982 and 1984, only coming to light when the case against Moore started to become inevitable.[41]

For Garrahy, all roads led back to one place: the commissioner's office. He relayed to Glasson information he had heard from another officer, who told him about a deputation of police who went to Lewis's office to complain after an "incident" on a trip that Moore was a part of. When the officers told Lewis that Moore was gay and needed to be disciplined, Lewis responded that he did not "give a stuff [care] what he does outside his working hours as long as he behaves himself" when he was at work.[42] Lewis's liberal feelings about Moore's sexuality were in direct contrast to the law of the time. As a gay man, Moore should have been subject to greater scrutiny by Lewis, with the potential that one of the QPF's most visible officers was, in fact, a sexual criminal. It was also in stark contrast with the public face that Lewis presented. At around the same time he argued against targeting Moore, in private Lewis was openly supporting the premier in his campaign to label gay men as "perverts" and shutdown gay bars through amendments to the Liquor Act. For Garrahy, the explanation for this dissonance is simple. Moore had survived because Lewis *needed* him to survive.

Losing Moore to a sex scandal involving the abuse of children was not simply a tragedy for the victims, but from Lewis's standpoint was a great embarrassment to the police force that put his own position in jeopardy. Cognizant of this, he turned a blind eye to Moore's illicit dealings and questionable relationships with people like Hurrey and Breslin, allowing him to continue working in a privileged position as a police officer for two years after the accusations of impropriety first came to light. More crucially, he permitted Moore to continue working on programs like *Super Saturday*, putting him in direct contact with young people who grew to idolize "Constable Dave." The allegations made against Hurrey and Moore in 1984 suggested that it was Moore's public profile that gave him the coverage to meet underage boys and lure them into his and Hurrey's clutches. It was also his job as a police officer that prevented his victims from speaking out against him, in fear of the reprisals if the police turned against them to protect one of their own. In protecting his own position and the reputation of the police force, it is likely the Lewis inadvertently put many young men at risk of being preyed on by Moore and his criminal associates.

Moore faced trial a matter of months after Hurrey was convicted. He was found guilty in November 1986 on all charges and was sentenced to six-years imprisonment.[43] A few months after that, in March 1987, the appeals court found that mistakes were made in the original trial and his conviction was overturned. It was a short-lived reprieve. In June 1987, he was tried again and found guilty on two charges of sexually assaulting a sixteen-year-old boy, for which he was sentenced to a term of thirty months in prison. He was in the minimum-security correctional facility at Numinbah, in the tranquil rainforest outside the Gold Coast, when the Fitzgerald Inquiry got underway. He was a focus of the inquiry on several occasions, when people like Lewis and Glasson were grilled over how much they knew about Moore's activities and why the police had not pursued the allegations when they were first raised in 1982.[44]

By that stage, the point was moot. Moore was in prison, and Lewis had been removed from his position as police commissioner to allow the Fitzgerald Inquiry to run its course. Moore was eventually released and offered a chance to reform as a private citizen, stripped of the uniform that once gave him power. Unfortunately, it was not to be the last time that the former Constable Dave faced the scrutiny of the court. Looking for a new career after the police force, he started a video production company in the quiet, leafy Brisbane suburb Aspley sometime after being released from prison. He might have faded into obscurity if not for a raid conducted by police on the business in May 2009, where a cassette recording featuring images of naked boys between twelve and fifteen years old was discovered. Moore pled guilty to possessing the video but claimed that he had forgotten about the tape. He said a client had left it there ten years prior.[45] The police were not buying his story this time. The tape, which appeared to have been produced in the 1970s, featured naked teenage boys rock climbing and swimming, as well as one performing a sexual act.[46] The prosecution argued that the tape was for Moore's sexual use, and he was ultimately handed a fifteen-month suspended sentence for possessing abuse material.[47]

The shadow cast by the Moore case cannot be understated. For an entire generation of Queenslanders, Constable Dave was a physical manifestation of the police force. He was the smiling, mustachioed man on television every Saturday morning, teaching them right from wrong. He taught them to trust the police, an important lesson that was completely undermined by the public revelations that Constable Dave himself was abusing that position of trust to abuse teen boys. His behavior was vulgar and certainly criminal, but his misconduct did not exist in vacuum. It was supported by a police force that, regardless of its mandate to impose moral order in Queensland, turned away when serious claims of impropriety were made against one of their own. Even at the very beginning, when Jones observed Moore associating with other gay men at the Hacienda, the police were obliged to investigate. State law made it illegal for men to engage in sexual acts with other men, and at the same time Moore was being watched in 1982, other less fortunate men were like sitting ducks being picked off by officers targeting the beats and gay bars around the city. Even so, it is possible to accept the concept (however unlikely) that Lewis and the QPF were taking a surprisingly progressive stance on Moore, choosing not to pursue him for his sexual preference whatever the law said. However, it does not explain the reluctance to act against Moore as the accusations around his sexual behaviors became increasingly more troublesome. By the end of 1982, the allegations had gone beyond whether or not he was a gay man. There was a statement from a victim who claimed Moore and Hurrey were working together to convince him to participate in a pornographic film shoot. Between this, the Jones report, and the discovery of his picture in Breslin's album, there was ample reason to at the very least remove Moore from his prominent, public-facing position. This did not happen, and as a result, Moore was given two more years to continue down the escalating path that he was already on in 1982.

The case of Moore is an example of just how much the blue brotherhood extends protection to officers on the other side of the law. There is a widespread view that pedophilia is an unforgivable crime, an affront on childhood innocence so serious that participating in child sexual abuse would see a person cast out from any social group, no matter how strong the bonds that exist are. Moore's case shows this to be partly true. There appears to have been a consensus from police ranging from Rat Packer Murphy to crusading JAB officer Garrahy that something needed to be done about Constable Dave. Yet, nothing was. Time after time, testimony and evidence was passed up the chain of command only to meet with inaction, if not outright obstruction, from senior police such as Atkinson and Lewis.

In part, this resulted from the commissioner's natural pragmatism, with Lewis reluctant to expose the force to the public scrutiny that criminal charges against Moore would bring. Even if this is the case from Lewis's perspective, though, it does not explain the fact that none of the officers who knew of the accusations against Moore were willing to go against the commissioner to publicly expose him to the media or Opposition politicians. As disgusted as they seemed to be, the socialization of the blue brotherhood remained strong, preventing them from speaking out against the Lewis administration for fear of ostracization and reprisal. The members of the QPF who knew about Moore may not have felt personal loyalty to him, convinced he was a child sex offender, but they *did* have loyalty to the organization that both he and they represented. If an attack on Moore gave critics a chance to attack the QPF, there was nothing else to be done. Loyal members of the blue brotherhood would remain silent, at least until the circumstances changed and the time to strike presented itself, as it did in late 1984 when it became clear to all that the institutional protection of Moore was no longer tenable.

When Rynne received Garrahy's report on Moore in late 1982, he said it came in the context of broader investigations into networks of child sexual offenders operating in Queensland at the time.[48] When it came to child abuse during this period, the Moore case was merely the tip of the iceberg. In supplying his report on Moore and Hurrey to Rynne, Garrahy asked for access to the Howard-Osborne files—material obtained by the QPF that outlined a ring of child sexual abusers operating out of Brisbane with connections around the world.[49] It was Garrahy's belief, and Rynne's (at least to some extent), that the accusations against Hurrey and Moore were not only believable but could be a part of a broader conspiracy at work in Brisbane that operated for years under the QPF's nose. Hurrey and Moore were not just accused of molesting boys. A consistent aspect of the allegations against them was the claim that it was part of their pattern to incite teenage boys to participate in pornographic photo shoots or films. There were no pornographic videos found among the materials in the raid on Hurrey's apartment. Where could these illicit films have gone? Was it possible that Gallagher's informant was right, that exploitation material was being produced in Brisbane and circulated around the country, amongst a clandestine network of child sex offenders? Though it sounds like an absurd conspiracy theory, there was good reason for police to believe that this may indeed be the case. Only a few years before, the Queensland police uncovered one of the biggest child exploitation networks in the world, operating out of the sleepy southern suburbs of Brisbane. It all started with a man who liked to take pictures named Clarence "Clarrie" Howard-Osborne.

CHAPTER 12

Dirt Files

C larence "Clarrie" Howard-Osborne loved to record things. The sixty-one-year-old worked in Parliament House as a shorthand reporter with the serious responsibility of making accurate records of what was said in the people's house. He got the job because of his experience with the notetaking skills of shorthand. Indeed, he was so good that Pitman College in London, named for the inventor of shorthand Isaac Pitman, often deferred to him for advice.[1] With his skills, he made a long career for himself in the public service, and had it ended there, he might have been preparing for a quiet retirement at his home in the southern Brisbane suburb Mt Gravatt. Howard-Osborne's fascination for recording things went beyond the professional, though. His home at 54 Eyre Street was rigged with recording equipment and, until the afternoon of 11 September 1979, was full of boxes holding thousands of photographs of young, naked boys. He was a predator, and proud of it. When police accused him of abusing boys, he was happy to speak to them about his sexual predilections. By the end of their search, police removed three carloads of illicit material. That was not even all of the files. There were more left at the house because there were so many boxes that it was impossible for police to take them all.

Howard-Osborne claimed a scientific interest in young boys. He was in the habit of not just taking nude photographs of his victims but making a range of notations for his "files" from the size of their penises to their biographical details.[2] He was so honest that the police were taken aback. The suspect in front of them was not ashamed. On the contrary, he seemed genuinely convinced that his "work" was legitimate, an admittedly unusual type of scientific research. Worse, Howard-Osborne was just as open in his zealous belief that, in spite of existing social taboos, adult–child sexual relationships were biologically normal. Unsure of how to deal with the strange person before them, the officers brought him into the station for questioning, where he continued to explain his interests freely and with some enthusiasm, like any hobbyist. The police who searched 54 Eyre Street were overwhelmed, in over their heads, and needed help. While they figured out what to do with Howard-Osborne, the officers told him that he was free to go home.

Howard-Osborne sat in his empty house that night, the threat of arrest looming. It was difficult to know what the next day would bring, but police were now in possession of his files. With all that evidence, there was no way that he was going to get away with his crimes against children. After all, he documented them so thoroughly that there was little doubt of his guilt. Ever the notetaker, Howard-Osborne picked up a pen. Surrounded by his remaining files, which he called his "life's work," he began to draft his final note. He explained what transpired with the police that afternoon, ominously writing that "this was the best way" to deal with the situation. He put his pen down and walked to his garage. He kept recording to the end, even after attaching a length of hose to his exhaust pipe and feeding it into his car. Just like the rest of his house, his car was fitted with devices once used to record the conversations he held with the young boys he preyed on. That night, the device recorded something else. Because of his habit for recording, we know that some time passed before he died. As the exhaust fumes filled the car his final words could be heard on the recording: "I've been sitting here ten minutes and I'm still alive."[3] Howard-Osborne was found dead the next day, never facing justice for his crimes. Even in death, though, the saga of the man believed to have preyed on at least two thousand young boys was just beginning.

If gambling and prostitution have traditionally been treated as "victimless crimes," then child sexual abuse is seen as the exact opposite. Crimes against children are universally condemned as "evil" by the community, criminal and civilian. Because of this, child abusers are set apart from the usual criminal class, ostracized and excluded by all. Most discussions of historical corruption do not cover the nexus between policing and pedophilia for a few reasons. For one, it is far less common than the involvement of corrupt police in victimless crimes such as gambling or of-age prostitution. The social sanction against child sexual abuse means that abusers are less able to identify officers willing to protect them, with police unable or unwilling to justify exercising their discretion when it comes to this area. Another reason is the lack of incentive for police to protect the run-of-the-mill abuser. Most cases of child sexual abuse occur within the home, and offenders do not profit from their crimes. This sets them apart from the vice traders of Fortitude Valley who profited enough from their illegal enterprises to provide the financial incentive required to buy protection from corrupt police. The combination of intense social stigma and the lack of a monetary incentive raises the question: why did police in Queensland have such a hard time enforcing the law when it came to child sexual abuse? Questions remain to this day as to the extent to which there was active protection of child sex abusers, but what is clear is that policing the area was fraught with challenges and, as seen in the David Moore case, a prevailing belief in some sectors of the Queensland Police Force (QPF) that efforts to bring offenders to justice were being curtailed by forces unknown.

A global moral panic about organized pedophilia began to take shape in the early 1980s, sparked by a series of prominent cases where multiple children accused groups of adults of sexual and physical abuse. With the benefit of hindsight, the conspiratorial belief in ritual or organized abuse has been attributed to several factors including the use of coercive interview techniques on children who were led to make false admissions to social workers and police.[4] Retrospective studies reveal that, fearful of the repercussions of being accused, many pragmatically decided to accept a plea bargain where they confessed in return for no jailtime.[5] Whatever the cause of this boom in organized abuse cases, the impact they had on the public's fear of organized pedophilia was profound. After allegations of Satanic ritual abuse at McMartin preschool in Los Angeles resulted in several adults being charged, more than one hundred daycares and preschools across the United States were investigated on accusations of organized abuse.[6] The McMartin case was largely the result of an investigation by social worker Kee MacFarlane, who made a name for herself in the years that followed as the world expert on ritual organized abuse. She pioneered the use of anatomically correct dolls, showing them to children and asking them to indicate where they were touched. Between these dolls and other leading, coercive questioning, she diagnosed sexual abuse in almost every child from the McMartin preschool that she interviewed.[7] As with process corruption in policing, flawed interrogation tactics used by social workers like MacFarlane have a detrimental impact on the criminal justice process. In this case, these techniques resulted not just in charges against innocent people, but they formed the basis of a moral panic that continued well into the 1990s.

The furor around organized abuse officially reached southern shores two years later when, in 1988, four employees of the Seabeach kindergarten in Sydney's Northern Beaches were charged with forty-nine counts of abuse on seventeen children aged between three and six years old.[8] The accusations were both serious and bizarre. In conversations with police, the children alleged that the staff of the Seabeach kindergarten routinely abused them, sometimes in the guise of a clown named "Mr Bubbles."[9] The case against the Seabeach employees was dismissed in 1988. The court found that police had used coercive techniques, like those used by MacFarlane in the McMartin preschool case, to elicit false accusations. Not only that, New South Wales police had leaked false information about the accused to the tabloid press, erroneously claiming that evidence of occult practices were found at the Seabeach kindergarten.[10] There were also unproven allegations that investigating police solicited a bribe from the accused and, when refused, set out to *create* proof to ensure they were sent to prison. The Mr Bubbles case complicated the Australian public's views on organized pedophilia. On one hand, the shocking allegations stoked panic that these abuse networks existed. On the other, the collapse of the trial and subsequent suggestion that the entire case was invented by police gave reason for pause, and reinforced the views of some in the community that organized pedophilia was no more real than Mr Bubbles himself. The conflicted perspective on organized abuse had a serious, detrimental impact on policing of child abuse in Queensland in the late 1980s. It allowed some in the police and the community to reject the valid accusations against people like Howard-Osborne and Constable Dave while, at the same time, prompting a quixotic campaign to root out elite pedophile rings that inevitably politicized and compromised policing of this area.

The police response to child sexual abuse in Queensland is a murky area. As the Royal Commission into Institutional Responses to Child Sexual Abuse (2013–2017) showed, the intense trauma often experienced by survivors is such that the true scope of the crimes only becomes clear many years after the offenses occurred, if ever.[11] For example, it was only recently that the details of the controversial case against University of Queensland academic Frederick "Doc" William Whitehouse began to emerge. An esteemed geologist, Whitehouse graduated from the prestigious St John's College, Cambridge, with the first ever doctoral degree awarded by the university's Department of Earth Sciences.[12] He returned to Brisbane after this, where he struck up a close friendship with one of the city's most prominent names: patron of the University of Queensland, Dr James Mayne. Whitehouse's new friend Mayne was the scion of a complicated dynasty. He was the son of the Butcher of Queen Street and former council member Patrick Mayne, who rumor had it earned his fortune through theft and murder in the 1840s.[13] Despite an almost four-decade age difference, Whitehouse and Mayne remained close up until Mayne's death in the late 1930s. Rosamond Siemon, expert on the Mayne family, claims that Mayne was gay and suggests that Whitehouse was a male companion who "would have brought a ray of sunshine to the colorless existence" of his later years. Newly returned to Brisbane, Whitehouse took up a position as coach at Toowong Rowing Club, where he coached many young men to success over the years. One of his students, who joined the club in 1940, was a young man named Howard-Osborne.[14]

By the early 1950s, Whitehouse was a busy man. Not only did he work as the state's top geologist, he was also lecturing in the subject at the University of Queensland, coaching the institution's rowers to state championships, and actively serving as deputy chief commissioner of the Boy Scouts Association.[15] In many ways, he was at his peak in 1955 when four police knocked on his door and accused him of committing indecent acts with underage boys. Leading the deputation? A young Criminal Investigation Branch detective named Tony Murphy. He had stumbled across the case earlier on Friday 15 April 1955, after bringing in a group of young people for questioning. One of the young men, Henry, had a story to tell. Why Henry chose to tell Murphy this story is not known, but there is a long tradition in the Queensland police (and indeed many law enforcement agencies around the world) of giving a "free pass" to petty criminals in return for intelligence leading to an even bigger arrest. It is possible that he saw an opportunity in accusing Whitehouse, an unquestionable "big fish," as part of a negotiation with police to avoid criminal charges of his own. He told Murphy that Whitehouse had picked him up at the Grosvenor Hotel in the central business district and drove him to his house, fondling the young man's penis during the car ride. When they got home, he fed the young man and gave him alcohol, before taking him into the bedroom where the sexual acts continued. Murphy and his colleagues, including future Deputy Commissioner Syd Atkinson, continued investigating and found at least two other teenage boys who said Whitehouse had done the same to them. Like Howard-Osborne more than twenty years later, Whitehouse intellectualized the accusations, telling Murphy that all men had a "dormant" same-sex tendency in them, and after being taken to the police station for questioning, he agreed that Henry's claims against him were true.[16] Interestingly, he told Murphy that he had an intellectual curiosity in the size of young men's genitals—a fascination that Howard-Osborne would also display in his meticulous files years later.

Murphy, a young detective on the rise, had Whitehouse dead to rights. The professor was admitting that not only was he a gay man (criminalized in 1955), but that he had also committed an indecent act on a teenage boy. Murphy needed to tread carefully, though. Whitehouse was no ordinary person. He was connected to some of the most powerful people in Brisbane, a group that included Murphy's boss and mentor Frank Bischof. Whitehouse worked with Bischof in a professional capacity on several cases, even analyzing soil found in the car at the center of the 1952 Southport Taxi Murder case that, in many ways, put Bischof on the map.[17] Before Murphy charged Whitehouse, he put a call in to Bischof to get his advice. It was alleged at the subsequent trial that, when Murphy returned, he told Whitehouse that he spoke to Bischof. The boss "told me [Murphy] that he admires you as a man," but that there was nothing he could do to prevent charges being laid. His young accuser, Henry, had already been charged with participating in an act of gross indecency with Whitehouse. If the case against Henry was going to proceed, the case against Whitehouse as his "co-offender" would have to as well.[18] With Bischof's hands tied, Murphy charged Whitehouse with one count of committing an act of gross indecency, a minor charge given the amount that he admitted to in the interview room. At trial that August, Whitehouse received a three-month suspended sentence, criticized in the media as lenient when compared to Henry's sentence of eighteen months in prison.[19] Bischof and Murphy were not able to prevent Whitehouse going to court, but there is no doubt that his public prominence contributed to the meager sentence that he received from the court. The impact of prominence on the policing of child sexual abusers in Queensland was to become a recurring theme in the years that followed, even more blatantly than it was in Whitehouse's case.

Whitehouse's case, although serious, pales in comparison to the crimes committed by his one-time rowing student Howard-Osborne. As a young man, Howard-Osborne grew up in a strict Mormon household. The young man was not able to play with other children from outside his faith, and he bristled under the repressive "rules" of the Howard-Osborne house.[20] When he left school and learned shorthand, a new world opened up to him. He started as a government court reporter in the 1960s, where he became well-known to many prominent figures in politics and the judiciary.[21] He was an unusual character for the time. He was open about his sexual behavior, unusual in an era where homosexuality was frowned upon. He spoke often about "picking up young hitchhikers" on the highway between Brisbane and the Gold Coast and showed pictures of the young men he was "friends" with to people at work.[22] Red flags were raised, and Howard-Osborne became the subject of two secret inquiries about his conduct in 1973, the result of which was that he was moved into the Hansard division at Parliament House where he could be closely monitored. The public service should have been more concerned, because his behavior went beyond a preference for youthful men. At the very time he was working in Parliament House, he was also operating as one of the world's most prolific producers of child sexual exploitation material.[23]

Howard-Osborne's files, discovered by the police in 1979, contained images and notations on at least two thousand young boys. More than that, he was also the Australian contact for the international Paedophile Information Exchange (PIE), an activist group dedicated to sharing exploitation material and abuse strategies among child sex offenders across the world, while at the same time publicly agitating to legalize sex between adults and minors.[24] He had been operating in Brisbane for a lengthy period before PIE was formed in 1974 and was seen by many international members as a "guru" of pedophilia. An excerpt from the PIE magazine in the 1970s refers to Howard-Osborne as the "member organizing the local PIE scene in Australia" and, most worryingly, reports that he was "taking up the cause there with great enthusiasm."[25] His pseudo-career as a producer of child exploitation material came to a crashing end almost by accident. A mother overheard her son discussing an incident where he was photographed naked by an elderly man, later ascertaining from her son that the man's name was "Clarrie Osborne" and that her child was not the only one in the pedophile's camera lens. The mother mentioned this, informally, to a friend with a husband in the police force.[26] Ordinarily, this type of investigation would have been taken on by the Juvenile Aid Bureau (JAB), but the unusual way that the incident was reported to police meant that it did not get passed along to that branch. Instead, the police responding conducted a sting operation to lure Howard-Osborne out using the initial informant's son as bait. After observing him taking fully clothed photos of boys in a local park, the officers took him into custody and went to his house to question him on the afternoon of 11 September 1979. By the next morning, he was dead.

Even with Howard-Osborne dead, the files he left behind provided police with ample opportunity to uncover the activities of other child abusers in Brisbane. There were more than two thousand young boys in the files, and even though they were compiled over a twenty-year period, it was highly unlikely that Howard-Osborne was solely responsible for taking every photo that was in his possession. Additionally, his role as the PIE liaison for Australia proved that he was in contact with other offenders both domestically and around the world, and there was hope his files might point police in the right direction to find these potential coconspirators. Indeed, one of the first steps taken by JAB officer Mike Garrahy in 1982 when the revelations about Moore and Bill Hurrey began to surface was to request access to the "Osborne files" to cross-reference his victims with those in the files, suggesting a suspected link between the Moore-Hurrey-Breslin ring and Howard-Osborne.[27] Garrahy never saw the Howard-Osborne files, as they had been removed from the JAB's possession long before 1982.

Survivors of Howard-Osborne were requested to come forward, but only two out of the thousands featured in his files did so. This is not uncommon in child sexual abuse cases. As the Royal Commission Into Institutional Responses to Child Sexual Abuse held in Australia in the mid-2010s (and other, similar historic abuse investigations like the United Kingdom's recent Operation Yewtree) made abundantly clear, young victims are often disinclined to report sexual abuse at the time it occurs and for many years after, in the belief that accusations against trusted adults would not be believed or would be investigated by doubtful authorities. Police-press liaison officer Ian Hatcher said, "Even before we got halfway into the stuff we realized there was potential for millions of dollars in blackmail," with many of the people identifiable in the images having moved on to positions of power and influence in Queensland society.[28] Howard-Osborne's files presented a real threat, not just to the offenders who operated in conjunction with him, but his victims too. Some police tried to use the files to launch a sting operation on the PIE, pretending to be Howard-Osborne to communicate with others in the group. The officers took some of his files out of the office to read them on a secluded hill north of the city, in fear that their attempts to expose child sexual offenders in Brisbane would make them a target. They might have been right. One of those officers later found a bullet in his drawer at work, a signal he took to mean that he should stop investigating the case.[29]

Another officer, who spoke anonymously to journalist Matthew Condon, claimed to have been part of the investigation into Howard-Osborne's files in the weeks after his death. He recalls the sense of panic in the QPF growing after a few weeks, when the full scope of the offenses began to be revealed. The officer said that, among the index cards and photographs, was a filing cabinet labelled "Associate" that held information of all the other child abusers who Howard-Osborne corresponded with, many of whom were local. One name that stood out was Kevin John Lynch, a guidance counsellor at one of Brisbane's elite schools who years later would be named as perhaps the most prolific child abuser in Queensland aside from Howard-Osborne himself.[30] As more familiar names began to surface in the files, Condon's source said a deputation from Special Branch arrived and took possession of the files and the case itself. From there, the files were taken from the JAB and not seen again.

The intervention of Special Branch, the state's intelligence unit, suggests that a decision was made in the QPF that the information in Howard-Osborne's files should be controlled and contained, not treated as evidence of the sexual offenses committed by Howard-Osborne and his associates. This decision would have been sanctioned by Commissioner Lewis, perhaps to control the fallout of the worst case of pedophilia ever seen in Australia to that point. Howard-Osborne's death and the QPF's discovery of his extensive files had been reported in the media. While no victims had been identified in the press, the continued investigation of the files no doubt sent a ripple of fear through those who were subject to his abuse, knowing that indecent images of them or their children were likely included in the cache of images now in police possession. Historically, child sexual abuse has been treated in conservative societies as a cause for shame, and Queensland was no different in 1979. To avoid being exposed as a victim of sexual abuse was powerful motivator to keep the Howard-Osborne files buried forever. Whatever the reason, the files' disappearance put an end to the investigation into a ring of child sexual offenders operating out of Brisbane, frustrating the efforts of the JAB in a manner that became routine in Lewis era.

During the 1980s, there was a belief held by many officers seconded to the JAB that investigations into prominent cases of child sexual abuse were destined to be scuttled by the powers that be in the police force. The Grenning incident was a prime example of this perspective in action, where officers in the JAB chose to not pursue a potential case of child sexual exploitation material being distributed for "political reasons."[31] Russell John Grenning was a senior political advisor to the ruling National Party, serving as press secretary for then-police minister Russell Hinze for much of the 1980s.[32] In March 1983, a letter was sent to the JAB from Victoria Police's Task Force Delta, a unit investigating the production and distribution of child exploitation material by self-described "pedophile advocacy groups" operating in the southern state. Delta was, for the most part, an aberration in Australian policing. As in Queensland, other state police forces were slow to respond to organized pedophilia until the international moral panic around such abuse reached Australian shores in the late 1980s. The letter Delta sent to the JAB in March 1983 was thus a reasonably early foray into the investigation of organized, interstate networks in Australia. It supplied information gathered during one of Delta's operations that suggested Grenning had purchased child exploitation material from a Victorian supplier by mail in 1981.[33]

Years later, *Courier-Mail* journalist Michael Ware claimed that the JAB intentionally decided not to investigate Delta's accusations, proven by a handwritten notation on Grenning's file stating, "No action to be taken. Political reasons."[34] The note was written by JAB officer Mark McCoy, the same person responsible for compiling a report on the allegations against Moore and Hurrey in 1984.[35] He admitted to writing the notation on Grenning's file, asserting that it was a way for the JAB to cover itself and avoid the potential repercussions from not investigating. He said that he was "concerned if Greening was a ped [pedophile], he would continue in his activities and someone later on would get this documentation and say 'hey, Mark McCoy did nothing about this whatsoever.'" In his 1990s inquiry, Justice John Patrick Kimmins described McCoy's actions as taking place in a "climate" of political exceptionalism where "it flourished in the minds of police officers ... that investigations concerning those with political influence could encounter some difficulty."[36] Grenning was never charged with offenses related to the letter from Task Force Delta and enjoyed a long and celebrated career in public service. Much later, in 2011, he was jailed for twelve months on unrelated charges of possessing exploitation material.[37]

Kimmins was right. In 1984, there was a real climate of apprehension about the way that the QPF was handling cases of child sexual exploitation. The Moore case, which came to a head with his arrest in December 1984, put the spotlight on the force's response to child sexual abuse cases. Around the same time, the *Courier Mail* published an article from journalists Tony Koch and Matthew Fynes-Clinton titled "The Men of Evil Who Prey on Children." Featured in the *Courier-Mail* on 10 December 1984, the article made startling claims that there were organized child exploitation rings operating in Queensland with the protection of certain members of the police force. Most allegations made in this period focused on the abuse of underage boys, but this is not to suggest that the sexual abuse of underage girls was not also taking place at the same time. In a statement offered to the Sturgess Inquiry in 1985, a Brisbane sex worker going by the alias "Dawn" told of how, with the protection of the corrupt Licensing Branch, "the girls [working at brothels] got younger and younger." Another sex worker, "Jennifer," told Des Sturgess that men would often call the brothels and "ask how old the youngest girl working there is."[38] When told there were none around ten or eleven years old, many customers would say they would try somewhere else where they knew girls that young were "available." Immediately after the *Courier-Mail* exclusive was published, the QPF jumped into action. Deputy Commissioner Atkinson ordered raids on two Brisbane brothels alleged to be involved in underage prostitution, Brett's Boys at Kelvin Grove and the House of Praetorian at Coorparoo. As part of the raid on Brett's Boys, police took possession of files that included credit card slips showing the identities of several of the brothel's customers. Rumors abounded in the years after the raid that some of this material was removed from the investigation's files by officers who took part in the raid, including receipts featuring the name of a high-profile National Party politician who would go on to have a long career in the Queensland Parliament.[39]

The suggestions that police intervened to protect powerful people associated with brothels who were offering underage prostitution remained no more than conjecture until April 1988, when senior QPF officer Kevin Dorries lay dying of cancer in hospital. Dorries called on long-serving police chaplain Walter Ogle, who came to visit him in his last days. Dorries had a confession to make, telling Ogle he had information on a pedophile ring operating of Brisbane. Dorries handed Ogle a folder full of documents, which reputedly included credit card receipts taken from Brett's Boys in 1984. Ogle, not wanting to keep the incriminating documents on him for security reasons, allegedly entrusted them to a friend, publican Neil McLucas. The owner of popular LGBTQI+ venue the Sportsman Hotel in Spring Hill, McLucas kept the files Ogle gave him in the basement of the hotel. When Ogle went to retrieve them years later, McLucas said that, at some point over the years, the box with the documents in it was accidentally thrown out.[40] The "proof" of police protection offered to Ogle, if it ever truly existed, was lost.

The impression that police had botched the policing of child sexual abuse and failed to protect young Queenslanders was at fever pitch. Neither the arrest of Moore nor the raid on Brett's Boys and House of Praetorian could satiate public concerns that not enough was being done on this issue. Meanwhile, the barrage of articles by reporters like Koch and Fynes-Clinton continued. The force announced that the Police Complaints Commission headed by Judge Eric Pratt was going to investigate the allegations made in "The Men of Evil" article. Still, it was not enough to satisfy the growing public rage at the QPF for not taking action against people like Moore who operated right under their very noses for years. Koch, Fynes-Clinton, and the other journalists were also painting a broader picture of the police force's failure in this area. A page-three article accompanying the original "The Men of Evil" feature on 10 December 1984 focused on the Howard-Osborne case, questioning why more wasn't done to address his criminal activity earlier, especially when the Public Service Board was aware of allegations against him several years prior. Eventually, the cabinet stepped in. Local barrister Sturgess, once the defense lawyer for Glen Hallahan, was named director of public prosecutions and was given the investigation into child pornography and prostitution as his "first official duty."[41]

The Inquiry into Sexual Offences Involving Children and Related Matters, better known simply as the Sturgess Inquiry, began straight away and continued well into 1985. In stark contrast to the restrictions placed on former commissioners like Harry Gibbs and Geoffrey Lucas, Sturgess claims there were few procedural limitations placed on him, and he was able to conduct his investigation largely autonomously. Even so, corruption played an incidental role in complicating his investigation. The unit responsible for policing brothels like Brett's Boys and the House of Praetorian was the Licensing Branch, and Sturgess admits, the fact that its activities were inextricably compromised by the Joke meant that the one group of police who should have provided the most information for his inquiry were untrustworthy and essentially useless.[42] Nevertheless, he made some headway in uncovering the main providers of sexual services in Brisbane. Unsurprisingly in a system where access was strictly controlled by the Joke, the providers that he came to investigate were the very same sex traders sanctioned by the Licensing Branch. Two police officers, Roland Dargusch and Brian Webb, were given the task of assisting Sturgess's investigation. The duo were, in fact, the only two officers appointed to assist the Sturgess Inquiry, and even then, Webb was also pulling double duty as liaison to another police taskforce at the same time, limiting the duo's ability to conduct a thorough investigation at Sturgess's direction.

Appointing Dargusch and Webb as Sturgess's investigators was a tactical move by Lewis. Both had strong reputations as internal affairs investigators, satisfying concerns that the QPF was not taking child sexual abuse seriously, but at the same time, offering Sturgess only two officers as support inevitably hamstrung the inquiry's ability to truly get to the bottom of the allegations made about the sex trade in Queensland. Despite these complications, Sturgess nevertheless managed to compose a compelling picture of the sex trade. He was able to identify the "main, protected players" in prostitution in Queensland, and the names his report offered were familiar ones: Anne-Marie Tilley, Hector Hapeta, Geraldo Bellino, Vic Conte, and Geoff Crocker.[43] The Sturgess report as well as the supplementary report from Dargusch and Webb were supplied to the Commissioner. No action was taken. Later, Lewis admitted that he did not even read the report, again showcasing an utter disregard for the policing of child sexual abuse on his watch. The Sturgess report became a "two-day tabloid wonder" and, while a harbinger of problems soon to come, quickly faded from the public memory.[44]

The Sturgess report has been largely overshadowed by the Fitzgerald Inquiry, which began only a year after Sturgess's findings were made public. The Fitzgerald Inquiry sent immediate shockwaves through the QPF, but for many police officers, the three-year period during which the commission existed was business as usual. In 1988, the second year of the Fitzgerald Inquiry, Brisbane played host to the World Exposition (Expo '88), a major six-month event that was a more modern version of past World Expositions like the one held in Paris in 1889 that gave us the Eiffel Tower and the one in Chicago four years later where the Ferris Wheel spun for the first time.[45] Expo '88 was one of the most significant events on Brisbane's calendar in the 1980s. This was a chance for the city to show itself off to the world, even as it faced the existential crisis of the Fitzgerald Inquiry. With the event, though, came the threat of interstate criminals preying on visitors. The QPF's Sexual Offenders Squad received intelligence from interstate agencies that a local branch of the Sydney-based Boy Lovers and Zucchini Eaters (BLAZE) pedophile organization was setting up in Brisbane during the event, with the intention of targeting young Expo visitors.[46] In response, the Sexual Offenders Squad established Operation Firefighter—a taskforce named for its goal of "putting out the BLAZE." The first incarnation of Operation Firefighter ended in August 1988 due to a lack of funding, but the investigation was struck up again in February 1989 by the newly formed Paedophile Task Force after intelligence suggested the same people involved in setting up a BLAZE chapter the previous year were still active in Queensland.[47]

One of the most important suspects targeted in Operation Firefighter was Desmond Patrick Kenafake, a public servant employed by the Police Complaints Tribunal. For the Paedophile Task Force, Kenafake presented a major risk. Because of his position at the tribunal, he had access to the photographs and personal information of all police employees. If he was involved in a group like BLAZE, it would make it challenging for police to conduct any type of undercover operations and could even put officers in personal danger if the subjects of their investigation were to discover where they and their families lived.[48] Kenafake was put under surveillance to try and avert these problems, as the Paedophile Task Force prepared to conduct raids against the pedophile ring on 4 April 1989. The raids were compromised, however, forcing the taskforce to bring the raids forward a day to 3 April 1989. Police discovered that information about the planned operation had been leaked, warning the suspects and giving them time to dispose of any incriminating evidence ahead of time.[49] Then Opposition spokesperson for the police, Terry Mackenroth, placed blame for the operation's failure on none other than Ronald Redmond, serving as acting commissioner during Lewis's suspension. Mackenroth told parliament that "Redmond summoned the detectives ... and demanded that they hand over the originals of all tapes and statements."[50] A senior officer attached to Operation Firefighter, Kym Goldup-Graham, supports Mackenroth's allegations. She said that she had secretly marked every copy of the Operation Firefighter files with a unique identifier and that when a copy was found during the raid on Kenafake, it matched the version supplied to Redmond.[51] Kimmins later found the Police Complaints Tribunal investigation into whether Redmond was a source of the information to be "rather perfunctory," possibly a result of having the same agency that employed one of the key subjects of Operation Firefighter investigate the causes of its failure.[52] In any case, Redmond was cleared by the tribunal of being involved in scuttling the operation, and Operation Firefighter concluded once and for all.

The experience of the Paedophile Task Force in the Operation Firefighter fiasco was the first domino in a series of interconnected events that would result in the unit being disbanded entirely within the next few years. While senior police believed there was "ample justification" for the Paedophile Task Force to continue, concerns were raised over what the QPF administration considered to be a somewhat obsessive targeting of prominent individuals by officers Garnett Dickson and Goldup-Graham. The officer in charge of the Sexual Offenders Squad and thus the Paedophile Task Force, Graham Williams, later told the Criminal Justice Commission that "it was quite obvious that things were going seriously wrong with the group ... they were making serious allegations against senior judges, ah politicians, the Commissioner of Police and senior members of the Queensland Police Service."[53] On one occasion, Williams said Dickson flew into a rage when told that he was not permitted to raid the house of a Supreme Court judge who he believed to be involved in abusing children. These were views that Dickson believed since at least October 1989, when he compiled a list of suspected members of an elite pedophile ring operating in Brisbane in the aftermath of Operation Firefighter.[54] The clash between Dickson and the QPF continued until the end of 1990, when Williams informed members of the Paedophile Task Force that its work would be taken over by a newly established Child Exploitation Unit.[55] No members of the Paedophile Task Force were transferred to this new unit, resulting in ongoing investigations being abruptly ceased and a profound loss in terms of institutional knowledge that officers like Dickson and Goldup-Graham could have brought to the table.

For a police officer like Dickson, on a moral crusade to root out child abusers in his state, the collapse of the Paedophile Task Force was a major setback. Luckily, Dickson was prepared. Knowing that at some point the powerful enemies he was courting might come after him, he made sure to take a dossier of sensitive documents with him before leaving the Paedophile Task Force. The documents related to several investigations where it was alleged that police had corruptly intervened in child sexual abuse investigations, such as the file from Task Force Delta about Grenning and eleven pages of a police file on Howard-Osborne. Also included was material related to aborted investigations into public servants and QPF employees suspected of criminal conduct. Originally, Dickson claimed that some of these documents were sent to him anonymously at some point during the Fitzgerald Inquiry, accompanied by a unsigned note that claimed the files were found when investigators with the inquiry raided Commissioner Lewis's safe. Dickson believed that, if these documents were found in Lewis's safe, it was proof that the commissioner was keeping "dirt files" related to prominent people suspected of crimes against children, either to use as blackmail or to prevent others from discovering the police's attempts to cover-up their behavior. Despite Dickson's claims, there is no evidence that these documents were ever found in Lewis's safe. In fact, Kimmins came to the position that the documents were copies made by officers in JAB in 1984, around the time that the Moore scandal was at its peak and the calls for an official inquiry into the policing of child sexual abuse were gathering steam. Kimmins believed that Dickson had come across the copies in the course of his work with the Paedophile Task Force and removed them from the office before handing over to the newly established Child Exploitation Unit.[56]

The "dirt files" became a central feature in a series of articles produced by Ware that were published in the *Courier-Mail* between 14 and 20 August 1997. Around the same time, on 18 August, veteran journalist Bob Bottom went on ABC Radio and claimed to have received information that no action had been taken against the producers of "snuff films" recorded on the banks of the Brisbane River, where young boys were sexually assaulted and afterwards murdered on film.[57] Bottom's informant was police officer James "Jim" Slade, who first came to prominence as the person who alerted ABC television reporter Chris Masters about corruption in the QPF, which as a result, triggered the Fitzgerald Inquiry.[58] The combination of the Ware articles and Slade's allegations, along with several other rumors about the policing of child sexual abuse, forced the state government to call on Justice Kimmins to preside over the Inquiry into Allegations of Misconduct in the Investigation of Paedophilia in Queensland, or the Kimmins Inquiry.

When the commission concluded and Kimmins reported his findings, the result was a whitewash. There were some occasions where Kimmins commented on questionable conduct, such as McCoy's annotation of the Grenning file and the Police Complaints Tribunal's haphazard investigation of the Operation Firefighter leaks, but for the most part the judge found that there was no reason to believe that police officers were derelict in their duty to protect Queensland children. He lambasted Ware's articles as being baseless, the product of imagination, and rejected any notion that former commissioner Lewis was complicit in protecting or, alternatively, blackmailing any criminal sex offenders with the "dirt files" that Ware claimed were discovered in his safe. Kimmins even discredited Slade's account of the "snuff movie" ring, painting the once highly respected whistleblower as a fantasist.[59] From a judicial perspective, the Kimmins Inquiry put an end to years of speculation about the QPF's involvement in protecting sexual predators. Kimmins had a reputation as a man who suffered no fools, expressed with an often "brutal directness."[60] The judge's characteristic distaste for people who took advantage of the system was seemingly reflected in his response to whistleblowers and journalists like Ware, Dickson, Goldup-Graham, and Slade. The ferocity with which Kimmins and the counsel assisting attacked these witnesses, undermining their credibility and dismantling their reputation, was warning enough for others not to speak out. Several whistleblowing police who made allegations before the Kimmins Inquiry had already left the QPF before the commission began, ushered out in the wave of reforms in the post-Fitzgerald era. It was easy, thus, for the inquiry to paint them as no more than disgruntled former police, taking potshots at a police force that, in the aftermath of Fitzgerald, became an easy target.

The Child Exploitation Unit that replaced the Paedophile Task Force in 1991 made way for a new unit, Task Force Argos, dedicated to investigating child abuse networks in the digital era. In the years since, Task Force Argos has become the gold standard for this area of law enforcement worldwide, responsible for collecting evidence to support thousands of prosecutions against suspected offenders around the world.[61] Their targets do not roam the halls of power, as those investigated by the defunct Paedophile Task Force did, but sit behind computer screens, lurking on the Dark Web. Though organized networks, these groups are far removed from the kind of elite pedophile rings that Dickson and Goldup-Graham pursued in the late 1980s or that Howard-Osborne seemed to preside over in the years before that. Because of this, it is hard to judge the recent success of the taskforce against the apparent failures of its predecessors in the QPF who made critical errors in their investigations of suspected abusers. There are, after all, major differences in pursuing a faceless enemy behind the screen in comparison to hunting suspects at the very pinnacle of the sociopolitical establishment.

Nevertheless, the recent good work of Task Force Argos has largely overshadowed the questions around how child sexual abuse was policed in Queensland prior to the Kimmins Inquiry, when real concerns existed about the extent to which sex offenders had infiltrated the public service, including the police force. Kimmins had written most of these allegations off as a mere fantasy, conspiracies pursued by a minority of obsessive police in the Paedophile Task Force based on flimsy or unreliable evidence. But, no matter whether their suspicions were true or not, Dickson and Goldup-Graham were scapegoated by Kimmins. Like the National Hotel Report before it, the Kimmins Report ended up being primarily concerned with discrediting witnesses. Again, an inquiry designed to probe police misconduct was weaponized against the very people who triggered it. Like David Young and John Komlosy, Dickson and Goldup-Graham were presented to the public as no more than ostracized police making accusations in pursuit of a long-standing professional vendetta. Kimmins failed to explore other allegations that would have shone a light on the protection of pedophilia in Queensland. He rejected the suggestion to revisit the Moore case and barely touched on the mystery of the Howard-Osborne files. Instead, Kimmins focused his attention on clearing the QPF of wrongdoing.

Unlike his predecessor Gibbs, fooled by the behind-the-scenes machinations of the Rat Pack in the National Hotel Inquiry, there is perhaps reason to believe that Kimmins, though misguided, had noble intentions in closing the door on pedophilia-related corruption allegations in his report. By the late 1990s, when the Kimmins Inquiry was held, the now-rebranded Queensland Police Service had been going through a decade-long period of rebuilding from the ashes of Fitzgerald. From one perspective, it is possible that Kimmins felt enough was enough, and that the disruption and mudslinging needed to stop in order for the police's ongoing reforms to have the chance to work. Though revealing the truth of corruption is usually seen as noble, there is a school of thought that sees no benefit in repeatedly trawling over the past rather than focusing on making positive change for the future. It is possible that Kimmins—a strong supporter of the state—was the type of person likely to adopt this view. Indeed, for both police and government the problems of the past were just that, in the past. What mattered was the future, a post-Fitzgerald police force that was cleansed of corruption and, once again, fit for purpose. So many victims of corruption waited so long for the QPF's reckoning to come. As the dramatic theme music to ABC's *Four Corners* began to boom across the nation on 11 May 1987, little did they know that they were about to get their wish. The endgame for the corrupt police of the QPF had arrived.

CHAPTER 13

Joke's Over

Even though he had flown from Sydney to Brisbane to meet his contact, Chris Masters still was not sure that there was a story here. The veteran reporter, now working with ABC's flagship current affairs program *Four Corners*, was certainly not naive about the state of policing in Queensland. The tropical north had a longstanding reputation, cultivated over the last thirty years, for being a place where corruption was rife. That was the problem, though. For Masters, it seemed like the story had been done over and over again, never making a real impact. Some journalists had come close. Back in 1982, ABC's *Nationwide* made a splash with the accusations of corruption levelled by the likes of Bob Campbell, including the first public naming of the "Rat Pack" at the head of the force.[1] The report claimed the scalp of Assistant Commissioner Tony Murphy, forcing him to retire slightly ahead of schedule, but besides that not much changed in the Queensland Police Force (QPF). Then there was the series of articles by Tony Koch and Matthew Fynes-Clinton in late 1984, consolidating the force's existing problems with David Moore by accusing police of protecting criminals who exploited children.[2] The articles put pressure on Commissioner Terry Lewis to act, and the state government enlisted Des Sturgess to investigate. The inquiry, for all its merits, was in the end a white elephant. The commissioner did not even read

Sturgess's final report, showing the level of seriousness with which the QPF took the issue. More recently, Phil Dickie had been making some noise on the ground in Brisbane, poring over building ownership records to trace the identities of the people who owned the brothels, massage parlors, and illegal casinos that dotted the city's landscape.[3] Masters was cynical. He knew that the man he was supposed to meet had a story to tell, but then again so did all the others who tried to blow the whistle on the Queensland police over the years. Whatever story he was about to hear, what difference could it possibly make?

Masters came to Brisbane with a man named Peter Vassallo, an analyst for the Australian Bureau of Criminal Intelligence (ABCI) in Canberra. Vassallo was a sharp operator, and he and Masters recently worked together on a report for *Four Corners* that aired on 23 June 1986 titled "The Family Business," which took aim at the connection between the Italian Mafia and the drug trade in Australia, including the group's suspected role in the death of anti-drug campaigner Donald Mackay in 1977.[4] After the report aired, Vassallo came to him again, telling him there was another, potentially even bigger, story to unravel in Queensland. Despite his initial reluctance, Masters trusted Vassallo, so he agreed to go with him to meet the person his informant said could steer him in the right direction: Jim Slade. The trio made plans to meet at a local pub on 27 September 1986. When Slade got out of his car, the reporter thought he looked more like a farmer than a police officer.[5] The three men sat down for a counter lunch at the pub, and Slade began to tell his story. It was a tale about the drug trade in north Queensland, a report that was ignored, and a protected class of criminals operating across the state with the support of corrupt members of the police force. After years of playing the good soldier, Slade was done. By the time he finished his story, Masters could see why Vassallo was so adamant that there was a story here. Slade was a good cop, doing his job, while senior QPF officers were doing everything in their power to silence him. Over a pub lunch, the seeds of Masters's explosive *Four Corners* report were sown. Within a year, the foundations that institutionalized corruption in Queensland was built on collapsed completely.

Slade came from a policing pedigree. When his great-grandfather emigrated from Ireland in the mid-nineteenth century, he became a New South Wales police officer, scouring the countryside hunting notorious bushranger bandits like Ben Hall. Slade's father was an undercover operative in Greece during World War II, and when Slade joined the Commonwealth Police in 1971, he also gravitated towards intelligence operations, in his case the photographic section. He moved his family to Queensland hoping the subtropical climate would be good for their health in 1976, arriving at the exact time that Raymond Whitrod was desperately holding on to his position as commissioner.

The next year, Slade was instructed to meet with Inspector Murphy at police headquarters in Brisbane. Lewis had just won the battle for control of the QPF and had placed his friend Murphy in charge of Whitrod's attack dog unit, the Crime Intelligence Unit (CIU). Murphy brought many of his protégés with him, and he told Slade he heard of his experience in photographic surveillance with the Commonwealth Police and wanted to bring him on board.[6] For all his faults, Murphy was a respected police officer. To this day, Slade continues to assert that he learned everything he knew about policework at the tutelage of Murphy. The CIU was soon rebranded, now called the Bureau of Criminal Intelligence (BCI) and turned its attention away from investigating corrupt police and towards major crimes such as murder and bank robberies. Slade claims there was little focus on the vice trade, recalling no investigations on prostitution and very few to do with illegal gambling.

Slade made a career at the BCI, developing a reputation as a strong undercover operative. He was good at undercover work for the very reasons Masters noticed when he first met him. He did not *look* like a police officer and could blend in to even some of the most unsavory environments. During his time at the BCI, Slade started coming up against the Bellino family, members of the Syndicate who were believed to have a hand in much of the vice activity occurring in Queensland. Part of the reason the Bellinos were so successful over the years was the protection they received from corrupt police by virtue of their participation in the Joke. Slade remembers one of the first interactions with the family. He was on an undercover job monitoring them in the late 1970s when the brothers came to him and told him they knew he was a police officer because they had "inside information."[7] He came across them once more in the early 1980s, this time far from the mean streets of Brisbane. By this point, Slade's mentor Murphy had been transferred to take control of the Far North region and brought him in to run an undercover operation into the drug trade in the tropics.

Slade threw himself into the task. For several years in the early 1980s, he worked to infiltrate drug rings and trace the importation of narcotics through the porous northern border, an area he described as the new "frontier." He ran across the name "Bellino" often and came to the view that they were one of the biggest players in the drug trade based in the north. Though he knew the risks of identifying them, Slade named the Bellinos in his report of Operation Trek that he supplied to his bosses at the BCI on 21 November 1984.[8] Slade's report featured a wealth of actionable information, so there was an expectation that the QPF would be able to use it to bust a gaping hole in the north Queensland drug trade. It was not to be. Slade's superiors at the BCI were not aware of it, but he was close to an analyst who worked the "Italian desk" at the ABCI in Canberra, Vassallo. Given the apparent involvement of the ethnically Italian Bellinos in the Queensland drug scene, Slade passed the report on to Vassallo. When Vassallo went into his systems to see the crucial intelligence, he was shocked to find it was not there. The BCI had never passed on the Operation Trek report to its partner agencies.

Slade and Vassallo began to suspect there were forces in the QPF who, once again, were working to protect the Bellinos. Their belief was confirmed when Slade's boss, fellow Murphy protégé Alan Barnes, approached him with an offer. While Slade was having a drink at the Police Club in Brisbane on 7 February 1985, Barnes offered him "a bit of extra money" that he said was organized by a group of officers who "met at Jack Herbert's place."[9] A month later, Barnes handed Slade $100, promising that he would receive the same amount every month so long as he played ball.[10] Slade knew the fix was in, and later, Barnes indicated that the money was coming from "Gerry"—a reference to one of Slade's targets in Operation Trek, Geraldo Bellino. Slade told his boss, Col Thompson, about the offer. The whole thing was swept under the carpet. The money was returned to Barnes, written off as a "loan" that was misconstrued, and Barnes was quietly transferred to rural Longreach. Slade was transferred, too, out of the BCI and sent to the "punishment" station at Beenleigh that also hosted Peter Gallagher when his agitation around David Moore and the Paul Breslin raids became an issue for senior police.[11] There, in Beenleigh, Slade stewed. He kept his friend Vassallo abreast of what was happening in Queensland, from the bribe attempt to his suspicions about the Operation Trek report being shelved by corrupt police. When Vassallo started working with Masters on "The Family Business" all of the pieces came together, and the basis for Masters's 1987 report "The Moonlight State" was formed.

The *Four Corners* team did not just rely on Slade's information to craft their report; they spoke to many other disgruntled police and participants in the vice trade. When conducting research in north Queensland, they met with former police officer Ross Dickson, brother of Paedophile Task Force officer Garnett Dickson and himself an outspoken opponent of the Lewis regime.[12] Afterwards, the team came to Brisbane to finish their investigation, setting up camp at the Tower Mill Motel, where police, more than a decade ago, clashed violently with protesters.[13] It was yet another case of a special synchronicity in Brisbane, still a small town at heart, where places and people intersect in sometimes unusual ways over time. Because of these intersections, it was inevitable that the QPF would soon hear about *Four Corners* being in town and speaking to enemies of the force to compile a story. Masters later learned that there were plans to discredit him, setting him up with an underage male sex worker and taking photos that could be used as blackmail to force him to stop his investigation if need be.[14] Knowing that *Four Corners* was closing in, the corrupt police in the Joke began to scramble to save themselves. It was too dangerous for the bagman Jack Herbert to be seen with any serving police or his criminal associates, but even so, he met with key members of the Joke such as Harry Burgess and Graeme Parker on several occasions to plan their next moves.[15] "The Moonlight State" aired on 11 May 1987 and, over the course of the hour, barely skimmed the surface of crime and corruption in Queensland. There was just too much to cover in one report, but it nevertheless exposed several key elements of how "the Joke" worked. The report made the connection between the Syndicate and Herbert and, in turn, corrupt elements of the police force going back to the Bischof era.

The *Four Corners* report may have ended up with no impact, just like the *Nationwide* episode in 1982, except for one thing. Deputy Premier Bill Gunn swiftly took control of the situation on 12 May, the day after the Masters report aired, and announced a commission of inquiry into the allegations raised by the program.[16] Initially, several police welcomed this, perhaps expecting the same type of whitewash that occurred in the National Hotel Inquiry, where the police came out of the proceedings completely vindicated. In the same way that Frank Bischof did then, Lewis set about trying to influence the inquiry's outcome before it even began. Unfortunately for Lewis, Gunn's announcement of the inquiry came at the precise time that Lewis's relationship with the premier failed. For most of the year to that point, Joh Bjelke-Petersen was engaged in a bizarre campaign to move directly from the premier's office to the prime minister's office by getting himself elected from outside of the federal parliament in a quixotic "Joh for PM" campaign.[17] When Lewis visited Bjelke-Petersen, he played to the premier's weaknesses, claiming the suggested commissioner Tony Fitzgerald was a Labor Party supporter and that rumors were that the inquiry was a political move by Gunn and Lewis's deputy Ron Redmond to depose both the premier and the commissioner in one fell swoop.[18] Usually, this plan would have worked. Bjelke-Petersen was distracted, though, his mind firmly set on his tilt at leading the country. The road to the inquiry had begun, and the only person who had the power to stop it, the premier, was completely disconnected with the threat such an investigation into police corruption could pose. On the 26 May 1987 the terms of reference for an inquiry into police misconduct related to the allegations made in "The Moonlight State" were published. The commission was to be overseen by Fitzgerald, a young barrister with none of the social or professional connections to police that could compromise his judgment.[19]

Though he might have been an unknown quantity to many before the inquiry began, Fitzgerald quickly made it clear that this commission was going to be different to the ones that came before it. On day one, he announced that the terms of reference had been extended to cover misconduct dating back ten years before the commission began, now encompassing the entire period of Lewis's tenure as commissioner.[20] He offered indemnities from prosecution for corrupt officers willing to testify about their misconduct. In his view, it was his mandate not to bring corrupt police to justice but to examine the systems that fostered corruption in as much detail as possible. By offering indemnity, he hoped that corrupt police would take the opportunity to dodge criminal charges in return for openness and transparency.[21] He was right. On 28 August 1987 Burgess, a central organizer of the Joke, resigned from the police force and accepted Fitzgerald's offer. Before he began testifying, though, Burgess made sure to meet with Anne-Marie Tilley and warn her about what he was going to do, telling her to flee before the police caught up with her.[22] When Burgess began telling his story on 31 August, the entire house of cards that was the Joke started to collapse. He implicated his bosses, Noel Dwyer and Parker, both of whom then went on to take indemnities to testify about other police in the system.[23] They both supported Burgess's evidence, named Herbert as the middleman between criminals and police and, importantly, implicated the commissioner as a recipient of corrupt monies. Lewis denied involvement, but his position was no longer sustainable. Gunn suspended him on 21 September 1987 and, as Lewis feared, replaced him with now acting commissioner Redmond.[24]

Herbert managed to dodge Fitzgerald for slightly longer than most. At first, he intended to stay in Queensland and ride out the drama, but a chance meeting with Jack Rooklyn a few weeks prior to the commission beginning gave him a wake-up call. Rooklyn told Herbert that the decision to stay would put him at great risk. After this conversation, Herbert and his wife fled to his native England, laying low and hoping that Fitzgerald's investigators would not find him.[25] For months, he and his wife kept slow profiles in the outer-London village Kingston-upon-Thames. Their luck ran out on 9 February 1988, when British police finally came knocking on their door and arrested the pair with the intention of extraditing them back to Australia. Over years working both sides of the law, Herbert had learned to play the angles, and he knew that he was backed into a corner. He instructed his solicitor to contact the inquiry and see if it was not too late to apply for one of Fitzgerald's indemnities. He was ready, now that he had been caught, to tell all.[26] His decision to testify to the Fitzgerald Inquiry was the death knell for the Joke. Here was a man who had learned the ropes of the first Joke, before his pyrrhic showdown with Arthur Pitts put an end to it, and had played an active role for more than a decade in organizing corruption from outside the force. There was next to nothing that Herbert did not know about the way corruption worked in the police force. Because of his position in the system, he was also in the best position to reveal all about Lewis's involvement in the racket. Like Dwyer and Parker, Herbert openly told of how the suspended commissioner was fully aware of the Joke and profited from it.[27]

Most of the police officers who admitted corruption to the Fitzgerald Inquiry walked free because of the indemnities. Some former police, such as Syd Atkinson, testified but managed to defend their reputation in the witness box.[28] Others, like Glen Hallahan, slipped the net of Fitzgerald thanks to the restrictions of the terms of reference, which limited investigators to a period long after both had left the force.[29] Some, such as Murphy, were never called to testify, despite the allegations made against them. Those senior police who did not take indemnity and stood their ground protesting their innocence fared the worst. Licensing Branch inspector Allen Bulger was sentenced to twelve years in prison on charges of corruption and perjury, and most shockingly, Commissioner Lewis received a fourteen-year sentence for the same crimes.[30] Don Lane, the former policeman who was Lewis's friend in state parliament, was convicted of misusing ministerial expenses as a result of the inquiry's investigation, also doing jail time.[31] The reach of the inquiry even entered Parliament House. Several months in, it became clear to Bjelke-Petersen that the Fitzgerald Inquiry was out of his control. In an attempt to salvage his position, the premier took the desperate step of attempting to fire his entire cabinet, a move that was denied by the governor, Wally Campbell.

It was the final straw for a National Party who had lost faith in Bjelke-Petersen's ability to steer the government through the crisis of Fitzgerald. The parliamentary party moved to vacate the leadership position and hold a vote to choose the new Nationals leader and, thus, premier of Queensland.[32] The vote was open for Bjelke-Petersen to renominate, but he refused, giving Sunshine Coast member of

Parliament Mike Ahern the chance to take the leadership from Bjelke-Petersen on 26 November 1987, almost twenty years after Bjelke-Petersen had succeeded Jack Pizzey in the position.[33] Ironically, Bjelke-Petersen's next move mirrored that of Vince Gair back in 1957. The deposed premier refused to give up his title and attempted to form a coalition of his former enemies to wrestle power away from Ahern and the National Party, to no avail.[34] Bjelke-Petersen, accepting defeat, announced his resignation on 1 December 1987. Exactly one year later, he was called to testify before the Fitzgerald Inquiry. Several years later, in 1991, the testimony he gave to Fitzgerald came back to bite him. The former premier was charged with perjury over his denials to the inquiry that he ever personally received corrupt money from developers. When the case went to trial, the jury was deadlocked, allowing him to escape justice. Later, it transpired that the jury foreman, Luke Shaw, was a member of the National Party's "Friends of Joh" movement, loyal to the former premier and dedicated to protecting his legacy.[35] Despite the obvious political influence exerted in Bjelke-Petersen's trial, prosecutors decided not to conduct a retrial considering that he was eighty-one years old at the time.[36] Unlike Lewis, Bjelke-Petersen avoided prison but was forced to live under the shadow of corruption until his death in 2005, forever intertwined with the police and political corruption that occurred on his watch.

When the Fitzgerald Report was released on 3 July 1989, it offered a damning account of a police force where mercenary corruption was not only entrenched, but directed from the very highest levels. In its later days, the inquiry turned its attention to political corruption and Fitzgerald's final report showed a state where corruption of all types was endemic, and not just limited to a few "rotten apples" in the police force. The inquiry explored, to varying degrees, some of the key intersections between politics and policing in Queensland in the Lewis era, giving officers like Peter Carmichael the platform to finally come out and reveal the former commissioner's intervention to prevent charges being laid against Ted Lyons. It set a trap for Supreme Court judge Angelo Vasta, catching him in a "gotcha" moment that indicated he had not been entirely truthful in previous sworn testimony. When it came to the QPF, Fitzgerald was able to salvage the reputation of officers like Alec Jeppesen who were run out of the force by the Lewis faction because they got in the way of corruption. The report's most important contribution was its rendering of how the Joke worked from the inside, made possible by the indemnities that Fitzgerald offered to key players such as Burgess, Parker, and, most importantly, Herbert. Because of Fitzgerald, the public was able to see a practical example of how mercenary corruption spreads through a police force and becomes institutionalized over time to the point that the lines between criminal and police officer are invariably blurred.

The exposure of corruption was, for Fitzgerald, a sideshow that was secondary to the *real* purpose of his inquiry. In his final report, Fitzgerald wrote that "the past misdeeds of individuals are of less concern, except as a basis for learning for the future... the main object of this report and its recommendations is to bring about improved structures and systems."[37] Unlike previous judicial commissions, both in Queensland and elsewhere, Fitzgerald adopted a holistic perspective on the causes of police corruption. He subscribed to the Chinese proverb that the fish rots from the head, and by that logic, it was a failure of *politics* that led to a corrupt police culture. All roads led back to the government. For Fitzgerald, the Licensing Branch's solicitation of bribes was a form of trickledown corruption that could trace its source to the top. Using executive prerogative to redraw the state's electoral map, the premier was able to manipulate the process in a manner that gave disproportionate power to voters in the areas where he enjoyed the most steadfast support. The gerrymander was so effective that, at one point, Bjelke-Petersen's National Party assumed power with 55 percent of the seats in the parliament—but just 39 percent of the overall vote.[38] On this, Fitzgerald identified that electoral malapportionment was a major precursor for political corruption, even more when the process was managed by political actors. He recommended stripping control of the electoral map from the government and giving it to a newly created, independent Electoral Commission. This was just one of Fitzgerald's recommendations for dealing with corruption from the top-down, starting with Parliament House.

Citing political transparency as another major risk area, Fitzgerald found that "without information... there can be no accountability." He pushed for the introduction of new Freedom of Information legislation that could be applied to the cabinet decision-making process, with subsequent reforms including the introduction of a mandatory public register of politicians' financial interests.[39] Despite open government being such a crucial aspect in the Fitzgerald reforms, the incoming Labor Party government quietly wound these reforms back after taking power in 1990. Exemptions were created to protect the very cabinet secrecy that Fitzgerald criticized and later extended to cover any materials that made even tangential reference to cabinet processes.[40] Before long, many of the key reforms to the political process suggested by Fitzgerald were abandoned or rendered benign. He had been very clear that, in his estimation, police corruption was reflective of wider, systemic problems. While state politicians on both sides would continue to praise the Fitzgerald reforms in public, their commitment to lasting structural change was, in private, a far more complicated matter.

For the most part, Fitzgerald believed in the improvement of bureaucratic structures that already existed rather than the creation of new agencies, a practice that only led to a more bloated, and often ineffective, civil service. There were some exceptions to this, however. Fitzgerald proposed the creation of a new organization with extensive responsibilities for oversight of crime and misconduct in Queensland. The foundation of the Criminal Justice Commission (CJC) in 1989 was one of the first steps taken to implement the Fitzgerald reforms. Uniquely, the CJC was the first and only state agency that had the unified responsibility for targeting organized crime, police misconduct, political corruption, and public sector oversight.[41] The CJC's sweeping mandate was reflective of the Fitzgerald doctrine that the branches of corruption and misconduct could not be extricated from each other, and the inquiry's findings that where one was found, the other was usually not far behind. Despite the promise of a permanent anti-corruption body for Queensland, the CJC was not without its own fatal structural problems. Successive state governments refused to provide the commission with the investigatory powers that an agency with its remit required, such as the power to conduct surveillance on telephones or coercive interrogations. The CJC was also not provided with the powers to discipline elected officials, except in criminal matters. This meant that often even when the CJC uncovered serious public service misconduct, it was powerless to act.[42] Finally, in outlining his vision for the CJC, Fitzgerald made clear that it was crucial that the new agency was staffed by a mixture of seconded police and specialist civilian staff, in order to avoid the pitfalls of "police investigating police" that had repeatedly emerged as a real failing of the QPF's disciplinary processes in the Lewis era.[43] With the allegations about Judge Eric Pratt and his management of the Police Complaints Tribunal still fresh in mind, the rationale for mixed staffing was obvious. Nevertheless, from its creation, the commission consistently relied on "a large posse of about 100 seconded police to conduct its investigations" and, in its next incarnation as the rebranded Crime and Misconduct Commission (CMC), began handing power over the police complaints process incrementally back to the QPF.[44] Again, as with Fitzgerald's proposed political reforms, the initial push for change waned significantly over the 1990s, and though still an improvement on the Lewis era, as the inquiry faded from the collective memory of Queenslanders, the Fitzgerald reforms were repeatedly watered down.

It was not long before Fitzgerald's warning of a political compact between the police and elected politicians was realized once more. After the 1995 state election saw the Labor Party's majority in parliament reduced to one seat, the Coalition Opposition forced a by-election in Mundingburra, an electorate in northern Queensland. As the election approached, Opposition Leader Rob Borbidge met with police union president Gary Wilkinson and agreed to a list of demands, including steps to limit the oversight of police by agencies like the CJC. In return, Wilkinson agreed to use the powers of his union to mount a campaign to criticize the government's policies on law and order in Mundingburra. The political partnership paid dividends, and the Coalition was able to win the seat and return to power.[45] Borbidge was good to his promise and used his short time as premier to dismantle the CJC. No longer a unified anti-corruption agency, Borbidge stripped it of its organized crime function and created a new agency, the Queensland Crime Commission (QCC), to handle this brief. Though Borbidge's intent was the disempower the CJC, Tim Prenzler argues that separating the CJC and QCC was "arguably the right thing to do"—the restructuring gave each organization the ability to refine their investigations on newly distinct foci.[46] The CJC-QCC split did not last long, however. After Borbidge was toppled in 1998 by a resurgent Labor Party government led by former student activist Peter Beattie, the two organizations were merged once more into yet another agency, the CMC. In 2014, the Queensland anti-corruption apparatus went through one more major rebranding, renamed the Crime and Corruption Commission to reflect a concerted reevaluation of its priorities to once more focus on serious or systemic corruption in the public sector.[47]

The road to implementing the Fitzgerald reforms has not been an easy one, characterized by speed bumps and deviations along the way. While the success of measures introduced to stem corruption at the highest levels has been mixed, other recommendations that were adopted have had a major impact on how corruption is practiced in Queensland. In focusing on unravelling the Joke, Fitzgerald was understandably concerned with combatting illicit relationships between police officers and the vice trade. Here, Fitzgerald proposed an innovative strategy. Instead of simply tightening the rules around corruption or expanding oversight, change the game to eliminate the *need* for corruption. His hearings had shown him that sex workers and gambling providers did not *want* to pay police their hard-earned profits just to stay in business. As a result of Fitzgerald's suggestions, Queensland law was changed to decriminalize many aspects of the vice trade, removing the need for "protection" entirely. Laws around gambling were liberalized, legal prostitution was gradually (albeit imperfectly) introduced, and, importantly, homosexuality was decriminalized.[48] This criminal justice reform was supplemented with a major restructuring of the QPF. Out were specialist squads like the Licensing Branch, Consorting Squad, and Special Branch, all of which had come in for criticism throughout the inquiry for engaging in misconduct and entrenched corrupt subcultures. The role of these specialist squads was assumed by newly established regional commands where constant exposure to "at-risk" areas of enforcement could be minimized or diffused.[49] By 1990, the QPF no longer existed. Now, reflecting its new commitment to the people of Queensland, it became the Queensland Police *Service*.

Reform is a tough business and even tougher in a place like Queensland where, over time, corruption became entrenched in so many corners of public life. When it came to previous reform attempts in Queensland, whether the National Hotel Inquiry in the 1960s or the Lucas Inquiry in the 1970s, the conditions needed to affect lasting change were simply not right. Pursuing an agenda of reform requires the collective will of the public and the bureaucracy—something that figures like Joh Bjelke-Petersen, Bischof, and Lewis had a vested interest in quashing. When working in conjunction with each other, the premier and the police commissioner had the ability to continue their hold on Queensland by using the powers of their positions to silence critics and repress dissent. Exposing corruption required a perfect storm: the whistleblowing of Slade; the journalistic prowess of Masters; the distraction of Bjelke-Petersen; the political bravery of Gunn; the steadfast tenacity of Fitzgerald; and the self-serving revelations of Burgess, Parker, and Herbert. Without each of these cogs, the Fitzgerald Inquiry may have fallen into obscurity in the same way as so many others before it. Even despite its transformative impact on policing in Queensland and the numerous corrupt scalps it claimed, the legacy of Fitzgerald has been compromised in the years since. Recommendations have been ignored and reforms quietly rolled back for reasons of political expediency. What Fitzgerald shows is that we must accept that even the most successful anti-corruption investigations require constant vigilance to see them through. It is undeniable that Fitzgerald helped purge the QPF of corruption, but even he admits that this was only a small part of what was needed to make real improvements for policing in Queensland. He always believed that police corruption was no island and instead was *symptomatic* of a broader, pervasive culture in the public service. Looking back on the Fitzgerald reforms, it is clear that progress was made, but by the same token, other crucial, systemic change was ignored, fading from memory as Queenslanders cast their eyes forward towards a brighter future.

Conclusion

In the end, there was little to separate Terry Lewis from all of the other defendants he had ushered into court in his career as a police officer. Just like them, he went down protesting his innocence to the end. He was suspended early in the Fitzgerald Inquiry, after it became clear that the investigation was not going to reflect well on the police commissioner. In fact, he had been the first person in the witness box, denying all involvement in police corruption. As more witnesses began to emerge—many of them indemnified police intimately aware of the corrupt networks in the Queensland Police Force (QPF)—the public began to come to the view that perhaps Lewis may not have been quite telling the truth. His suspension became a termination and, worse, led to fifteen charges of corruption. His trial began in the Brisbane District Court on 18 March 1991, where a jury was told it was going to hear from a literal cavalcade of Queensland's most prominent (in some cases, notorious) citizens. At least 110 witnesses came forward to testify about Lewis's corruption, liberated from the fear of reprisal that dominated before the Fitzgerald Inquiry, when Joh Bjelke-Petersen and his cronies were at the helm. The witnesses included Jack Herbert, once again telling the secrets of the Joke. Other admittedly corrupt police also came forward to put this old boss behind bars, including former Licensing Branch boss Noel Kelly.[1] They told of receiving tens of thousands of dollars in bribes from the Syndicate and Hapeta-Tilley consortium every single month, and that a cut of that money always went to the police commissioner. Lewis's cut was never a major percentage of the take, but it added up over the years. At one point, Herbert recounted how the police commissioner often repeated the maxim "little fish are sweet" when Herbert handed over his share of bribes, referring to his belief that getting too greedy could lead to the whole system falling apart.[2] It might have been something Lewis learned from his former mentor Frank Bischof, who was forced out of the QPF not because of an internal affairs probe, but because the bookmakers he extorted became frustrated with the ever-increasing demands of corrupt police. Despite the testimonial evidence against him, Lewis remained firm, pleading not guilty to all charges.

On 5 August 1991, just over four years after the Fitzgerald Inquiry was called, the jury returned its verdict: guilty on all counts. Lewis was sentenced to fourteen years in prison. He was spirited away to the infamous Boggo Road prison for processing, later settling in for a long stretch at the Wacol medium security prison, where he shared a home with the likes of now-incarcerated vice kingpins Geraldo Bellino and Hector Hapeta. He continued to plead his innocence, keeping detailed notes of his theories that he was "set up" to take the fall for corruption. Lewis's former Rat Pack colleague, Tony Murphy, visited him occasionally and kept him updated on the latest news from the outside. His other Rat Pack colleague, Glen Hallahan died after a long battle with cancer in June 1991, still young at fifty-nine years old.[3] Lewis, on the other hand, suffered on in prison until April 1996, when he was released to a community corrections facility in South Brisbane, his old stomping grounds as part of Bischof's Criminal Investigation Branch in the 1950s.[4] Two years later, on 11 May 1998, Lewis finally got his wish and was approved for home detention. It was almost eleven years to the day since "The Moonlight State" had aired and had torn his world apart.

Now in his nineties, Lewis reappears on occasion, still fighting to clear his name, with mixed success. His pitch to have Brisbane journalist Matthew Condon write his official biography backfired, resulting in Condon publishing some of the most seismic allegations against Lewis since his trial.[5] The former police commissioner was not pleased. Rumor has it he continues to operate in some of his old QPF networks, too. Former Australian Border Force chief (and before that, QPF officer) Roman Quaedvleig wrote in his memoirs of being approached by Lewis around 2015 to request Quaedvleig consider his son for a job. Despite the two only ever meeting once, Lewis reached out to Quaedvleig as an old friend, playing on the notions of the police bond. Queensland's blue brotherhood continues to permeate. Quaedvleig recalls that the initial request to talk to Lewis's son about a job came not from the former Rat Packer but federal Liberal minister Peter Dutton who, before entering politics, was also a Queensland police officer.[6]

In the late 1980s, Tony Fitzgerald dismantled a system of mercenary corruption that had persisted in Queensland for decades. So many corrupt officers were excised from the force, made to resign as a condition of indemnity or, worse, convicted on corruption-related charges. There is an interesting observation made by Fitzgerald, deep in the report, that requires attention, however. On page 206 of his final report, he notes that "perhaps the more widespread" form of corruption observed in Queensland was "based upon the refusal by police to comply with the law and allow the criminal justice system to operate as intended."[7] Here, he refers to "noble cause" corruption, where police misuse their position and operate outside the system to bring what they consider to be "justice" in the community. Despite his acknowledgment of the fact that this form of corruption was more pervasive than mercenary corruption, it is the narrative of the Joke that dominated the public's attention in the wake of the Fitzgerald Inquiry. Queenslanders could be excused for thinking that the Joke was the singular focus of the Fitzgerald Inquiry. It was the subject of many of the commission's most salacious revelations, at the heart of "The Moonlight State," and the reason for the charges ultimately brought against senior police like Bulger and Lewis. This was partly an inevitable outcome of the inquiry's reliance on the testimony of indemnified police, who unwittingly directed Fitzgerald towards the Joke in their rush to save themselves. Because of the wealth of detail provided by these witnesses, Fitzgerald was able to continue pulling on a string that eventually unraveled the Joke entirely. Though his good work taking on the Joke cannot be understated, one of the by-products of this was that the extent of noble cause corruption in Queensland never received the attention it deserved, overshadowed by the overt criminal conduct of the Jokers.

Narratives are important, who controls them even more so. The narrative that has emerged about police corruption in Queensland over the years has often been one that is skewed in some fashion—at times inadvertently but often intentionally. What results is an understanding of corruption that is at best incomplete or at worst outright untrue. Police power is not just in the ability to arrest a suspect, but comes from the trust that most of the general public implicitly has in law enforcement to do the right thing. This is why, in the National Hotel Inquiry, it was easy for corrupt police to shift the narrative in such a way as to protect themselves. Bischof limited the investigation itself to one venue, one set of allegations, excluding all others. With the fallout limited, it was a simple task for the Rat Pack and its allies to target the small group of whistleblowers willing to speak out against the police, tarring them in public as criminals and deviants, abortionists, and communists. By the time it reached its end, the National Hotel Inquiry was in many ways a benefit to corrupt police. Rather than a risk, their participation in such a manipulated inquiry had given them the opportunity to shape the narrative in their favor, purportedly clearing them of wrongdoing and staving off any real anti-corruption attempts for more than a decade.[8] Turning the National Hotel Inquiry into a whitewashing campaign rather than the truth-seeking endeavor that it was supposed to represent was not possible without process corruption, again highlighting the intersectionality between diverse misconduct in a corrupt system like twentieth-century Queensland.

Time after time, the corrupt elements of the Queensland police sought to reinforce their position by taking control of the narrative. Whether it was Herbert convincing another officer to wear a wire to cast his nemesis, Arthur Pitts, as a villain, or the subversive campaign to undermine Commissioner Raymond Whitrod to force him out of his job, there was a strong tradition of storytelling in the QPF that provided a layer of protection for many corrupt police. It is often easier to operate in plain sight when those who call you a villain are themselves cast as the madmen. It was only when Fitzgerald took control of that narrative that corruption in the QPF, and the state more generally, was revealed for all to see. Even then, the inevitable result of Fitzgerald's inquiry is that the narrative on police corruption has once again been constructed in such a way that it ignores its full scale. The stories coming from the inquiry of brothels and brown bag payments are intriguing and shocking but are only one part of the rich tapestry of misconduct in the QPF. The narrative established by Fitzgerald has understandably dominated but has been less successful in tying the corruption and anomic policing culture he revealed to other types of misconduct in the same era. It is vital to emphasize the connections that exist between all forms of process corruption, regardless of whether they are motivated by personal benefit or the "greater good." In the vast majority of cases of noble cause corruption involving the QPF, there is a common factor: police misconduct was sanctioned, implicitly or explicitly, by figures in the state government who believed a strong police force was essential to maintaining the social order.

When it came to the bodgie threat in the 1950s, police were given a roving brief to assert conformity, profiling young people who appeared to be "delinquent" and asserting dominance over them. The Bodgie Squad was, in some ways, a precursor of what was to come in the 1960s and 1970s, the spiritual predecessor to units like the Regional Task Force, purpose-built to suppress dissent on the streets. The Regional Task Force worked hand in glove with its more covert counterpart, the Special Branch—a unit that Fitzgerald found problematic enough to recommend that it be disbanded in the inquiry's final report as part of a full restructuring of the police force.[9] Designed as an intelligence-gathering unit, Special Branch was coopted in the Bjelke-Petersen era to serve at the pleasure of the premier, using police powers and resources to serve the political interests of the government, rather than the people of Queensland. When the police are working to support the interests of the government, participating in misconduct can seem justifiable.

The interplay between politics and policing is virtually inescapable in Queensland, symbolized by the looming specter of Bjelke-Petersen. For almost twenty years, the premier was arguably the greatest driver of process corruption for the QPF—despite never having worn a police uniform. Bjelke-Petersen would likely agree with his contemporary, the U.S. president Richard Nixon, when he asserted that "when the President [or, in this case Premier] does [crime], that means that it is *not* illegal."[10] For twenty years, Bjelke-Petersen ruled over Queensland as his own personal fiefdom, and by that logic, the police were an extension of the government's will. It was the police's main purpose to ensure the stability and continuity of the state government. If that meant the liberal use of a baton to teach protesters a lesson, so be it. Even if it meant hiding the illegal conduct of "friends" of the government, so be it. Because the premier's end also came at Fitzgerald's hand, his mercenary corruption is often conflated with that of Lewis or the Joke. For the most part, this is a misconception. While Bjelke-Petersen ultimately did go on trial for perjury regarding his receiving bribes, the case in question involved property developers and thus had little to do with police corruption.[11] The criminal prosecution of the premier was, in a sense, incidental.

The fact that Bjelke-Petersen's charges were not related to policing does not, however, mean that his role in presiding over Queensland's corrupt system is overstated. His mercenary corruption may have been separate to Lewis's in practice, yet the growth of police corruption in the 1970s and 1980s owes much to the culture of permissiveness he fostered as premier. Though Bjelke-Petersen may not have received a "cut" of illegal bribes like Lewis did, he benefitted from police misconduct in other, potentially more important ways. His use of the QPF to quash political dissent and target enemies consistently strengthened his position as "the Hillbilly Dictator." The corrupt bargain he struck with police, indirectly, contributed to corruption. While Lewis was willing to do his bidding, no amount of criticism could force Bjelke-Petersen to remove him from the commissioner's office. But Bjelke-Petersen's legacy is not, ultimately, a brown paper bag, as so many of the narratives would suggest. His legacy was a police state that criminalized those who deigned to speak out against the state government. Under this regime, the QPF was a law unto itself, answerable only to a government that had little interest in taking action against police officers guilty of misconduct. Lack of oversight or consequences for police struck fear in Queenslanders. The police state emboldened corrupt officers to roam the streets with relative impunity, partaking in ever more bold expressions of corruption.

When corruption is endemic in the very system that is intended to provide oversight, it can result in a complete abdication of responsibility. A corrupt polity, over time, *becomes* the system. A state of anomie develops where the norms of the government and, indeed, the norms of the police force are no longer in alignment with the expectations of the community. In such a context, process corruption, both mercenary and noble cause, can become the system, not an aberration of it. When Bjelke-Petersen suspended the police rules by issuing a state of emergency during the 1971 Springboks tour, he gave a formal approval to police to use whatever means necessary to achieve their objectives. Was this illegal? No, it was sanctioned by the state government. But the excuse of "just following orders" does not absolve participants of moral responsibility. It only makes it more difficult to bring formal sanctions against them in retrospect. More insidious were the subtle, unspoken signs from the government that process corruption was tolerated so long as it did not contradict Bjelke-Petersen's ambitions. The state of emergency did not last, but the premier left no question where he stood on violence against protesters when he scuttled the internal investigations into the Rosemary Severin assault and the Cedar Bay raid. As long as the QPF did the premier's bidding, he remained loyal to the man tasked with leading it: Lewis. Other police commissioners would not have survived the 1982 *Nationwide* allegations or the David Moore scandal. Lewis did, not because of his innocence in these matters, but because he enjoyed the full support of the premier. Because of this compact, corruption was given the chance to flourish on his watch, eventually reaching the pervasive stage it was in when Fitzgerald began to take to it with an axe in 1987.

The story of twentieth-century Queensland is one of a place that was characterized by rampant corruption, but it is also the story of a people's refusal to accept repression and control. What emerged from Bjelke-Petersen's police state was a pushback from the subsections of society most impacted by the state's corruption. When pursued from venue to venue by police out for blood, the punks fought back—both with fists and in their art. Resistance to the state drove punk music, and the image of "Pig City" was revealed on airwaves around the country.[12] Repeated targets of state violence, the gay community could have buckled under the pressure. From at least the 1940s, police had labelled them "deviants" and set out to hunt them down wherever they gathered in the city's bars and beats.[13] But Queensland's gay community persisted and, when decriminalization occurred in 1990, emerged from the crucible ascendant. When Bjelke-Petersen and Lewis committed to crushing political opposition and told protesters to not bother applying for permits, the protest movement did not retreat. In fact, the Right to March campaign only served to fuel the public rage against the government, and after years of struggle, it was the *government* that was forced to backdown, not the people.[14] The story of corruption in Queensland is one of serious abuse of power, but it is also a tale of hope because despite all that Queenslanders went through at the hands of the state and its police force, they endured.

Too often, though, the focus of corruption in Queensland has reduced it to the mutualistic relationship between Lewis and Bjelke-Petersen. This is partly due to the ever-present influence of the Fitzgerald Inquiry, limited by its terms of reference to investigating only corruption that occurred in Lewis's time as commissioner. Far from this being the case, corruption has, to some degree, been a staple factor of policing in Queensland. Before Herbert even arrived in the Licensing Branch, there was already "a joke on" in the branch, and Bischof's use of process corruption techniques like the verbal to boost his career extended back into the pre-war period. Special Branch was the invention of Labor Party premier Ned Hanlon in 1948, not the personal political vanguard of Bjelke-Petersen. The larrikins in pre-federation Brisbane gave way for the bodgies in the 1950s who, in turn, gave way to the punks in the 1970s and 1980s. The gay beats in Brisbane have lengthy histories, some being used for anonymous sexual encounters for at least one hundred years in the criminalization period. Even the Bischof era, which many point to as the origin point for the corruption that was revealed by Fitzgerald, only came to pass because of the perception that a non-Catholic needed to be chosen as commissioner to cleanse the force of nepotism and political cronyism. The question of corruption has always been central to policing in Queensland, as it has in other jurisdictions all over the world. The organized misconduct seen in Queensland is one of the most well-defined examples of endemic, institutionalized corruption in recent history, yet the conditions that drive and perpetuate this system reverberate in many police forces that have had some experience of corruption. The problems Queensland faced in stamping out corruption should serve as a lesson to these other places, a roadmap of the pitfalls to avoid that let corruption become so essential to the system in the state throughout the twentieth century.

More than anything, exploring historical police corruption in Queensland shows that the division between mercenary and noble cause corruption is often an arbitrary distinction. Some police have been able to rationalize their actions, treating their own misconduct and that of their "blue brothers" as justifiable if part of a utilitarian pursuit for justice, but not if it is undertaken for personal gain. Perhaps for this reason, what Queensland shows is that noble cause corruption is more prolific than mercenary corruption. It also shows that this is not a binary proposition. Rarely are police involved in mercenary corruption not also engaged in noble cause corruption. For police to ignore vice crime because they are being paid to do so is unquestionably bad practice, but corruption is not a zero-sum game. Just because mercenary corruption is "bad" does not mean that noble cause corruption is not equally as bad, if not worse. Pursuing justice via noble cause corruption and rejecting the presumption of innocence until *proven* guilty does not serve the "greater good." It, too often, leaves bodies in its tragic wake. While all eyes were on the collapse of the Joke and the protection of vice in Queensland, the question of a police culture that sustained this Dirty Harry problem was left largely unanswered. Ultimately, the battle against corruption cannot be won unless *both* mercenary and noble cause corruption are addressed effectively.

It would be easy to write off the events of Queensland's past as an aberration—a case of rotten apples coming together at a singular moment in history, poisoning the profession of policing in Queensland. This characterization fits comfortably alongside the popular concept of rotten barrels, where rogue operators are able to corrupt other officers who have the misfortune of coming into contact with them. To suggest that a single person, or even a small group of people, was the vector for all of the Queensland police's problems in the twentieth century ignores the lessons of Fitzgerald, however. Bischof did not invent corruption, nor did Herbert or Lewis. History shows that where power over others is bestowed on certain people, the potential for the misuse of that power also exists. However, this risk is not restricted to police. Systemic corruption can emerge from all corners of the public service and political milieu. Queensland's experience shows us that corrupt police cultures do not exist in a vacuum, informed instead by factors from police leadership and political strategy to personal values and broader notions of collective social identity.

Fitzgerald was clear that, despite the popular perceptions of what his inquiry was about, the real solution to the problems facing Queensland was not a matter of restricting the police force or purging corrupt officers. The solution could be found in an honest, holistic assessment of the entire system of governance that gave rise to police corruption. It was not simply a matter of blowing apart the corrupt bargains between criminal and police officer. It was about blowing apart the same sort of corrupt deal made between premier and police commissioner. For Fitzgerald, the latter was more problematic, because blurred lines between police and politics put not just community safety that at risk, but democracy itself. The endemic corruption that Fitzgerald revealed was just one small part of a long history of corruption in the state, a mere ripple on the surface. But where there is a ripple, there is usually something beneath it, something causing a disruption to the otherwise tranquil water. For years, brave police officers, journalists, sex workers, bookmakers, politicians, and regular citizens created ripples, trying to expose the QPF for the corruption that was taking place within its ranks. Eventually, those ripples made waves that swept through the state in a way that transformed our understanding of how not just police corruption, but *all* corruption, is able to take root in policing institutions and, in doing so, compromise the justice system for all citizens.

Acknowledgments

This is a book several years in the making, and over that time, so many people have played a role in getting this project ready for release. First and foremost, I would like to express my gratitude to Catherine Cocks and her team at Michigan State University Press, who took a chance on a first-time author coming to them with a story about regional police corruption in far-flung Australia. I cannot tell you how much your support on this project means to me. Thank you for seeing the vision for *Under a Bad Sun* and helping me to realize it.

I would never have been able to finish this book without the support of the Department of Criminology and Sociology at Middlesex University, where I have worked while working on this project. Your advice and insight has been invaluable during this time. The research that forms the backbone of this book owes so much to my team of doctoral supervisors at the University of New England (Australia). I would not be here without the constant support of my principal supervisor, Dr. Matthew Allen, who took me on as a student and then worked with me to unravel the story of police corruption in Queensland. Matt, you showed a lot of trust in me to get this research right, and I cannot thank you enough. Credit also belongs to Dr. Erin Ihde, who was with me on this project from day one and who was always there with sage advice on not just how to complete this project, but how to tell a good story as well. Rounding out the team, I owe an immense amount of gratitude to Dr. Thomas J. Kehoe, not just a supervisor but a true mentor even beyond my studies. Tom, you have shown me not just how historical criminology should be done, but how we should *think* about what it is. You have taken so many chances on me since we first started working together, and your advice on how to pitch a clunky doctoral dissertation into an appealing book spurred me on to complete *Under a Bad Sun*. The book would simply not exist without your guidance and support.

I would like to thank the many police, journalists, authors, researchers, public servants, and so many others who took the time to speak with me as I put this book together. You were all so very supportive of what I was trying to do here and never hesitated to offer advice or leads to follow up as I pulled together this complicated story. I also thank the Queensland state government and, particularly, the Queensland State Archives for providing the archival materials that made this work possible.

I have been lucky enough to have a strong support team that have been an active part of this process from the beginning. This is for my grandmother, Gloria Bleakley. My love of books and stories is because of you, and your endless faith in me means so much. Thanks to my mother, Cindy Bleakley, for helping me believe that not only was something like this possible but that I was the one to do it. Your proofreading and feedback on the early drafts of this book also kept me on the right track, and this book owes a lot to you. To Taylor Kehoe, my forever "partner in crime" (and in life). You are an endless source of support and inspiration. You never cease to boost me up when things fall apart, and I would not be the person I am without you.

Finally, and perhaps most importantly, *Under a Bad Sun* is about corrupt police, but it is not *for* them. This book is dedicated to the legion of honest police who fought against misconduct and often suffered because of it. Without you, we would never have been able to tell the story of corruption. Your courage must never be forgotten.

Notes

INTRODUCTION

1. Matthew Condon, *Jacks and Jokers*, Brisbane, University of Queensland Press, 2014, p. 13.
2. Ibid., p. 187; Phil Dickie, *The Road to Fitzgerald*, Brisbane, University of Queensland Press, 1988, p. 75.
3. Matthew Condon, *All Fall Down*, Brisbane, University of Queensland Press, 2015, p. 295.
4. Chris Masters, "The Moonlight State," *Four Corners*, ABC Australia, 11 May 1987.
5. Ibid.
6. Janet Ransley and Richard Johnstone, "The Fitzgerald Symposium: An Introduction," *Griffith Law Review 18*(3), 2009, pp. 537–538.
7. Gerald E. Fitzgerald, *Report of a Commission of Inquiry Pursuant to Orders in Council*, Brisbane, Commission of Inquiry into Possible Misconduct and Associated Police Misconduct, 1989, p. 206.
8. James Wood, *Final Report of the Royal Commission into the New South Wales Police Service*, vol. 1, Sydney, Royal Commission into the New South Wales Police Service, 1997, pp. 20–21.
9. Carl Klockars, "The Dirty Harry Problem," *Annals of the American Academy of Political and Social Science 452*(1), 1980, p. 33.
10. Raymond Evans, "Springbok Tour Confrontation," in Raymond Evans and Carole Ferrier

(eds.), *Radical Brisbane: An Unruly History*, Brisbane, Vulgar Press, 2004, p. 278.
11. Jerome H. Skolnick, "Enduring Issues of Police Culture and Demographics," *Policing & Society 18*(1), 2008, p. 38.
12. Mark Lauchs, Robyn Keast and Daniel Chamberlain, "Resilience of a Corrupt Police Network: The First and Second Jokes in Queensland," *Crime, Law and Social Change 57*(2), 2012, p. 196.
13. Paul Bleakley, "'No Action Required': A Historical Pattern of Inaction and Discretion Towards Child Sexual Abuse in Queensland Policing," *Police Journal: Theory, Practice and Principles 93*(2), 2019, https://doi.org/10.1177/0032258X19839281, p. 2.
14. Paul Knepper and Anja Johansen, "Introduction," in Paul Knepper and Anja Johansen (eds.), *The Oxford Handbook of the History of Crime and Criminal Justice*, New York, Oxford University Press, 2016, p. 4.
15. Jay S. Berman, "The Taming of the Tiger: The Lexow Committee Investigation of Tammany Hall and the Police Department of the City of New York," *Police Studies: International Review of Police Development 4*(3), 1980, p. 55.
16. Queensland Cabinet, decision no. 47272, 14 October 1985, Queensland State Archives, Runcorn, Item ID2446312, Cabinet minutes—Transplantation and Anatomy Act regulations, p. 1.
17. Paul Bleakley, "Cleaning up the Dirty Squad: Using the Obscene Publications Act as a Weapon of Social Control," *State Crime Journal 8*(1), 2019, p. 19.
18. Richard Boyd, "Representing Political Violence: The Mainstream Media and the Weatherman 'Days of Rage,'" *American Studies 41*(1), 2000, p. 143.
19. Zelman Cowan, report, 31 August 1971, Queensland State Archives, Runcorn, Item ID381773, Correspondence—police, p. 2.

CHAPTER 1. SOMEWHERE ON THE RIVER BEND

1. Chris Pearce, *Through the Eyes of Thomas Pamphlett: Convict and Castaway*, Brisbane, Australian eBook Publisher, 2014.
2. From around 1790, a rum economy existed in Australia. Rum was imported and controlled by a small group of wealthy settlers and, as such, was very valuable. It was used as currency in a form of bartering.
3. Margaret Cook, *A River with a City Problem: A History of Brisbane Floods*, Brisbane, University of Queensland Press, 2019.
4. John T. Bigge, *Report of the Commissioner of Inquiry into the State of the Colony of New South Wales*, no. 68, Sydney, Government Printer, 1822.

5. Pearce, *Through the Eyes of Thomas Pamphlett*; Raphael Cilento and Clem Llewellyn Lack, "'Wild White Men' in Queensland," *Journal of the Royal Historical Society of Queensland* 6(1), 1959, pp. 74–75.
6. Cilento and Lack, "Wild White Men," p. 77.
7. Geoffrey A. Ginn, "Impressions and Inscriptions: Making Brisbane Town," *Queensland History Journal* 21(12), 2013, p. 791.
8. Raymond Evans, "The Mogwi Take Mi-an-jin: Race Relations and the Moreton Bay Penal Settlement 1824–42," in Rod Fisher (ed.), *Brisbane: The Aboriginal Presence, 1824–1860*, Brisbane, Brisbane History Group Papers, 1992, p. 12.
9. Indeed, Australia owes its very existence (in its current form, at least) to the United States. The outbreak of the American Revolution in 1775 forced the British to suspend convict transportation to the Americas. As a result, the hunt was on for a new colonial outpost to transport convicts to. Australia was chosen as this location, and European settlement commenced in 1788.
10. Douglas W. Fraser, "Settlement in Queensland in the 'Logan' Period," *Journal of the Royal Historical Society of Queensland* 7(3), 1965, p. 305.
11. Louis Radnor Cranfield, "Life of Captain Patrick Logan," *Journal of the Royal Historical Society of Queensland* 6(2), 1960, p. 321.
12. Raymond Evans, *A History of Queensland*, Cambridge, Cambridge University Press, 2007, p. 40.
13. Libby Connors, "Traditional Law and Indigenous Resistance at Moreton Bay, 1842–1855," *Australia and New Zealand Law and History E-Journal*, 2005, p. 109.
14. "Murder of Mr Stapylton by the Blacks at Moreton Bay," *Sydney Gazette and New South Wales Advertiser*, 29 August 1840, p. 2; Arthur Laurie, "The Black War in Queensland," *Journal of the Royal Historical Society of Queensland* 6(1), 1959, p. 107.
15. Patrick Wolfe, "Settler Colonialism and the Elimination of the Native," *Journal of Genocide Research* 8(4), 2006, p. 388.
16. Jonathan Richards, *The Secret War: A True History of Queensland's Native Police*, Brisbane, University of Queensland Press, 2008, p. 7.
17. Laurie, "The Black War," p. 171.
18. Bernadette Turner, "Mayne, Patrick (1824–1865)," *Australian Dictionary of Biography*, supplementary vol., 2005, http://adb.anu.edu.au/biography/mayne-patrick-13088.
19. K. L. Fry, "Boiling Down in the 1840s: A Grimy Means to a Solvent End," *Labour History: A Journal of Labour and Social History* (25), 1973, p. 1.
20. Turner, "Mayne, Patrick (1824–1865)"; Rosamond Siemon, *The Mayne Inheritance: A Gothic Tale of Murder, Madness and Scandal Across Generations*, Brisbane, University of

Queensland Press, 2003, p. 179.
21. Rosamund Siemon's book *The Mayne Inheritance*, first published in 1997, was been heavily criticized for using unsubstantiated historical evidence to connect Patrick Mayne to Robert Cox's murder. It is a controversial, yet influential, piece of work on Queensland history.
22. Siemon, *The Mayne Inheritance*, p. 7; Turner, "Mayne, Patrick (1824–1865)."
23. Letters Patent 1859, *Queensland Government Gazette*, 1859, p. 1.
24. Norman S. Pixley, "An Outline of the History of the Queensland Police Force, 1860–1949," *Journal of the Royal Historical Society of Queensland 4*(3), 1950, pp. 348–350.
25. Evans, *A History of Queensland*, p. 97.
26. "Central Police Court," *Brisbane Courier*, 22 September 1866, p. 4.
27. Peter Karsten, "Law and Politics in British Colonial Thought," *Settler Colonial Studies 1*(2), 2011, p. 163.
28. Denver Beanland, *The Queensland Caesar: Sir Thomas McIlwraith*, Brisbane, Boolarong Press, 2013, pp. 212–213; "Sir Thomas McIlwraith's Address," *Daily Northern Argus*, 27 March 1888, p. 3.
29. Noreen Kirkman, "Chinese Miners on the Palmer," *Journal of the Royal Historical Society of Queensland 13*(2), 1987, pp. 49–62.
30. "The Chinese on the Gold-Fields," *The Age*, 20 October 1856, p. 3; Myra Willard, *History of the White Australia Policy to 1920*, Melbourne, Melbourne University Press, 1923, p. 31; Mae M. Ngai, "Chinese Gold Miners and the 'Chinese Question' in Nineteenth-Century California and Victoria," *Journal of American History 101*(4), 2015, p. 1082.
31. R. Scott Baxter, "The Response of California's Chinese Populations to the Anti-Chinese Movement," *Historical Archaeology 42*(3), 2008, pp. 29–30; John Soennichsen, *The Chinese Exclusion Act of 1882*, Santa Barbara, ABC-CLIO, 2011, p. 8.
32. Beanland, *The Queensland Caesar*, p. 213.
33. Raymond Evans, "Anti-Chinese Riot, 1888," in Raymond Evans and Carole Ferrier (eds.), *Radical Brisbane: An Unruly History*, Brisbane, Vulgar Press, 2004, pp. 68–69.
34. C. P. Dorland, "Chinese Massacre at Los Angeles in 1871," *Annual Publication of the Historical Society of Southern California 3*(2), 1894, p. 23.
35. Erika Lee, "Review of *The Chinatown War: Chinese, Los Angeles and the Massacre of 1871* (2012), by Scott Zesch," *Journal of American History 100*(1), 2013, p. 217.
36. Evans, "Anti-Chinese Riot, 1888," p. 69.
37. Laurie, "The Black War," p. 171.
38. "The True History of the Hideous Gatton Murders," *Truth*, 27 June 1926, p. 23.
39. "Police Inquiry: Report of Commission," *Toowoomba Chronicle and Darling Downs General*

Advertiser, 5 December 1899, p. 3.
40. Ibid.; "Inspector Urquhart: What a Commission Thought," *Daily Standard*, 4 January 1917, p. 3.
41. W. Ross Johnston, "Urquhart, Frederic Charles (1858–1935)," *Australia Dictionary of Biography 12*, 1990, http://adb.anu.edu.au/biography/urquhart-frederic-charles-8901.
42. Alan Jenkins, "Attitudes Towards Federation in Queensland," MA thesis, University of Queensland, 1979, p. i.
43. Lyndon Megarrity, *Northern Dreams: The Politics of Northern Development in Australia*, North Melbourne, Australian Scholarly Publishing, 2019, pp. 26–27.
44. R. Gollan, "The Trade Unions and Labor Parties, 1890–94," *Australian Historical Studies* 7(25), 1955, p. 28; "Great Shearer's Strike: Episodes of 1891 Recalled," *Zeehan and Dundas Herald*, 3 August 1920, p. 4.
45. Raymond Evans, "Baton Friday 1912," in Raymond Evans and Carole Ferrier (eds.), *Radical Brisbane: An Unruly History*, Brisbane, Vulgar Press, 2004, p. 143.
46. Ibid.
47. Ibid., p. 144. Urquhart's use of a motor vehicle as a means of dispersal was opportunistic and a method that has been used in more recent cases of civil unrest like the 2020 protests against police brutality in the aftermath of George Floyd's death.
48. *Industrial Peace Act 1912* (QLD) 3 Geo V, No. 19, http://classic.austlii.edu.au/au/legis/qld/hist_act/ipao19123gvn19254/; Thomas William McCawley, "Industrial Arbitration in Australia," *International Labour Review 5*, 1922, p. 385.
49. "Queensland News," *Morning Bulletin*, 6 January 1917, p. 7; Johnston, "Urquhart, Frederic Charles (1858–1935)."
50. Raymond Evans, "Red Flag Riots of 1919," in Raymond Evans and Carole Ferrier (eds.), *Radical Brisbane: An Unruly History*, Brisbane, Vulgar Press, 2004, pp. 47–48.
51. Ibid., p. 130; "Down with Bolsheviks: Brisbane Soldiers' Mission," *Newcastle Sun*, 25 March 1919, p. 2.
52. Evans, "Red Flag Riots," p. 172. The cliché "reds under the beds" did not enter into the common discourse for several years to come, popularized during the Red Scare of 1950s McCarthyism. Nevertheless, in the 1919 siege of Russian Hall the cliché was made reality by a police force willing to accede to mob rule.
53. J. R. Laverty, "Town Planning in Brisbane, 1842–1925," *Royal Australian Planning Institute Journal* 9(1), 1971, p. 20.
54. Laverty, "Town Planning in Brisbane," p. 20; Peter Spearritt, "The 200km City: Brisbane, the Gold Coast and Sunshine Coast," *Australian Economic History Review* 49(1), 2009, p. 90.

55. Robert Menzies, "Menzies Speech: Declaration of War," *National Film and Sound Archive of Australia*, https://www.nfsa.gov.au/collection/curated/menzies-speech-declaration-war.
56. Walter R. Borneman, *MacArthur at War: World War II in the Pacific*, New York, Little Brown, 2017, pp. 167–168.
57. Prime Minister John Curtin denied being involved in the Brisbane Line plan and called a royal commission to investigate if his predecessor, Robert Menzies, had considered such a plan. The commission found no evidence to suggest the plan existed, but this finding has been disputed by many, including Douglas MacArthur in his memoirs.
58. Paul Burns, *The Brisbane Line Controversy: Political Opportunism versus National Security, 1942–45*, St Leonards, Australia, Allen & Unwin, 1998, 205.
59. Douglas MacArthur, *Reminiscences of General of the Army Douglas MacArthur*, Annapolis, Blue Jacket Books, 1964, pp. 152–153.

CHAPTER 2. THE END OF THE GREEN MAFIA

1. Meredith A. Harmes, Marcus K. Harmes, and Barbara Harmes, "Power at the Periphery: Sectarianism and the 1957 Labor Party Split in Regional Queensland," *Queensland History Journal* 21(9), 2012, p. 626.
2. Phil Dickie, *The Road to Fitzgerald*, Brisbane, University of Queensland Press, 1988, p. 4; Gerald E. Fitzgerald, *Report of a Commission of Inquiry Pursuant to Orders in Council*, Brisbane, Commission of Inquiry into Possible Misconduct and Associated Police Misconduct, 1989, p. 30.
3. *Parliamentary Debates*, 6 March 1958, LA, QLD, p. 1708.
4. Stuart Andrews, *Irish Rebellion: Protestant Polemic, 1798–1900*, Basingstoke, UK, Palgrave Macmillan, 2006, p. 5.
5. Michael Hogan, "Whatever Happened to Australian Sectarianism?," *Journal of Religious History* 13(1), 1984, p. 83.
6. Jenny Fleming and Monique Marks, "Reformers or Resisters? The State of Police Unionism in Australia," *Employment Relations Record* 4(1), 2004, p. 1; Georgina Sinclair, "The 'Irish' Policeman and the Empire: Influencing the Policing of the British Empire-Commonwealth," *Irish Historical Studies* 36(142), 2008, pp. 173–174. It was not just Australia where Irish migrants flocked to a career in policing. Former New York City Police Commissioner George W. Matsell claimed in 1855 that almost 17 percent of police officers in the city were Irish. By the turn of the twentieth century, that number had risen to five out of six NYPD officers being Irish-born or having Irish heritage. Michael W.

Flamm, "New York's Night of Birmingham Horror: The NYPD, the Harlem Riot of 1964, and the Politics of Law and Order," in Richard Bessel and Clive Emsley (eds.), *Patterns of Provocation: Police and Public Disorder*, Oxford, Berghann Books, 2000, p. 87.
7. Fitzgerald, *Report of a Commission*, p. 30.
8. Australia has had six changes in prime minister since 2007. Only two of these changes were the result of an election; the other four were all internal party disputes that resulted in the party leadership being ousted.
9. John Wanna and Tracey Arklay, *The Ayes Have It: The History of the Queensland Parliament, 1957–1989*, Canberra, ANU E Press, 2010, p. 35.
10. Ibid., p. 38.
11. *Parliamentary Debates*, 6 March 1958, p. 1707.
12. Matthew Condon, *Three Crooked Kings*, Brisbane, University of Queensland Press, 2013, p. 54.
13. "Runs on the board" is an Australian colloquialism that means someone has wins to their name. It is equivalent to the American "notch in the belt."
14. W. Ross Johnston, "Bischof, Francis Erich (Frank) (1904–1979)," *Australian Dictionary of Biography 13*, 1993, http://adb.anu.edu.au/biography/bischof-francis-erich-frank-9513.
15. Dickie, *The Road to Fitzgerald*, p. 268.
16. "Mt. Isa Greek Charged with Murder," *Courier-Mail*, 8 September 1941, p. 1.
17. Condon, *Three Crooked Kings*, p. 55.
18. Ibid., p. 21.
19. Johnston, "Bischof, Francis Erich (Frank)"; Matthew Condon, *Little Fish Are Sweet*, Brisbane, University of Queensland Press, 2016, p. 48.
20. G. A. G. Lucas, *Report of the Committee of Inquiry into the Enforcement of Criminal Law in Queensland*, Brisbane, Committee of Inquiry into the Enforcement of Criminal Law in Queensland, 1977, Queensland State Archives, Runcorn, Item ID2236744, Commission of Inquiry—reports, p. 9; Tim Anderson, "Miscarriages—What Is the Problem?," *Current Issues in Criminal Justice 5*(1), 1993, p. 76.
21. Dylan J. French, "The Cutting Edge of Confession Evidence: Redefining Coercion and Reforming Police Interrogation Techniques in the American Criminal Justice System," *Texas Law Review 97*, 2019, p. 1034.
22. "Murder Charge in Brisbane," *Argus*, 13 January 1947, p. 20; Condon, *Little Fish*, p. 48.
23. "'They Beat Me!' Inside Stories on Suicide in Brisbane Prison Cell," *Truth*, 23 March 1947, p. 1.
24. "Detective's Allegation: Halliday Found He Killed Taxi-Driver for 'Two Quid,'" *Morning Bulletin*, 10 December 1952, p. 1.

25. Trent Dalton, "Houdini and Me," *The Australian*, 16 June 2018.
26. *Parliamentary Debates*, 27 February 1951, LA, QLD, p. 1752; "Action on Bulimba Fraud," *Northern Miner*, 1 March 1951, p. 1.
27. "Arrest of Chief Electoral Officer in Queensland," *West Australian*, 9 March 1951, p. 1.
28. *Parliamentary Debates*, 6 March 1958, p. 1717.
29. Condon, *Three Crooked Kings*, p. 59.
30. "Two Constables for Trial on Manslaughter Charge," *Central Queensland Herald*, 19 July 1956, p. 13; *Parliamentary Debates*, 6 March 1958, pp. 1717–1718.
31. Condon, *Three Crooked Kings*, p. 37.
32. Dickie, *The Road to Fitzgerald*, p. 268.
33. Condon, *Three Crooked Kings*, p. 55.
34. Ibid., p. 56.
35. "Supreme Court: Criminal Sittings," *Townsville Daily Bulletin*, 27 November 1941, p. 7.
36. Condon, *Little Fish*, p. 36.
37. *Parliamentary Debates*, 6 March 1958, p. 1742.
38. Ibid., p. 1717.
39. "Made Statement Under Pressure, Says Constable," *Central Queensland Herald*, 12 July 1956, p. 24; *Parliamentary Debates*, 6 March 1958, p. 1718.

CHAPTER 3. RATS IN THE RANKS

1. Steve Bishop, *The Most Dangerous Detective: The Outrageous Glen Hallahan*, Charleston, CreateSpace, 2012, pp. 27–30.
2. "Bailey Found Guilty of Sundown Murder," *Canberra Times*, 21 May 1958, p. 3.
3. Bishop, *The Most Dangerous Detective*, pp. 30–31.
4. "'Took My Rifle'—Witness at Sundown Trial," *The Age*, 16 May 1958, p. 3.
5. Glendon Patrick Hallahan and Raymond John Bailey, transcript, 22 January 1958, quoted in Bishop, *The Most Dangerous Detective*, pp. 34–35.
6. "Bailey Found Guilty," p. 3; Hallahan, statutory declaration, 19 October 1988, Queensland State Archives, Runcorn, Item ID2548831, Commission of Inquiry—legal advice, p. 1; Bishop, *The Most Dangerous Detective*, p. 297.
7. Bishop, *The Most Dangerous Detective*, p. 336.
8. Samantha L. Thomas, Sophie Lewis, Colin McLeod and John Haycock, "'They Are Working Every Angle': A Qualitative Study of Australian Adults' Attitudes Towards, and Interactions with, Gambling Industry Marketing Strategies," *International Gambling Studies* 12(1), 2012, p. 111.

9. Stephen Letts, "Chart of the Day: Are Australians the World's Biggest Gambling Losers? You Can Bet on It," *ABC News* (Australia), 20 November 2018, https://www.abc.net.au/news/2018-11-20/australians-worlds-biggest-gambling-losers/10495566.
10. Leanne White, "The Role of the Horse in Australian Tourism and National Identity," in Elspeth Frew and Leanne White (eds.), *Tourism and National Identities: An International Perspective*, Oxford, Routledge, 2011, p. 66.
11. *Parliamentary Debates*, 3 October 1923, LA, QLD, p. 1426; *Racecourses Act 1923* (QLD) 14 Geo V, No. 23, http://classic.austlii.edu.au/au/legis/qld/hist_act/rao192314gvn23228/.
12. Max Bingham, *Report on S.P. Bookmaking and Related Criminal Activities in Queensland*, Brisbane, Criminal Justice Commission, 1991, p. 11.
13. Paul E. Gabriel and James R. Marsden, "An Examination of Market Efficiency in British Racetrack Betting," *Journal of Political Economy* 98(4), 1990, pp. 874–875.
14. Phil Dickie, "Organising Crime in Queensland," *Melaleuca Media*, http://www.melaleucamedia.com.au/_dbase_upl/Organising%20crime%20in%20Qld.pdf.
15. Ibid.
16. Bennett Liebman, "Horseracing in New York in the Progressive Era," *Gaming Law Review and Economics* 12(6), 2008, p. 561.
17. Bingham, *Report on S.P. Bookmaking*, p. 11.
18. W. J. Riordan, *Royal Commission Appointed to Inquire Into Whether It Is Desirable to Make Legal the Method of Betting and Wagering Commonly Known as Off-The-Course Betting*, transcript, 1951, Queensland State Archives, Runcorn, Item ID92059, Papers—Royal Commission, p. 3; Dickie, "Organising Crime," p. 6.
19. B. Grant Stitt, "Victimless Crime: A Definitional Issue," *Journal of Crime and Justice* 11(2), 1988, p. 87.
20. Matthew Condon, *Little Fish Are Sweet*, Brisbane, University of Queensland Press, 2016, p. 35.
21. Matthew Condon, *Three Crooked Kings*, Brisbane, University of Queensland Press, 2013, p. 21.
22. Glendon Patrick Hallahan, statutory declaration—appendix H, 19 October 1988, Queensland State Archives, Runcorn, Item ID2548831, Commission of Inquiry—legal advice, p. 1.
23. W. Ross Johnston, "Bischof, Francis Erich (Frank) (1904–1979)," *Australian Dictionary of Biography 13*, http://adb.anu.edu.au/biography/bischof-francis-erich-frank-9513.
24. Condon, *Three Crooked Kings*, pp. 8–9.
25. Bishop, *The Most Dangerous Detective*, p. 27.
26. *Parliamentary Debates*, 6 March 1958, LA, QLD, p. 1717; Bishop, *The Most Dangerous*

Detective, p. 28.
27. Raymond Evans, *A History of Queensland*, Cambridge, Cambridge University Press, 2007, p. 84.
28. Joan M. Jensen and Darlis A. Miller, "The Gentle Tamers Revisited: New Approaches to the History of Women in the American West," in Mary Ann Irwin and James F. Brooks (eds.), *Women and Gender in the American West*, Albuquerque, University of New Mexico Press, 2004, p. 19.
29. Yorick Smaal, "Queer Pleasure: Masculinity, Male Homosexuality and Public Space," *Queensland Historical Atlas*, 2010, https://core.ac.uk/download/pdf/143889667.pdf.
30. Yorick Smaal, "Coding Desire: The Emergence of a Homosexual Subculture in Queensland, 1890–1914," *Queensland Review* 14(2), 2007, p. 15.
31. Yorick Smaal, "Prostitution, 1880s-1900s," *Queensland Historical Atlas*, 2010, https://core.ac.uk/download/pdf/143889666.pdf.
32. Susan Pinto, Anita Scandia, and Paul Wilson, "Prostitution Laws in Australia," *Trends and Issues in Crime and Criminal Justice* 22(1), 1990, p. 2.
33. Smaal, "Prostitution."
34. Pinto, Scandia, and Wilson, "Prostitution Laws," p. 2; Smaal, "Prostitution."
35. Raymond Evans and Jacqui Donegan, "The Battle of Brisbane," *Politics and Culture* (4), 2004, https://politicsandculture.org/2010/08/10/the-battle-of-brisbane-by-raymond-evans-and-jacqui-donegan-2.
36. John Hammond Moore, *Over-sexed, Over-paid & Over-here: Americans in Australia, 1941–1945*, Brisbane, University of Queensland Press, 1981, p. 100.
37. "1 Man Killed, 8 Injured in City," *Courier-Mail*, 27 November 1942, p. 3; Evans and Donegan, "The Battle of Brisbane."
38. Donald Friend, diary, 7 March 1943, Box 2, Item 13, MS5959, National Library of Australia, Canberra; Clive Moore, *Sunshine and Rainbows: The Development of Gay and Lesbian Culture in Queensland*, Brisbane, University of Queensland Press, 2001, p. 107.
39. Condon, *Three Crooked Kings*, pp. 42, 45.
40. Ibid., p. 84.
41. Bishop, *The Most Dangerous Detective*, p. 84.
42. Condon, *Three Crooked Kings*, p. 85.
43. Ibid.
44. "Shake-up in CIB Vice Team," *Sunday Truth*, 18 October 1959, p. 3.
45. Carl Klockars, "The Dirty Harry Problem," *Annals of the American Academy of Political and Social Science* 452(1), 1980, p. 33; James Wood, *Final Report of the Royal Commission into the New South Wales Police Service*, vol. 1, Sydney, Royal Commission into the New

South Wales Police Service, 1997, p. 28.
46. Phil Dickie, *The Road to Fitzgerald*, Brisbane, University of Queensland Press, 1988, p. 5; "Commissioner Denies 'Close-Knit Friendship,'" *Canberra Times*, 29 January 1964, p. 6.
47. Bishop, *The Most Dangerous Detective*, pp. 85–86; Condon, *Three Crooked Kings*, p. 87.
48. "Commissioner Denies 'Close-Knit Friendship,'" p. 6.
49. Bishop, *The Most Dangerous Detective*, p. 86; Condon, *Three Crooked Kings*, p. 107.
50. Ronald Weitzer, "New Directions in Research on Prostitution," *Crime, Law & Social Change 43*(4–5), 2005, pp. 227–228.

CHAPTER 4. CHECKING IN AT THE NATIONAL HOTEL

1. William Marshall, "The Creation of Yorkshireness: Cultural Identities in Yorkshire c. 1850–1918," PhD thesis, University of Huddersfield, 2011, p. 14; Steve Bishop, *The Most Dangerous Detective: The Outrageous Glen Hallahan*, Charleston, CreateSpace, 2012, p. 92.
2. "Allegations About 2 Women Withdrawn," *Canberra Times*, 6 December 1963, p. 6; Bishop, *The Most Dangerous Detective*, p. 92.
3. Matthew Condon, *Three Crooked Kings*, Brisbane, University of Queensland Press, 2013, pp. 147–148.
4. "Witness Admits Lack of Proof on Hotel Girls," *Canberra Times*, 4 December 1963, p. 3; Condon, *Three Crooked Kings*, p. 74.
5. "Police Union Seeks Inquiry into Force," *Canberra Times*, 7 November 1963, p. 2.
6. Condon, *Three Crooked Kings*, p. 73.
7. Clare Wright, *Beyond the Ladies Lounge: Australia's Female Publicans*, Melbourne, Text Publishing, 2003, p. 106.
8. Condon, *Three Crooked Kings*, p. 73.
9. "Shake-up in CIB vice Team," *Sunday Truth*, 18 October 1959, p. 3; Condon, *Three Crooked Kings*, p. 85.
10. Condon, *Three Crooked Kings*, p. 144.
11. *Parliamentary Debates*, 29 October 1963, LA, QLD, p. 1062.
12. Condon, *Three Crooked Kings*, pp. 147–148.
13. "Hotel Scandal: New Witness Fobbed Off; Ready to Tell," *Sunday Truth*, 10 November 1963, p. 1.
14. George Gilligan, "Royal Commissions of Inquiry," *Australian & New Zealand Journal of Criminology 35*(3), 2002, p. 303.
15. Mike Rowe and Laura McAllister, "The Roles of Commissions of Inquiry in the Policy Process," *Public Policy and Administration 21*(4), 2006, p. 100.

16. Ross Fitzgerald, "Judicial Culture and the Investigation of Corruption: A Comparison of the Gibbs National Hotel Inquiry 1963–64 and the Fitzgerald Inquiry 1987–89," in Scott Prasser, Rae Wear and John Nethercote (eds.), *Corruption and Reform: The Fitzgerald Vision*, Brisbane, University of Queensland Press, 1990, p. 64.
17. Condon, *Three Crooked Kings*, p. 73.
18. Phil Dickie, *The Road to Fitzgerald*, Brisbane, University of Queensland Press, 1988, p. 9.
19. Matthew Condon, *Little Fish Are Sweet*, Brisbane, University of Queensland Press, 2016, p. 87.
20. "Investigation of Police Begins," *Canberra Times*, 21 November 1963, p. 2.
21. Michael Kirby, "The Centenary of Sir Harry Gibbs: Constitutional Methodology, Lawmaking and the Marriage Plebiscite," *University of Queensland Law Journal 35*, 2016, pp. 286–287.
22. *Parliamentary Debates*, 28 August 1963, LA, QLD, p. 100; "Battle Ahead for Liberal of Independence," *Canberra Times*, 13 October 1969, p. 8.
23. Bishop, *The Most Dangerous Detective*, pp. 94–95.
24. Ibid., p. 112.
25. Greg McCarthy, "The HIH Royal Commission and the Tangled Web of Truth," *Australian Journal of Public Administration 60*(3), 2001, p. 111.
26. "Hotel Scandal," p. 1.
27. Bishop, *The Most Dangerous Detective*, p. 99.
28. "Hotel Scandal," p. 1.
29. Bishop, *The Most Dangerous Detective*, p. 99.
30. "Hotel Scandal," p. 1; Bishop, *The Most Dangerous Detective*, p. 93.
31. Raymond Evans, "Red Flag Riots of 1919," in Raymond Evans and Carole Ferrier (eds.), *Radical Brisbane: An Unruly History*, Brisbane, Vulgar Press, 2004, p. 47.
32. "Waiter Challenged on Threats Against PM," *Canberra Times*, 11 December 1963, p. 6; Condon, *Three Crooked Kings*, pp. 159–160.
33. "Waiter Challenged," p. 6.
34. Bishop, *The Most Dangerous Detective*, p. 100.
35. Ibid., p. 101.
36. Condon, *Little Fish*, p. 80.
37. Harry Talbot Gibbs, *Report of the Royal Commission Appointed to Inquire into and Report on Certain Matters Relating to Members of the Police Force and the National Hotel, Petrie Bight*, Brisbane, 10 April 1964, Queensland State Archives, Runcorn, Item ID415488, Cabinet papers, p. 84.
38. Bishop, *The Most Dangerous Detective*, p. 95.

39. "Witness Admits Lack of Proof," p. 3; Condon, *Three Crooked Kings*, p. 74.
40. Bishop, *The Most Dangerous Detective*, pp. 97, 107.
41. "Probe Witness Tells of Threat," *Courier-Mail*, 4 December 1963, p. 1; Condon, *Three Crooked Kings*, p. 162.
42. *Parliamentary Debates*, 13 October 1971, LA, QLD, p. 1053.
43. "Commissioner Denies 'Close-Knit Friendship,'" *Canberra Times*, 29 January 1964, p. 6; Bishop, *The Most Dangerous Detective*, p. 109.
44. Bishop, *The Most Dangerous Detective*, p. 111.
45. Condon, *Three Crooked Kings*, p. 165.
46. Bishop, *The Most Dangerous Detective*, p. 114.
47. Dickie, *The Road to Fitzgerald*, p. 5.

CHAPTER 5. JOKERS' WILD

1. Manfred Cross, "Hiley, Sir Thomas Alfred (Tom) (1905–1990)," *Australian Dictionary of Biography 17*, http://adb.anu.edu.au/biography/hiley-sir-thomas-alfred-tom-12634.
2. Matthew Condon, *Three Crooked Kings*, Brisbane, University of Queensland Press, 2013, p. 20.
3. Phil Dickie, *The Road to Fitzgerald*, Brisbane, University of Queensland Press, 1988, p. 5.
4. In 2020, the large town fee of AUD$80,000 equates to AUD$1.18 million (USD$794,000) when adjusted for inflation. The small-town price of AUD$20,000 is equal to AUD$295,000 (USD$199,000).
5. Dickie, *The Road to Fitzgerald*, pp. 5–6.
6. Ibid., p. 6.
7. Ibid., p. 274.
8. Gerald E. Fitzgerald, *Report of a Commission of Inquiry Pursuant to Orders in Council*, Brisbane, Commission of Inquiry into Possible Misconduct and Associated Police Misconduct, 1989, p. 32.
9. Ibid., pp. 22–23.
10. Stephanie St. Clair, the African American numbers boss of Harlem in the 1930s, found this out first hand when police arrested her and sentenced her to eight months in a workhouse after she went public accusing them of taking bribes to protect her gambling interests. LaShawn Harris, "Playing the Numbers Game: Madame Stephanie St. Clair and African-American Policy Culture in Harlem," *Black Women, Gender and Families* 2(2), 2008, pp. 53–54.
11. Patrick Glancy, statutory declaration, 5 October 1988, Queensland State Archives,

Runcorn, Item ID2548827, Commission of Inquiry—legal advice, pp. 1–2.
12. Domenico Cacciola and Ben Robertson, *Who's Who in the Zoo? A Story of Corruption, Crooks and Killers*, Brisbane, University of Queensland Press, 2014, pp. 38–39.
13. Fitzgerald, *Report of a Commission*, p. 33.
14. Matthew Condon, *Little Fish Are Sweet*, Brisbane, University of Queensland Press, 2016, p. 35.
15. Fitzgerald, *Report of a Commission*, p. 33; Condon, *Three Crooked Kings*, p. 182.
16. Elena Jeffreys, "Australia and New Zealand," in Melissa Hope Ditmore (ed.), *Encyclopedia of Prostitution and Sex Work*, vol. 1, Westport, Greenwood Publishing, 2006, p. 53; Matthew Condon, *The Night Dragon*, Brisbane, University of Queensland Press, 2019, p. 187.
17. Janice G. Raymond, Donna M. Hughes, and Carol J. Gomez, "Sex Trafficking of Women in the United States," in Leonard Territo and George Kirkham (eds.), *International Sex Trafficking of Women and Children: Understanding the Global Epidemic*, Flushing, NY, Looseleaf Law Publications, 2010, p. 5.
18. Ronald Redmond, statutory declaration, 29 July 1988, Queensland State Archives, Runcorn, Item ID1278190, Commission of Inquiry—Exhibit, pp. 5–6; Cacciola and Robertson, *Who's Who in the Zoo?*, p. 50.
19. Cacciola and Robertson, *Who's Who in the Zoo?*, p. 50.
20. Raymond Wells Whitrod, *Before I Sleep*, Brisbane, University of Queensland Press, 2001, p. 93.
21. Fitzgerald, *Report of a Commission*, p. 38.
22. Ibid., p. 37.
23. "Lawyer Says a Clean Police Force Wanted," *Canberra Times*, 20 May 1976, p. 3; Fitzgerald, *Report of a Commission*, p. 38.
24. "Lawyer Says a Clean Police Force Wanted," p. 3.
25. "$1,500 a Month Bribe Offer Alleged," *Canberra Times*, 2 September 1975, p. 7; In 2020, AUD$1500 equates to AUD$13,843 (USD$9,320).
26. Fitzgerald, *Report of a Commission*, p. 38; In 2020, AUD$50 million equates to AUD$461,417,412 (USD$310,626,202).
27. G. A. G. Lucas, *Report of the Committee of Inquiry into the Enforcement of Criminal Law in Queensland*, Brisbane, Committee of Inquiry into the Enforcement of Criminal Law in Queensland, 1977, Queensland State Archives, Runcorn, Item ID2236744, Commission of Inquiry—reports, pp. 22–23.
28. Ibid.
29. Dickie, *The Road to Fitzgerald*, p. 69.

30. James Wood, *Final Report of the Royal Commission into the New South Wales Police Service*, vol. 1 Sydney, Royal Commission into the New South Wales Police Service, 1997, p. 29.
31. *Parliamentary Debates*, 13 October 1971, LA, QLD, p. 1053; Condon, *Three Crooked Kings*, p. 70.
32. Steve Bishop, *The Most Dangerous Detective: The Outrageous Glen Hallahan*, Charleston, CreateSpace, 2012, p. 123; Condon, *Three Crooked Kings*, p. 70.
33. Bishop, *The Most Dangerous Detective*, pp. 127–128.
34. "Sydney's Richest Call-Girl," *Sunday Mirror*, 8 June 1969, p. 1; Bishop, *The Most Dangerous Detective*, p. 127.
35. *Parliamentary Debates*, 13 October 1971, p. 1052; Condon, *Three Crooked Kings*, pp. 233–234.
36. *Parliamentary Debates*, 13 October 1971, p. 1053.
37. Whitrod, *Before I Sleep*, pp. 136–137.
38. *Parliamentary Debates*, 13 October 1971, p. 1053.
39. Ibid., pp. 1052–1053.
40. Dickie, *The Road to Fitzgerald*, p. 270.
41. Glendon Patrick Hallahan, statutory declaration—appendix C, 19 October 1988, Queensland State Archives, Runcorn, Item ID2548831, Commission of Inquiry—legal advice, p. 1; Bishop, *The Most Dangerous Detective*, p. 215; Condon, *Three Crooked Kings*, pp. 283–284.
42. "Corruption Is Alleged," *Canberra Times*, 20 December 1971, p. 7; Condon, *Little Fish*, p. 117.
43. "Decision on Charge Deferred," *Canberra Times*, 20 May 1972, p. 8; Condon, *Three Crooked Kings*, p. 271; In 2020, AUd$20 is equivalent to AUD$233 (USD$156) when adjusted for inflation.
44. Bishop, *The Most Dangerous Detective*, p. 164; Condon, *Three Crooked Kings*, pp. 272–273.
45. Condon, *Three Crooked Kings*, p. 273.
46. Bishop, *The Most Dangerous Detective*, pp. 175, 178.
47. Condon, *Three Crooked Kings*, p. 293.
48. Bishop, *The Most Dangerous Detective*, pp. 183–184; Condon, *Three Crooked Kings*, pp. 293–294.
49. "Police in the Land of Papa Joh," *Tribune*, 5 September 1972, p. 6; Glendon Patrick Hallahan, statutory declaration—appendix C, 19 October 1988, Queensland State Archives, Runcorn, Item ID2548831, Commission of Inquiry—legal advice, p. 6.

CHAPTER 6. VICE CITY

1. Steve Bishop, "Chapter 1: Why Bob Declared War," *Bob Campbell's War*, http://www.stevebishop.net/chapter-1-why-bob-campbell-declared-war.html.
2. Amanda Davies, "A Case of Community Safety: Displacing Complex 'Social' Problems in Fortitude Valley," PhD thesis, Queensland University of Technology, 2011, p. 5.
3. *Parliamentary Debates*, 4 March 1982, LA, QLD, p. 4421; Bishop, "Chapter 1."
4. Glendon Patrick Hallahan, statutory declaration—appendix H, 19 October 1988, Queensland State Archives, Runcorn, Item ID2548831, Commission of Inquiry—legal advice, p. 1; Bishop, "Chapter 1."
5. Roman Quaedvleig, *Tour de Force: From Rookie to Top Cop*, read by the author, Carlton, Melbourne University Publishing, 2019, chapter 2.
6. Steve Bishop, *The Most Dangerous Detective: The Outrageous Glen Hallahan*, Charleston, CreateSpace, 2012, p. 43.
7. *Parliamentary Debates*, 6 March 1958, LA, QLD, p. 1717; Bishop, *The Most Dangerous Detective*, p. 297; Matthew Condon, *Little Fish Are Sweet*, Brisbane, University of Queensland Press, 2016, p. 35.
8. "An 'Outsider' with Inside Experience," *Canberra Times*, 19 January 1970, p. 2; Matthew Condon, *Three Crooked Kings*, Brisbane, University of Queensland Press, 2013, p. 206.
9. Raymond Whitrod, *Before I Sleep*, Brisbane, University of Queensland Press, 2001, pp. 93, 137, 142.
10. Ibid., p. 145.
11. Mark Lauchs, Robyn Keast, and Nina Yousefpour, "Corrupt Police Networks: Uncovering Hidden Relationship Patterns, Functions and Roles," *Policing & Society 21*(1), 2011, p. 122.
12. Queensland Police Union of Employees to Francis Bischof, letter, 16 July 1963, Queensland State Archives, Runcorn, Item ID373745, Administration file, police, p. 1.
13. William D. Simpson, "The Control of Deviant Behaviour in Australia: A Police Approach," paper presented to the Seminar on the Control of Deviant Behaviour in Australia, Canberra, 30 January–23 February 1968, Queensland State Archives, Runcorn, Item ID380908, Administration file, police, p. 4.
14. Allen Maxwell Hodges, press statement, 2 November 1972, Queensland State Archives, Runcorn, Item ID373748, Administration file, police, p. 1.
15. Raymond Wells Whitrod to David Longland, letter, 3 January 1973, Queensland State Archives, Runcorn, Item ID373748, Administration file, police, p. 1.
16. Ibid.
17. Condon, *Three Crooked Kings*, p. 252.
18. Gerald E. Fitzgerald, *Report of a Commission of Inquiry Pursuant to Orders in Council*,

Brisbane, Commission of Inquiry into Possible Misconduct and Associated Police Misconduct, 1989, p. 37.
19. Queensland Police Force, "Regulation 2.25," Police Rules, n.d., Queensland State Archives, Runcorn, Item ID540963, Protest demonstrations—general, p. 1; Matthew Condon, *Jacks and Jokers*, Brisbane, University of Queensland Press, 2014, p. 26.
20. Owen Kelly to Johannes Bjelke-Petersen, letter, 10 August 1976, Queensland State Archives, Runcorn, Item ID540963, Protest demonstrations—general, p. 1.
21. Whitrod, *Before I Sleep*, p. 180.
22. "Two Constables for Trial on Manslaughter Charge," *Central Queensland Herald*, 19 July 1956, p. 13; *Parliamentary Debates*, 6 March 1958p. 1717.
23. Whitrod, *Before I Sleep*, pp. 184–185.
24. Fitzgerald, *Report of a Commission*, p. 46.
25. Condon, *Jacks and Jokers*, p. 67.
26. Selwyn Raab, "New York's Police Allow Corruption, Mollen Panel Says," *New York Times*, 29 December 1993, https://www.nytimes.com/1993/12/29/nyregion/new-york-s-police-allow-corruption-mollen-panel-says.html?pagewanted=all&src=pm.
27. G. A. G. Lucas, *Report of the Committee of Inquiry into the Enforcement of Criminal Law in Queensland*, Brisbane, Committee of Inquiry into the Enforcement of Criminal Law in Queensland, 1977, Queensland State Archives, Runcorn, Item ID2236744, Commission of Inquiry—reports, pp. 214, 34–35.
28. Fitzgerald, *Report of a Commission*, p. 48.
29. Lucas, *Report of the Committee of Inquiry*, p. 18; Fitzgerald, *Report of a Commission*, p. 51.
30. *Vagrants, Gaming and Other Offences Amendment Act 1971* (QLD), part 2, s. 5, https://www.legislation.qld.gov.au/view/whole/html/asmade/asmade/act-1971-069.
31. Fitzgerald, *Report of a Commission*, p. 66.
32. Domenico Cacciola and Ben Robertson, *Who's Who in the Zoo? A Story of Corruption, Crooks and Killers*, Brisbane, University of Queensland Press, 2014, p. 188.
33. Salvatore Di Carlo, testimony, 17 May 1988, Queensland State Archives, Runcorn, Item ID2548522, Commission of Inquiry—legal advice, p. 9349.
34. Phil Dickie, *The Road to Fitzgerald*, Brisbane, University of Queensland Press, 1988, p. 70.
35. Di Carlo, testimony, p. 9349.
36. "Three Machine Operators Allegedly Ordered to Pay $50,000 Each," *Canberra Times*, 17 May 1988, p. 7; Fitzgerald, *Report of a Commission*, p. 55.
37. Dickie, *The Road to Fitzgerald*, p. 276.
38. Ibid.
39. Evan Whitton, *The Hillbilly Dictator*, Crows Nest, Australia, ABC Books, 1989, p. 53.

40. Fitzgerald, *Report of a Commission*, p. 67.
41. Noel Dwyer, testimony, 19 May 1988, Queensland State Archives, Runcorn, Item ID2548524, Commission of Inquiry—legal advice, p. 9515.
42. Dickie, *The Road to Fitzgerald*, pp. 32, 98.
43. Ibid., p. 75; Condon, *Jacks and Jokers*, p. 187.
44. Dickie, *The Road to Fitzgerald*, pp. 82–83; Fitzgerald, *Report of a Commission*, p. 65.
45. Dickie, *The Road to Fitzgerald*, pp. 84–85; In 2020, a payment of AUD$23,000 in 1987 equals around AUD$65,255 (USD$43,212) while AUD$17,000 comes to AUD$44,536 (USD$29,492).
46. Steve Bishop, "Chapter 2: First Salvos," *Bob Campbell's War*, http://www.stevebishop.net/chapter-2-first-salvos.html.
47. *Parliamentary Debates*, 13 October 1981, LA, QLD, p. 2507.
48. Bishop, "Chapter 2."
49. *Parliamentary Debates*, 2 March 1982, LA, QLD, p. 4294; Condon, *Jacks and Jokers*, p. 393.
50. Steve Bishop, "Chapter 4: Campbell's War Attracts TV Coverage," *Bob Campbell's War*, http://www.stevebishop.net/chapter-4-campbells-war-attracts-tv-coverage.html.
51. Condon, *Jacks and Jokers*, p. 419.
52. T. S. C. Atkinson, statutory declaration, 11 July 1988, Queensland State Archives, Runcorn, Item ID2548800, Commission of Inquiry—legal advice, p. 7.
53. Ibid.
54. Roy Clapper, testimony, 12 May 1988, Queensland State Archives, Runcorn, Item ID2548520, Commission of inquiry—legal advice, p. 9101; Serge Pregliasco, testimony, 12 May 1988, Queensland State Archives, Runcorn, Item ID2548520, Commission of inquiry—legal advice, pp. 9106–9107.
55. Condon, *Jacks and Jokers*, p. 271.

CHAPTER 7. THE BODGIE SQUAD HITS THE STREET

1. "Girls Were the Curse of Danny's Life," *Mail*, 5 May 1951, p. 3.
2. "Danny Simmons on Points," *Argus*, 8 June 1945, p. 13.
3. "Girls Were the Curse," p. 3.
4. "Bookie's Clerk Shot Dead in Sydney House," *Barrier Miner*, 2 May 1951, p. 1.
5. "Girls Were the Curse," p. 3; "Stamp Out Bodgie Cult," *Townsville Daily Bulletin*, 7 June 1952, p. 1.
6. Fiona Allon, "At Home in the Suburbs: Domesticity and Nation in Postwar Australia," *History Australia* 11(1), 2014, p. 13.

7. Andrew Clark, "The Push to Return Australia to an Era of Social Conservatism," *Australian Financial Review*, 20 September 2019, https://www.afr.com/politics/federal/the-push-to-return-australia-to-an-era-of-social-conservatism-20190920-p52t7t.
8. Robert Menzies, "The Forgotten People: A Speech by Robert Menzies on, 22 May, 1942," Liberals.net, http://www.liberals.net/theforgottenpeople.htm.
9. Ibid.
10. John Rickard, "Lovable Larrikins and Awful Ockers," *Journal of Australian Studies* 22(56), 1998, p. 81.
11. Melissa Belanta, *Larrikins: A History*, Brisbane, University of Queensland Press, 2012, p. xx.
12. Philip Gooderson, "'Noisy and Dangerous Boys': The Slogging Gang Phenomenon in Late Nineteenth-Century Birmingham," *Midland History* 38(1), 2013, p. 58.
13. Belanta, *Larrikins*, p. 28.
14. Ibid., pp. 9–10.
15. "City Police Court," *Brisbane Courier*, 18 October 1884, p. 3.
16. Rickard, "Lovable Larrikins," p. 79; Murray Johnson, "Larrikin Push 1902," in Raymond Evans and Carole Ferrier (eds.), *Radical Brisbane: An Unruly History*, Brisbane, Vulgar Press, 2004, p. 124.
17. *Vagrancy Act 1835* (NSW), no. 6, s. 1.
18. "The Fatal Affray," *Brisbane Courier*, 28 December 1891, p. 5.
19. Johnson, "Larrikin Push," pp. 125–126.
20. Gooderson, "Noisy and Dangerous Boys," pp. 58–59.
21. Larry Ford, "Geographic Factors in the Origin, Evolution, and Diffusion of Rock and Roll Music," *Journal of Geography* 70(8), 1971, p. 456.
22. Milton Moon, "Radio Round-Up," *South Coast Express*, 16 March 1951, p. 5.
23. "1500 Saw 500 Dance," *Courier-Mail*, 24 July 1951, p. 5.
24. "Bookie's Clerk Shot Dead," p. 1; "Girls Were the Curse," p. 3.
25. "Man Wounded: Shots Fired from Car," *Sydney Morning Herald*, 19 February 1938, p. 11; James Morton and Susanna Lobez, *Gangland Australia*, Carlton, Victory Books, 2007, p. 133.
26. "Bookie's Clerk Shot Dead," p. 1.
27. "Girls Were the Curse," p. 3; Grace Garlick, "Six Discharged from Their Jobs in the City," *Sunday Mail*, 16 December 1951, p. 2.
28. "Girls Were the Curse," p. 3.
29. "'Entitled to Shoot Lee' says Hayes," *Sydney Morning Herald*, 29 August 1951, p. 5; Morton and Lobez, *Gangland Australia*, p. 132.

30. "Entitled to Shoot Lee," p. 5.
31. "A Detective Denied 'Putting on the Verbal,'" *Daily Telegraph*, 2 December 1951, p. 35; Morton and Lobez, *Gangland Australia*, p. 133. Ray Kelly was close to another familiar Queensland police officer with a reputation for verbals. During an interstate manhunt in the 1960s, Kelly became friends with Rat Pack member Glen Hallahan—a relationship that continued until Hallahan's resignation in 1972.
32. Morton and Lobez, *Gangland Australia*, p. 135.
33. "Bodgies Refused Time," *Brisbane Telegraph*, 5 December 1951, p. 16.
34. Ibid.
35. "Brisbane Bonds for a 'Bodgie,'" *Advocate*, 15 December 1951, p. 29.
36. Garlick, "Six Discharged," p. 2.
37. Ibid.
38. Eugene Toker, "The Scapegoat as an Essential Group Phenomenon," *International Journal of Group Psychotherapy* 22(3), 1972, p. 320.
39. "Rigid Police Action," *Northern Miner*, 20 December 1951, p. 1.
40. "Truculent Bodgies: Youth Carrying Weapon Jailed," *Brisbane Telegraph*, 17 May 1954, p. 9.
41. "Police Order to Smash Bodgie Gangs," *Warwick Daily News*, 19 May 1954, p. 1.
42. Ibid.
43. "Police Drive on Bodgies Is Welcome," *Brisbane Telegraph*, 19 May 1954, p. 20.
44. "Order Out on City Gangs: Police to Smash 'bodgies,'" *Courier-Mail*, 19 May 1954, p. 1.
45. "Bodgie in City Wild Sex, Liquor 'Parties' Are Held," *Truth*, 4 July 1954, p. 3; "Campaign to Beat Bodgies: Police See Parents," *Courier-Mail*, 16 July 1954, p. 3.
46. Raymond Evans, "Rock 'n' Roll Riot 1956," in Raymond Evans and Carole Ferrier (eds.), *Radical Brisbane: An Unruly History*, Brisbane, Vulgar Press, 2004, pp. 250, 251.
47. Ibid., p. 251.
48. Condon, *Three Crooked Kings*, p. 75.
49. Evans, "Rock 'n' Roll Riot," pp. 249–250.
50. Geoffrey Walden, "It's Only Rock 'n' Roll But I Like It: A History of the Early Days of Rock 'n' Roll in Brisbane as Told by Some of the People Who Were There," PhD thesis, Queensland University of Technology, 2003, pp. 232–233.
51. Ibid., p. 234.
52. John Wayne Ryan, *I Survived: True Stories of Brisbane's Underbelly*, Coopers Plains, Book Pal, 2012, p. 138.
53. Ross Fitzgerald, "Judicial Culture and the Investigation of Corruption: A Comparison of the Gibbs National Hotel Inquiry 1963–64 and the Fitzgerald Inquiry 1987–89," in Scott Prasser, Rae Wear, and John Nethercote (eds.), *Corruption and Reform: The Fitzgerald*

Vision, Brisbane, University of Queensland Press, 1990, p. 75.
54. *Parliamentary Debates*, 27 October 1959, LA, QLD, p. 950.
55. "Bodgie Threat Beaten," *Courier-Mail*, 29 July 1957, p. 3.
56. Elijah Wald, *How The Beatles Destroyed Rock 'n' Roll: An Alternative History of American Popular Music*, New York, Oxford University Press, 2009, p. 182.
57. Raymond Evans, "'Real Gone Town': Popular Music and Youth Culture in 1960s Brisbane," in Shirleene Robinson and Julie Ustinoff (eds.), *The 1960s in Australia: People, Power and Politics*, Newcastle-upon-Tyne, UK, Cambridge Scholars Publishing, 2012, p. 5.
58. Glenn A. Baker, *The Beatles Down Under: The 1964 Australia and New Zealand Tour*, Sydney, Wild & Wooley, 1982, p. 87.
59. Anthony James Taylor, "Beatlemania—A Study in Adolescent Enthusiasm," *British Journal of Social and Clinical Psychology* 5(2), 1966, p. 81.
60. Norwin Bauer, letter, 25 August 1964, Queensland State Archives, Runcorn, Item ID318753, Correspondence, police, p. 2.
61. Andrew Stafford, *Pig City: From the Saints to Savage Garden*, Brisbane, University of Queensland Press, 2006, p. 57.
62. Terence Lewis, *Annual Report 1978*, Brisbane, Queensland Police Department, 1978, p. 14.
63. Allan Gardiner, "Punks and Police," in Raymond Evans and Carole Ferrier (eds.), *Radical Brisbane: An Unruly History*, Brisbane, Vulgar Press, 2004, pp. 300–301.
64. Stafford, *Pig City*, p. 57.
65. Thomas Vuleta, "Ups and Downs: Music Venues and Popular Music in Brisbane 1959–1989," Honors thesis, University of Queensland, 2010, pp. 11–12.
66. Michael Ewen Kitson, "The Sex Pistols and the London Mob," PhD thesis, University of Western Sydney, 2008, p. 7.
67. Stafford, *Pig City*, pp. 148–149.
68. Mark Thewlis, *Thirty Years of Anger: One Man's Journey through the Australian Underground Hardcore Punk & Extreme Metal Scenes*, Brisbane, Boolarong Press, 2016, p. 96.
69. Rob Cameron, "Pub Rock Revived," *Semper Floreat*, 7 June 1978, p. 33.
70. Gardiners, "Punks and Police," p. 300.

CHAPTER 8. TAKING THE FIGHT TO THE STREETS

1. Rae Wear, *Johannes Bjelke-Petersen: The Lord's Premier*, Brisbane, University of Queensland Press, 2002, p. 137.
2. official log, 14 July 1971, Queensland State Archives, Runcorn, Item ID318772,

Correspondence, police, p. 23.
3. Zelman Cowan, report, 31 August 1971, Queensland State Archives, Runcorn, Item ID381773, Correspondence, police, pp. 5–6, 8.
4. "Down with Bolsheviks: Brisbane Soldiers' Mission," *Newcastle Sun*, 25 March 1919, p. 2.
5. "No More Picketing: Police Given Wider Powers By New Law," *Courier-Mail*, 10 March 1948, p. 1.
6. "Police, Strikers in Street Fracas," *Townsville Daily Bulletin*, 18 March 1948, p. 1.
7. "Police Clash with Reds' City March," *Courier-Mail*, 18 March 1948, p. 1.
8. Raymond Evans, "Fred Paterson Bashing, 1948," in Raymond Evans and Carole Ferrier (eds.), *Radical Brisbane: An Unruly History*, Brisbane, Vulgar Press, 2004, pp. 226–227.
9. *Parliamentary Debates*, 17 March 1948, LA, QLD, p. 2062.
10. *Parliamentary Debates*, 27 April 1950, House, Commonwealth, p. 1997.
11. *Parliamentary Handbook Part 5: Referendums and Plebiscites*, Canberra, Parliament of Australia, 2014, p. 393.
12. Troy Reeves, "Queensland's Nicklin Government 1957–68: Modernisation, Industrialization and Education," *Queensland History Journal* 22(5), 2014, pp. 423–424.
13. Grant Farred, "Endgame Identity? Mapping the New Left Roots of Identity Politics," *New Literary History* 31(4), 2000, p. 627.
14. Jon Piccini, "'Up the New Channels': Student Activism in Brisbane During Australia's Sixties," *Crossroads* 5(2), 2011, p. 79.
15. Frank Brennan, *Too Much Order With Too Little Law*, Brisbane, University of Queensland Press, 1983, pp. 58, 61.
16. Van Gosse, *Rethinking the New Left: An Interpretive History*, New York, Palgrave Macmillan, 2005, p. 89.
17. Sven Condon, letter, 1 July 1967, Queensland State Archives, Runcorn, Item ID540961, Protest demonstrations—general, p. 1. In 1967, AUD$1 was equal to AUD$13.37 (USD$8.85) in 2020.
18. Condon, letter, p. 1.
19. Francis Bischof, report, 7 July 1967, Queensland State Archives, Runcorn, Item ID540961, Protest demonstrations—general, p. 2.
20. Francis Bischof, memorandum, 7 September 1967, Queensland State Archives, Runcorn, Item ID540961, Protest demonstrations—general, p. 1.
21. "Called a Halt—90 Police Turn Back Marchers," *Courier-Mail*, 6 September 1967, p. 3.
22. Glendon Patrick Hallahan, statutory declaration—appendix A, 19 October 1988, Queensland State Archives, Runcorn, Item ID2548831, Commission of Inquiry—legal advice, p. 1.

23. "Called a Halt," p. 3.
24. Queensland Cabinet, decision no. 10671, 7 September 1967, Queensland State Archives, Runcorn, Item ID540961, Protest demonstrations—general, p. 1.
25. Brennan, *Too Much Order*, p. 102.
26. Frank Nicklin, ministerial statement, 12 September 1967, Queensland State Archives, Runcorn, Item ID540961, Protest demonstrations—general, p. 3.
27. Colin Arkell, letter, 14 September 1967, Queensland State Archives, Runcorn, Item ID540961, Protest demonstrations—general, p. 1.
28. Waterside Workers Federation, telegram, 9 September 1967, Queensland State Archives, Runcorn, Item ID540961, Protest demonstrations—general, p. 1.
29. Mitch Thompson, circular, 28 June 1968, Queensland State Archives, Runcorn, Item ID540961, Protest demonstrations—general, p. 1.
30. John Wanna and Tracey Arklay, *The Ayes Have It: The History of the Queensland Parliament 1957–1989*, Canberra, ANU E Press, 2010, p. 203.
31. "Premier of Qld Dead," *Canberra Times*, 1 August 1968, p. 1.
32. "Chalk Leads State for a Week," *Canberra Times*, 2 August 1968, p. 3; Rae Wear, "Chalk, Gordon William (Chalkie) (1913–1991)," *Australian Dictionary of Biography*, 2014, http://adb.anu.edu.au/biography/chalk-gordon-william-chalkie-15168.
33. Wanna and Arklay, *The Ayes Have It*, p. 230; Wear, "Chalk, Gordon."
34. Rae Wear, *Johannes Bjelke-Petersen: The Lord's Premier*, Brisbane, University of Queensland, 2002, p. 6.
35. Neroli Roocke, "Kingaroy, Still the Peanut Capital of Australia," *ABC News*, https://www.abc.net.au/news/2012-06-13/kingaroy-still-the-peanut-capital-of-australia/6162660.
36. Wear, *Johannes Bjelke-Petersen*, p. 39.
37. "Queensland's New Premier," *Canberra Times*, 9 August 1968, p. 2; Wear, *Johannes Bjelke-Petersen*, p. 74.
38. Johannes Bjelke-Petersen, *Don't You Worry About That!*, North Ryde, Australia, Angus & Robertson, 1990, p. 76.
39. Wear, *Johannes Bjelke-Petersen*, p. 79; Wanna and Arklay, *The Ayes Have It*, p. 209.
40. Jon Piccini, "'Australia's Most Evil and Repugnant Nightspot': Foco Club and Transnational Politics in Brisbane's '68,'" *Dialogue* 8(1), 2010, p. 1.
41. Thomas Vuleta, "Ups and Downs: Music Venues and Popular Music in Brisbane 1959–1989," Honors thesis, University of Queensland, 2010, p. 14.
42. Piccini, "Australia's Most Evil," p. 1.
43. "Police Bash, Kick Woman," *Tribune*, 25 January 1967, p. 1.
44. Carole Ferrier and Ken Mansell, "Student Revolt, 1960s and 1970s," in Raymond Evans and

Carole Ferrier (eds.), *Radical Brisbane: An Unruly History*, Brisbane, Vulgar Press, 2004, p. 268.
45. James Barnard Prentice, "The Brisbane Protests 1965–72," PhD thesis, Griffith University, 2005, pp. 127–128.
46. "Thousands Join in Moratorium, Few Incidents," *Canberra Times*, 9 May 1970, p. 1; Charlie Gifford, "The 'Laver Incident,'" *Tribune*, 24 June 1970, p. 4.
47. "Manhunt Follows Action on QLD University Campus," *Tribune*, 16 September 1970, p. 4.
48. Prentice, "The Brisbane Protests," p. 202.
49. Piccini, "Up the New Channels," p. 86.
50. George Katsiaficas, *The Imagination of the New Left: A Global Analysis of 1968*, Cambridge, South End Press, 1987, p. 5.
51. "Central Police Court," *Brisbane Courier*, 22 September 1866, p. 4.
52. Raymond Evans, "Springbok Tour Confrontation," in Raymond Evans and Carole Ferrier (eds.), *Radical Brisbane: An Unruly History*, Brisbane, Vulgar Press, 2004, p. 278.
53. Matthew Condon, *Three Crooked Kings*, Brisbane, University of Queensland Press, 2013, p. 245.
54. official log, 14 July 1971, p. 23.
55. police radio transcript, 21 July 1971, Queensland State Archives, Runcorn, Item ID381772, Correspondence, police, p. 1.
56. *Parliamentary Debates*, 31 March 1971, LA, QLD, pp. 3393–3394.
57. Cowan, report, p. 2.
58. police radio transcript, 21 July 1971, pp. 2–3.
59. Cowan, report, pp. 5–6.
60. official log, 22 July 1971, Queensland State Archives, Runcorn, Item ID381772, Correspondence, police, p. 56; Cowan, report, p. 8.
61. official log, 22 July 1971, p. 56.
62. official log, 23 July 1971, Queensland State Archives, Runcorn, Item ID381772, Correspondence, police, p. 64.
63. official log, 24 July 1971, Queensland State Archives, Runcorn, Item ID381772, Correspondence, police, p. 73.
64. Cowan, report, p. 10.
65. Raymond Wells Whitrod, police radio transcript, 24 July 1971, Queensland State Archives, Runcorn, Item ID381772, Correspondence, police, p. 3.
66. Cowan, report, p. 10.
67. *Ibid.*, pp. 11–12.
68. Evan Whitton, *The Hillbilly Dictator*, Crows Nest, Australia, ABC Books, 1989, p. 10.

69. Owen Kelly to Johannes Bjelke-Petersen, letter, 10 August 1976, Queensland State Archives, Runcorn, Item ID540963, Protest demonstrations—general, p. 1.
70. *Parliamentary Debates*, 30 November 1976, LA, QLD, p. 1916.
71. Brennan, *Too Much Order*, p. 126.
72. Ronald H. Matthews, *Report by the Honourable R H Matthews QC on His Investigation into the Allegations of Lorelle Anne Saunders Concerning the Circumstances Surrounding Her Being Charged with Criminal Offences in 1982, and Related Matters*, Brisbane, Criminal Justice Commission, 1994, p. 77.
73. Jeff Rickertt, "Right to March Movement," in Raymond Evans and Carole Ferrier (eds.), *Radical Brisbane: An Unruly History*, Brisbane, Vulgar Press, 2004, p. 296.
74. Ibid.
75. Russell Hinze to Johannes Bjelke-Petersen, letter, 1 September 1980, Queensland State Archives, Runcorn, Item ID540966, Protest demonstrations—general, p. 1; Brennan, *Too Much Order*, p. 126.
76. Hugh Lunn, *Joh: The Life and Political Adventures of Sir Johannes Bjelke-Petersen*, Brisbane, University of Queensland Press, 1987, pp. 287–288.
77. Andrew Stewart, "Queensland Police Show They Plan a Tough Stance Against Games Protesters," *Canberra Times*, 21 September 1982, p. 2.

CHAPTER 9. IF YOU WANT A FRIEND IN POLITICS

1. *Parliamentary Debates*, 2 March 1982, LA, QLD, p. 4292; Matthew Condon, *Jacks and Jokers*, Brisbane, University of Queensland Press, 2014, p. 392.
2. "Policeman Lied over Lyons Charge," *Canberra Times*, 11 October 1988, p. 3.
3. "Fraser 'Feared Qld Casino Whitewash,'" *Canberra Times*, 27 October 1988, p. 3; Condon, *Jacks and Jokers*, p. 356.
4. "Policeman Lied," p. 3.
5. Dan Rottenberg, "About that Urban Renaissance . . . ," *Chicago Magazine*, 1 May 1980, p. 154.
6. Dianne Dredge, "Tourism Reform, Policy and Development in Queensland, 1989–2011," *Queensland Review* 18(2), 2011, pp. 154–156.
7. Matthew Condon, *All Fall Down*, Brisbane, University of Queensland Press, 2015, p. 27.
8. Jean-Paul Brodeur, "High Policing and Low Policing: Remarks about the Policing of Political Activities," *Social Problems* 30(5), 1983, p. 507.
9. *Parliamentary Debates*, 1 September 1948, LA, QLD, pp. 197–198.
10. "Batons, Clubs Used in Wild Q'ld Battle," *Sun*, 17 March 1948, p. 1; Raymond Evans, "Fred

Paterson Bashing, 1948," in Raymond Evans and Carole Ferrier (eds.), *Radical Brisbane: An Unruly History*, Brisbane, Vulgar Press, 2004, pp. 226–227.
11. *Parliamentary Debates*, 1 September 1948, pp. 197–198.
12. Domenico Cacciola and Ben Robertson, *Who's Who In The Zoo? A Story of Corruption, Crooks and Killers*, Brisbane, University of Queensland Press, 2014, p. 87.
13. John Edward Deukmedjian, "Making Sense of Neoliberal Securitization in Urban Policing and Surveillance," *Canadian Review of Sociology 50*(1), 2013, p. 64.
14. Ross Fitzgerald, "Judicial Culture and the Investigation of Corruption: A Comparison of the Gibbs National Hotel Inquiry 1963–64 and the Fitzgerald Inquiry 1987–89," in Scott Prasser, Rae Wear, and John Nethercote (eds.), *Corruption and Reform: The Fitzgerald Vision*, Brisbane, University of Queensland Press, 1990, p. 61.
15. *Parliamentary Debates*, 20 September 1960, LA, QLD, p. 389.
16. A "double dissolution election" is when both houses of parliament (House of Representatives and Senate) are dissolved, and all seats are immediately put up for contest. Gough Whitlam, *The Truth of the Matter*, Carlton, Melbourne University Press, 1979, p. 16.
17. Paul Davey, *Joh for PM: The Inside Story of an Extraordinary Political Drama*, Sydney, NewSouth, 2015, pp. 7–8.
18. *Parliamentary Debates*, 27 August 1975, LA, QLD, p. 210.
19. Hedley Thomas, "Stolen Police Chief's Dossier Aided Gough Whitlam's Dismissal," *Australian*, 11 November 2015, http://www.theaustralian.com.au/national-affairs/stolen-police-chiefs-dossier-aided-gough-whitlamsdismissal/news-story/102d640c36fd183f6750946a000277a7.
20. Raymond Whitrod, *Before I Sleep*, Brisbane, University of Queensland Press, 2001, pp. 174., 175.
21. Dickie, *The Road to Fitzgerald*, p. 276; Matthew Condon, *Three Crooked Kings*, Brisbane, University of Queensland Press, 2013, p. 28.
22. Condon, *Three Crooked Kings*, p. 28.
23. Glendon Patrick Hallahan, statutory declaration, 20 October 1988, Queensland State Archives, Runcorn, Item ID2548831, Commission of Inquiry—legal advice, p. 1.
24. Dickie, *The Road to Fitzgerald*, p. 277.
25. *Parliamentary Debates*, 22 August 1974, LA, QLD, p. 270.
26. Dickie, *The Road to Fitzgerald*, p. 277; Gerald E. Fitzgerald, *Report of a Commission of Inquiry Pursuant to Orders in Council*, Brisbane, Commission of Inquiry into Possible Misconduct and Associated Police Misconduct, 1989, p. 116.
27. Fitzgerald, "Judicial Culture," p. 65.

28. Dickie, *The Road to Fitzgerald*, p. 30.
29. *Parliamentary Debates*, 10 March 1976, LA, QLD, p. 2661; *Parliamentary Debates*, 9 November 1976, LA, QLD, pp. 1383–1384.
30. *Parliamentary Debates*, 9 November 1976, p. 1384.
31. *Parliamentary Debates*, 30 November 1976, LA, QLD, p. 1932.
32. Gregory Early, unpublished memoir, quoted in Condon, *Jacks and Jokers*, p. 66.
33. Gregory Early to Terry Lewis, letter, quoted in Condon, *Jacks and Jokers*, p. 58.
34. In 1983, AUD$331 million would be worth AUD$1.145 billion (around USD$758 million) in 2020; *Parliamentary Debates*, 2 August 1983, LA, QLD, p. 18; Evan Whitton, *The Hillbilly Dictator*, Crows Nest, Australia, ABC Books, 1989, p. 82.
35. Whitton, *The Hillbilly Dictator*, p. 82.
36. Condon, *Jacks and Jokers*, pp. 243, 244.
37. *Parliamentary Debates*, 26 February 1986, LA, QLD, p. 3855; Whitton, *The Hillbilly Dictator*, p. 59.
38. "Fraser 'Feared,'" p. 3; Steve Bishop, "Chapter 3: Top Level Trouble," *Bob Campbell's War*, http://www.stevebishop.net/chapter-3-top-leveltrouble.html.
39. Condon, *Jacks and Jokers*, p. 392.
40. Bishop, "Top Level Trouble."
41. "Policeman Lied," p. 3.
42. Condon, *Jacks and Jokers*, p. 393.
43. Ric Allen, "Knight Faces Drive Charge," *Sunday Mail*, 20 December 1981, p. 1.
44. *Parliamentary Debates*, 2 March 1982, p. 4294.
45. In 1982, AUD$175 would be worth AUD$673 (around USD$445) in 2020. Phil Dickie, *The Road to Fitzgerald*, Brisbane, University of Queensland Press, 1988, p. 118.
46. Fitzgerald, *Report of a Commission*, pp. 79–80.
47. "Policeman Lied," p. 3.
48. *Parliamentary Debates*, 4 March 1982, LA, QLD, p. 4421; Bishop, "Top Level Trouble."
49. Condon, *All Fall Down*, p. 73.
50. K. J. Morrison, letter, 6 September 1982, Queensland State Archives, Runcorn, Item ID2549063, Commission of Inquiry—legal advice, p. 1; Condon, *All Fall Down*, p. 73.
51. Fitzgerald, *Report of a Commission*, p. 79.
52. Whitton, "Dishing the Libs."
53. Condon, *All Fall Down*, p. 75.
54. Terence Lewis, letter, 25 August 1986, Queensland State Archives, Runcorn, Item ID2548995, Commission of Inquiry—legal advice, pp. 1–2; Fitzgerald, *Report of a Commission*, p. 325.

55. Fitzgerald, *Report of a Commission*, p. 325.
56. Harry Gibbs, *First Report of the Parliamentary Judges Commission of Inquiry*, Brisbane, Parliamentary Judges Commission of Inquiry, 1989, Queensland State Archives, Runcorn, Item ID2692389, Commission of Inquiry—reports, pp. 22–23.
57. "Judge Stands Down, Sues the Media," *Canberra Times*, 25 October 1988, p. 1.
58. Dickie, *The Road to Fitzgerald*, p. 277.
59. Serge Pregliasco, testimony, 12 May 1988, Queensland State Archives, Runcorn, ID2548520, Commission of inquiry—legal advice, pp. 9106–9107; Dickie, *The Road to Fitzgerald*, p. 251.
60. Condon, *Jacks and Jokers*, pp. 271, 88.
61. Dickie, *The Road to Fitzgerald*, p. 251.
62. In 2020, AUD$10,000 in 1988 is equal to AUD$24,418 (USD$16,205). Roy Clapper, testimony, 12 May 1988, Queensland State Archives, Runcorn, Item ID2548520, Commission of inquiry—legal advice, p. 9101.
63. Condon, *Jacks and Jokers*, p. 88.
64. *Parliamentary Debates*, 7 March 1989, LA, QLD, p. 3346.
65. Donald Frederick Lane, testimony, 15 November 1988, Queensland State Archives, Runcorn, Item ID2548512, Commission of inquiry—legal advice, p. 19677; Rae Wear, *Johannes Bjelke-Petersen: The Lord's Premier*, Brisbane, University of Queensland Press, 2002, p. 191.
66. Dickie, *The Road to Fitzgerald*, p. 221.
67. In 2020, AUD$4538.17 in 1990 is equal to AUD$9,555 (USD$6,339). Evan Whitton, "God Has Judged Me," *The Hillbilly Dictator*, http://netk.net.au/Whitton/Hillbilly48.asp.

CHAPTER 10. MARCHING TO A DIFFERENT BEAT

1. Clive Moore, *Sunshine and Rainbows: The Development of Gay and Lesbian Culture in Queensland*, Brisbane, University of Queensland Press, 2001, pp. 128–129.
2. Ibid.
3. Ross Barber, "Capital Punishment in Queensland," BA honors thesis, University of Queensland, 1967, p. 18; *An Act to Consolidate and Amend the Statute Law of Queensland Relating to Offences Against the Person 1865* (QLD), 29 Vic. No. 11.
4. *Parliamentary Debates*, 26 October 1891, LA, QLD, p. 1734.
5. *Criminal Code 1899* (QLD), 63 Vic. No. 9, ss. 208–211, https://digitalcollections.qut.edu.au/4801/1/CrimCode1899_63Vic_9.pdf.
6. Raymond Evans, *A History of Queensland*, Cambridge, Cambridge University Press, 2007,

p. 270.
7. Robert Aldrich, "Homosexuality in the French Colonies," *Journal of Homosexuality* 41(3–4), 2002, p. 201.
8. There were, in fact, *many* women in the Wild West. By the standards of the time, however, these women were not seen as "acceptable" choices. Many were Native American or Mexican women who were either sex workers for European settlers, or were otherwise embedded in their own cultural marital structures and thus unavailable to the American cowboy. Jana Bommersbach, "Homos on the Range: How Gay Was the West?," *True West Magazine*, 1 November 2005, https://truewestmagazine.com/old-west-homosexuality-homos-on-the-range.
9. Yorick Smaal, "Queer Pleasure: Masculinity, Male Homosexuality and Public Space," *Queensland Historical Atlas*, 2010, p. 1.
10. Laud Humphreys, *Tearoom Trade: Impersonal Sex in Public Places*, London, Duckworth, 1970, p. 125.
11. Richard Tewksbury, "Cruising for Sex in Public Places: The Structure and Language of Men's Hidden, Erotic Worlds," *Deviant Behavior* 17(1), 1996, pp. 1–2.
12. Moore, *Sunshine and Rainbows*, pp. 101–103; Brisbane Magistrates Court (1925, 18 September), *Case 290*, Queensland State Archives, Runcorn, Item IDJUS/S17.
13. Moore, *Sunshine and Rainbows*, pp. 101–103; Smaal, "Queer Pleasure," p. 1.
14. Allan Berube, *Coming Out Under Fire: The History of Gay Men and Women in World War Two*, Chapel Hill, University of North Carolina Press, 1990, p. 3.
15. Ibid.
16. Moore, *Sunshine and Rainbows*, p. 125.
17. "Pink Elephant Affair: Man Charges Bashing by Policemen," *Truth*, 27 October 1946, p. 20.
18. "Pink Elephant Appeal Succeeds," *Evening Advocate*, 7 August 1947, p. 1.
19. Moore, *Sunshine and Rainbows*, p. 128.
20. William Eskridge Jr., *Gaylaw: Challenging the Apartheid of the Closet*, Boston, Harvard University Press, 2002, p. 94.
21. Richard Weinmeyer, "The Decriminalization of Sodomy in the United States," *American Medical Association Journal of Ethics* 16(11), 2014, p. 917.
22. *Lawrence v Texas*, 539 US 558 (2003).
23. Brian Lewis, *Wolfenden's Witnesses: Homosexuality in Postwar Britain*, Basingstoke, UK, Palgrave Macmillan, 2016, p. 275.
24. *Sexual Offences Act 1967* (UK), c. 60.
25. Tim Reeves, "Dr Duncan Revisited," *Journal of the Historical Society of South Australia* (44), 2016, p. 117.

26. Shirleene Robinson, "Homophobia as Party Politics: The Construction of the 'Homosexual Deviant' in Joh Bjelke-Petersen's Queensland," *Queensland Review* 17(1), 2010, p. 37.
27. Destiny Rogers, "Cold Case: What Happened to Brisbane Man Gary Venamore?," *Q News*, 11 December 2018, https://qnews.com.au/cold-case-brisbane-man-gary-venamore.
28. "Detectives Gaoled for 5 Years," *Canberra Times*, 25 July 1968, p. 8.
29. Ibid.
30. Rogers, "Cold Case."
31. "'Police Trap' Set, Court Told," *Canberra Times*, 15 November 1967, p. 10.
32. Moore, *Sunshine and Rainbows*, p. 143.
33. Matthew Condon, *Three Crooked Kings*, Brisbane, University of Queensland Press, 2013, p. 191.
34. Rogers, "Cold Case."
35. Ibid.
36. Ellie Sibson, "Bundaberg Man Charged Over 1976 Cold Case Murder of Rex Keen," *ABC News*, 1 July 2019, https://www.abc.net.au/news/2019-07-01/bundaberg-man-charged-over-1976-cold-case-murder-of-rex-keen/11268360.
37. Jack McKay, "Lennons Plaza Hotel Murder: Hunt Still on for Rex Keen's Killer 40 Years On," *Courier-Mail*, 26 August 2016, http://www.couriermail.com.au/news/queensland/crime-and-justice/crime-read-how-to-get-awaywith-murder/news-story/adc5d01f107a89d42894baad81428c79.
38. Sibson, "Bundaberg Man Charged."
39. Matthew Condon, *Little Fish Are Sweet*, Brisbane, University of Queensland, 2016, p. 140.
40. Hallahan was charged for soliciting protection payments from sex worker Dorothy Knight on 30 December 1971. These charges were eventually dropped, but Hallahan immediately resigned from the force in disgrace.
41. David Alexander, "Former Bjelke-Petersen Government Reveal QLD AIDS Response 'Bastardry,'" *Star Observer*, 7 January 2016, http://www.starobserver.com.au/news/national-news/queensland-news/released-cabinetdocuments-of-former-bjelke-petersen-government-reveal-qld-aids-response-bastardry/144283.
42. Queensland Cabinet, decision no. 47272, 14 October 1985, Queensland State Archives, Runcorn, Item ID2446312, Cabinet minutes—Transplantation and Anatomy Act regulations, p. 1.
43. *Parliamentary Debates*, 19 November 1985, LA, QLD, p. 2477.
44. Bjelke-Petersen was not alone in seeing the closure of gay-venues as a way to combat "gay-related" problems. In the same year that he sought to amend the *Liquor Act* to

criminalize gay bars, New York City Mayor Ed Koch famously backed the city Health Department's move to shut down gay bathhouses across the city as part of its campaign to stop the spread of HIV/AIDS. Hannah Szapary, "More Than Miles: An Analysis of the Different Bicoastal Responses to the Early AIDS Epidemic," *Intersect: The Stanford Journal of Science, Technology and Society* 12(1), 2018, p. 3.

45. "Police Seize Campus Condom Machines," *Canberra Times*, 2 September 1987, p. 8.
46. Felicity Caldwell, "Queensland Attempted to Tackle AIDS While Sodomy Remained a Crime," *Brisbane Times*, 1 January 2019, https://www.brisbanetimes.com.au/politics/queensland/queensland-attempted-to-tackle-aids-while-sodomy-remained-a-crime-20181220-p50ngv.html.

CHAPTER 11. THE CURIOUS CASE OF CONSTABLE DAVE

1. Matthew Condon, *All Fall Down*, Brisbane, University of Queensland Press, 2015, p. 90.
2. Roland Dargusch, report, 20 December 1984, Queensland State Archives, Runcorn, Item ID2549029, Commission of Inquiry—legal advice, p. 5; Condon, *All Fall Down*, p. 91.
3. Condon, *All Fall Down*, p. 92.
4. "Fresh pursuit" dictates that when a crime has just been committed responding officers have the right to pursue the suspect regardless of jurisdiction or the lack of a warrant.
5. Dargusch, report, p. 5; Condon, *All Fall Down*, p. 93.
6. Matthew Condon, *Jacks and Jokers*, Brisbane, University of Queensland Press, 2014, p. 191.
7. Phil Dickie, *The Road to Fitzgerald*, Brisbane, University of Queensland Press, 1988, p. 70.
8. Condon, *Jacks and Jokers*, pp. 189–191.
9. Ronald H. Matthews, *Report by the Honourable R H Matthews QC on His Investigation into the Allegations of Lorelle Anne Saunders Concerning the Circumstances Surrounding Her Being Charged with Criminal Offences in 1982, and Related Matters*, Brisbane, Criminal Justice Commission, 1994, p. 66.
10. Jill Bolen, "An Older Lesbian's Story of Discrimination and Acceptance in 1970s Queensland," *Star Observer*, 28 October 2014, http://www.starobserver.com.au/opinion/soapbox-opinion/an-older-lesbians-story-ofdiscrimination-and-acceptance-in-1970s-queensland/129457.
11. Condon, *Jacks and Jokers*, pp. 36–37.
12. Dickie, *The Road to Fitzgerald*, p. 108; Condon, *Jacks and Jokers*, p. 332.
13. Toby Crockford, "'The Most Successful Accident': Adults-Only Agro Its Road for Birthday," *Brisbane Times*, 26 November 2019, https://www.brisbanetimes.com.au/national/queensland/

the-most-successful-accident-adults-only-agro-hits-road-for-birthday-20191125-p53dy6.html.
14. Condon, *Jacks and Jokers*, p. 333.
15. Ibid., p. 334.
16. G. M. Jones, report, 20 April 1982, Queensland State Archives, Runcorn, Item ID2549029, Commission of Inquiry—legal advice, p. 1.
17. N. S. Collins, addendum, 20 April 1982, Queensland State Archives, Runcorn, Item ID2549029, Commission of Inquiry—legal advice, p. 1.
18. Condon, *All Fall Down*, p. 41.
19. Dargusch, report, p. 3; Condon, *Jacks and Jokers*, p. 410.
20. Condon, *All Fall Down*, p. 43.
21. T. S. C. Atkinson, statutory declaration, 26 September 1988, Queensland State Archives, Runcorn, Item ID2549029, Commission of Inquiry—legal advice, p. 2.
22. Victim 1, interview transcript, 4 September 1982, Queensland State Archives, Runcorn, Item ID2549029, Commission of Inquiry—legal advice, p. 3.
23. Mike Garrahy, memo, 6 September 1982, Queensland State Archives, Runcorn, Item ID2549029, Commission of Inquiry—legal advice, p. 1; In 2020, AUD$200 in 1982 would be worth AUD$770 (USD$512).
24. Garrahy, memo, p. 1.
25. Ibid.
26. Victim 1, interview transcript, p. 3.
27. Francis Rynne, statutory declaration, 5 October 1988, Queensland State Archives, Runcorn, Item ID2549029, Commission of Inquiry—legal advice, pp. 2–4.
28. Kerry Kelly, statutory declaration, 21 September 1988, Queensland State Archives, Runcorn, Item ID2549029, Commission of Inquiry—legal advice, pp. 1 2.
29. Dargusch, report, p. 5.
30. Condon, *All Fall Down*, p. 173.
31. Ibid., pp. 173–174.
32. Dargusch, report, p. 5.
33. Mark McCoy, report, 9 November 1984, Queensland State Archives, Runcorn, Item ID2549029, Commission of Inquiry—legal advice, p. 1.
34. "Hurrey: 5 Years for Sex Offences," *Canberra Times*, 6 July 1986, p. 3; Condon, *All Fall Down*, p. 438.
35. McCoy, report, p. 1.
36. Victim 1, interview transcript, p. 1; McCoy, report, p. 2.
37. McCoy, report, pp. 2–4.

38. William Glasson, statutory declaration, 20 October 1988, Queensland State Archives, Runcorn, Item ID2549029, Commission of Inquiry—legal advice, p. 2.
39. Terence Lewis, memo, 26 November 1984, Queensland State Archives, Runcorn, Item ID2549029, Commission of Inquiry—legal advice, p. 1.
40. Dargusch, report, p. 7.
41. Mike Garrahy, interview transcript, 19 December 1984, Queensland State Archives, Runcorn, Item ID2549029, Commission of Inquiry—legal advice, pp. 1, 21–22, 7.
42. Ibid., p. 17.
43. Condon, *All Fall Down*, p. 315.
44. Glasson, statutory declaration, p. 1; Condon, *All Fall Down*, p. 438.
45. Jared Owens, "Former Children's TV star and Cop David Moore Avoids Jail for Child Porn," *Australian*, 3 November 2010.
46. Jason Rawlins, "Former Policeman Pleads Guilty to Possessing Child Pornography," *ABC News*, 2 November 2010, https://www.abc.net.au/news/2010-11-02/former-policeman-pleads-guilty-to-possessing-child/2320972.
47. Owens, "Former Children's TV Star."
48. Rynne, statutory declaration, p. 1.
49. Garrahy, memo, p. 1; Rynne, statutory declaration, p. 1.

CHAPTER 12. DIRT FILES

1. David Crystal, "Isaac Pitman: The Linguistic Legacy," *English Today* 14(3), 1998, p. 12; Matthew Condon, *Little Fish Are Sweet*, Brisbane, University of Queensland Press, 2016, p. 164.
2. Matthew Condon, *All Fall Down*, Brisbane, University of Queensland Press, 2015, pp. 218–219.
3. Matthew Condon, *Jacks and Jokers*, Brisbane, University of Queensland Press, 2014, p. 303.
4. Kamala London, Maggie Bruck, Stephen J. Cecci, and Daniel W. Shuman, "Disclosure of Child Sexual Abuse: A Review of Contemporary Empirical Literature," in Margaret-Ellen Pipes, Michael E. Lamb, Yael Orbach, and Ann-Christin Cedarborg (eds.), *Child Sexual Abuse: Disclosure, Delay and Denial*, New York, Routledge, 2007, p. 20.
5. Debbie Nathan and Michael R. Snedeker, *Satan's Silence: Ritual Abuse and the Making of a Modern American Witch Hunt*, New York, Basic Books, 1995, p. 24.
6. Jeffrey S. Victor, *Satanic Panic: The Creation of a Contemporary Legend*, Chicago, Open Court, 1993, p. 117.

7. Nathan and Snedeker, *Satan's Silence*, pp. 79–80.
8. James Wood, *Final Report of the Royal Commission into the New South Wales Police Service*, vol. 4, Sydney, Royal Commission into the New South Wales Police Service, 1997, pp. 183–185.
9. Witness SB41, statement, 27 October 1988, Royal Commission into the New South Wales Police Service, Exhibit 2304C.
10. Wood, *Final Report*, pp. 190–191.
11. Peter McClellan, *Report of the Royal Commission into Institutional Responses to Child Sexual Abuse*, vol. 3, Canberra, Australian Government, 2017, p. 10.
12. Frederick W. Whitehouse, "Australian Cretaceous Fauna," PhD thesis, University of Cambridge, 1925, p. 1.
13. Rosamond Siemon, *The Mayne Inheritance: A Gothic Tale of Murder, Madness and Scandal Across Generations*, Brisbane, University of Queensland Press, 2003, p. 7.
14. Rosamond Siemon, quoted in Condon, *Little Fish*, pp. 176, 178.
15. "Dr. Whitehouse Now Associate Professor," *Queensland Times*, 8 November 1948, p. 2; "New River Pairs Title," *Brisbane Telegraph*, 8 November 1951, p. 35; "Lamington Jungle Adventure," *Beaudesert Times*, 14 January 1955, p. 3; Condon, *Little Fish*, p. 185.
16. Condon, *Little Fish*, pp. 188, 189, 192.
17. "Detective's Allegation: Halliday Found He Killed Taxi-Driver for 'Two Quid,'" *Morning Bulletin*, 10 December 1952, p. 1; Condon, *Little Fish*, p. 193.
18. Condon, *Little Fish*, p. 195.
19. "Alleged Indecency with Professor," *Canberra Times*, 6 May 1955, p. 2; "Professor to Stand Trial on Indecency Charge," *Central Queensland Herald*, 19 May 1955, p. 17; Condon, *Little Fish*, p. 204.
20. Condon, *Little Fish*, p. 164.
21. *Parliamentary Debates*, 1 November 1984, LA, QLD, p. 2116; Condon, *Little Fish*, pp. 164–165.
22. Paul Wilson, *The Man They Called a Monster*, North Ryde, Australia, Cassell, 1981, pp. 8–9.
23. "Monster Snared by His Own Camera," *Sunday Mail*, 30 September 1979, p. 1; Wilson, *The Man They Called a Monster*, p. 7.
24. Home Office (UK), "Independent Investigation into the Alleged Payment of Home Office Funding to the Paedophile Information Exchange," UK Government, https://assets.publishing.service.gov.uk/government/uploads/system/uploads/attachment_data/file/327927/InvestigationFundingPIE.pdf.
25. Condon, *Little Fish*, p. 168.
26. "Sex Monster's 2000 Boy Victims," *Truth*, 29 September 1979, p. 1; Condon, *Jacks and*

Jokers, p. 303.
27. Mike Garrahy, memo, 6 September 1982, Queensland State Archives, Runcorn, Item ID2549029, Commission of Inquiry—legal advice, p. 1.
28. "Sex Monster's 2000 Boy Victims," p. 1.
29. Condon, *Little Fish*, p. 169.
30. Kevin Lynch, "BSE and Kevin Lynch," Royal Commission into Institutional Responses to Child Sexual Abuse, 1996, Exhibit ASQ.232.006.0127_R; Condon, *Little Fish*, p. 243.
31. Mark McCoy, notation, 1984, Criminal Justice Commission file 104/01/07/004, p. 1.
32. John Patrick Kimmins, *Report of the Inquiry into Allegations of Misconduct in the Investigation of Paedophilia in Queensland*, Brisbane, Criminal Justice Commission, 1998, p. 21.
33. Task Force Delta, letter, 29 March 1983, Criminal Justice Commission file 104/01/07/004, p. 1.
34. McCoy, notation, p. 1.
35. Mark McCoy, report, 9 November 1984, Queensland State Archives, Runcorn, Item ID2549029, Commission of Inquiry—legal advice, p. 1.
36. Kimmins, *Report of the Inquiry*, pp. 33, 27.
37. Tony Keim, "Former Liberal Advisor Russell John Grenning Jailed for 12-Months for Child Porn," *Courier-Mail*, 29 August 2011.
38. Condon, *All Fall Down*, pp. 193–195.
39. Kimmins, *Report of the Inquiry*, pp. 149, 156; Robert Borbidge, quoted in John Wanna, "Queensland: July to December 1997," *Australian Journal of Politics and History* 44(2), 1998, p. 269.
40. Condon, *All Fall Down*, pp. 412–413.
41. Ibid., p. 163.
42. Kimmins, *Report of the Inquiry*, p. 155.
43. Roland Dargusch and Brian Webb, report, 25 April 1986, Queensland State Archives, Runcorn, Item ID2549020, Commission of Inquiry—legal advice, pp. 1–2.
44. Phil Dickie, *The Road to Fitzgerald*, Brisbane, University of Queensland Press, 1988, pp. 109–110.
45. Norm Bolotin and Christine Laing, *The World's Columbian Exposition: The Chicago World's Fair of 1893*, Urbana, University of Illinois Press, 2002, p. vii.
46. Robert Sawford, report, 13 September 1988, quoted in Kimmins, *Report of the Inquiry*, p. 86.
47. Kimmins, *Report of the Inquiry*, p. 88.
48. Kimmins, *Report of the Inquiry*, p. 89; Condon, *All Fall Down*, p. 387.

49. Kimmins, *Report of the Inquiry*, p. 90.
50. *Parliamentary Debates*, 4 April 1989, LA, QLD, p. 3935.
51. Condon, *All Fall Down*, p. 484.
52. Kimmins, *Report of the Inquiry*, p. 93.
53. Graham Williams, interview transcript, 6 March 1996, quoted in Kimmins, *Report of the Inquiry*, p. 97.
54. Garnett Dickson, report, 19 October 1989, quoted in Kimmins, *Report to the Inquiry*, p. 104.
55. Kimmins, *Report to the Inquiry*, p. 124.
56. Ibid., pp. 16, 42, 42–44, 41.
57. Ibid., pp. 44, 59.
58. Gerald E. Fitzgerald, *Report of a Commission of Inquiry Pursuant to Orders in Council*, Brisbane, Commission of Inquiry into Possible Misconduct and Associated Police Misconduct, 1989, p. 204.
59. Kimmins, *Report of the Inquiry*, pp. 54, 63–64.
60. "Obituary: John Patrick 'Jack' Kimmins," *Courier-Mail*, 12 April 2012, https://www.couriermail.com.au/ipad/obituary-john-patrick-jack-kimmins/news-story/be7215c68a6cfede5381e61a7e670b01?sv=7c3ebaed76c74464557931fb63fed1d5.
61. Kimmins, *Report of the Inquiry*, p. 79; Paul Bleakley, "Watching the Watchers: Taskforce Argos and the Evidentiary Issues Involved with Infiltrating Dark Web Child Exploitation Networks," *Police Journal: Theory, Practice and Principles* 92(3), 2019, pp. 222–223.

CHAPTER 13. JOKE'S OVER

1. Steve Bishop, "Chapter 4: Campbell's War Attracts TV Coverage," *Rob Campbell's War*, http://www.stevebishop.net/chapter-4-campbells-war-attracts-tv-coverage.html.
2. Tony Koch and Matthew Fynes-Clinton, "The Men of Evil Who Prey on Children," *Courier-Mail*, 10 December 1984, p. 1.
3. Phil Dickie, "A Year after Sturgess, Sex-for-Sale Business Thrives Unchallenged," *Courier-Mail*, 12 January 1987, p. 1; Phil Dickie, *The Road to Fitzgerald*, Brisbane, University of Queensland Press, 1988, p. 124.
4. "Mackay Shot Dead by Mafia Order: Crown," *Canberra Times*, 6 March 1986, p. 3; Matthew Condon, *All Fall Down*, Brisbane, University of Queensland Press, 2015, p. 260.
5. Condon, *All Fall Down*, p. 261.
6. Matthew Condon, *Jacks and Jokers*, Brisbane, University of Queensland Press, 2014, pp. 23 84–86.

7. Ibid., p. 280.
8. Condon, *All Fall Down*, p. 147.
9. James Slade and Allan Barnes, transcript, 7 February 1985, Queensland State Archives, Runcorn, Item ID1276355, Commission of Inquiry—Exhibit, pp. 1–2.
10. In 2020, AUD$100 in 1985 would be worth AUD$310 (USD$196); Condon, *All Fall Down*, pp. 178–179.
11. Condon, *All Fall Down*, p. 174.
12. *Parliamentary Debates*, 20 September 1984, LA, QLD, p. 741.
13. Zelman Cowan, report, 31 August 1971, Queensland State Archives, Runcorn, Item ID381773, Correspondence, police, pp. 5–6; Condon, *All Fall Down*, p. 274.
14. Condon, *All Fall Down*, p. 273.
15. Dickie, *The Road to Fitzgerald*, p. 168.
16. Gerald E. Fitzgerald, *Report of a Commission of Inquiry Pursuant to Orders in Council*, Brisbane, Commission of Inquiry into Possible Misconduct and Associated Police Misconduct, 1989, p. 3.
17. Christine Jennett, "Political Review," *Australian Quarterly 59*(1), 1987, p. 102.
18. Condon, *All Fall Down*, p. 302.
19. Fitzgerald, *Report of a Commission*, p. 3.
20. Eric Bigby, "Order in Council of 24 June 1987," *Queensland Government Gazette Extraordinary 285*(73A), pp. 1840B.
21. Fitzgerald, *Report of a Commission*, p. 12.
22. Dickie, *The Road to Fitzgerald*, p. 208; Condon, *All Fall Down*, p. 335.
23. Noel Dwyer, testimony, 19 May 1988, Queensland State Archives, Runcorn, Item ID2548524, Commission of Inquiry—legal advice, p. 9515; Dickie, *The Road to Fitzgerald*, p. 220.
24. William Gunn to Terence Lewis, letter, 21 September 1987, Queensland State Archives, Runcorn, Item ID2548981, Commission of Inquiry—legal advice, p. 1.
25. Fitzgerald, *Report of a Commission*, pp. 70–71.
26. Condon, *All Fall Down*, p. 403.
27. Jack Reginald Herbert, ledger, 12 September 1988, Queensland State Archives, Runcorn, Item ID1277500, Commission of Inquiry—Exhibit, p. 1; Fitzgerald, *Report of a Commission*, p. 72.
28. Condon, *All Fall Down*, pp. 410–411.
29. Glendon Patrick Hallahan, statutory declaration, 19 October 1988, Queensland State Archives, Runcorn, Item ID2548831, Commission of Inquiry—legal advice, p. 1; Condon, *All Fall Down*, p. 411.

30. Tony Moore, "Before Fitzgerald: How the Band of Brothers Gathered as Whistleblowers," *Brisbane Times*, 21 July 2019, https://www.brisbanetimes.com.au/national/queensland/before-fitzgerald-how-the-band-of-brothers-gathered-as-whistleblowers-20190718-p528iy.html.
31. Evan Whitton, "God Has Judged Me," *The Hillbilly Dictator*, http://netk.net.au/Whitton/Hillbilly48.asp.
32. Anne Twomey, *The Veiled Sceptre: Reserve Powers of Heads of State in Westminster Systems*, Cambridge, Cambridge University Press, 2018, p. 303.
33. "Premier of Qld Dead," *Canberra Times*, 1 August 1968, p. 1; "Chalk Leads State for a Week," *Canberra Times*, 2 August 1968, p. 3.
34. Evan Whitton, *The Hillbilly Dictator*, Crows Nest, Australia, ABC Books, 1989, pp. 137–139.
35. William Carter, *Report by the Honorable WJ Carter QC on his Inquiry into the Selection of the Jury for the Trial of Sir Johannes Bjelke-Petersen*, Brisbane, Criminal Justice Commission, 1993, pp. 1–3.
36. Rae Wear, *Johannes Bjelke-Petersen: The Lord's Premier*, Brisbane, University of Queensland Press, 2002, p. 110.
37. Fitzgerald, *Report of a Commission*, p. 8.
38. Queensland Parliamentary Record, "Table 1: Precis of Results of Queensland State Elections 1932–2017," *Queensland Parliament*, https://www.parliament.qld.gov.au/documents/explore/parliamentaryrecord/sections/Part%202.21.pdf. In the American presidential system, it is possible for candidates to win the popular vote and yet still lose the election because of the Electoral College system, as occurred with the 2016 election of Donald Trump. John Sides, Michael Tesler and Lynn Vavreck, "The 2016 US Election: How Trump Lost and Won," *Journal of Democracy* 28(2), 2017, pp. 34–35.
39. Fitzgerald, *Report of a Commission*, pp. 123–124.
40. Greg Chamberlin, "Corruption Watchdog Seems to Be Losing Its Bite," *Courier-Mail*, 21 September 2009, p. 24.
41. Ross Homel, "Integrating Investigation and Prevention: Managing the Transformation of the Queensland Criminal Justice Commission," *Queensland Review* 4(2), 1997, pp. 37–39.
42. Tim Prenzler, "Reform in Politics, Criminal Justice and the Police in Post-Fitzgerald Queensland: An Assessment," *Griffith Law Review* 18(3), 2009, p. 582.
43. Fitzgerald, *Report of a Commission*, p. 313.
44. Prenzler, "Reform in Politics," p. 587.
45. Mark Finnane, "Police Unions in Australia: A History of the Present," *Current Issues in Criminal Justice* 12(1), 2000, p. 7.

46. Prenzler, "Reform in Politics," p. 581.
47. Michael Briody, "Establishing the Crime and Corruption Commission: The Reformation of Queensland's Premier Crime-Fighting Agency," *Journal of Policing, Intelligence and Counter Terrorism* 10(2), 2015, pp. 136–137.
48. Fitzgerald, *Report of a Commission*, p. 149; Prenzler, "Reform in Politics," p. 583.
49. Fitzgerald, *Report of a Commission*, pp. 233–244; John Patrick Kimmins, *Report of the Inquiry into Allegations of Misconduct in the Investigation of Paedophilia in Queensland*, Brisbane, Criminal Justice Commission, 1998, pp. 124–125.

CONCLUSION

1. Matthew Condon, *All Fall Down*, Brisbane, University of Queensland Press, 2015, p. 486.
2. Jack Herbert, transcript, 31 August 1988, quoted in Matthew Condon, *Little Fish Are Sweet*, Brisbane, University of Queensland Press, 2016, p. i.
3. Condon, *All Fall Down*, pp. 501–508, 491–492.
4. *Parliamentary Debates*, 12 May 1998, LA, QLD, pp. 1007–1008; Condon, *All Fall Down*, p. 525.
5. Condon, *Little Fish*, pp. 3–4.
6. Roman Quaedvleig, *Tour de Force: From Rookie to Top Cop*, read by the author, Carlton, Melbourne University Publishing, 2019, chapter 13.
7. Gerald E. Fitzgerald, *Report of a Commission of Inquiry Pursuant to Orders in Council*, Brisbane, Commission of Inquiry into Possible Misconduct and Associated Police Misconduct, 1989, p. 206.
8. Steve Bishop, *The Most Dangerous Detective: The Outrageous Glen Hallahan*, Charleston, CreateSpace, 2012, p. 114.
9. Fitzgerald, *Report of a Commission*, p. 243; Daniel Hurst, "Inside Queensland's Spy Unit," *Brisbane Times*, 7 April 2010, https://www.brisbanetimes.com.au/national/queensland/inside-queenslands-spy-unit-20100406-rpbg.html.
10. David Frost and Bob Zelnick, *Frost/Nixon*, London, Pan Books, 2007, p. 88.
11. William Carter, *Report by the Honorable WJ Carter QC on His Inquiry into the Selection of the Jury for the Trial of Sir Johannes Bjelke-Petersen*, Brisbane, Criminal Justice Commission, 1993, pp. 1–3.
12. Andrew Stafford, *Pig City: From the Saints to Savage Garden*, Brisbane, University of Queensland Press, 2006, p. 57.
13. "Pink Elephant Affair: Man Charges Bashing by Policemen," *Truth*, 27 October 1946,

p. 20; Shirleene Robinson, "Homophobia as Party Politics: The Construction of the 'Homosexual Deviant' in Joh Bjelke-Petersen's Queensland," *Queensland Review* 17(1), 2010, p. 37.

14. Frank Brennan, *Too Much Order with Too Little Law*, Brisbane, University of Queensland Press, 1983, p. 126.

Index

Atkinson, Syd "Sippy," 101, 103–104, 197, 203, 217; David Moore and, 182, 184, 190; Jeppesen investigation and, 100

Bailey, Raymond John, 47–48, 54
Battle of Brisbane, 56–57
Bauer, Norwin "Norm," 73, 83, 93, 148; The Beatles tour and, 119; student protests and, 128–129
Beattie, Peter, 123–124, 135, 221
Bellino, Geraldo, 2, 101–103, 204, 213–214, 224
Bennett, Colin, 64–67
Bischof, Francis "Frank," 32, 48, 128, 198, 229; becoming police commissioner, 11, 34, 37, 41–46; Bodgie Squad and, 115–118; Bulimba election fraud and, 40–41, 78; closing the brothels, 58–60; early life of, 37–40; Jorgensen affair and, 44–45; Juvenile Aid Bureau and, 94–95; National Hotel Inquiry and, 60–61, 63–69, 72–75; Rat Pack and, 52–54; resignation of, 78–79, 81

Bjelke-Petersen, Johannes "Joh," 6–7, 9–11, 120, 227–228; anti-gay campaign, 11, 167–168, 174–175, 229; becoming premier, 130–131; early life of, 130–131; Fitzgerald Inquiry and, 2–3, 215, 217–218, 222; resignation of, 217–218; Right to March and, 12, 137–138, 229; selecting a new police commissioner, 96–99, 104–106; Special Branch and, 149–150; Springboks 1971 tour and, 123, 133–134, 136, 228; Ted Lyons and, 142–143, 155–156
Bodgie Squad, 116–120, 226–227
Bracken, Len, 141–142, 151–152
Breslin, Paul, 177–178, 182, 184–185, 214

Brifman, Shirley, 60, 63, 65, 86–88, 172–173; National Hotel testimony of, 73–74, 87–88; suspicious death of, 88
Burgess, Harry, 4, 102, 104, 215–216, 218, 222

Cacciola, Domenico, 82–83, 99, 145
Cairns, 103–104
Campbell, Bob, 91–92, 102–103, 151–152, 211
Carmichael, Peter, 141–142, 151–152, 218
Civil Liberties Co-ordinating Committee (CLCC), 127–129
Colston, Mal, 146–147
Consorting Squad, 57–58, 81, 94, 98–99, 116, 148, 166, 222
Conte, Vic, 2, 101–102, 205
Corner, Charlie, 43–44, 51, 81, 93
Crime Intelligence Unit (CIU), 83, 88–89, 94–95, 99, 104, 213
Criminal Justice Commission (CJC), 3, 220–221
Crocker, Geoff, 101, 103–104, 204

Denham, Digby, 28–29
Dewar, Alexander, 79. 118
Dickson, Garnett, 206–209, 214
Donovan, Jim, 33–35, 37, 43–44, 52; Jorgensen affair and, 41–42, 45, 96; Leigh Hamilton case and, 58–59, 88–89
Duncan, Abe, 87–88
Dwyer, Noel, 100–101, 216–217

Eddington, Ron, 134, 149

Fitzgerald, Tony, 3–5, 215–216, 225
Fitzgerald Inquiry, 10–13, 99–101, 152–154, 188, 205, 207–208; foundation of, 3, 215–223; impact of, 225–227, 229, 231
Fortitude Valley, 112–113, 149, 179, 183, 185; vice trade and, 1–2, 91–93, 99, 101–103, 195
Four Corners, 2–5, 8, 210–212, 214–216, 224–225
4ZZZ radio, 120–121
Freier, Neil, 84–85
Fulton, John, 169–170, 172

Gair, Vince, 33–37, 50, 126
Gallagher, Peter, 177–178, 182, 184–185, 190, 214
Garrahy, Mike, 182–183, 186–187, 190, 200
Gibbs, Harry Talbot, 68–69, 71–72, 74–75, 78, 204, 209
Glasson, Bill, 186–188
Gold Coast, 58–59, 65, 84, 114, 143, 188, 199
Goldup-Graham, Kym, 206–209
Green Mafia, 33–37, 40–46, 52, 78
Grenning, Russell, 201–202, 207–208
Gulbransen, Norm, 83, 88–89, 96, 98
Gunn, Bill, 3, 215–216, 222

Hallahan, Glendon "Glen," 61, 117, 128, 148, 217, 224; Dorothy Knight sting and, 88–90, 94, 104; Gary Venamore case and, 171–173; Leigh Hamilton case and, 58–59; National Hotel Inquiry and, 64–65, 70, 74–74, 86–87; Sundown murders and, 47–48, 53–54, 93
Hamilton, Leigh, 58–59, 65, 88–90
Hanlon, Ned, 49–50, 125, 144, 229
Hapeta, Hector, 1–3, 101–103, 105, 204, 224
Harold, Thomas William, 33–34, 37, 42–45, 78, 96, 118

Hayes, Brian, 100
Hayes, John "Chow," 111–113
Herbert, Jack, 79–84, 95–98, 100–102, 154–155, 214, 223–224, 229–230; Fitzgerald Inquiry and, 215–218, 222; Southport bookmakers case and, 84–86, 104, 226
Hiley, Thomas, 38, 43, 51–52, 59, 74–75, 77–79, 81
Hodges, Allen Maxwell "Max," 83, 93–95, 149
Hooper, Kevin, 102–103, 151
Howard-Osborne, Clarence, 191, 193–194, 197–199, 204, 207, 209; death of, 194, 199; Howard-Osborne files, 190, 198–201, 209
Hurrey, William "Bill," 181–183, 185–190, 200, 202

Jeppesen, Alec, 98–101, 103, 178–179, 218
Jorgensen, Michael, 41–45, 53, 93, 96
Juvenile Aid Bureau (JAB), 94–95, 182–185, 187, 199–202, 207; conflict with EDLU, 95, 104

Kangaroo Point homosexuality case, 159–160, 168
Keen, Rex Kable, 172
Kimmins Inquiry, 202, 206–210
Knight, Dorothy, 88–90
Komlosy, John, 66, 69–72, 74, 148, 209

Lane, Donald "Don," 105, 116, 149, 157; Fitzgerald Inquiry and, 154–155, 217; Special Branch and, 147–149
Laver, Brian, 127, 131–133, 135
Leslie, William Nation, 169–170, 176
Lewis, Terence "Terry," 8, 74, 82, 120, 179; after Fitzgerald, 223–225; becoming police commissioner, 92, 97–100, 104–106, 149, 213; Bjelke-Petersen and, 11, 227–230; Bob Campbell and, 102–104; David Moore case and, 183–190; early life of, 53, 61; Fitzgerald Inquiry and, 2–3, 153–154, 215–218; investigating child sexual abuse, 201, 204–205, 207–208, 211; Juvenile Aid Bureau and, 94–95; Leigh Hamilton case and, 58–59, 65, 89–90; Right to March and, 137–139; Ted Lyons and, 142–143, 150–152, 156–157
Licensing Branch, 2–3, 9, 11, 43, 57, 73, 95, 103–104, 223; Alec Jeppesen and, 97–101, 178–179; Arthur Pitts and, 83–86; Fitzgerald Inquiry and, 217, 219, 222; Jack Herbert and, 79–82, 229; underage prostitution and, 202, 204
Logan, Patrick, 18–19
Lucas Inquiry, 97–98, 204, 222
Lyons, Ted, 103, 142–143, 150–153, 156, 218

MacArthur, Douglas, 31, 55–56
Marlin, Brian, 99, 178–179, 181
Masters, Chris, 2–3, 207, 211–215, 222
Mayne, Patrick, 21–22, 70, 197
McCoy, Mark, 185, 202, 208
McIlwraith, Thomas, 24–25
Menzies, Robert, 30–31, 71, 108–109, 126
Moore, David, 178, 181, 184–185, 190, 202–203, 211, 228; arrest and trial of, 186, 188–189; Garrahy investigation of, 183–184, 187, 200; TV career of, 180–182
Morris, Ken, 44–45, 77
Mount Isa, 21, 38, 81, 128, 148, 179; Jorgensen case and, 41, 45, 96; Sundown murders

and, 47–48, 53–54, 93
Murphy, Anthony "Tony," 58, 92, 94–95, 117, 149, 213, 224; allegations of corruption and, 99–101, 103–104, 211, 217; early years, 52–53; joining the Licensing Branch, 81–82; National Hotel Inquiry and, 64, 68–74, 86–88, 90, 148; policing the gay community, 179, 183, 189–190, 197–198
Murray, Douglas Morton, 166

National Hotel, 60, 63–65; Inquiry, 66–75, 78–79, 82–83, 86–87, 91, 118, 148, 225–226
Nicklin, Francis "Frank," 29, 34, 41–46, 64, 66–68, 77–78, 130–131, 145; becoming premier, 36–37; student protests and, 126–129

Ogle, Walter, 203
Operation Firefighter, 205–206, 208
Oxley, John, 16–19

Paedophile Task Force, 205–209, 214
Pamphlett, Thomas, 15–19
Parker, Graeme, 3, 215–218, 222
Paterson, Fred, 125–126, 144
Pink Elephant Café, 165–166
Pitts, Arthur, 83–86, 95–96, 98, 149, 154, 217, 226

Quaedvlieg, Roman, 92, 224–225

Redmond, Ronald, 116, 215–216; Operation Firefighter, 206
Regional Task Force, 120–121, 137, 227
Risch, Cecil, 113–114

Roberts brothers, 63–67, 69–70, 72–74
Rooklyn, Jack, 105, 154–155, 216
Ryan, Lily, 60, 73
Rynne, Francis "Frank," 183, 190

Scanlan, Charles Hackett, 159–160, 166
Seymour, David, 23, 26
Simmons, Danny, 107–108, 111–113
Slade, Jim, 207–208, 212–214, 222
Special Branch, 120, 144–145, 156, 173, 201, 222, 227, 229; Colston affair and, 146–147; Donald Lane and, 148–149; protest and, 133, 135
Springboks 1971 tour, 12, 123–124, 133–136, 139, 149, 228
Spring Hill, 2, 91, 110, 163–164, 203
Students for Democratic Action (SDA), 127, 131–132, 135
Sturgess, Des, 89; Sturgess Inquiry, 202–205, 211–212

Thompson, Mitch, 127, 129, 131, 135
Tilley, Anne-Marie, 1–3, 101–103, 105, 204, 216, 224
Traffic Branch, 96, 114, 128–129
Turrbal people, 18, 20

University of Queensland, 123, 127, 129, 133–134, 174, 196–197
Urquhart, Frederic, 21; 1899 royal commission and, 26; Native Mounted Police and, 21, 26; 1912 general strike and, 28–29; Red Flag riots and, 29–30

Vassallo, Peter, 212, 214
Vasta, Angelo, 152–154, 156, 218

Venamore, Gary, 170–173, 176

Ware, Michael, 202, 207–208
Weidinger, Val, 60, 70, 72–74
Welldon, Lawrence, 169–170, 172
Whitehouse, Frederick William, 196–198
Whitrod, Raymond Wells, 90, 94–96, 104, 147, 179–180, 213; becoming police commissioner, 83, 87, 92–94; Springboks 1971 tour and, 134–136; resignation of, 96–97, 105–106, 137, 147–149, 226
Woolloongabba, 102–103, 110, 114–115, 185

Young, David, 63–66, 72–74, 148, 209